MANAGING ONLINE REFERENCE SERVICES

Edited by ETHEL AUSTER

Neal-Schuman Publishers, Inc.
New York   London

Published by Neal-Schuman Publishers, Inc.
23 Cornelia Street
New York, NY 10014

Printed and bound in the United States of America.

Library of Congress Cataloging-in-Publication Data
Main entry under title:

Managing online reference services.
    Bibliography: p.
    Includes indexes.
    1. Reference services (Libraries)—Automation—
Addresses, essays, lectures. 2. Information services—
Management—Addresses, essays, lectures. 3. Bibliographical services—Automation—Addresses,
essays, lectures. 4. On-line bibliographic searching—Addresses,
essays, lectures. 5. Information storage and retrieval
systems—Addresses, essays, lectures. 6. Library
administration—Addresses, essays, lectures. I. Auster,
Ethel.
Z711.M35   1986   025.5'2'0285   85-21542
ISBN 0-918212-93-6

Contents

Preface

During the past decade online searching has become an integral part of the services offered by library and information centers. Indeed, the growth of the online industry—the proliferation of vendors, suppliers, databases—has lived up to if not exceeded the optimistic predictions made by experts in the early years. Concomitant with this activity in both the profit and nonprofit sectors has been the growth of a diversified and prolific literature documenting everything from the most intricate configurations of hardware to the changing roles of information specialists precipitated by the new technology.

Meanwhile, faculties of library and information science, recognizing that the major changes in the practice of the profession must be reflected in the way professionals are trained, have devoted significant portions of their curriculum to ensuring that their graduates are able to play effective roles in the new technologically based information environment.

Although faculty members have by and large done their best to ensure that the new information scientists would be well prepared to enter a highly competitive environment, their efforts have been handicapped by the paucity of relevant texts available. Specifically, the need for a book of readings such as this one became clear to me from my experience in teaching the online reference course to MLS students at the Faculty of Library and Information Science, University of Toronto. As I compiled course reading lists, I became aware that the literature was scattered across numerous sources, not all of which were readily available. Students brought to my attention the costs of duplicating these materials and the library impressed upon me the problems posed by copyright issues. It occurred to me that the difficulties we faced were not unique to me or my students but must be being experienced by faculty and students elsewhere as well. Hence the impetus for compiling *Managing Online Reference Services*.

The approach taken is an administrative one. The choice of topics was determined not only by traditional management concerns but with a view to providing the persons responsible for setting up, justifying, or operating such a service with useful materials to bolster their position. Ephemeral and soon-dated items as well as descriptions of overly specific situations have been avoided. The emphasis has been on selecting articles from major referred journals.

The articles that are included span the years 1975 through 1984. The configuration of the literature on online information retrieval changed considerably during those years, reflecting the changes that were occurring in the online field. The number of articles on the management of online services peaked in 1978 while articles published in the 1980s have focussed on such current interests as microcomputers, searching by end users, development of user-friendly front ends and expert systems, and the availability of sophisticated telecommunications and data storage technologies.[1]

The range of articles in this volume mirrors these trends in the literature and the field. Some earlier writings have been included, such as those on planning and promotion, for example, not only because of the scarcity of appropriate recent articles on these topics, but because they remain as pertinent today as when they were written. Topics that have just recently come to prominence, the legal issues surrounding downloading for example, are represented by the latest material available through 1984.

Managing Online Reference Services is intended for the following audiences: library and information science faculty and students involved in courses dealing with online reference services (these may be reference, special library, information retrieval, special literatures, or online courses) and those practitioners working in the field who are either starting an online reference service or those who wish to improve their own management of such a service or justify the implementation of such a service to senior management.

Managing Online Reference Services is divided into eight parts, each part representing a prime administrative concern. Introductory overviews summarize the main thrust of the material presented and place it in the broader context of the topic treated. Since space does not permit the inclusion of all items that might be of potential interest, a selected bibliography of additional readings has been included. Name and subject indexes complete the volume.

Footnotes

1. Donald T. Hawkins, "The Literature of Online Retrieval: An Update," *Online Review* 8 (1984): 153-64.

Acknowledgments

I owe a great deal to the students who enrolled in my Online Information Retrieval course at the Faculty of Library and Information Science, University of Toronto in 1984 and 1985. When the idea was first broached of putting together a book of readings, the students reacted with enthusiasm and encouragement. They offered incisive critical opinions about items being considered for inclusion, they volunteered to check references and perform the myriad tasks involved in verifying bibliographic citations. But most of all, they made clear through their dedicated and selfless actions that they believed in the need for such a reader. Witnessing their determination provided me with the incentive to carry out the project to its completion. I hope they are pleased with the result.

From the inception of the project, a number of students played key roles. Gina McOuat tracked down the original articles, traced the location of items missing from library shelves, and duplicated what must have seemed like endless articles so that they could be reviewed, classified, and, in many cases, ultimately rejected. Carol Ann O'Brien monitored the progress of correspondence with publishers, prodded me to pursue somewhat casual correspondents, and suggested including a section on microcomputers. Patricia Bellamy became editorially indispensable as she applied her intricate knowledge of the Chicago *Manual of Style* to the idiosyncratic practices of twenty-nine authors and eleven publishers. Denise Bruno compiled the index. Not content with a mere author-subject listing, she examined each item in exquisite detail to determine the precise importance given to each name included and then developed a weighting scheme to aid users in determining whether the reference was suited to their particular needs. To these four MLS students I would like to express my very special appreciation.

Thanks also to the many publishers and authors who granted copyright permission to use their material. Without their understanding and cooperation, this project could not have been realized.

Final appreciation is reserved for Andrea Pedolsky, editor, and Patricia Schuman, publisher, whose encouragement, advice, and experience proved invaluable to me throughout this undertaking.

Planning is the first step of the management process. It is critical to the ultimate success of the activity being undertaken but, ironically, is often overlooked in the pressures of coping with current operations. Managers, being for the most part action oriented, tend to give planning short shrift, regarding it as a nebulous exercise in dealing with intangibles. Yet planning is a far cry from soothsaying or fortune telling. It is a method of determining in advance what actions should be taken and how human and other resources should be allocated in order to achieve identified goals.

Planning takes place at different levels in the organization. While senior executives are more likely to be concerned with factors in the external environment such as economic, governmental, and legal issues, and social, technological, and market influences that impinge on the organization as a whole, middle managers and supervisors are usually more interested in how changes in these areas will affect their own daily functioning. To help predict these events, a variety of forecasting techniques are available. These range from qualitative techniques such as the Delphi method and market surveys, to the projection of historical trends into the future, to casual modeling using regression and econometric models. But no matter which approach is used, the planning process involves the setting of goals and objectives, the collection of data regarding prevailing conditions, the analysis of these data to determine the advantages and disadvantages that apply to the particular courses that might be pursued, the choice among these alternatives, the implementation of the chosen alternative, the evaluation of the implemented plan in light of the goals and objectives set earlier, and, finally, the possible adjustment of the plan to provide a closer fit between the envisioned ideal and the actual reality.

Planning is, then, an ongoing activity engaged in by managers at all levels of the organization. Plans may vary in the time span to which they apply and may cover the short, medium, or long term. They appear in all shapes and sizes: policies, procedures, programs, projects, budgets, and schedules are all examples of plans that vary in complexity, time span, and management level at which they are prepared.

Although planning is absolutely necessary to ensure that goals and objectives are met, the planning process itself is not free from its own pitfalls. It stands to reason that an activity whose outcome will determine the allocation of staff and resources must have the support of senior management. It is also abundantly clear that a planning program will founder if goals and objectives have not been adequately defined. Nor can it be successful if those closest to its ultimate implementation are not involved in the process or if the plan itself becomes so paper-ridden and rigid as to become unworkable.

The most preliminary of plans is the proposal that is usually made to senior management before a new service, such as online reference, is introduced. The basic purpose of such a document is to present convincing evidence as to why such a service should be undertaken. In her article, Jean K. Martin first describes the steps that must be taken in the preparation of the proposal and then goes on to outline the components of the actual document. She emphasizes the importance of careful data gathering and analysis. Information must be collected about the needs of potential users; the estimated volume of usage; the effectiveness, staff time, and cost of online searching compared with manual; the appropriateness of various databases, vendors, and types of equipment; the impact and benefits of online services; alternatives to operating one's own service; and the changes, if any, that will be needed to cover costs. If, after analyzing all of this information, the planner is convinced that online services should be introduced, a proposal to the next higher level of management is prepared. Martin goes on to suggest a basic outline for a proposal and gives advice on how it might be effectively presented.

Magdeleine L. Moureau alerts the reader to some of the difficulties that may be encountered by both managers and users of an online service. She pinpoints physical, economic, technical, and social constraints and issues related to vendors, telecommunications, and suppliers. Problems created by existing organizational structures and those arising from the use of a new technique are also identified. Her article also provides insight into the additional problems encountered by Europeans using products developed primarily for an American market—problems related to disparities in distance, language, and information infrastructures and national economies.

Though the advice given in both these articles is sound and distills the experiences of seasoned professionals, they cannot hope to provide all the information needed for the effective planning of online services. The Additional Readings list general overviews, texts, and monographs, as well as a few articles that deal with specific situations, to supplement the background needed by planners to ensure that their efforts have an optimal chance of meeting with success.

Preparation of Proposals for Online Bibliographic Services in Academic, Government, and Industrial Libraries

Jean K. Martin

INTRODUCTION

With the budgetary restrictions library managers are facing in all types of libraries today, it becomes increasingly important to justify new expenditures. The initiation of online search services by the library represents an item within the budget which comes under close scrutiny, partially because it is a nontraditional service. In an academic setting, top management within the library often feels that costs of such services must be either wholly or partially recovered through user fees. In the special library in industry or government, there is perhaps less emphasis on cost recovery.

However, search service costs are likely to represent a significant part of a library budget, particularly start-up costs. Regardless of the extent of the prospective user population, all sizes and types of libraries will incur such basic costs as computer terminal purchase or lease, staff training and manuals. Even in a small to moderate-sized library such costs may be nearly equal to those in a much larger organization. Once the service is underway, costs in those libraries serving larger user populations are likely to be higher than those in smaller organizations, assuming that any assessment of user fees will not deter prospective clientele from utilizing online searching.

Therefore, a process of data gathering and careful analysis is essential to determine the feasibility of offering online search services within the library. Along with the preliminary analysis will come the selecting and

Reprinted with permission of Haworth Press from *Science and Technology Libraries* 1 (Fall 1980):7-15.

planning which must precede the preparation of a final proposal to management.

ANALYSIS AND PLANNING

The responsibility for gathering supporting documentation, analysis, and preparation of a proposal will vary with the type and size of library. In a small to moderate-sized industrial or government library, the library manager is likely to assume the responsibility for analysis and planning. In a large special library or academic library, the head of the reference department or a departmental library may assume this role.

Whether top management requires a formal written proposal, merely a verbal presentation/demonstration, or no information, it is important that the librarian responsible for the proposed service not skip the planning stage.

Needs Assessment

The planner must determine whether a need exists for such a service. Many times such an assessment is an intuitive one—made on the basis of recognized weaknesses in the library's collection and the realization that online search services could offer far more to meet the literature needs of users than could the current staff without such services. The assessment may take the form of a survey of prospective users or informal discussions with key clientele of reference services.

Anticipated Usage

Perhaps one of the most difficult parts of the preliminary study is to estimate volume of usage of the online service. Much will depend on the type of library and clientele and the extent to which services are promoted. Although an estimate may be based on experiences of other libraries with similar characteristics, professional judgment plays a large role in estimating volume of usage.

Comparison with Manual Searching

Various authors have conducted comparative analyses of manual and online searching to determine their respective degree of effectiveness, staff time, and costs. The planner may be able to utilize some of the data provided by others, or may wish to develop his or her own estimates. Among the articles which may be useful are those by Bivans,[1] Calkins,[2] Cooper and DeWath,[3] Elchesen,[4] Elman,[5] and Johnson.[6] There is considerable evidence that online searching is cost-effective, though in some situations this may not be true.

Database and Vendor Selection

One must assess one's needs for the various databases available, based upon user population, relative costs, and accessibility through database vendors. Christian's book, *The Electronic Library*,[7] provides information on databases and vendor services, to aid the planner. One may also want to read the articles by Williams[8] and by Weiss,[9] as well as pages 35-39 in Atherton and Christian,[10] which aid in evaluating and selecting such services. The directory of databases published by Cuadra Associates[11] and the one edited by Williams[12] will also prove useful.

Terminal Selection

Among the factors one will want to consider when choosing a terminal are degree of quietness desired and speed. Terminals currently most widely used for online searching generally operate at a speed of 30 or 120 characters per second. Portability may be desirable, if one foresees the need to move the terminal occasionally from one location to another. Searchers seem unanimous that a terminal must provide hardcopy. If one anticipates providing many online demonstrations, particularly to groups of people, one may wish to select a cathode ray tube (CRT) terminal with hardcopy terminal attachment. The option of the purchase or rental of a terminal will depend on the individual situation. However, many library managers believe that a purchase is more cost-effective, since lease or rental prices for good terminals over a couple of years would equate to the purchase price. The reader is referred to articles by Radwin,[13] Stewart,[14] and to *Online Terminal Guide and Directory*[15] for comparative information. Bonn and Heel[16] provide a useful discussion of terminology which one encounters in descriptions of terminals.

Impact of Online Services

Perhaps one does not fully realize the impact on one's staffing, budget, and other services until one has had actual experience with online search services. However, a number of articles have been written within the last few years which point out some considerations for the planner of such services. Among references to general impact of services are those by Atherton and Christian,[17] DeGennaro,[18] and Hawkins.[19] For the effect on professional and clerical staff, especially see Atherton and Christian.[20] An increased volume of interlibrary loan requests has been noted by Calkins,[21] Hawkins,[22] and Martin.[23] Calkins also reported significant increases in circulation of books and periodicals, after online search services were initiated. Collection development is another area in which changes have been reported. Wanger's survey[24] noted that 28% of library managers had to make such adjustments, primarily through increasing the number of journal subscriptions, but a few also reported adjustments in collecting monographs and technical reports. Additional recordkeeping is required by both professional and clerical staff.[25]

Benefits in Offering Services

No matter whether the library has a modest collection serving a small organization or is part of a large academic system, the positive effects of offering online services are considerable. Through use of online search services, the library can provide much greater access to literature, particularly if one selects database vendors offering a large number of databases. Librarians report a more positive self-image,[26] as well as greater esteem on the part of library users, once online searching is provided. Not only can libraries provide access to a broader base of literature, but they can do it in a fraction of the time which would be required by a manual search. The speed and ease of access are very impressive, particularly to first-time users.

Alternatives to Online Searching

In addition to the two options of continuing with the traditional, manual searches, or accessing online search services through an inhouse terminal, one should consider other alternatives. It may not be economically feasible to operate one's own service, because of a low volume of searches needed, or having to pay minimum guaranteed fees for access to specialized databases, for instance. Therefore the manager may consider occasionally utilizing the search services of an information broker on an informal basis, or may enter into a contractual agreement. McCann and Burgess[27] provide guidelines adopted by their government agency in securing proposals from outside sources to provide search services for them.

Charging for Services

Depending upon the philosophy of the host organization and the ready availability of funds for providing a supplementary service of online searching, the library may elect to provide services without charge, or on a full or partial cost-recovery basis (the latter often meaning the library absorbs staffing costs). Since most academic libraries traditionally have not conducted extensive manual literature searches for faculty and students, they are more likely to gain authorization to initiate services only if at least some costs are passed on to users. However, in an industrial or government library which historically has prepared bibliographies for users, librarians can more readily show that the service is cost-effective so that the library could bear all costs. Some considerations to aid the planner are provided by Atherton and Christian,[28] Cooper and DeWath,[29] and by Huston.[30] Drinan[31] provides excellent guidelines for pricing online services.

PROPOSAL PREPARATION

After analyzing the data gathered, the planner must make a decision whether or not the library should offer an online search service. If the decision is in favor of implementation, the next step is preparing a proposal for the next higher level of management. One has to know one's management in order to determine the degree of formality of the proposal, or whether one is even needed.

A few librarians have found that no proposals were necessary. For instance, Valerie Noble[32] at The Upjohn Company Business Library initiated online services in 1973 without having prepared a proposal, based upon her assessment of the need for such a service, and she projected costs into her library budget. Connie Steward[33] at the General Electric Electronics Park Library also reports that no written proposal was prepared when services were initiated in the mid-1970s. Otherwise, some prorating of costs to departments may be required. Written proposals were prepared by Urban Sweeney[34] at General Dynamics Corporation, Convair Division, and by the author at the USDA Russell Research Center and her present company. One gains the impression, in reading Atherton and Christian's book,[35] as well as various articles, that academic librarians generally must write proposals. This has been reaffirmed in conversations the author has had with academic librarians.

The online search service planner will find several good references available to aid in assessing needs and preparing proposals, some of which have already been mentioned, and others are in the list of references at the end of this paper. Particularly useful are the article by Hoover[36] and books by Atherton and Christian[37] and by Wax.[38] Not only is the textual material valuable, but the publications contain many useful examples of budgets, fee schedules, and forms for search requests and internal record-keeping.

The length of the proposal and the topics to be included will vary from one type of environment to another. The library manager who prepares the final proposal for submission to upper management of the organization should tailor the proposal to fit his or her own situation. If one's superior does not want to be bothered with details, the report should contain only essential information, such as proposed plan for service, benefits, and cost data. Fiscally-oriented managers will want to see detailed cost analyses on which the budget is based, etc. The following is suggested as a basic outline for a proposal.

1. Introduction
2. Plan for Service
3. Benefits of Online Services
4. Impact of Services on the Library
5. Budget
6. Recommendations

A discussion of each section is presented below. Much of the information required by the library manager will have been obtained during the planning stage discussed previously.

Introduction

This section may include a brief history or overview of computer literature searching as well as prospects for the future and implications for the library in one's own institution.

Plan for Service

The library manager should carefully outline the mode of operation which is proposed, including staffing, primary user groups, user interface, estimated volume, and projected date of initiation. This would also be an appropriate place to indicate databases which are expected to be more highly relevant to the needs of primary users, and database vendors which may best meet those needs. If cost recovery is part of the plan, it should be discussed in this section. Plans for promotion of the online services and staff training may be included in this section too.

Benefits of Online Services

This section should include the positive aspects which have been ascertained during the planning stage, presenting statements as to the cost-effectiveness of providing online search services. This is a very important section of the proposal, which may well "sell" management on the initiation of services, so much thought and careful preparation are needed.

Impact of Services on the Library

This section should include some indication of the possible effect on staffing. One example of this would be an assessment of how readily the present staff can handle the increased workload, not only that created by the search service interaction, but also the aftereffects, such as increased use of books and periodicals and interlibrary loan services. The acquisitions policy may need to be modified by adding new subscriptions and dropping old ones, as well as perhaps changing the emphasis of the monograph collection, and purchasing more technical reports. The service will affect the library budget, not just direct costs in providing the services, but also in increased purchases of materials and interlibrary loan charges.

Budget

Librarians who have written about budgeting for online services tend to agree that one needs to prepare a two-part budget. One part should outline the costs of initiation of such services, which would cover perhaps a six-month or a one-year period. This will include many of the large, one-time costs, such as purchase of equipment and manuals, as well as staff training, possible modifications to the facility to accommodate the terminal and staff to operate it, additional telephone lines for terminals, etc. Of course, recurring costs such as online charges incurred during the start-up period should be included also. The second part of the budget should consist of a one-year estimate (following the start-up budget) of recurring costs. Several authors have prepared guidelines for estimating costs and preparing a budget. Among them are Atherton and Christian,[39] Drinan,[40] and Cooper and DeWath.[41] Needless to say, this section should be prepared with great care and as accurately as possible. Probably the most difficult part to estimate will be the vendor costs, which will have to be based on a projected volume of usage. One may find it valuable to consult with other librarians in a similar environment when estimating such costs. After a year or so of experience, it of course becomes easier to make cost projections for the budgets of succeeding years.

Recommendations

The final section may contain a brief summary of the important points discussed earlier in the proposal. It should, of course, include a firm recommendation that the plan for initiation of online search services be implemented within the library.

PRESENTATION OF THE PROPOSAL

The degree of formality of the presentation and the intended audience will vary from organization to organization. Some managers prefer having something in hand (the proposal) to read and evaluate and will make a decision solely on the basis of the written proposal. Others will appreciate a verbal presentation in addition to the written proposal. Of course, there are some who want only an informal verbal presentation, with perhaps a copy of the proposed budget or total dollar investment figure. Some organizations will require evaluation by a committee. In some instances it may be desirable to borrow a terminal and arrange for access to a relevant database so that one may provide a demonstration of the capabilities of the service. A well-executed online search can be very impressive in convincing management of the desirability of initiating online search services.

PERSONAL OBSERVATIONS AND CONCLUSIONS

After working in academic, government, and industrial libraries, and maintaining communication with other librarians in all three types of libraries, the author concludes that one may make specific recommendations only in relation to specific situations. Broad generalizations about introduction of online search services can be misleading. There are too many types and sizes of libraries and many other factors which one must take into account. For instance, librarians in some organizations have a high degree of authority and can initiate services without obtaining prior approval from higher echelons of the organization. Others are able to take advantage of subsidies to initiate such services in order to generate interest and enthusiasm among users.

The author, while head of The University of Texas Physics-Math-Astronomy Library in the early 1970s, was able to offer inhouse searching (without cost to users) of the American Institute of Physics SPIN tapes, partially because of a grant from the University Research Institute. It was not necessary to present a written proposal.

As head of the USDA Russell Research Center Library the author began online service following approval of a written proposal. One favorable factor was due to the National Agricultural Library having offered at that time a six-month subsidy of terminal and vendor costs, which created a stimulus to initiate online searching. However, it is felt that the proposal would have been approved, even without the subsidy, since interest was very strong. During the initial six-month period enthusiasm spread among the researchers at the organization, and there was never any question about continuing the service after the subsidy ended.

More recently as manager of the library at Molycorp, Inc. the author found management receptive to a carefully documented written proposal. Management supported the view that such a service is cost-effective and valuable to the various groups whom the library serves.

The librarian who is interested in initiating online search services has many resources from which to draw in conducting an analysis and planning for online searching. If it is determined that online searching is feasible and desirable within the organization, the library planner must convince management, often through a proposal. With a well-prepared proposal, the library manager should be able to convince top management that online searching provides an invaluable extension to traditional reference services.

Footnotes

1. Margaret M. Bivans, "A Comparison of Manual and Machine Literature Searches," *Special Libraries* 65 (May/June 1974):216-22.
2. Mary L. Calkins, "Online Services and Operational Costs," *Special Libraries* 68 (January 1977):13-17.
3. Michael D. Cooper and Nancy DeWath, "The Cost of Online Bibliographic Searching," *Journal of Library Automation* 9 (September 1976):195-209.
4. Dennis R. Elchesen, "Cost-Effectiveness Comparison of Manual and Online Retrospective Bibliographic Searching," *Journal of the American Society for Information Science* 29 (March 1978):56-66.
5. Stanley A. Elman, "Cost Comparison of Manual and Online Computerized Literature Searching," *Special Libraries* 66 (January 1975):12-18.
6. Susan M. Johnson, "Choosing between Manual and Online Searching: Practical Experience in the Ministry of Agriculture, Fisheries and Food," *Aslib Proceedings* 30 (October/November 1978):383-93.
7. Roger W. Christian, *The Electronic Library: Bibliographic Databases, 1978-79*, rev. 2d ed., Professional Librarian Series (White Plains, N.Y.: Knowledge Industry Publications, 1978).
8. Martha E. Williams, "Criteria for Evaluation and Selection of Databases and Database Services," *Special Libraries* 66 (December 1975):561-69.
9. Irvin Weiss, "Evaluation of ORBIT and DIALOG Using Six Databases," *Special Libraries* 67 (December 1976):574-81.
10. Pauline Atherton and Roger W. Christian, *Librarians and Online Services* (White Plains, N.Y.: Knowledge Industry Publications, 1977), pp. 35-59.
11. *Directory of Online Databases* (Santa Monica, Calif.: Cuadra Associates, 1979).
12. Martha E. Williams, ed., *Computer Readable Databases: A Directory and Data Sourcebook*, 2d ed. (White Plains, N.Y.: Knowledge Industry Publications, 1979).

13. Mark S. Radwin, "The Intelligent Person's Guide to Choosing a Terminal for Online Interactive Use," *Online* 1 (January 1977):11-17, 64-66.
14. Alan K. Stewart, "The 1200 Baud Experience," *Online* 2 (July 1978):13-18.
15. *Online Terminal Guide and Directory, 1979-80*, (Weston, Conn.: Online, 1979).
16. Jane H. Bonn and Philipp R. Heer, "Terminal Equipment for Online Interactive Information Retrieval Using Telecommunications," *Special Libraries* 67 (January 1976):30-39.
17. Atherton and Christian, *Librarians and Online Services*, pp. 5-9.
18. Richard DeGennaro, "Providing Bibliographic Services from Machine-Readable Databases: The Library's Role," *Journal of Library Automation* 6 (December 1973):215-22.
19. Donald T. Hawkins, "Impact of Online Systems on a Literature Searching Service," *Special Libraries* 67 (December 1976):559-67.
20. Atherton and Christian, *Librarians and Online Services*, pp. 18-21, 58-59.
21. Calkins, "Online Services and Operational Costs," p. 14.
22. Hawkins, "Impact of Online Systems on a Literature Searching Service," p. 566.
23. Jean K. Martin, "Computer Based Literature Searching: Impact on Interlibrary Loan Service," *Special Libraries* 69 (January 1978):1-6.
24. Judith Wanger, Carlos A. Cuadra, and Mary Fishburn, *Impact of Online Retrieval Services: A Survey of Users, 1974-75* (Santa Monica, Calif.: System Development Corporation, 1976).
25. Atherton and Christian, *Librarians and Online Services*, p. 21.
26. Ibid., pp. 21-22.
27. Anne McCann and Jonathan G. Burgess, "Procurement of Literature Searching Services," *Online* 3 (January 1979):36-48.
28. Atherton and Christian, *Librarians and Online Services*, pp. 22-23.
29. Michael D. Cooper and Nancy DeWath, "The Effect of Users Fees on the Cost of Online Searching in Libraries," *Journal of Library Automation* 10 (December 1977):304-319.
30. Mary M. Huston, "Fee or Free: The Effect of Charging on Information Demand," *Library Journal* 104 (September 1979):1811-14.
31. Helen Drinan, "Financial Management of Online Services: A How to Guide," *Online* 3 (October 1979):14-21.
32. Personal communication with Valerie Noble, February 15, 1980.
33. Personal communication with Connie Steward, February 18, 1980.
34. Personal communication with Urban J. Sweeney, February 18, 1980.
35. Atherton and Christian, *Librarians and Online Services*.
36. Ryan E. Hoover, "Computer Aided Reference Services in the Academic Library: Experiences in Organizing and Operating an Online Reference Service," *Online* 3 (October 1979):28-41.
37. Atherton and Christian, *Librarians and Online Services*.
38. David M. Wax, *A Handbook for the Introduction of Online Bibliographic Search Services into Academic Libraries*, Office of University Library Management Studies, Occasional Papers, no. 4 (Washington, D.C.: Association of Research Libraries, 1976).

39. Atherton and Christian, *Librarians and Online Services*, especially pp. 30-31 and 55-62.
40. Drinan, "Financial Management of Online Services."
41. Cooper and DeWath, "The Cost of Online Bibliographic Searching."

Problems and Pitfalls in Setting Up and Operating an Online Information Service

Magdeleine L. Moureau

1 INTRODUCTION

In setting up an online retrieval facility, one meets problems and difficulties stemming from natural constraints and specific or national interests which oppose one another, together with the economic problems they entail and the need for standardization they require. Information networks do not escape from any of these pitfalls, and this is particularly true of online retrieval services.

In the following sections, these pitfalls are examined firstly from the point of view of those who provide the service and determine how it operates, i.e. the suppliers, and secondly from the point of view of those who give life to the retrieval service and justify its existence, i.e. the users.

2 THE SUPPLIERS

The first series of problems and pitfalls are part of the overall service itself. A second series of difficulties stem from the individual components of the system.

2.1 Structure of the Service

The various difficulties encountered depend on the nature of the service, e.g. whether it is international or national, multidisciplinary, interdisciplinary or specialized. Usually they have identical causes, i.e. too much physical, economic, technical or social heterogeneity between

Reprinted with permission of Learned Information Ltd. from *Online Review* 2 (1978):237-244.

different points in the network. This leads to elements that are too disparate and which cannot all be fused together in the same system.

(1) Physical Pitfalls

(a) Existing monopolies forbidding the use of the service at one or several points (e.g. *Excerpta Medica* on Lockhead Dialog inaccessible to German users).

(b) Linguistic problems created by the existence of different languages or, even worse, different scripts.

(c) Hardware problems resulting from the use of too dissimilar equipment.

(d) Problems of methodology arise when operational modes are so difficult to make compatible that they have to be partially or totally abandoned.

(e) Problems of geographic location and the time and money constraints resulting from too great distances.

(2) Economic Problems

(a) The difficulty in equitably dividing up the charges of the service and in obtaining a consensus on this matter.

(b) The disparity of the resources of the various participants.

(c) The problem of subsidies (e.g. one participant may be subsidized, and another not).

(d) A difference in the evaluation of the cost effectiveness by the different parties involved, with some often feeling more affected by the additional work load than by the new services rendered.

(e) The problem of pricing, with the same product priced differently by different services.

(3) Technical Problems

These are associated with the large differences that exist in
(a) Subject coverage (energy, geology, chemistry, medicine etc.).
(b) Communication systems (networks, teleprocessing etc.).
(c) Information technology (thesaurus, indexing, semantics etc.).

(4) Social Problems

These are mainly problems of leadership:
(a) To work properly, a service must have an executive structure which, no matter how light it may be, involves a certain delegation of power. If such an organization does not already exist, or if a body is

already performing this function, this delegation of power generally leads to problems of *precedence*, with two extreme cases: (1) positive precedence, with each wanting command; (2) negative precedence, with no one wanting to command and yet not accepting the least subordination.

(*b*) Mention should also be made of the conflicts and risks of secession involved.

(*c*) The smooth functioning of a network. Some participants are linked to other components or other authorities. This makes them incapable of taking any decision or upholding a decision taken by the other participants without first referring it to consultation, a process that may take months and hold up the operation of the entire service.

It can now be seen that the pitfalls are structural and do not arise from the nature of a network. An international service should logically be more difficult to set up and operate than a national service, and specialized service more difficult than a multidisciplinary one. This is not always the case. Everything depends on the service's homogeneity and on the willingness of the parties involved to make it succeed.

Also, whereas an international service generally has to take linguistic difficulties into consideration, it will often have less difficulty in avoiding economic, technical and social pitfalls because of the technical and economic similarity of the partners involved.

2.2 Components of the Network

We indentify three components: (i) online vendors; (ii) telecommunications; and (iii) database suppliers.

(1) Online Vendors

Rather than pitfalls, we shall refer to constraints with regard to such problems as defining the product, its maintenance and its price:

(*a*) Definition of the software product and its comparison to other existing systems.

(*b*) Choice of hardware.

(*c*) Choice of databases.

(*d*) Maintenance of the software in the face of new requirements.

(*e*) Maintenance of the databases: (i) its cleanness and absence of defects associated with the online vendor's manipulation of the data. (ii) the need for rapid updating.

(*f*) Need to keep users informed on all improvements, changes or problems with the operation of the system: (i) by a series of messages supplied online on the vendor's system; (ii) by the publication of newsletters announcing and explaining any changes; (iii) by the presence of specialists able to answer any request for information or assistance by telephone and this can mean up to 12 hours per day in systems operating in several time zones.

(g) Standardization problems which might entail a partial or total rewriting of the system (e.g. the common command language set being studied by the European Commission for Euronet.

(h) The problem and cost of user training, the writing of instruction manuals, training sessions with the attendant problems of distance, dispersion and language.

(i) Financial problems.

(2) Telecommunications

Data transmission depends more and more on 'public' telecommunication systems over which it has no control and almost no influence. Yet this transmission is the umbilical cord joining the online vendor and its users. It can be considered as the most vulnerable element in the chain, whereas in reality it should be entirely transparent.

(a) The telecommunication network may be considered as an essential infrastructure for a country's development, with all the resulting facilities, but it may also be considered as a luxury item and hence be reserved for a lucky few who are able to pay the price.

(b) Either telecommunication and datatransmission networks are in the hands of private firms, with a policy for competing with one another, and with minimum government control (this is the situation in the USA), with all the problems generated by free enterprise; or these networks are in the hands of national PTT services and operate on a monopolistic basis (this is the situation in Europe), with all the problems generated by a monopoly.

(c) The pricing policy: (i) depending on distance (like the telephone at present); (ii) independent of distance but priced by the hour, per character transmitted, or subscription; (iii) with minimum charge.

Some combinations penalize users more than others. The main problem lies in knowing what organization, authority or association will be able to talk directly with the bodies providing the telecommunication services and to attempt to influence them and make them responsive to user needs.

Whatever the case may be, the unsatisfactory operation of this intermediate but essential part, or its operation at too high a price, can be enough to kill new, struggling online services and their associated databases.

(3) Databases

(a) The first problem is the adequacy of the database for online processing. This depends on (i) the type and refinement of its indexing, (ii) the type and number of identifying fields used, (iii) the language of the database, (iv) the choice of the processing systems software permitting optimum exploitation of the database.

(b) The maintenance of an online database entails responsibilities such as better indexing and the necessary evolution toward greater standardization of the nomenclature and format (cf. *Reference Manual for Machine Readable Bibliographic Description*), rapidity of updating and the control of changes in the online system.

(c) Training raises the same problems as those already mentioned for online vendors.

(d) The pricing policy must take account of the way costs are broken down among the different conventional and new products that are distributed. It must be borne in mind that the loss of a single subscription to the paper version of the bibliographic bulletin can cost more than the royalties paid for several months' use of the online system. Therefore, putting a database online may threaten its very existence.

In the operation of a traditional database (bibliographic bulletin on paper), the cost of compiling the database itself represents about 80 per cent of the total costs, and the distribution costs including printing, represent about 20 per cent.

For operating computerized online databases, distribution costs (processing system + telecommunications system) represent from 70 to 90 per cent of the price paid by the user. There is therefore an economic transfer to the detriment of those who supply the product and to the benefit of those who transmit it.

Confronted with this new problem, the producer of the database can react in three different ways : (i) by increasing the royalties for each reference retrieved; (ii) by limiting access to the database to users who are already subscribers (e.g. API Refining Abstracts); (iii) by practising differential pricing according to the different types of users, i.e. subscribers and nonsubscribers (e.g. Derwent, Petroleum Abstracts). Other restrictions can be considered (e.g. the number of hours of use).

In any case, the survival of a database depends of an effective planning policy. The lack of antecedents furthur accentuates the uncertainty with regard to pricing and promotion strategies that will give it the best long-range viability.

3 THE USERS

Roughly speaking, two types of users can be considered, namely intermediate users who search for information at the request of others, and end users who search for their own purposes.

Among the problems and pitfalls encountered or caused by these two types of users, a distinction must be made between two problems, namely those inherent in already existing structures, and those that arise from the use of a new technique.

3.1 Problems Inherent in Already Existing Structures

(1) From the Point of View of Intermediaries:

(a) The presence of a traditional documentaion/library function that is reasonably satisfactory.

(b) The presence of an in-house computerized system with which the online information service enters into conflict, and a desire to defend and perpetuate the existing system.

(c) The presence of one or several online systems already in place, already used and hence well known and satisfactory and which supply the same type of service as the new system that is proposed, so that investment in training to use the new system does not seem justified.

(2) From the Point of View of End Users:

(a) Satisfaction with their own documentation method.

(b) Unshakable belief in the 'invisible college' and in the inefficiency of any documentation system, whether computerized or not.

3.2 Problems Arising from the Use of a New Technique

(1) Intermediate Users

(a) When the system is not introduced. This refusal may have various causes: (i) Negative attitudes by the intermediary himself:

— a critical attitude, whether right or wrong, with regard to the new method, which is assumed to be unable to solve the problems at hand;
— apprehension with regard to a new system and fear of being incompetent in using it;

— fear that a new system will create too much of an additional work load and upset existing habits.

(ii) Positive attitude countered by:

— the absence of support by the management in the face of a service which generates new charges;
— the absence of apparent user needs.

(b) *When the system is introduced:* (i) Problem of training the existing staff to use it: At present training is mainly based on individual and solitary efforts by users by way of manuals and instructions provided by the systems as well as on trial and error searches via the terminal. The types of training that exist are: That provided by the online vendors. It may be reproached for

— lacking any critical outlook with regard to its product;
— poorly understanding the products it distributes.

That provided by the database suppliers. It can be reproached for

— lacking any critical outlook with regard to its product and a failure to see the product weaknesses;
— not providing any comparative information on databases that may compete with the product;
— too many trainees at a time;
— trainees at too many different levels of competence;
— training sessions given in a foreign language.

(ii) Problems of hiring skilled searchers—on the level of higher education two problems arise : the need to start from scratch and the absence of a technically competent teaching staff, for using both systems and databases—hindering the setting up of institutionalized teaching. It is very difficult to know what sort of demand there will be for qualified specialists. In any case, the nonexistence of such specialists remains an obstacle to the use of such services.

(ii) Economic problems: There is no doubt that the price per reference found online is very much lower than the price per reference found by manual methods. In our own documentation center, calculations reveal a ratio of at least 1 to 10 for the most favourable manual search cases (i.e. bibliographic tools used for manual searching that are available on the spot).

However, for a search done online the user experiences an outflow of money, whereas for a manual search the costs incurred are all inhouse. Everything depends on the relative value of the time saved by computerized searching.

As a result, online bibliographic services are greatly underused because users think, rightly or wrongly, that they cannot pay current prices, although they are very low in absolute value.

The second problem capable of seriously handicapping the development of an information transmission network is the pricing policy followed by all or part of the network.

A user who is convinced that he must pay a fair price for information may be entirely discouraged by an invoicing and control policy that is too complex or restictive.

— An annual subscription, even one not costing very much, deters small new users who do not yet know whether they will be able to amortize this investment.
— A subscription per identification number, i.e. per system to be interrogated as operated by some European PTT's, will discourage users from subsribing to a new system on the market. They will be inclined to remain with the 'supermarket' services offering the most databases, such as Lockheed, SDC or SDS/ESRIN at present.
— Minimum fee for a certain number of minutes will force users to group small questions together, and so they will lose the benefit of the immediate availability of online information.
— Invoicing on the basis of the number of characters transmitted raises the problem of both how to control this number and its reinvoicing if needs be.
— A database that places too many restrictions and controls on its use risks either seeing its rules infringed, even in good faith, or of seeing its use decrease.

The pricing structure, no matter what it stems from, must be as absolutely simple as possible. A complicated formula offers not the slightest guarantee of greater income for the vendor, but it automatically entails higher operating expenditures. It increases the cost of services without providing any supplementary income. In addition, since operating expenditure is on manpower, computerization results in transferring the work load from bibliographers to accountants.

(2) The End User

The end user is the one who is supposed to benefit the most from online networks. However, statistics show that the user who makes the most use of systems to fulfil solely his own needs represents hardly 5 per cent of the total number of users.

(a) *Training*

The reason for this is that for only a few questions per year it is not justifiable to invest the time and effort required to assimilate the system whose procedures are quickly forgotten if not used regularly.

The end user who acquires and maintains some expertise will quickly be consulted by his colleagues and will take on the status of an intermediary.

However, faced with the growth of available systems (for the IFP Documentation Center alone, five systems can be used: SDC, Lockheed, SDS, Control Data and General Electric), with the increasing appearance of non-bibliographic databases and with the promises of Euronet, an intermediary cannot indefinitely increase his range of action, especially with regard to databanks supplying not only data but also the means of inserting them into calculations and models. As was generally the case with manual systems, those that are too specific will have to be left to the end user. Therefore, promoters of highly specialized databanks will have to hunt for their users and to provide this type of clientele with suitable training.

(b) *Research Secrecy*

An end user may also refuse to make use of an outside system, whether national or foreign (the latter case being all the more serious), out of fear of revealing what he is up to and hence jeopardizing the secrecy of his research.

(c) References without Quality Control

The end user may even suffer from the excellence of the system, through which he can receive all publications available in his field.

A National Bureau of Standards study asserts that 50 per cent of the data supplied by scientific literature are unusable for one reason or another. Therefore, a selection has to be made, which is in turn time consuming. As a result, the end user prefers selectivity to exhaustiveness and is content with a few journals or publications by institutions considered to be predominant in the field.

(d) Difficulty of Obtaining Primary Documents

Online information systems result in a greater demand for primary documents and for more and more exotic documents that are often hard to find.

But ·faced with the problem of demands for the reproduction of primary documents, publishers appear to be acting more and more vigorously to impose copyright regulations that will close many doors on specialized institutions who will have to eliminate their reproduction services as too heavy a load to bear.

If primary documents become too difficult to acquire easily and quickly, part of the benefit of online systems will disappear, and their utilization will suffer in consequence.

This has been a quick rundown of the problems and pitfalls that computerized information systems are facing. Such systems are still undergoing a phase of development, and their existence is characterized by the search for an equilibrium and for the critical mass that will enable them to sustain their forward progress.

Additional Readings—
Planning for Online Reference

Atherton, Pauline, and Christian, Roger W. *Librarians and Online Services.* White Plains, N.Y. Knowledge Industry Publications, 1977.

Borgman, Christine L., Moghdam, Dineh, and Corbett, Patti K. *Effective Online Seaching: A Basic Text.* New York: Marcel Dekker, 1984.

Chen, Ching-chih. *Online Bibliographic Searching: A Learning Manual.*New York: Neal-Schuman, 1981.

Fenichel, Carol H., and Hogan, Thomas H. *Online Searching: A Primer.* Marlton, N.J.: Learned Information, 1981.

Hawkins, Donald T. "Online Information Retrieval Bibliography Seventh Update Part 1." *Online Review* 8 (June 1984): 247-277. 'Part II.' *Online Review* 8 (August 1984): 325-381.

Henry, W.M. et al. *Online Searching: An Introduction.* London: Butterworth. 1980.

Hoover, Ryan E., ed. *Library and Information Managers' Guide to Online Services.* White Plains, N.Y.: Knowledge Industry Publications, 1980.

Katz, Bill, ed. *Reference and Online Services Handbook: Guidelines, Policies and Procedures for Libraries.* New York: Neal-Schuman, 1982.

Katz, Bill, and Fraley, Ruth A., eds. *Video to Online: Reference Services and the New Technology.* New York: Haworth Press, 1983.

Lee, Joann H., ed. *Online Searching: the Basics, Settings, and Management.* Littleton, Colo.: Libraries Unlimited, 1984.

Maloney, James J., ed. *Online Searching Technique and Management.* Chicago: American Library Association, 1983.

Meadow, Charles T. and Cochrane, Pauline A. *Basics of Online Searching.* Toronto: John Wiley & Sons, 1981.

Nichol, Kathleen M. "Database Proliferation: Implications for Librarians." *Special Libraries* 74 (April 1983):110-118.

Palmer, Roger C. *Online Reference and Information Retrieval.* Littleton, Colo.: Libraries Unlimited, 1983.

Pensyl, Mary E. "The Online Policy Manual . . . " *Online* 6 (May 1982): 46-49.

Roose, Tina. "Going Online: The Ten Most-Asked Questions." *Library Journal* 109 (Sept. 1, 1984): 1614-1615.

Wax, D.M. *A Handbook for the Introduction of Online Bibliographic Search Services Into Academic Libraries.* Washington, D.C.: Association of Research Libraries, Office of University Library Management Studies, 1976.

It is by now commonplace to refer to the growth of the online industry during the 1970s as explosive. Whereas in the early part of that decade barely a handful of databases were available through two or three commercial vendors, now well over a thousand databases are produced by a plethora of public and private, for-profit and not-for-profit organizations. Virtually every subject is or soon will be retrievable online. With this seemingly endless range of possibilities to contemplate, the choice of what to offer users would now appear to be a daunting task. Nor is it made easier by recent trends in the literature. For as systems, services, and features have proliferated, so have the sources that document their development. Articles in online journals tend to concentrate on specific database characteristics and search strategy techniques while reflective, comprehensive, and general-izable treatments of the field as a whole have become increasingly rare. While this trend is understandable and may be viewed as meeting the needs of information specialists for detailed explan-atory aids to help them cope with the increasing complexity and sophistication of their field, it does little to provide a coherent, unified perspective for the provision of online services as a whole. For discussions of some of the broader, more general questions raised, one must return to the literature of the mid-seventies.

Martha E. Williams has tracked the developments in the online industry virtually since its beginning. In the article included here, she not only provides criteria for evaluating databases and database services and centers, but also suggests the kinds of questions that planners must ask about the relationship of online services to the needs of their host organization.

Most of the issues she raises are as pertinent today as when they were originally written. With regard to database evaluation she suggests that subject coverage, types of original materials indexed, depth of indexing, use of controlled vocabulary and codes, and inclusion of abstracts are among some of the features that need to be considered. If the number of searches performed does not warrant the direct use of a commercial vendor, she points to the purchase of online services from an information center as a more economical alternative and provides guidelines to help make the choice among the different options available. One of the most useful parts of her article asks the planner to consider how increased demands for service will be handled, a frequent occurrence that affects staffs, budgets, and resources but is not usually handled in a systematic manner.

A somewhat different approach to the selection and use of commercially available online bibliographic retrieval services is taken by Doris B. Marshall. From a review of the literature and as a result of her own experiences in introducing online services, she has compiled a checklist of 120 variables that she feels warrant consideration by those responsible for planning and managing online services. These variables are subdivided into the following categories: needs of the user, hardware selection, transmission, system and the vendor, databases, search strategy and evaluation measures, and user-system interface. It is the author's hope that by giving some thought to these matters managers can avoid needless mistakes and help to ensure the successful selection, use, and evaluation of online services.

While the Williams and Marshall articles draw on the literature of the field and the experiences of the authors themselves for their insights, Carol Tenopir represents a more empirical approach. She presents the findings of a research study she carried out to compare the efficacy of two methodologies to evaluate the coverage of bibliographic databases. The focus of her comparison is the bibliography method and the subject profile method. In the former, the citations listed in subject specialized bibliographies or review articles are searched for in databases. In the latter, a profile of terms representing the subject is run against the relevent databases. The subject Tenopir used was volcanology and the databases Geological Reference File (GeoRef) and GeoArchive. She found that both methodologies yielded the same results with respect to amount of coverage in the two databases. She concludes that both these methodologies allow comparisons of databases to discover which includes more literature on a given subject but that the subject profile method is the preferred one since it is less costly to use.

The purpose of presenting these articles has been to provide readers with general guidelines and approaches that would facilitate the process of choosing the most appropriate services and databases from the multitude of resources available. To this end, references to specific vendors and files has been avoided as much as possible. It is recognized, however, that after philosophical issues have been debated and evaluative criteria exhausted, there remain to be made choices among existing vendors and databases that will form the backbone of a real service offered to live users. The references in the Additional Readings to specific vendors and files are meant to aid in those choices.

Criteria for Evaluation and Selection of Databases and Database Services

Martha E. Williams

Database, in the context of this paper, is a term that refers to machine readable collections of information. Although databases may contain numerical, representational, or bibliographic information, the focus will be on bibliographic databases and their potential relationship to libraries. Most of the databases of this type were not created for the purpose of information storage and retrieval but came into existence as a by-product of a publication activity, i.e., when it became economical to use computer-generated tapes to produce abstract and indexing publications. Although these tapes were not initially designed for retrieval purposes, numerous centers began to process them and put them in a form that was more usable for searching. More recently, the "database approach" to management of information has been adopted by many publishers. This approach makes the database central to a wide variety of purposes in an organization and provides properly formatted information for such uses as indexing, abstracting, sequencing of processes, composing, distributing, and searching.

Why should computers be used to search major bibliographic collections? Because it is no longer feasible to search them manually. The size of these collections is voluminous. *Chemical Abstracts* now includes roughly 310,000 abstracts a year. *Biological Abstracts* is producing 250,000 a year. The Institute for Scientific Information in Philadelphia puts out 450,000 yearly citations of source material and then, for each of the source titles listed on their tape, they include an average of ten references cited by the original article. Years ago it was possible to search by hand through documents such as *Chemical Abstracts*. Today it is not readily possible. It is even difficult to determine which section will be appropriate for a particular need. If you are interested in an inter-

Reprinted from *Special Libraries* 66 (12):561-569 (December 1975). © Copyright Special Libraries Association.

disciplinary field such as environmental chemistry, you can not predict that the item of interest will be found in a particular section of *Chemical Abstracts*. One article might legitimately belong to five or six sections within the same secondary source. For example, if an article deals with a particular chemical, that chemical itself may be an organic chemical and belong to organic chemistry; or that chemical may be detected by a particular analytical instrument and belong to analytical chemistry; or it may be something that is released into the air and therefore belongs to air pollution. It may fall on the ground and become part of soil chemistry; it may wash into a stream and become part of water pollution. There are numerous ways to look at the same publication.

Currently, most of the major fields in science and technology and a few fields in the social sciences and humanities, have machine readable databases. In general, these bases fall into four classes, either disciplinary databases such as CAS Condensates, COMPENDEX or BIOSIS Previews, mission-oriented databases such as those produced by NASA or the Energy Research and Development Administration (ERDA, formerly Atomic Energy Commission); problem-oriented databases such as those dealing with transportation, environment, or pollution; or multi-disciplinary databases such as those produced by the Institute for Scientific Information (ISI).

Initially, most of the generation and processing of sizable databases was restricted to or funded by federal agencies such as NASA, the Energy Research and Development Administration, and the National Library of Medicine. A little later the government became involved in the establishment of centers for processing and providing services from databases. In the past few years the trend has changed somewhat. There has been a diminution in the amount of money the government is putting into the establishment of centers and more of this financing has been taken over by other organizations such as state governments through their universities. In addition, a new phenomenon has occurred; computer based processing of information has become a commercial activity in the United States as well as in some other countries.

The Institute for Scientific Information, a commercial organization that provides searching from its own databases, is evidence of this trend. It is a for-profit commercial organization that is entirely dependent on information products and services. The IIT Research Institute in Chicago, the only one of the NSF funded centers that is now self-supporting, is another example. Although many years ago users simply would not have paid for these services, times have changed and now all services provided from machine readable tapes are supported by outside money from users. Another commercial information service, EDITEK in Chicago, which provides services to users via online systems, is almost self-supporting after only two years of operation.

Although the increase in the use of databases has occurred gradually, it took a quantum jump in 1974. In a survey done in 1971 for the Association for Scientific Information Dissemination Centers, we found that there were roughly 50,000 SDI (selective dissemination of information) profiles being run in the United States. The number of computer based retrospective searches was considerably smaller. Currently, the number of online retrospective searches being conducted in the United States and Canada is about 700,000, and the projection for next year is around a million. These statistics are for bibliographic searches and do not include library automation activities such as OCLC (Ohio College Library Center) searches. Presumably this great increase is due partly to the fact that users are more familiar with databases and their services and partly to the fact that now more information has been collected in machine readable form for retrospective searches.

Many organizations can do some processing of information but none can process all databases and most must rely on outside information centers. The centers themselves rely on other centers, and the resources of various databases are shared in an information network.

Traditionally, of course, libraries have been the source of stored information. In recent years, with the proliferation of publication and governmental involvement in research, databases have evolved as separate entities, indexing, abstracting, and storing much of the same information found in libraries. As the quantity of recorded information increases, libraries will be forced to rely on these databases to search the accumulated knowledge if they are to retrieve it efficiently (or at all). Many libraries are now considering providing database services to their patrons, but few of them know where to begin. How does one evaluate an information center and its services? Some criteria for database selection will be provided here and some questions which libraries should ask both of the the potential services and of themselves will be suggested.

DATABASE SERVICES

Database services are classified as either batch mode or online services depending on the method of processing the information; however, it is the content of the database and the means of searching it which are of primary importance to a potential user. The three main types of services are SDI, which can be tailored to an individual or a group profile, retrospective searches of stored bibliographic data, and what is called a "private library" service. In the latter, a user can have output from any machine search stored for him on a separate disc file along with his own judgments about citations he has received. This feature is now available from several organizations that process databases. For an extra fee, users can maintain personal files, at their own discretion they may discard unwanted references, add new material, or even augment the file with additional indexing terms for the references already selected. This type of service can be provided on a personal basis or on a company basis. It would be possible, in this way, for a company to generate its own machine readable files without having to develop its own database or search strategy.

DATABASE EVALUATION

The potential user of database services will have to evaluate not only the searching methods available but the content of the database itself. The subject coverage of these bases may be discipline-oriented, mission-oriented, problem-oriented or multidisciplinary, as indicated before. In evaluating them you must first know how their coverage matches the objectives and the breadth of your own organization. Does the database cover material such as government reports, journal articles, patents, monographs, theses, preprints and news items? If it does, how complete is this coverage? That is, if they claim to cover a particular journal, will it be covered in its entirety or only selected issues or selected articles? This information can be hard to find although many database producers can provide lists of the journals and other items indexed.

Another important consideration is the time lapse between the item as it appears in the primary source, in the secondary source (or index), and finally in the database. In some cases a citation will appear on a tape before it is produced in a hard copy secondary source because the hard copy publication is produced from the tape.

In addition, you need to question the indexing and coding practices. Do they include free language key words on the tape? Do they include controlled thesaurus or hierarchical vocabulary terms? Are titles given exactly as the author provided them, or are they augmented titles as in the case of BIOSIS where additional terminology is added to the author's title? Do they include other kinds of codes to indicate subject matter or any other criteria about the item itself? Are abstracts and extracts available on tape for search and display or do you have to go back to the hard copy to obtain them?

You may be interested in knowing what the size of the database is, and its growth rate. This will tell you something about the number of citations you should be able to get from a year's worth of that file. You may want to know how the tape version corresponds with the hard copy version. In some cases there is a one to one correspondence; that is, for every abstract or reference contained on the hard copy there is a tape representation.

In many cases the database itself is a subset of the hard copy version, or the reverse may be true. Or the database may contain more citations than the hard copy. And, in other cases, such as the MARC tapes from the Library of Congress, there is no corresponding hard copy publication (except the collection of LC cards) and consequently no easy way to check to see if you are retrieving everything you should. If there is a corresponding hard copy, you can occasionally do both computer and manual searches of an issue as a cross check to be sure you are using the right terminology and really getting what you wanted.

PROCESSOR CONCERNS

If you are going to be doing the processing of tapes internally, you will be interested in the consistency and quality control exercised by the database supplier. Although it is a unique case, I have found error rates as high as 10%. This is extremely high and could result in the loss of entire data entries. For example, if a term such as *dog* is spelled *dgo*, there is no way that your search term is going to match the term on the tape.

As a processor, you will also be interested in the frequency with which changes are made in the database and even in the various provisions for notification of these changes. If the supplier lists forenames of authors by first initials and then decides later to add full first names instead, this is going to affect your own processing. If new data elements are added, this will also affect processing time and possibly require a change in the search program.

Another processing concern is the compatability among various databases. There are about as many database formats as there are databases. They have different data elements and different kinds of tags to indicate the data element types. There can be differences in character codes, recording densities, number of tracks, blocking factors and labeling. The variability complicates processing for those who are handling these databases and want to convert all incoming databases to a standard format. There have been some attempts at standardization; for example many databases are beginning to adhere to the ANSI Z39.2 standard for formatting databases for distribution. This standard specifies a directory and character string format. Standardization efforts, however, are slow and the standards are voluntary.

Adherence to a delivery schedule is another concern of the processor. If the database supplier sends his tapes to you late, then you are going to be providing output to the customers late. Although he may only send one tape to you, you may have to send out a notice to several hundred people saying that this week's output is going to be delayed.

Another consideration in looking at databases, if you plan to use more than one, is the occurrence of overlap between databases. Years ago it was thought that duplication was going to be a serious concern to the user but that has not proved to be the case. The real problem with overlap and redundancy lies with the data producer. There are costs associated with intellectual processing (indexing and abstracting) and manual inputting of citations. If the same citation is handled more than once, this can represent wasted time and effort (money). Also, the processor wastes money by having to search for the same material on more than one set of tapes. There are a few processing centers that now merge serveral databases to create one common database. This is being done at Ohio State University and for the pollution database (Pollution Information Program-PIP) at the National Science Library in Canada, but in general most of the centers search each database as an individual entity.

CENTER EVALUATION

The actual processing of data is an extremely expensive activity and the majority of libraries will be interested in buying these services from an information center. There are a number of questions a library will need to ask of itself and of each center under consideration, when evaluating the merits of available centers.

First of all, you need to know if they have the database or mix of databases that you need to satisfy your own clientele. After you have found a center with the appropriate databases, you need to know whether that center retains all the citations from the databases you are using. Some centers strip off certain parts of the tape, others retain all of it. You may think you are covering all of the information in *Chemical Abstracts*, for example, when actually you are not.

You will also need to know whether they have a standard internal format; whether all databases will be processed the same way; and whether the output will look (be formatted) the same. If the center uses several different search programs, the output may look different and you may not be able to put together a bibliography, for instance, in a compatible format without reworking some of the citations. If a single standard is adhered to internally, it may be possible for you to use the same search profile in multiple databases. If not, you may have to write a different profile to search each database. Theoretically, if there is a standard internal format, it is possible to write one profile for multiple databases. This can be wasteful, however, because certain databases have elements that are not contained on other databases. For example, a Library of Congress class number on a MARC tape is an element that cannot be found on a tape from INSPEC; in this case an identical search profile might be impractical. The decision is usually based on cost. There is a trade-off between personnel time for tailoring profiles versus machine time for processing duplicates.

Another question pertinent to the evaluation of a center is that of document delivery. Does the center provide any kind of document back-up? Most centers do not because of the cost associated with resource location and acquisition. ISI, however, provides document backup for anything that is in their *Current Contents* through Lockheed's Dialog and System Development Corporation's ORBIT online systems. Anyone searching ISI tapes on these systems can enter a request for a document. The requests are saved by the systems and transmitted back to Philadelphia every night. Documents are mailed out the following day. A similar system is available for NTIS (National Technical Information Service) tapes. The Ohio State University's MIC (Mechanized Inform-ation Center) system also provides document delivery from its own collections.

There are other services which a center may provide. They may supply off- or on-site training for your personnel, or provide user aid manuals to assist you in writing profiles and search strategies. They may provide free demonstration searches to give you an idea of what is happening and how to write a search question. You will need to know whether they allow you to revise search profiles and whether this imposes an added cost. They may provide dictionaries or vocabulary lists for controlled vocabulary, term frequency lists for title terms, and free language key words or thesauri for controlled terms. Some centers supply a newsletter to keep the user informed about changes in indexing practices or the addition of new data elements so that the user can modify his search strategy to accommodate to the changes. In some instances there is a provision for feedback or database monitoring to help in calculating the precision rating for searches. All these things relate to the general cooperativeness of the center staff and their accessibility to the patron.

The elements provided in the output are also of interest to the patron. What data elements will be included in the actual printout or display? Will you see just the title and the author name or do you also see the key words? Are you told which of the terms in your search caused this particular item to be a "hit"?

On what media is output provided? There are many possible answers to the latter question. Some centers display the information on cathode ray tubes, in which case, the user is likely to require that hard copy also be printed offline and sent to him. Some centers can generate microform output directly from the tape. Or the output can be supplied on magnetic tape itself for later in-house use. Most suppliers require, however, that the output be provided on hard copy both to avoid copyright difficulties and to provide records of the citations for the purposes of reimbursing the suppliers with appropriate royalties. Assuming that the output will be provided on hard copy, there are still many possibilities to choose from. Some centers can produce output on multilith masters for further reproduction. This feature would be especially useful to libraries, for example, in the production of bulletins. The output may be on IBM cards, 3 in. × 5 in. cards, 4 in. × 6 in. cards, or 5 in. × 8 in. cards; or it may be on computer paper of various sizes. If it is on cards, it will be easily separable into unit records; false hits can be discarded and citations can be interfiled with other material. If it is on computer printout paper, the whole group of citations may have to be retained or the desired references cut out of the pages.

How will the data elements be arranged on the output medium? How many citations will there be per page? If large computer paper is used, will the citations be printed in two adjacent columns?

Are there options available for sorting the output? For example, can one specify that the output be sorted alphabetically by author's name; numerically by reference number; in descending order according to weight or value; or by date of publication? Will the output from various databases be displayed in a standard format for easy visual scanning? Will both upper and lower case characters be used? All of these features may be of considerable importance to your particular institution.

SEARCH FEATURES

When considering the search that is done by a center, it is important to ask what data elements are searched on? There is a difference between the data elements used in searching and those displayed in the output. Searchable elements are often a subset of those that are displayed. Abstracts are seldom searched but often displayed. The use of an abstract provides context information to permit the user to determine whether the terms in his search have succeeded in locating an article he will need to order. In some cases abstracts themselves may be searched but this is seldom done because it significantly increases the search time and cost, usually with little added benefit. However, the number of access points available for searching can greatly influence your ability to achieve high recall and precision in searching. Some centers permit you to search only on subject terminology, words found in the title and key words or index terms. Others permit you to search on author, company affiliation, Library of Congress class number or Dewey Decimal number, report numbers of various types, languages, countries of origin, or other types of data elements. (Obviously, some data elements are specific to certain databases, e.g., Engineering Index card-a-lert codes are found only in COMPENDEX and Biological Abstracts CROSS code numbers are found only in BIOSIS tapes.) It is important to ask whether hierarchical terms can be used in searching, as in the case of MEDLINE. You will need to know whether there is a way to distinguish between the data elements. For example, can you distinguish an author word from a subject term? You may need to know this to avoid retrieving false hits due to homographs. If you were interested in paint and searching on the term *white* for white pigments, you would not want to produce references by an author named Sam White or by a company named White Star Chemical Company. The term may be the same but found as a different element in a different field on the tape. You should be able to specify in your search question which elements or fields you want to search.

What kind of logic is permitted in your search? Are you provided with full Boolean logic, using *and*, *or*, and *not* operators, or are you restricted in some way? Some services provide adjacency logic, i.e., they permit specification of the context in which a term occurs. For example, the searcher can indicate that a term must occur within one or two words of another term as opposed to being found anywhere in the record. This feature is available in several systems.

Another feature to look for is the availability of truncation, that is the ability to search on a term fraction. For example, a user interested in the concept *analysis* can include in the search question the fraction *analy*, (truncating after the y) and thereby retrieve all occurrences of the terms analysis, analytical, analytics, etc., all of which contain the common string *analy*. Without this feature, it is necessary to specify all the forms of a word that an author may have used. In most databases the title terms are not controlled but contain freely generated natural language terms. The searcher then must be able to adjust to the variability that is provided. Most centers provide right truncation only, however left truncation can be extremely useful. For example, if a person is interested in antibiotics and entered under the fraction *mycin* he would hit about 40 different terms, which is probably more than he would have been able easily to think up initially. It is also important to ascertain the limit to the number of characters that can be truncated and whether truncation is available for other term types than subject words. Truncation can be useful in the identification of transliterated author names or for searching on embedded codes such as those found in ASTM (American Society for Testing Materials) CODEN. By truncating on either side of the XX in the CODEN for patents, all patents can be easily identified.

Another important searching question is whether the system can provide ranges for numeric data. Could you search for items published between 1972 and 1975, for example. And, finally in the case of online systems, is the capability there for one to review his searching strategy, or save search inquiries for later use? Can the system answer inquiries about the system, e.g., explain commands and responses, etc. Many new features are being added to online systems. One must keep up-to-date with all of them in order to be able to make effective use of the tools provided.

COST FEATURES

Cost features, although often looked at first, should be secondary considerations after the selection of the appropriate databases and centers that provide suitable searching and output features. Generally costs do not vary greatly. Most center operators seem to look at the prices charged by competitors in establishing their own charges.

Charges can be made on various bases. Does a center charge as an annual service? Does it charge for the actual writing of a profile as well as for the provision of the search service over the year? Is there a charge for the number of terms used in a search? Or, are you allowed some maximum number of terms and then assessed when this number is exceeded? Are you charged on the basis of the number of hits received in the searching? Or is a maximum established and a charge levied only after the maximum is achieved? Is there an additional charge for postage? Is there an additional charge for user aids or for the media on which you receive your output? Is there a higher charge if your output is on cards rather than on paper? If you are using an online system, are you charged for connect time? Are you charged for the use of the terminal? Are you charged for additional hard copy output requested for material you do not want to print on your own terminal? Some systems have different fees for different types of search terms based on the frequency with which a term occurs. A high frequency term costs more to search than a low frequency term. There are many ways charges can be levied.

Is there a base fee for the service? There are several organizations which will charge a base fee within which you can charge up various kinds of services, each associated with a certain number of units. For example, an SDI profile might cost 5 units a year and a retrospective search 2 units per volume. You can buy a package of 100 units for example, and then use them in any desired manner. This is done at two of the NASA centers, ARAC (Aerospace Research Application Center) in Indiana, and NERAC (New England Research Application Center) in Connecticut.

There are many different ways of charging users. The purchaser should become familiar with them in order to compare services.

EVALUATING YOUR ORGANIZATION

In looking at your own position with respect to adding database services, there are several questions to ask. How does the proposed service meet the needs of your own organization? You know what services are currently available and what your users will and will not accept. How will this new service affect your journal acquisition policy? It may tell you that you can not provide adequate document back up for your users from your own collection. It may point out that some of your journals are never used, or seldom produce useful hits. (Obviously, there are some journals that are not included in the indexing services which does not necessarily mean that they are of no value to you.) It may indicate journals that should be added to the collection or for which multiple copies are needed. In any event, the new service probably will have an impact on your journal acquisition policy. In some cases the introduction of computer based services has an impact on interlibrary loan activities. It also usually affects staff assignments if many people previously did manual current awareness work or retrospective searches. In most cases the real effect is that many more searches get done.

You will probably have to justify the cost of the new service to your own management. What is the difference between the old searching methods and the new method? What is the ability of your staff to sell the services in-house? Obviously, the new service will have to be introduced to people who have never heard of computer based retrieval systems before. If you want to provide a service, you will have to justify its cost.

How are these services usually financed? In some organizations an individual scientist or user will actually pay for his own services, but this is by far the least popular method. In some cases the service is purchased through a library budget, in others, through a departmental budget. Specific projects, grants, or contracts may pay for the services they use. In some cases the overhead for the total organization pays for them. You know your own organization and you know which is the most likely source of funds.

How are you going to handle increased demands for service? If it becomes popular, will this mean the acquisition of new staff? How will you handle the feedback and evaluation of this service? Feedback regarding coverage, cost, turn-around time and user satisfaction can be helpful. You will have to keep records to evaluate the success of the service, and at the end of the year justify its continuation for a second year. Who is going to keep the output? Are you going to keep duplicates of the material or will the end user himself keep all the output material? In some cases a library may want to keep a machine readable record of everything that was received. It is doubtful that a library would want to clutter its files with additional hard copy output.

These are just a few of the considerations involved in the acquisition of database services. The questions that are appropriate to you will depend on your own organization, its accounting system and its service orientation, but it is essential that you know what questions to ask.

In general, libraries choose to have data processing done by outside centers. The patron or end user in the library is not usually the person who operates the system or writes the search profile even in the case of online systems. Searches are usually delegated to information specialists or reference librarians. This is important for the effective searching of databases both to control the costs and to insure that the searching is being done by someone who is up-to-date with respect to changes made in the databases, center services, and the command languages of online systems.

Reference librarians have traditionally provided information regardless of the form or media on which it is recorded.

Future librarians must be involved in the searching of databases if they are to avail themselves of the most current and useful tools for providing information services to users.

Bibliography

Keenan, Stella, ed. *Key Papers on the Use of Computer Based Bibliographic Services*. Washington, D.C.: American Society for Information Science, 1973; Philadelphia: National Federation of Abstracting and Indexing Services, 1973.

Lancaster, Frederick W., and Fayen, Emily G. *Information Retrieval Online*. New York: John Wiley & Sons, 1973.

Marron, Beatrice; Fong, Elizabeth; Fife, Dennis W.; Rankin, Kirk. *A Study of Six University-Based Information Systems* NBS Technical note 781. Washington, D.C.: National Bureau of Standards, Institute for Computer Sciences and Technology, 1973.

Mauerhoff, Georg R. "Selective Dissemination of Information." In *Advances In Librarianship*, vol. 4, pp. 25-26. Edited by Melvin Voigt. New York: Academic Press, 1974.

Schneider, John H., Gechman, Marvin; and Furth, Stephen E., eds. *Survey of Commercially Available Computer Readable Bibliographic Databases*. Washington, D.C.: American Society for Information Science, Special Interest Group for Selective Dissemination of Information, 1973. (ED 072 811. Available from American Society for Information Science, Washington, D.C.)

Williams, Martha E. "Use of Machine Readable Databases." In *Annual Review of Information Science and Technology*, vol. 9, chap. 7, pp. 221-84. Edited by Carlos A. Cuadra and Ann W. Luke. Washington, D.C.: American Society for Information Science, 1974.

Williams, Martha E., and Brandhorst, W.T. "Databases: A Review of the Reviews." *Bulletin of the American Society for Information Science* 1 (June/July 1974): 21-22.

Williams, Martha E., and Stewart, Alan K. *ASIDIC Survey of Information Center Services.* Chicago, Ill.: IIT Research Institute, 1972.

User Criteria for Selection of Commercial Online Computer Based Bibliographic Services: An Industrial Practical Case Study

Doris B. Marshall

King and Palmour[1] have indicated, as reported by the American Chemical Society, that industrial chemists spend nearly 12 hours per week in literature searching and current awareness reading. Since the figures have indicated that the scientists spend only about 5% of their time using formal primary media, and an even smaller time using abstracting and indexing media, the implication is that even small improvements could result in large gross savings in scientific manpower utilization, assuming the saved time would be reallocated to useful pursuits.

In describing the benefits of networking, Greenberger and colleagues[2] have listed four developments which are applicable to interactive online retrieval: the greater variety and richness of available resources; improved computer communications technology reflected in the widened availability regardless of size, location, or financial status; the decreasing cost per unit of information stored or processed; and payment for information processed as it is obtained, with virtual elimination of huge capital costs and budgetary uncertainties. In the industrial environment of the author, the latter was one of the deciding factors for trying online bibliographic data retrieval.

In the case under study, information has been of great value many times. Provision of the right information at the right time has saved time and money, but no attempt has ever been made to quantify it. The

Reprinted from *Special Libraries* 66 (11):501-508 (November 1975). © Copyright Special Libraries Association.

industry has also found that the absence of necessary information can be costly—as in the duplication of its own work and the work of others—with regard to manpower, equipment, time, and patents. Costs must be considered in obtaining objectives.

In trying to find reasons engineers were not using external bibliographic retrieval services, Rippon[3] found lack of encouragement by management to make use of the services as one reason. In the author's case, management approved, encouraged, and gave the final impetus toward the use of online bibliographic data retrieval.

METHODOLOGY

The development of the methodology gives a breadth of process observation that is characteristic of case studies. Rae[4] in discussing the use of the SUNY biomedical network pointed out that pioneers have to learn by experience, as this author found. Townley[5] was not able to find any examples of successful solutions of practical problems in using external information services, and she wished that many people would be prompted to come forward with their own experiences, in order to shed light on a number of problems, which are also applicable to online retrieval. Cooper[6] found that the value of information cannot be ascertained until examined. The value of the use of online services has, therefore, to be determined by experience.

In this report, prior research or experiences linking the use of each system component to ultimate value or effectiveness have been noted. Applications to prior studies have been made to online data retrieval as possible criteria for selection and use of components of the total system. Applications have been related to case history experience. The selection process and implementation of commercial online computer based bibliographic services in an industrial environment are related to many separate factors that are interrelated. These factors are considered under the component interactive parts of the total retrieval system.

THE NEEDS OF THE USER

Garvey and colleagues[7] found that users had variation of needs at various stages of research. A rather exhaustive search prior to the beginning of a project, a detailed but narrow search needed where only methodology was in question. Information needed varied with scientific discipline, and workers in applied sciences had needs varying from theoretical and research scientists. Needs for browsing and broad scientific knowledge were noted. The experience and educational background of the users varied the needs. The information scientist has to have some feeling or understanding of what a user does know, as well as what he wants to find. Burton[8] has reported the selective dissemination of information service that was user-dependent met the needs of the users both in research support and for educational purposes.

McCarn and Leiter[9] found that a large percentage of online users were not seeking complete information or exhaustive bibliographies. They considered measures of perfomance of information and retrieval systems based on precision and recall to be somewhat inappropriate. A fellow participant of the author's at a recent workshop[10] remarked that her staff referred to online searches as "quick and dirty," because they were done quickly with incomplete recall, but with sufficient recall to fill the need. The author has had the experience of trying to meet a request, "Do what you can for $100." The pertinence of a particular document to a particular need can be decided only by the person with the need, according to Kemp[11]. In the author's experience, information systems were of less value when new or novel applications were required.

HARDWARE SELECTION

At the time of the decision to "go online," the author had had no experience with any type of terminal used for data or document retrieval. Management sought advice from systems and data processing personnel who were knowledgeable about data retrieval, final computations, but not familiar with intermediary, often changing, search strategy statements. The author had to emphasize repeatedly the absolute necessity of having print capability; a leased cathode ray tube (CRT) was useful for scanning and group demonstrations, but not for retaining the search strategy. Problems followed of not being able to break leasing contracts, not being permitted to upgrade contracts, not being able locally to interface one company's printer with another company's CRT. The teletype that was used to "fill in" was slow, ten characters per second, and noisy, being an impact rather than a thermal printer. To use the CRT, a dataphone had to be installed. Users need to consider the number of characters per line a terminal can handle, installation and rental or purchase costs, cost of supplies, availability of supplies, service availability. In the author's case, the terminal has been moved four times, and will possibly be moved again, so relative portability should be considered. If the service will be used extensively, a backup facility may be needed.

TRANSMISSION

The author found little information in the published literature. The transmission agent should have a local number or be geographically close so that the transmission system can be accessed. WATS (Wide Area Transmisssion Systems) use is at lower rates than direct long distance, but more expensive than use of a transmission agent such as Tymshare. If direct long distance is used, the costs are directly proportional to the geographical distance from the computer. Atmospheric conditions sometimes influence transmission fidelity, and this can be detected from the printout. Transmission by satellite had been available. If search strategy is lost due to transmission difficulties, determine in advance if the cost is recoverable in some way.

THE SYSTEM AND THE VENDOR

Brandhorst and Eckert[12] have listed several features of good system design, which are: 1) ability to enter any command any time; 2) ability to select which records or elements to print; 3) ability to qualify retrievals by date or language or other qualifiers; 4) ability to print online or offline; 5) unrestricted use of Boolean operators and number of search terms; 6) online thesaurus; 7) ability to link search statements; 8) protection against file or program destruction; 9) user query language as close to natural as possible. The author could cite problems encountered with almost any of the nine features! Ability to use word adjacency is also important.

Training procedures are desirable, and also tutorials built into the system, if they can be bypassed by the constant user. Training manuals and word lists and database descriptions should be provided by the vendor. Some free online learning time should also be provided.

Fast response time is desirable and a minimum of "down" time, when the computer is not operating[13]. The flexibility provided by a system has to be judged by experience, but its ability to handle more than one database or its ability to update searches readily would be two indications.

The terms of the contract with respect to cost should be examined critically. On a subscription basis the user must pay for a specified number of hours whether use is made of them or not. Some vendors have combinations of subscription rates and use rates, or for only certain initial periods. Some require purchase of hard copy material or combinations of hard copy subscriptions up to a specific sum. Most charges are made by connect time only, which is most economical, and the user pays only for the time actually used. These charges vary not only from one vendor to another, but also by database used. Direct assistance is essential from a contact person or subject specialist. The vendor should demonstrate sensitivity to users' needs.

DATABASES

Back[14] and Kabi[15] have indicated that completeness of coverage within the time period covered, and keeping the database as current as possible are the most important criteria for measurement of an information service. Corbett[16] asked if the database covers the core journals of the specific discipline, and Helliwell[17] felt that index changes affected the database user. Various investigators[18] have considered time lag in abstracting, number of indexing terms, accuracy of data as criteria for selection. Consistency should also be a consideration; Tate[19] explained that grouping the first twenty *Chemical Abstracts* sections into a subject-interest field called "Biochemistry" indicated concentration, not exclusivity. Natural language used has been touched upon. Degree of overlap must be considered because a searcher must make the decision to search more than one database with the full realization that duplicate results indicate waste of time and money. Abstracts as well as bibliographic data are also helpful. The present costs range from $25 per hour to $150 per hour.

SEARCH STRATEGY AND EVALUATION MEASURES

Recall and precision have been the primary evaluation criteria for systems for several years. These relate not only to the system, however, but the search strategy used, the searcher performing the task, and the judgment of the user as to pertinence of material retrieved. It is not within the province of this report to describe search strategy using Boolean operators, or index language devices such as coordination, term weighting, or links and roles, but it is important for the search strategist to understand the concepts, and to be aware of how the system utilizes them. Carmon and Park[20] have related the familiarity of the searching personnel with the database, the ability to structure a search question properly, and the interaction between the end user and the searcher as critical to successful use. The searcher must have some knowledge of which database contains relevant material and be relatively familiar with the search terms within a database. In addition to structuring his strategy before he goes online, the searcher must analyze results. Examples of failures noted in the literature were terms retrieved in wrong context, wrong correlation of terms, deficiency in statement of interest, use of ambiguous terms, inadequate concept expansion, too restrictive statement, mistakes in spelling or keypunch errors in the database, inadequate titles, inadequate or improper indexing[21]. An overriding "NOT" term may produce a failure, particularly in a comparison. The author found that the user did not always state what he really needed, or how his need fitted into a larger problem. The searcher has a choice of approaches directly related to the flexibility of the system, which greatly influences total cost and efficiency. In the author's case exhaustive searches have been minimally requested. The value may be inherent in the information found, or the cost benefits in the method of finding it, or the value of finding the amount of information, or the value of finding no information.

USER-SYSTEM INTERFACE

Summit[22] has stated that truly interactive information retrieval systems properly depend on the terminal operator as an intellectual decision maker not as merely a clerical keyboard operator answering computer initiated questions. Bennett[23] related user acceptance of interactive systems to many factors: 1) the "bullying" effect of the terminal prodding the user to move at a faster pace than optimal, 2) the consciousness of the high costs being incurred, 3) the resentment of the user being watched by colleagues, and 4) the human eye as a limiting factor in CRT design and use. According to Cuadra[24], the user first regards the system as remote and mysterious, then he may feel "molded and manipulated." Totally different systems have to be learned and assimilated in order to access different databases. Lancaster and co-workers[25] found that casual users never became expert users, and consequently experience was a factor. Fox[26] has stressed the importance of the physical environment directly relating to noise, lighting, placement of the terminal too high or too low, and so on. Melnyk's article[27] about frustration was classic, relating the user's fear of appearing foolish, fear of destroying the system, and fear of asking for help—and the author's experience of finding few persons locally or at a distance who knew the answers anyway! Special frustrations of the author have been distance required to gain access to the system, not enough work space near the terminal, time delays in accessing the database, special knowledge of special languages or special codes needed, inability to duplicate printout, permanence of output (some Hi-Liters react with thermal print paper), and allowing the time for use to override all other time requirements. A new corollary to Murphy's Law would be, "During any given demonstration, *some* problem will develop."

Table 1 is a quick checklist for criteria for selection, use, and evaluation of commercial online computer based bibliographic services, relating to the needs of the user, hardware selection, transmission, system and vendor, databases, search strategy and evaluation measures, and user-system interface. It is hoped that these experiences, these selection criteria, these correlations, will help others make the selection

TABLE 1   Quick Checklist for Criteria for Selection, Use, and Evaluation of Commercial Online Computer Based Bibliographic Services

Needs
of
the
User
	Varies with:
	    Background education
	    Background experience
	    Subject discipline
	Value to user:
	    Effectiveness
	    Efficiency
	    Convenience
	    Time savings
	    Cost savings
	Encouragement of
	    management
		Function of use:
		    Research support, theoretical
		    Research support, applied
		    Short query
		    Exhaustive retrospective
		        search
		    Extension of subject expertise
		    Extension of broad scientific
		        interest

Hardware
Selection
	Systems compatibility
	Print capability
	    Characters per line
	    Upper and lower case
	Speed of operation
	Noise of operation
	Need for visual scanning
	    Black on white screen
	    White on black screen
	    Positioning of cursor
	    Information flow
	    Demonstrations
	    Ease of visual use
		Ease of installation
		Location
		Ease of moving; portability
		Ease of manual use
		Servicing
		Availability of supplies
		Cost of supplies
		Ease of duplicating printed copy
		Need for back-up facility
		Rental cost
		Purchase cost
		Can contract be changed?
		Terms of contract

Transmission	Long distance, direct
	Long distance, WATS
	Transmission vendor
	    Local accessibility
	    Local representative
		Dataphone necessary
		Installation
		Rental cost
		Noise or interference
		Satellite
		Cost recovery for lost strategy?

System
and
the
Vendor
	Training provision
	    Manuals
	    Indexes
	    Workshops
	        Cost, transportation
	        Cost, housing
	        Cost, workshop
	    Other aids
	    Cost of all above
	Ability to print off-line and
	    on-line
	Compatibility with hardware
	Ability to select records to
	    print
	Ability to qualify retrievals
	Cost by subscription
	Cost by computer time
	    used
	Must hard copy data base
	    be purchased?
		Flexibility with single data base
		Flexibility with multiple data bases
		Protection of privacy
		Protection of file
		Natural query language
		Option of level of use
		Availability of assistance
		Fast response time
		Number of search terms unlimited
		Availability during day
		Use of Boolean operators not restricted
		Ability to link search statements
		Ability to command system readily
		Off-line print charge by page, citation,
		    or number of lines
		Must back-up files be purchased or
		    leased?
		Sensitive to user's needs

Data Bases	Time-span covered	Number of journals covered
	Extent of articles covered	Core journals in discipline covered
	Time lag from date of publishing to date of indexing	Time lag in updating data base
		Document types covered; e.g., patents?
	Indexing aids available	Exhaustivity in indexing
Data Bases (contd.)	Thesaurus available	Number of errors or fidelity
	Abstracts included?	Users notified of index procedures changes
	Limitations	
	Time availability	Reference to hard copy
	Cost	Allowance for time zone differences
Search Strategy and Evaluation Measures	Knowledge of data base construction	Precision failures of terms in wrong context
	Experience with system	Precision failure of use of non-specific word fragments
	Knowledge of search terms	
	Communication with user	Precision failure in use of ambiguous words
	Ability to structure search statement	Inadequate concept expansion failure in recall
	Analytical evaluation of results	Statements too restrictive
	Recall failure in having NOT terms present	Mistakes in spelling
		Recall failure with inadequate indexing
	Search strategy not logical	Interest statement deficient
	Wrong terms combined	Value of information found
	New uses learned	Cost-benefits
	Value of time saved	Value of finding no information or amount published
	Time saved permitting more searches made	
User-System Interface	Noise disturbs operator	Visual disturbances
	Improper lighting	Physical placement of terminal, high or low
	Temperature	
	Privacy from onlookers	Distance of terminal from user's office
	Space for demonstrations	
	Place for concentration	General comfort during operation
	Not "bullied" by speed of operation	Fear of making expensive errors
		Frustration by not obtaining a telephone line
	Fear of destroying system	
	Initial distrust	Fear of making "ridiculous" errors
	Inexperience cuts efficiency	Frustration of having transmission problems
	Frustration with delayed responses	Frustration by not being able to access computer
	Instruction manuals being unavailable	Forgetting special terms or "lingo"
		Available time for use overrides other user considerations

and use of online systems, workable, practical, valuable, and enjoyable.

One of our research staff members stated that the author had been far too negative in this report. He suggested that the author tell how within six minutes, eleven precisely pertinent references had been found by entering just one term, thereby making a "believer" of the staff member, after he had searched manually for a long time. In conclusion, therefore, it is not all frustration—if you have faith, and are facile, you will find online searching fast, factual, fruitful, frugal, fabulous, fun, fascinating, and seldom a failure!

Footnotes

1. Donald W. King and Vernon E. Palmour, "User Behavior," in *Changing Patterns in Information Retrieval*, ed. Carol Fenichel (Washington, D.C.: American Society for Information Science, 1974), pp. 7-33
2. Martin Greenberger et al., "Computer and Information Networks," *Science* 182 (October 1973): 29-35.
3. John S. Rippon, "Manpower Implications: Skills Required to Select, Interact with and Exploit External Services to fit the User's Needs," *Aslib Proceedings* 25 (February 1973): 65-76.
4. Patrick D.J. Rae, "Online Information Systems: Experience of the Parkinson Information Center in Using the SUNY Biomedical Communication Network," in *Proceedings of the Annual Meeting*, vol. 7, (Washington, D.C.: American Society for Information Science, 1970), pp. 173-76.
5. Helen M. Townley, "Pitfalls and Problems," *Aslib Proceedings* 25 (February 1973): 51-64.
6. Michael D. Cooper, "The Economics of Information," in *Annual Review of Information Science and Technology*, vol. 8, ed. Carlos A. Cuadra and Ann W. Luke (Washington, D.C.: American Society for Information Science, 1973), pp. 1-40.
7. William D. Garvey, Kazuo Tomita and Patricia Woolf, "The Dynamic Scientific Information User," *Information Storage and Retrieval* 10 (March/April 1974): 115-31.
8. Hilary D. Burton, "A User Dependent SDI System: They Said It Could Not Be Done," *Special Libraries* 64 (December 1973): 541-44.
9. Davis B. McCarn and Joseph Leiter, "Online Services in Medicine and Beyond," *Science* 181 (July 1973): 318-24.
10. Special Libraries Association, San Diego Chapter, "Preconference Workshop on Computer Based Information Systems" (San Diego, Calif.: Special Libraries Association, 1974).
11. D.A. Kemp, "Relevance, Pertinence and Information System Development," *Information Storage and Retrieval* 10 (February 1974): 37-47.
12. Wesley T. Brandhorst and Philip F. Eckert, "Document Retrieval and Dissemination Systems," in *Annual Review of Information Science and Technology*, vol. 7, ed. Carlos A. Cuadra (Washington, D.C.: American Society for Information Science, 1972), pp. 379-437.
13. Carlos A. Cuadra, "Online Systems: Problems and Pitfalls," *Journal of the American Society for Information Science* 22 (March/April 1971): 107-14.
14. Harry B. Back, "What Information Dissemination Studies Imply Concerning the Design of Online Reference Systems," *Journal of the American Society for Information Science* 23 (May/June 1972): 156-63.
15. A. Kabi, "Use, Efficiency and Cost of External Information Services," *Aslib Proceedings* 24 (June 1972): 356-62.

16 L. Corbett, "Problems in Using External Information Services: Attitudes of the Special Library and Its Users," *Aslib Proceedings* 24 (February 1972): 96-110.

17. B.F.M. Helliwell, "Experiences of BP's Patents Information Branch in Using Commercial Patent Documentation Services," *Aslib Proceedings* 25 (January 1973): 18-21.

18. Peter B. Schipma, Martha E. Williams, and Allan Shafton, "Comparison of Document Databases," *Journal of the American Society for Information Science* 22 (September/October 1971): 326-32; E.J. Scott, H.M. Townley, and B.T. Stern, "A Technique for the Evaluation of a Commercial Information Service," *Information Storage and Retrieval* 7 (November 1971): 149-65.

19. Fred A. Tate, "Access to the Biomedical Literature through Services Produced at Chemical Abstracts Service," *Federation Proceedings* 33 (June 1974): 1712-14.

20. James L. Carmon and Margaret K. Park, "User Assessment of Computer Based Bibliographic Retrieval Services," *Journal of Chemical Documentation* 13 (February 1973): 24-26.

21. Frances H. Barker, Barry K. Wyatt, and Douglas C. Veal, "Report on the Evaluation of an Experimental Computer Based Current Awareness Service for Chemists," *Journal of the American Society for Information Science* 23 (March/April 1972): 85-99.

22. Roger K. Summit, "Dialog and the User--An Evaluation of the User Interface with a Major Online Retrieval System, in *Interactive Bibliographic Search: The User/Computer Interface*, ed. Donald E. Walker (Montvale, N.J.: AFIPS Press, 1971), pp. 83-94.

23. John L. Bennett, "The User Interface in Interactive Systems," in *Annual Review of Information Science and Technology*, vol. 7, ed. Carlos A. Cuadra (Washington. D.C.: American Society for Information Science, 1972), pp. 159-96.

24. Carlos A. Cuadra, "Online Systems: Problems and Pitfalls," p. 112.

25. Frederick W. Lancaster, Richard L. Rapport, and J. Kiffin Penry, "Evaluating the Effectiveness of an Online, Natural Language Retrieving System," *Information Storage and Retrieval* 8 (October 1972): 223-45.

26. J.G. Fox, "Ergonomics and Information Systems," *Aslib Proceedings* 24 (March 1972): 178-86.

27. Vera Melnyk, "Man-Machine Interface: Frustration," *Journal of the American Society for Information Science* 26 (November/December 1972): 392-401.

Evaluation of Database Coverage: A Comparison of Two Methodologies

Carol Tenopir

1. INTRODUCTION

A variety of methods for evaluating the coverage of bibliographic databases or printed indexes and abstracts has been described in the literature.[1] These methods vary in assumptions, complexity, effort, and results, yet they have rarely been compared with each other. The identification of one inexpensive, relatively easy and reliable method of database coverage evaluation would be of great help to users and searchers who are faced with an ever-increasing number of databases from which to choose.

Two methods commonly recommended for evaluating and comparing database coverage of a specific subject are the 'bibliography' method and the 'subject profile' method. This report will examine these two methodologies by applying them to the same subject. It will look at the assumptions behind them, the way they are applied, and some of the studies that have used one or the other of them. The findings suggested by both will be analyzed and compared. The differences in time, cost, and results achieved between the two will also be compared, in an attempt to discover if the two methods allow the same conclusions about database coverage to be drawn, and if so, if one is easier, less costly, or more reliable than the other.

This project was started as part of a contract to develop a model Directory of Databases of pertinence to the Federal Emergency Management Agency. The subject profile technique was employed in that project.[2]

Reprinted with permission of Learned Information Ltd. from *Online Review* 6 (1982): 423-441.

2. METHOD A—BIBLIOGRAPHY METHOD

The bibliography method uses specialized bibliographies or review articles in a specific subject area. The citations in them are looked for in databases. A database that contains a larger percentage of these citations is considered to have more extensive coverage of the materials actually used and needed by researchers in the specific field. Citations that have been systematically chosen by a reviewer in the field imply some quality judgement of these articles. Citations chosen by a bibliographer may or may not imply quality judgement. The evaluation literature does not always clearly differentiate between bibliographies and review articles so they are treated interchangeably in this article.

This methodology was first used to evaluate the coverage of printed indexes and was applied often enough to be called the "standard method of estimating the coverage of a given base in relation to a specific topic" by Yska and Martyn.[3] John Martyn has used the bibliography methodology on several occasions to test the coverage of printed indexes.[4] F.W. Lancaster also recommended using this approach for evaluating the National Library of Medicine's recurring bibliographies because "we can obtain a very good idea of coverage by the use of review articles covering various aspects of the broad subject field" and "it is an adequate method of studying coverage and arriving at a meaningful coverage factor."[5] In his doctoral dissertation, Virgil Diodato provides a comprehensive survey of the studies that have used this method or variations on it to test coverage of printed indexing and abstracting tools.[6]

More recently, the bibliography method has been applied to test how the coverage of *databases* matches the citations in subject specific review articles. John Martyn used a comprehensive bibliography on biodeterioration to test and compare the coverage of Science Citation Index, Biological Abstracts, Chemical Abstracts, Medlars, and Food Science and Technology Abstracts on that subject.[7] He measured coverage of the bibliography citations in each database, as well as how most of these citations could be retrieved by a subject search in the file (recall) without retrieving other irrelevant citations (precision). Martyn found that twenty-three percent of the literature of biodeterioration was not covered by any database, a figure that was similar to his earlier studies of printed indexes. He used this study to justify establishment of a Biodeterioration Information Centre that would create a database of the literature.

Pranas Zunde and John M. Gehl obtained a "representative sample" of fire-relevant bibliographies to test the coverage of fire-relevant literature in eleven databases.[8] No one database contained more than 15.6% of the citations in this multidisciplinary field. Zunde and Gehl analyzed the sample citations and the retrieved citations by document type and concluded "there is a significant discrepancy between, on the one hand, the needs of authors of publications on fire and, on the other, the type of information on fire available in the selected information (sources)."[9] Researchers showed a preference for reports in their citations, while the primary document type available in databases was journal articles.

Tests such as these using the bibliography method of database evaluation obviously allow a variety of conclusions to be drawn about how databases meet the needs of authors and researchers in specific disciplines. There are some problems with the methodology, however.

For this methodology to be successful, either a comprehensive bibliography must exist for the subject to be tested or sufficient review articles or bibliographies must exist to give an overview of all aspects of the subject. In order to avoid bias, the review articles or bibliographies must not have been compiled from the databases to be tested. It is easy to ensure that the review articles are not selected from the databases to be tested; it is more difficult to ensure they were not used by the author in his compilation.

Another deficiency pointed out by Martyn is that the "bibliography approach necessarily gives a picture of the situation obtaining at some time in the past."[10] He points out that because of the time required to compile a bibliography the citations included are normally several years older than the bibliography itself.

The bibliography methodology also assumes that compilers of review articles examine the full body of literature on a subject, exercise quality judgement and select those items that are of the most use to researchers in the field. This is a difficult assumption to confirm. If judgement is exercised, some bias by the author is inescapable.

Perhaps the biggest drawback to the bibliography methodology is the amount of time (and, therefore, cost) required. After bibliographies or review articles are located, a minimum of 300–400 randomly selected citations from the articles must each be searched in each database to be tested. This requires many hours of online connect time. Although some of the studies reported in the literature search a printed equivalent rather than the database itself, in most cases this cannot be considered a complete coverage test of the database. Many databases include more citations than their printed equivalents, merge several printed indexes, have different update schedules, or, increasingly, do not even have a printed equivalent.

In spite of these problems, the bibliography method can provide detailed information about how well a database covers the information cited in review articles or bibliographies on specific subjects.

3. METHOD B—SUBJECT PROFILE METHOD

In its simplest form, the subject profile method involves developing a comprehensive profile of terms that together represent a broad overview of the subject to be tested, running this profile on the databases to be tested, and comparing the number of citations retrieved in each database. The database with the most citations on the subject is judged to be the most useful for the subject.

Elaborations on this methodology are possible. If a random sample of retrieved citations from each database is printed, it allows: (1) calculation of the percent of false drops so an adjusted total number can be calculated, (2) analysis of more detailed characteristics of the contents of each database. This more detailed analysis of the type of information available in a database allows better comparisons among databases and more closely approximates the kind of analyses possible with the bibliography method.

The subject profile method is assumed to provide information on a database's coverage of the "core" material in a field. Thus, in contrast to the assumed purpose of the bibliography method, the subject profile method will show which databases contain more information directly on a topic, but will not reflect the peripheral materials used by researchers in the field.

Gerda Yska and John Martyn used the simplified subject profile technique in their analysis of forty-five databases for coverage on environmental topics. The method was chosen because it is "economical of manpower and . . . of its equivalent in machine time and [was] able to produce some meaningful [sic] in a very short time."[11] Terms that collectively represented environmental interests were chosen for searching in databases of potential relevance. "From the user viewpoint, the results provide an indication of the search product to be expected over a number of areas of each base, and indications of the relative specialisations of the bases studied."[12]

This approach was first used by Martha Williams in her development of an automatic Data Base Selector.[13] Williams proposed using an extended subject profile technique that involves printing and analyzing random samples for citations in an analysis of the coverage of databases of potential interest to the Federal Emergency Management Agency, (FEMA).[14] This analysis was completed by Tenopir and Williams under the direction of FEMA.[15]

The major advantage of the subject profile methodology is its simplicity and relatively low costs. Once a subject profile is developed, the online costs of running the typical profile of ten to thirty terms and printing a sample of citations are much less than individually checking 300–400 citations. It also removes from consideration any bias on the part of a bibliographer or reviewer.

The major disadvantages of this method are its reliance on subject terms that may vary from database to database due to indexing procedures, the variation of searching techniques among searchers, and the problem of constructing a profile that will balance retrieving the most citations (recall) with retrieving the fewest false drops (precision).

In spite of these problems, the subject profile technique can provide a relatively easy and inexpensive method of measuring and comparing the coverage of databases in a specified subject area.

4. APPLICATION OF THE TWO METHODOLOGIES

The bibliography and subject profile techniques were both applied to the field of volcanology to compare the results obtained with each.[16] The two primary geologic databases, Geological Reference File and Geo-Archive, were compared using both methods.

Volcanology includes the study of terrestrial and extraterrestrial volcanic activities and is especially concerned with eruptions of volcanoes, movement or flows of lava, and ash falls.

The Geological Reference File (GeoRef) database provides international coverage of the full range of geological literature. It is produced by the American Geological Institute and is aimed at the professional geoscientist. It corresponds to five printed indexes: *Bibliography and Index of North American Geology, Bibliography of Theses in Geology, Geophysical Abstracts, Bibliography and Index of Geology Exclusive of North America*, and the *Bibliography and Index of Geology*. Forty percent of the GeoRef database citations originate in the United States; approximately eighty percent of its coverage is journal articles. Coverage is from 1961 to the present, with a size (as of March 1982) of approximately 700,000 citations. GeoRef is available through Dialog Information Services, Inc. as file 89 and through System Development Corporation's Orbit System.[17]
the geosciences, but it includes citations to both the formal and informal literature. GeoArchive is produced by Geosystems (London). Information from journals, magazines, conference proceedings, doctoral dissertations, technical reports, maps and books is included "regardless of quality of substantive contribution."[18] Coverage is from 1974 to the present, with a size (as of March 1982) of approximately 420,000 citations. GeoArchive is available through Dialog Information Services, Inc. as file 58.[19]

The coverage, characteristics and indexing features of GeoRef and GeoArchive were compared by C. Oppenheim and S. Perryman.[20] Their analysis employed the question array technique (described by Lancaster and Yska). Oppenheim's and Perryman's conclusions could also be compared to the conclusions reached in the two methodologies tested in the present study. This would expand this comparison to include three out of the five methodologies described by Yska and Martyn for evaluation of database coverage.

Method A

Review articles on volcanology were taken from the Science Citation Index Database (Dialog files 34, 94 and 186—SciSearch). They are identified as document type "REV" or "BIB" in SciSearch, and were combined with the subject terms volcan (o, ism, ology, etc.) or lava or lavas or ash flow(s) or ash fall(s). Twenty-three review articles were retrieved, with publication dates ranging from 1973-81. These twenty-three articles yielded a total citation pool of 2254. The review articles are listed in the Appendix.

Each citation was assigned a consecutive number and a random number table was used to draw slightly over 300 random numbers between 1 and 2254. The 305 unique citations that corresponded to the random numbers were selected as the sample to be checked in the two databases.

TABLE 1   Type of Material in Random Sample from Review Articles

Type of Material	Absolute Frequency	Relative Frequency (percent)	Cumulative Frequency (percent)
Journal articles	201	65.9	65.9
Books	23	7.5	73.4
Chapters in books	20	6.6	80.0
Paper in conference proceedings	20	6.6	86.6
Technical reports	15	4.9	91.5
Maps	10	3.3	94.8
USGS papers or reports	6	2.0	96.8
Special publications of societies	6	2.0	98.8
Theses	4	1.3	100.0
Totals	305	100.0	100.0

TABLE 2   Language of Material in Random Sample from Review
Articles

Language	Absolute Frequency	Relative Frequency (percent)	Cumulative Frequency (percent)
English	295	96.7	96.7
Other	9	3.0	99.7
Unknown	1	.3	100.0
Totals	305	100.0	100.0

Tables 1-3 show the characteristics of the sample citations. It can be
seen that nearly sixty-six percent of the literature cited in the review
articles is journal articles, almost ninety-seven is in English, and
seventy-five percent was published after 1967.

Every sample citation was checked online in Dialog's version of both
the GeoRef and GeoArchive databases. The titles were searched first
using Dialog's word adjacency feature, but if a title was not found, author
searches were attempted. Each citaton that was found was printed in the
full format to allow subsequent analysis.

TABLE 3   Dates of Material in Random Sample from Review Articles

Date	Absolute Frequency	Relative Frequency (percent)	Cumulative Frequency (percent)
1845–1894 (50 years)	1	.3	.3
1895–1944 (50 years)	9	2.7	3.3
1945–1959 (15 years)	12	3.8	7.2
1960–1964 (5 years)	20	6.5	13.8
1965–1969 (5 years)	52	17.1	30.9
1970–1974 (5 years)	87	28.5	59.5
1975	21	6.9	66.4
1976	33	10.8	77.3
1977	25	8.2	85.5
1978	21	6.9	92.4
1979	18	5.9	98.4
1980	5	1.6	100.0
Unknown	1	.3	
Totals	305	100.0	

One hundred and eight (35.4%) of the citations were found in both databases. GeoRef contained 225 (73.8%), 117 (38.4% of the total) of which were unique to GeoRef. GeoArchive contained 115 (37.7%) of the citations, seven of which were unique to it (2.3% of the total). Seventy-

TABLE 4   Type of Material from Review Articles Found in One, Both or Neither Databases

Type	Count Row PCT Col. PCT	In Both	In Neither	GeoRef only	GeoArc only	Row total
Journal		74	41	83	3	201
		36.8	20.4	41.3	1.5	65.9
		68.5	56.2	70.9	42.9	
Book		5	11	6	1	23
		21.7	47.8	26.1	4.3	7.5
		4.6	15.1	5.1	14.3	
Chapter in book	11	4	5	0	20	
		55.0	20.0	25.0	0	6.6
		10.2	5.5	4.3	0	
Map	2	2	6	0	10	
		20.0	20.0	60.0	0	3.3
		1.9	2.7	5.1	0	
Conference Proc.		11	3	3	3	20
		55.0	15.0	15.0	15.0	6.6
		10.2	4.1	2.6	42.9	
USGS paper or report		3	0	3	0	6
		50.0	0	50.0	0	2.0
		2.8	0	2.6	0	
Special pubs of societies		1	1	4	0	6
		16.7	16.7	66.7	0	2.0
	0.9	1.4	3.4	0		
Thesis		0	2	2	0	4
		0	50.0	50.0	0	1.3
		0	2.7	1.7	0	
Tech.rept		1	9	5	0	15
		6.7	60.0	33.3	0	4.9
		0.9	12.3	4.3	0	
	Column Total	108	73	117	7	305
		35.4	23.9	38.4	2.3	100.0

three (23.9%) of the citations were not found in either database, a figure consistent with coverage figures found in studies done by Martyn.

Tables 4-6 present a breakdown of the citations found in both, neither, or one database by type of document, language of the original article, and year of publication. This breakdown allows certain conclusions about the coverage of each database to be drawn. It can be concluded from the application of the bibliography method that the GeoRef database provides nearly twice the coverage of the volcano literature than does GeoArchive. Seventy-six percent of the literature needed by researchers in the field of volcanology can be found if both databases are accessed, yet almost seventy-four percent can be found by accessing GeoRef alone.

Both GeoRef and GeoArchive have good (seventy-five percent or better) coverage of the journal articles, conference proceedings, and book chapters cited in review articles, but theses, books and technical reports are less well covered. GeoRef has much better coverage of a variety of materials (maps, government special publications, society reports) than does GeoArchive.

Older materials cannot be found in either database, although GeoRef does include items from the early 1960s forward. Neither database seems to have picked up many materials prior to its announced coverage dates (1961 for GeoRef, 1974 for GeoArchive).

GeoRef seems to be the better source for foreign language materials, but the inclusion of non-English materials in the review articles is so

TABLE 5 Language of Materials from Review Articles Found in One, Both or Neither Databases

Language	Count Row PCT Col. PCT	In Both	In Neither	GeoRef only	GeoArc only	Row total
	0	0	0	1	0	1
		0	0	100.0	0	.3
		0	0	.9	0	
		108	67	113	7	295
English		36.6	22.7	38.3	2.4	96.7
		100.0	91.8	96.6	100.0	
		0	6	3	0	9
Other		0	66.7	33.3	0	3.0
		0	8.2	2.6	0	
	Column	108	73	117	7	305
	total	35.4	23.9	38.4	2.3	100.0

TABLE 6 Date of Material from Review Articles Found in One, Both or Neither Databases

Year	Count Row PCT Col. PCT	GeoRef In Both 1.	GeoArc In Neither 2.	only 3.	only 4.	Row total
1845–1894		0 0 0	1 100.0 1.4	0 0 .0	0 0 0	1 .3
1895–1944		0 0 0	9 100.0 12.5	0 0 0	0 0 0	9 3.0
1945–1959		0 0 0	11 91.7 15.3	1 8.3 0.9	0 0 0	12 3.9
1960–1964	0	0 55.0 0	11 45.0 15.3	9 0 7.7	0 6.6 0	20
1965–1969		1 1.9 0.9	13 25.0 18.1	37 71.2 31.6	1 1.9 14.3	52 17.1
1970–1974		22 25.3 20.4	17 19.5 23.6	47 54.0 40.2	1 1.1 14.3	87 28.6
1975		15 71.4 13.9	1 4.8 1.4	4 19.0 3.4	1 4.8 14.3	21 6.9
1976		26 78.8 24.1	2 6.1 2.8	4 12.1 3.4	1 3.0 14.3	33 10.9
1977		16 64.0 14.8	5 20.0 6.9	4 16.0 3.4	0 0 0	25 8.2
1978		15 71.4 13.9	1 4.8 1.4	5 23.8 4.3	0 0 0	21 6.9
1979		10 55.6 9.3	1 5.6 1.4	5 27.8 4.3	2 11.1 28.6	18 5.9
1980		3 60.0 2.8	0 0 0	1 20.0 0.9	1 20.0 14.3	5 1.6
	Column Total	108· 35.5	72 23.7	117 38.5	7 2.3	304 100.0

small, that no definitive conclusions about the database's coverage by language can be reached. What can be concluded is that non-English materials are of little interest to compilers of English language review articles.

In terms of number of useful citations, variety of types of materials, and range of dates, the bibliography evaluation method shows GeoRef to be the better database in the field of volcanology.

Method B

The other methodology, the subject profile technique, was tested by creating a subject profile of the field of volcanology by combining broad volcanology terms. Volcan(ism, o, oes, ology, etc.) or lava or lavas or ash flow(s) or ash fall(s) was searched on Dialog's GeoRef and GeoArchive databases and a systematic random sample of approximately sixty citations from the retrieved set was printed. A sample size of sixty allows a confidence interval of ninety percent.[21]

GeoRef contains 33,028 volcanology citations, while GeoArchive has 10,324.[22] Because GeoRef contains material from 1961 to the present while GeoArchive contains material only from 1974 to the present, the number of volcano citations per year of coverage was computed. GeoRef contains 1560 citations per year of coverage; GeoArchive has 1251, indicating that GeoRef has an edge in coverage each year as well as in total coverage.

The citations in each database were analyzed to compare document types, date of citations, and languages. Tables 7-9 summarize this comparison of the volcano materials included in GeoRef and Geo-Archive.

Based on the subject profile evaluation methodology, the GeoRef database appears to have better coverage of the subject of volcanology. It includes three times as many total citations per year of coverage, and has a much more extensive coverage of older materials. Both databases have a similar majority of journal articles (66.7% for GeoArchive, 72.7% for GeoRef), but they have an almost equal spread of coverage of other types of materials. GeoArchive has more Conference Proceedings and GeoRef has a wider variety of types of non-article materials. Nearly forty percent of the citations in GeoRef are in languages other than English, as compared to approximately twenty-seven percent in GeoArchive. (Seventy-nine percent of the GeoArchive database on the whole is English language, while seventy percent of the journal articles in GeoRef are in English). This again illustrates GeoRef's more diverse coverage in this field.

TABLE 7 Type of Material Found in Subject Search of GeoRef and GeoArchive

Type	Count Row PCT Col. PCT	GeoArc	GeoRef	Row Total
Journal article		40 45.5 66.7	48 54.5 72.7	88 69.8
Book		1 50.0 1.7	1 50.0 1.5	2 1.6
Chapter in book		0 0 0	3 4.5 4.5	3 2.4
Map		0 0 0	2 100.0 3.0	2 1.6
Conference Proc.		14 66.7 23.3	7 33.3 10.6	21 16.7
USGS paper or report		2 50.0 3.3	2 50.0 3.0	4 3.2
Special pubs. of societies		2 100.0 3.3	0 0 0	2 1.6
Thesis		1 33.3 1.7	2 66.7 3.0	3 2.4
Tech rept		0 0 0	1 100.0 1.5	1 0.8
	Column Total	60 47.6	66 52.4	126 100.0

TABLE 8   Language of Material Found in Subject Search of GeoRef and GeoArchive

Language	Count Row PCT Col. PCT	GeoArc	GeoRef	Row Total
English	1.	44 52.4 73.3	40 47.6 60.6	84 66.7
Other	2.	16 38.1 26.7	26 61.9 39.4	42 33.3
	Column Total	60 47.6	66 52.4	126 100.0

5. COMPARISON OF THE TWO METHODOLOGIES

The two tested methodologies allow similar conclusions to be drawn about the two databases being compared. Each method shows GeoRef to have more coverage of the field of volcanology, with the bibliography method showing GeoRef to have nearly twice the coverage of GeoArchive, and the subject profile method showing GeoRef to have three times the coverage. These conclusions are not startling since GeoRef has 700,000 total citations to GeoArchive's 420,000.

The format of each database is in part responsible for the much larger number of citations found in GeoRef by the subject profile technique. GeoRef includes some abstracts or short descriptions of article coverage, while GeoArchive does not, and GeoRef typically assigns more subject headings to each record. In subject searching it can therefore be concluded that GeoRef will yield a much higher recall. Although it will still be higher than in GeoArchive, known item searching in GeoRef will not be quite as dramatically better. Indexing and database formatting policies have a bigger impact on the subject profile technique (and on subject searching). These indexing differences also affect how many of the bibliography sample citations would have been retrieved in the subject profile method. Of the 305 citations in the bibliography method random sample, 21.3% contained a subject term somewhere in the citation that would result in its being retrieved by the subject profile method in both databases. 24.3% would have been retrieved in GeoRef only, and 1.3% retrieved in GeoArchive only. A total of 46.9% of the random sample citations are therefore also represented in the subject profile methodology.

TABLE 9 Date of Material Found in Subject Search of GeoRef and Geo Archive

Year	Count Row PCT Col. PCT	GeoArc	GeoRef	Row Total
1945–1959		0 0 0	2 100.0 3.0	2 1.6
1960–1964		0 0 0	3 100.0 4.5	3 2.4
1965–1969	0	0 22.7 0	15 22.7	15
1970–1974	52.8	19 47.2 31.7	17 28.6 25.8	36
1975	50.0	3 50.0 5.0	3 4.8 4.5	6
1976		5 50.0 8.3	5 50.0 7.6	10 7.9
1977	37.5	3 62.5 5.0	5 6.3 7.6	8
1978	55.6	10 44.4 16.7	8 14.3 12.1	18
1979		4 44.4 6.7	5 55.6 7.6	9 7.1
1980		1 84.6 18.3	2 15.4 3.0	13 10.3
1981		5 83.3 8.3	1 16.7 1.5	6 4.8
Column Total		60 47.6	66 52.4	126 100.0

The other characteristics measured are also very similar in each method. Both methods showed a similar percentage of journal article coverage (between sixty-seven and seventy-three percent), with GeoRef having a slightly better percent of journal articles in each method. If the other types of materials are considered as a whole, the ratio of journal article coverage to other types of materials is the same in each method. The breakdown by specific types of other materials differed slightly, however. Unfortunately, the numbers represented by each type are too small to draw many conclusions, but it appears that conference proceedings are not cited in proportion to their coverage in the databases and books or chapters in books are cited much more by volcanologists. Both methods show GeoRef to have a slightly wider variety of material types.

The conclusions on English or non-English language coverage in the two databases varies greatly between the two methodologies. The bibliography method sample is 96.7% English language with no non-English materials found in GeoArchive. This methodology allows the erroneous conclusion to be drawn that GeoArchive contains very few foreign language materials. The subject profile technique reveals that 26.7% of GeoArchive citations in volcanology and 39.4% of GeoRef citations in volcanology are in non-English languages.

This finding casts doubts on the representative nature of the citations in review articles. It seems that the compilers of these articles are heavily biased toward English language materials and reliance on this technique would virtually exclude coverage comparisons of the significant body of non-English language material.

Both methods point to the same conclusions regarding dates of materials. GeoRef has many more older citations than does GeoArchive, a fact that is in agreement with their stated coverage. Both methods show that neither database has retrospectively indexed many materials published before their stated starting dates. Over seven percent of the works cited in review articles were published prior to the coverage dates of these databases. Both methodologies suggest that neither database provides access to materials published prior to 1961 and that GeoRef is the preferred database for materials published prior to 1974.

The bibliography method required approximately 6.5 hours of online time (for a cost of approximately $465). In addition, it required the time to locate review articles, photocopy them, compile a random number table, and select the random sample of citations.

The subject profile method required approximately .75 hours of online time (for a cost of approximately $55). In addition, it required the time to develop the subject profile. If a larger sample was taken to allow a ninety-five percent confidence interval, an additional offline printing cost of approximately $100.00 and approximately .5 additional online hours ($35.) would be necessary. Obviously, the subject profile technique is much less costly and less time consuming.

6. CONCLUSION

This study has compared two *methodologies* for database evaluation by applying each to one subject. Its purpose is not to compare databases, but to analyze two of the possible methodologies that can be used to evaluate databases. Test results from the field of volcanology should not be extrapolated to comparisons of other subjects or to GeoRef and GeoArchive on the whole.

The test comparison of databases by amount of coverage, type of materials included, and dates of coverage show virtually the same results using either methodology. Both methods show GeoRef to have significantly more citations in the field of volcanology, a slightly higher percentage of journal articles, and more coverage of older materials. Because the review articles tested cited literature predominantly in English, the bibliography method does not allow fair comparisons of the language coverage in the tested databases.

Is it fair to compare the two methodologies? The two methods do not test exactly the same thing. The bibliography method relies on the assumption that authors of review articles or bibliographies have selected the best and most useful in the field. Applications of this method have often confused the distinction between a review article that could indeed be expected to reflect this judgement and a comprehensive bibliography that covers all literature on a topic, regardless of quality. It is thus difficult to know how much quality selection has occurred in a sample of citations from a sample of review articles or bibliographies. The SciSearch database from which the sample was drawn in this study labels an article a review or bibliography if it contains over a certain number of references.

If quality selection has occurred in the review articles used, application of this method reveals how the coverage of databases reflects the biases or judgements of a certain compiler. Because the needs of practitioners in the field may vary and quality judgement is a subjective thing, use of review articles eliminates from consideration much of the literature of potential interest on a topic.

The subject profile method is not biased in this way. It tests databases for coverage of all literature on a topic (within the confines of the database selection policy). This method thus eliminates quality judgement from consideration. The subject profile method only tests for literature that contains terms within the subject profile in each database. It can therefore be affected by database indexing policies and includes only literature relevant specifically to the topic being tested. Peripheral literature that may be cited in review articles but is not directly on a topic (e.g. general geology textbooks) is not reflected in the subject profile method.

If the purpose of coverage evaluation is to analyze how one database covers the literature cited by authors of review articles or bibliographies in a given field, the two methodologies cannot be compared. Only the bibliography method will provide information on how much of this literature is contained in a given database.

If the purpose of coverage evaluation is to compare databases to discover which database has more literature on a given subject, the two methodologies can be compared. It appears that either method will allow the same general conclusions to be drawn. Since the subject profile method is so much less costly, it must be considered the preferred method in such a comparison study.

7. SUGGESTIONS FOR FURTHER STUDY

The underlying assumption that compilers of review articles cite the best materials of use in a field is unproven, but is beyond the scope of this project. The wide discrepancy between citing non-English language materials and their proportion in the literature suggests that authors of review articles and bibliographies are biased toward English materials (or that practitioners in the field underuse non-English articles). It would be useful to know if this assumption is correct when evaluating the bibliography method, but would be difficult to test.

Comparisons of coverage evaluation methodologies should be expanded to include more methods using a larger number of databases. Also, comparisons of other types of evaluation techniques would be helpful in identifying the most reliable, but least costly, evaluation method for a given project.

This study is just a beginning to the needed comparisons of database evaluation methodologies. Considering that the literature of database evaluation has been established for a decade, it is time to compare methodologies, test assumptions, and seek the best ways to evaluate database coverage.

Footnotes

1. Gerda Yska and John Martyn, *Databases Suitable for Users of Environmental Information* (London: Aslib, 1976); Frederick W. Lancaster, "The Evaluation of Published Indexes and Abstract Journals," *Bulletin of the Medical Library Association* 59 (July 1971): 479-94; Virgil P. Diodato,

"Author Indexing in Mathematics" (Ph.D. dissertation, University of Illinois, 1981), pp. 25-38.

2. Martha E. Williams, "A Proposal for FEMA Database Requirements Assessment and Resource Directory Model," Coordinated Science Laboratory, University of Illinois, 1981; Carol Tenopir and Martha E. Williams, *FEMA Database Requirements Assessment and Resource Directory Model* (Coordinated Science Laboratory Report No. R942, prepared for the Federal Emergency Management Agency, 1982).

3. Yska and Martyn, *Databases Suitable for Users*.

4. John Martyn and Margaret Slater, "Tests on Abstracts Journalism," *Journal of Documentation* 20 (December 1964):212-35; John Martyn, "Tests on Abstracts Journals; Coverage, Overlap and Indexing," *Journal of Documentation* 23 (March 1967):45-70; John Martyn, *Services to an Interdisciplinary Need-Group from Computerized Secondary Services* (London: Aslib, 1975).

5. Lancaster, "The Evaluation of Published Indexes," p. 482.

6. Diodato, "Author Indexing," p. 25-38.

7. Martyn, *Services to an Interdisciplinary Need-Group*.

8. Pranas Zunde and John M. Gehl, "Fire-Relevant Literature and Its Availability," *Information Processing and Management* 12 (1976): 53-61.

9. Ibid.

10. Martyn, *Services to an Interdisciplinary Need-Group*, p. 4.

11. Yska and Martyn, *Databases Suitable for Users*.

12. Ibid.

13. Martha E. Williams, "Feasibility Study for an Automatic Database Selector," *Newsdic* 20 (Summer 1976):14; Martha E. Williams and Scott Preece, "Database Selector for Network Use: A Feasibility Study," in *Proceedings of the ASIS Annual Meeting* (White Plains, New York: Knowledge Industry Publications, fiche no. 10C-13, 1977).

14. Williams, *A Proposal for FEMA Database Requirements*.

15. Tenopir and Williams, *FEMA Database Requirements Assessment*.

16. One possible problem resulting from choosing a geologic field should be mentioned, although it is unresolved in this study. Geology tends to be a somewhat static field that probably uses a larger amount of older materials than other sciences. The conclusions drawn from these comparisons may not, therefore, be transferable to more dynamic fields.

17. Lockheed Dialog Information System, *Guide to Dialog Searching* (Palo Alto, Calif.: Lockheed, 1979); T.N. Smalley, "GeoRef: A Description of a Database," *Catholic University of America Report* LSC B19, 1977; Richard D. Walker, "Database Review: GeoRef," *Online* 1 (April 1977): 74-78.

18. Richard D. Walker, "GeoArchive: A Brief Review," *Online* 2 (October 1978): 42.

19. Lockheed Dialog Information System, *Guide to Dialog Searching*; Walker, "GeoArchive: A Brief Review;" Walker, "GeoArchive Online," *Database* 1 (December 1978): 35-45.

20. C. Oppenheim and S. Perryman, "GeoRef/GeoArchive," *Database* 3 (December 1980): 41-46.

21. To achieve a confidence interval of 95%, a sample size of nearly 300 would be

necessary. The cost of printing such a large sample was beyond my means for this project.
22. As of March 20, 1982.

Appendix

Review Articles

Cadle, R.D. "A Comparison of Volcanic with other Fluxes of Atmospheric Trace Gas Constituents." *Reviews of Geophysics and Space Physics* 18 (1980): 746-752.

Cole, J.W. "Structure, Petrology, and Genesis of Cenozoic Volcanism, Taupo Volcanic Zone, New Zealand—A Review." *New Zealand Journal of Geology and Geophysics* 22 (1979):631-57.

Dittberner, G.J. "Climatic Change—Volcanos, Man-made Pollution, and Carbon Dioxide." *IEEE Transactions on Geoscience Electronics* 16 (1978):50-61.

Ewart, A. "An Outline of Geology and Geochemistry, and Possible Petrogenic Evolution of Volcanic Rocks of Tonga Kermadec New Zealand Island Arc." *Journal of Volcanology and Geothermal Research* 2 (1977):205-250.

Ferguson, A.K. "Petrological Aspects and Evolution of Leucite Bearing Lavas from Bufumbira, South West Uganda." *Contributions to Mineralogy and Petrology* 50 (1975):25-46.

Furumoto, A.S. "Status of Research Leading toward Volcano Energy Utilization." *CRC Critical Reviews in Environmental Control* 6 (1976):371-402.

Gage, D.R. "Laser Raman Spectrometry for the Determination of Crystalline Silica Polymorphs in Volcanic Ash." *Analytical Chemistry* 53 (1981):2123-27.

Greeley, R. "Volcanism on Mars." *Reviews of Geophysics and Space Physics* 19 (1981):13-41.

Head, J.W. "Lunar Volcanism in Space and Time." *Reviews of Geophysics and Space Physics* 14 (1976):265-300.

Jarrad, R.D. "Implications of Pacific Island and Seamount Ages for Ages for Origin of Volcanic Chains." *Reviews of Geophysics and Space Physics* 15 (1977): 57-76.

Kay, R.W. "Volcanic Arc Magmas—Implications of a Melting-Mixing Model for Element Recycling in the Crust-Upper Mantle System." *Journal of Geology* 88 (1980):497-522.

Luhr, J.F. "Colima Volcanic Complex, Mexico." *Contributions of Mineralogy and Petrology* 71 (1980):343-72.

McBirney, A.R. "Volcanic Evolution of Cascade Range." *Annual Review of Earth and Planetary Sciences* 6 (1978):437-56.

Miyashiro, A. "Volcanic Rock Series and Tectonic Setting," *Annual Review of Earth and Planetary Science* 3 (1975):251-69.

Piermatt, R. "Historical Review of Seismic Studies on Structure of Volcanoes." *Annali di Geofisica* 26 (1973):525-59.

Pilger, R.H. "Pacific-North-American Plate Interaction and Neogene Volcanism in Coastal California." *Tectonophysics* 57 (1979):189-209.

Sato, H. "Diffusion Coronas around Quartz Xenocrysts in Andesite and Basalt from Tertiary Volcanic Region in Northeastern Shikoku, Japan." *Contributions to Mineralogy and Petrology* 50 (1975):49-64.

Simkin, T. "Volcanology." *Reviews of Geophysics and Space Physics* 17 (1979): 872-87.

Solomon, S.C. "Lunar Mascon Basins—Lava Filling, Tectonics, and Evolution of the Lithosphere." *Reviews of Geophysics and Space Physics* 18 (1980):107-141.

Sugisaki, R. "Chemical Characteristics of Volcanic Rocks—Relation to Plate Movements." *Lithos* 9 (1976):17-30.

Sun, S.S. "Petrogenesis of Archaen Ultrabasic and Basic Volcanics." *Contributions to Mineralogy and Petrology* 65 (1978):301-25.

Suppe, J. "Regional Topography, Seismicity, Quaternary Volcanism, and Present-day Tectonics of Western United States." *American Journal of Science* A275 (1975):397.

Tomblin, J. "Earthquakes, Volcanos and Hurricanes—A Review of Natural Hazards and Vulnerability in the West Indies." *Ambio* 10 (1981):340-45.

Additional Readings— Choosing Services and Databases

Blue, Richard I. "Question for Selection of Information Retrieval Systems." *Online Review* 3 (March 1979):77-83.

Buckel, William L. "Literature Searching Services—Choosing the Contract with the Best Discount Plan." *Online* (September 1982):59-64.

Folke, Carolyn. "Optimizing Search Costs: A Comparative Study of Three Systems to Find the Best One . . . or Two . . . " *Online* 4 (April 1981):38-43.

Hunter, J.A. "Quantifiable Characteristics of Bibliographic Databases." *Information Services and Use* 1 (March 1981):31-43.

Janke, Richard V. "Databases and Search Services North of the Border." *Online '82 Conference Proceedings*, pp. 1-16. Weston, Conn.: Online Inc., 1982.

Klingensmith, Patricia J., and Duncan, Elizabeth E. *Easy Access to DIALOG, ORBIT, and BRS.* New York: Marcel Dekker, 1984.

Kritchman, Albert. "Command Language Ease of Use: A Comparison of DIALOG and ORBIT." *Online Review* 5 (June 1981):227-40.

McCann, Anne and Burgess, Jonathan G. "Procurement of Literature Searching Services." *Online* 3 (January 1979):36-48.

Rouse, Sandra H., and Lannom, Lawrence W. "Some Differences Between Three Online Systems: Impact on Search Results." *Online Review* 1 (June 1977):117-32.

Tenopir, Carol. " 'Other' Bibliographic Systems." *Library Journal* 109 (Nov. 1, 1984):2008-9.

Tenopir, Carol. "Newspapers Online." *Library Journal* 109 (March 1, 1984):452-53.

Tenopir, Carol. "Full-text Databases." In *The Annual Review of Information Science and Technology*, (Vol. 19), pp. 215-46. Edited by Martha E. Williams. White Plains, N.Y.: Knowledge Industry Publications, 1984.

Wanger, Judith. "Multiple Database Use: the Challenge of the Database Selection Process." *Online* 1 (October 1977):35-41.

Weiss, Susan. "Online Bibliographic Services: A Comparison." *Special Libraries* 72 (October 1981):379-89.

PART 3   STAFF SELECTION AND TRAINING

The field of online searching has changed dramatically over the past decade and with it the role and function of the search analyst. It has become a specialization in its own right requiring special education and training. Searchers have, of course, known this for a long time. Managers have been somewhat slower to recognize this, for it implies a reallocation of human and financial resources to meet the demands of technological change and perhaps a re-examination of the goals and objectives of the organization as well.

Should enlightened managers attempt to set up the ideal search service, they will obtain little help from the literature. While there are numerous definitions of what constitutes a good search and lengthy lists of positive attributes that the model searcher should possess, in general the literature is exploratory rather than definitive, speculative rather than conclusive. Moreover, it is probable that characteristics deemed effective in one setting would be judged less appropriate in another.

The wide range of skills, knowledge, and behaviors that combine to produce competent searchers are matched by the variety of agencies that offer programs, courses, and workshops to educate and train them. Database suppliers, search services, online user groups, professional associations, inhouse staff, university extension, and faculties of library and information science all provide some form of instruction, though there is little consistency among them and limited control over the quality of the staff, the subject content, the techniques used, the duration of the program, the size of the classes, or the fees. In most cases distinctions are made between education and training. University faculties generally view education as the inculcation of the principles and theories of online searching and thus a legitimate part of their intellectual domain. Training is somewhat differently defined as the mastery of specific skills and techniques best left to database producers and vendors. This is not a universally accepted division of responsibilities, however.

The proliferation of training sources and methods serves to underline the fact that the information environment is changing rapidly, that the demand for online searchers and searches continues to grow, and that it is incumbent upon managers to recognize, plan for, and meet the needs of users for computer-based information through the provision of quality services by expert staff.

The quality of online searching is the focus of the article by William J. Jackson. The key to providing an excellent service is the competence of the searcher, but ensuring a high degree of skill is not, as he points out, an easy task. Not only are we uncertain about which skills, knowledge, and behaviors comprise the competent searcher, but we do not know whether these are the same or different from those attributes exhibited by good reference librarians, we do not possess reliable and valid instruments for ascertaining the presence of these characteristics in individuals and, finally, we do not have accepted methods for evaluating the quality of the searches themselves. Even given these areas of uncertainty, however, Jackson maintains that quality searching can be ensured through the careful selection and training of potential searchers. He suggests that further research be undertaken into the qualities possessed by excellent reference librarians and competent online searchers. He proposes two variables for examination: locus of control and abstract reasoning. He postulates that the searcher with an internal locus of control would feel more responsible for the results of the search, ask more questions, and take a more active role in the search process than one with an external locus of control, who would be less likely to pursue the user's true needs. While he urges the faculties of library and information science to provide a thorough background in the principles of online searching, he feels that employers also have an important role to play in on-the-job staff training. He describes the mentor method used in his library and reports on the encouraging results of that program in improving overall searcher quality.

Mary M. Hammer has taken the more conventional issue of whether reference librarians make competent searchers and reversed it to ask whether searchers can become successful reference librarians. To provide an answer, she examines five areas that she believes are critical: training, experience, personal characteristics, marketing skills, and user evaluations. She takes the view that meeting the user's need for information requires a combining of the reference and online functions into an integrated service. The searcher must be able to distinguish between those requests that may best be answered by using databases, those that require manual sources, and those that would benefit from both approaches. If online searching is seen as one aspect of the total information provision picture, it becomes incumbent upon the searcher to operate as a complete information specialist.

While practitioners attempt to accommodate online searching into their own environments, educators struggle to define the place that online searching has in library and information science education. A survey of faculties of library and information science found that while most offered some form of online instruction, the type and extent of training and education were by no means uniform. While there was general agreement about the importance of covering the concepts, principles, and techniques of online searching, the provision of hands-on practice time was somewhat more problematic ranging in consciousness-raising courses from six minutes to ten hours per student. Most schools taught one system, Lockheed, with ERIC being the most utilized database. Topics covered in the online searching courses included the nature and types of machine-readable databases, searching, structure of the online industry, the negotiation interview, and management of an online search service. The authors, Stephen P. Harter and Carol H. Fenichel, note the emergence of three educational patterns: the most prevalent they call the "Single Online Course"; the second they refer to as "Large Component"; and, finally, there is the "Integrated Approach." Although the latter was the one most often advocated by educators, it was the approach least often used. The researchers speculate about the reasons for this discrepancy between what is offered and what is perceived to be ideal and conclude that the ultimate fate of the online searching component in library and information science curricula will result from the goals of the schools, the needs of the marketplace, the competence of available faculty, financial considerations, and advances in online searching techniques.

Of interest to readers concerned with staff selection and training will be the relationship between searcher background and behavior, the role of the computer, examples of inhouse training programs, and preliminary attempts at tests to control the quality of searchers. For discussions of these issues and others, the reader is referred to the Additional Readings.

Staff Selection and Training for Quality Online Searching

William J. Jackson

In a field as new as online searching, it is not surprising that training methods have not been standardized. Online searchers are in such demand that even those with minimal training are acceptable. What inhibits progress in the development of online training is a lack of understanding or, at the very least, a lack of agreement on what differentiates an adequate searcher from an excellent searcher. Little research has been done in this area, and no generally accepted theories of online education or personnel evaluation have emerged.

One possible reason for this lack of theory is a similar lack of understanding about what makes an excellent reference librarian. Online searching may be considered an extension of basic reference librarianship. The lack of theory about performance standards of reference librarians becomes clear when one examines the literature concerning evaluation of the reference product. No theory exists here because we do not yet know what we are trying to evaluate. We continue to ask whether an answer to a reference question is correct without discovering why it is or is not correct.

This paper will discuss the relationship between online searching and reference librarianship and the need to examine the educational theories of both together. It will also discuss the need to discover success factors of online searchers and apply that knowledge to the selection and training of reference librarians.

SELECTING STAFF

Any good reference librarian should be able to learn to search online, and most are eager to try. The personal qualifications for an online searcher are no different from those for a reference librarian: a high degree of intelligence, resourcefulness, excellent interpersonal skills, diligence, problem-solving ability, organization, and a careful approach to tasks.[1]

The above statement offers one of the more precise lists of skills in library literature concerning online searching. Some would shorten it to "Any reference librarian, should be able to learn to search online," and, doubtless, there are few who believe that anyone can learn to search. The problem of who should be selected to learn to search is critical. Since training is an expensive investment, and evaluation of a searcher's work is not easy, it may be difficult to justify removal of a person from searching once he has been trained. The damage done to the reputation of online searching will last long after the deficient searcher has departed, especially if the search service operates on a fee-recovery basis.

The first four words of the quotation are the most critical: "Any good reference librarian." This immediately causes one to ask for a definition of "good reference librarians" and how they are selected. The current method of selecting a reference librarian permits anyone who expresses an interest in reference work to apply; i.e., we allow people to volunteer for the work. Little attempt is made to evaluate whether a candidate has the necessary skills to provide quality reference service, and it would be difficult to devise a test since "there is no totally satisfactory definition or theory of the reference process." [2] To allow anyone who is a reference librarian to search is to select as searchers second-generation volunteers. This method, "as capricious as a Ouija board,"[3] cannot assure quality.

The question of whether every reference librarian is going to make a competent searcher is answered by Ann Van Camp with a "limited no."[4] She lists several qualities which some may not always consider necessary in order to be a competent reference librarian, including self-confidence with man-machine interaction and "the ability to think in a logical and analytical manner."[5]

Donna Dolan and Michael Kremin go a step further by listing competence in concept analysis, the ability to think in synonyms, and the ability to anticipate variant word forms and spellings.[6] They propose that a good searcher has a certain cognitive style, an inherent quality that cannot be taught, and believe that a person lacking the proper cognitive style will never grasp the essentials necessary to become a good searcher. Dolan and Kremin have developed a short pretest as a method of determining who should and should not be trained to search.

Even this test has its shortcomings. Scoring some of the answers is a subjective process, and the test does not address the human-machine interaction problem—machine phobia. Furthermore, as Dolan and Kremin point out, the test measures only the basics of online searching—the ability to analyze, conceptualize, and expand concepts. The good searcher is one who can perform all of these functions simultaneously and synthesize the results with ease. No one has identified a method of testing that ability.

It is not unreasonable to state that any good reference librarian should be able to learn to search, nor is it unreasonable to state that the personal qualifications for an online searcher are no different from those for a reference librarian. However, until we move from speculation about what those characteristics are to answers based on validated research, it seems necessary to impose additional requirements or tests to identify potentially good searchers. The methods proposed by Dolan and Kremlin offer a possible solution.

TRAINING OF STAFF

An effort is made in the literature of online searching to distinguish between "training" and "education." For example, Harold Borko states:

> Education is concerned with the foundations, principles and basic know-ledge of information science and other disciplines as these relate to such things as database structures, database management systems, file structures, logic, formulation of search strategies in a generic sense, systems analysis and design, vocabulary structures, and user needs. The concerns of training are the content and structure of specific databases, design of search strategies as these are implemented within specific online or batch systems, and techniques for utilizing specific services offered by individual service centers.[7]

Borko contends that the university should concern itself with education, implying that training is somehow unworthy of consideration at the university level. He assumes that other sources are adequately providing what he classifies as training.

Excellence in online searching demands both education and training, and it seems artificial and unnecessary to separate the two aspects when many of their objectives complement one another. Search strategies in a generic sense (education) become more meaningful when illustrated by actual strategies performed within specific systems (training). The contents and structure of specific databases (training) are easier to comprehend when they are shown to be an application of the general theory of file structures and database structures (education).

While there are some courses in library schools that address the total education and training needs of online searchers, they are elective courses. Borko reported an unexpected enrollment in such a course at UCLA of thirty to forty students during the 1977-78 school year.[8] Clearly, even in those schools offering a separate course in online searching, few students benefit from extensive university-level instruction on the topic.

Most persons who search online have been trained in a setting other than a library school. This may have included vendor-supplied training, in-house on-the-job training, self-training, or training provided by database producers. This combination has produced searchers, but it has not always resulted in searching with consistent quality.

Searchers themselves perceive a lack of needed instruction or information. A recent survey indicates a need for system-specific database seminars and training in the formulation of search strategies. Many searchers responding to the survey claimed that they feel they do not understand file structures, are not familiar with database content and lack the ability to gain this knowledge from the vendor-supplied documentation or other printed sources.[9]

EVALUATION OF STAFF

Staff evaluation, whether of online searchers, reference librarians, or both, cannot escape imperfection. Most current evaluation methods measure input—space and equipment available, size of the reference collection, number of reference librarians on the staff, etc. Guidelines addressing these issues have been developed. For example, the Education and Training of Search Analysts Committee of the Machine-Assisted Reference Section, Reference and Adult Services Division, American Library Association, has published guidelines for online training sessions.[10] Most quantifiable methods of evaluation are simple measures: How many questions were answered? How much time was used? and How many people were served?

Charles Bunge provides a thorough review of methods of evaluating reference services in a recent publication.[11] Although Bunge concludes his essay with the hopeful suggestion that various imperfect methods, used together consistently, might result in acceptable evaluation standards, the pages preceding this optimism are a catalog of flawed attempts to evaluate the reference product. Bunge carefully reviews numerous methods of evaluation to be found in the literature, including asking the librarian, asking the user, unobtrusive evaluation, having an informed "anonymous shopper" ask questions, and anonymous telephone calls. All of these methods are approaches to evaluating the output of reference services, but none is judged reliable either because it is contrived or because, due to the type of question asked, the answer given cannot be ascertained to be the best or most accurate answer.

Librarians have tended to believe, more often than their users, that they have given the best of all possible answers.[12] Librarians cannot evaluate themselves, since they often do not perceive their failings, and users are not able to evaluate accurately the answers they receive, since they seldom know the extent to which service is possible. Users of online services are even less able to evaluate accurately whether an online searcher has provided the best possible service. If the user views the library as a "black box," as Orr et al.[13] claim, then the online search is the epitome of the user's inability to understand how needed information is provided. The fact that a computer has done the work so amazes most users that they do not think to question the completeness or accuracy of the results or the skill of the person providing those results. Even the mediocre searcher appears impressive when seated at a terminal. Surveys of users, therefore, are often futile and are likely to detect problems only when a searcher is grossly deficient. Other methods of evaluating search output are either lacking in completeness (for example, examining search strategies on completed request forms) or virtually impossible (for example, observing the searcher on a regular basis) due to the individualized, almost private nature of searcher-user interaction. Simply stated, what is true for reference librarians is true for online searchers: No accepted method of evaluating the quality of output is known, and none appears likely to be found in the immediate future.

IMPLICATIONS OF THE LACK OF EVALUATION METHODS

The lack of precise methods of evaluating the reference product forces us to reexamine selection and training processes. As currently used methods of evaluation have hinted, if it is impossible to measure the quality of output, we must do more to regulate the quality of input. Searchers must be selected based upon measurable qualities or criteria and must receive training designed to enhance the knowledge and skills necessary for quality performance.

Library schools could play an important role in this process by the full integration of online searching into the reference training of library school students. Currently, many librarians and library users view online searching as a separate activity: if information cannot be found in books or journals, perhaps the computer will solve the problem. The computer, with its amazing credibility in our society, at times seems to serve as a convenient way out of searching for answers to difficult questions. Users are often advised to search for information by computer without regard to whether it is the best method to address their information needs or whether it can address those needs at all. Instead, librarians should view online searching as another method of accessing available information, or perhaps as providing alternate access points for information. Manual and online databases could be viewed as alternate file structures for similar information. Library school students would gain an understanding of how the differences between manual and online searching affect the user's ability to select and manipulate informaton in the database.[14] If a user wants information that can be found in ERIC, and the subject is one in the controlled vocabulary, manual searching is fine. However, subjects not included in the controlled vocabulary are usually more easily searched by computer. Teaching students to judge the most efficient method of accessing information that is available through various methods is an important task of contemporary reference instruction. As information becomes increasingly available in multiple formats, this judgment becomes more essential.

In order to develop an understanding of the appropriate role of online searching in reference services, all reference students should be taught online searching. Online education should be integrated into reference courses rather than taught separately. The appearance of comprehensive, well-written texts, such as the recent one by Meadow and Cochrane,[15] makes this task easier. So many skills needed by good reference librarians are also needed by good searchers; it seems inappropriate to separate the two.

In addition, traditional reference education would be improved by a thorough introduction to online searching. Online searchers are aware of information sources not available in many libraries, and they are familiar with alternate methods of accessing information which is available. They are thus more able to meet information needs.

Online searchers are more aware of alternate access points for information as a result of their study of vendor-supplied or database-producer-supplied documentation. Understanding the documentation is a necessity for searching, and it gives the searcher a more detailed, precise knowledge of what is in each database, including what is in the printed versions of online databases. A comparison of the description of *Psychological Abstracts* in the authoritative *Introduction to Reference Work* by Katz[16] with the same in the *Guide to Dialog Databases*[17] will reveal important differences. Katz is descriptive, telling the types of materials included, the frequency of publication, the types of indexes, and similar information. The *Guide to Dialog Databases* chapter tells when the controlled vocabulary was changed, when a certain type of document was deleted from the printed index, and other analytical information that gives the librarian a better understanding of changes that have actually occurred in the printed index. Both are needed, and both should be taught.

NEED FOR FURTHER RESEARCH

One might suspect that not all students taking reference courses have the ability to learn online searching. Such students, if they are planning to seek jobs as reference librarians, should be encouraged to reevaluate their career decisions. While not every reference librarian has the inclination to search, a lack of the abilities needed to search online is a clue that the librarian may lack some of the abilities necessary to achieve excellence in reference librarianship. In addition, choosing whether to search will soon be out of the control of individual librarians. Online searching is likely to be the only way of accessing some types of information in the future.[18] Persons lacking that ability will have some employment opportunities closed to them.

Research is needed to identify those qualities or abilities that excellent reference librarians and online searchers possess. This will not be easy, since "excellence" must be judged subjectively and imperfectly. However, the task will be more easily accomplished than a judgment of excellence in the reference product, and it cannot wait until the problem of evaluation of the reference product has been solved. I propose that two variables be examined: locus of control, and abstract reasoning ability.

Locus of control refers to whether an individual perceives events as determined internally, by his own behavior, or externally, by fate, luck, or external forces. I suspect that reference librarians with external locus of control are less likely than others to pursue true user needs during the reference interview, less likely to feel that they have an important role in reducing the barriers to information that exist in many settings, and more likely to give users what they say they want rather than what they really need. The online searcher with external locus of control may have the additional problem of machine phobia. In contrast, librarians with internal locus of control, believing that rewards come from one's own behavior, should be more likely to take an active role in the successful resolution of a search. These librarians will be proactive in the search process, ask more probing questions and share in the resulting success or failure, rather than accepting the user's statements without question.

Abstract reasoning ability is probably the key to whether a searcher is able to progress from understanding the processes of searching to synthesizing all of those processes into a good search. A searcher lacking good abstract reasoning ability might score well on Dolan and Kremin's pretest yet still not be able to search well. This is the searcher who never progresses past the beginning stages of training.

Research on these and other factors may allow us to select potential searchers who have ability rather than hoping that those who volunteer will somehow "work out." The researcher will need access to a larger number of beginning searchers than is normally found in one location, making this research difficult to accomplish.

A third method of screening applicants that might be tested is an examination of standardized aptitude test scores, such as Graduate Record Examination scores. Dolan has stated that searchers might need to have "ambidextrous" lateral dominance,[19] suggesting that successful searchers will probably be found to have equally strong verbal and quantitative scores on aptitude tests. This method of testing could be done as a follow-up study by anyone with access to the scores of a large number of students.

COPING WITH THE PRESENT

Lacking any concrete research data on which to base training methods has not prevented online searchers from realizing that certain types of training are needed and are lacking in most standard training programs offered by online vendors. Many libraries and local user groups supplement vendor training with training programs that allow experienced searchers to share their knowledge. At the University of Houston Central Campus all searchers participate in an in-house program designed to supplement training received at the vendors' introductory training seminars. New searchers (or those who are beginning to search after a long lapse) are presented a set of questions and asked to prepare strategies for online retrieval. Questions used are actual questions from searches done within the past two years and require the new searcher to examine some of our most frequently used databases: *ERIC, Psychological Abstracts, Management Contents, ABI/Inform, and Sociological Abstracts*. As needed, additional questions have been prepared to give searchers experience with databases in their specific field. For example, ten questions to be answered using *PAIS, U.S. Political Science Documents, Historical Abstracts, America: History and Life, and GPO Monthly Catalog* were prepared at the request of the political science librarian. Questions are chosen to illustrate a specific database feature (e.g., limiting by date), how to handle an especially complex question, or a vocabulary or thesaurus problem.

Searchers are asked prepare two or three strategies at a time. These strategies are discussed with the trainer before additional questions are prepared. The trainer has prepared a strategy, often the strategy actually used when the question was originally asked by the user. The two strategies are compared, and a discussion ensues as to why the strategies are different and what effect the differences would have on recall and precision. The new searcher is also encouraged during this period to observe various members of the staff as they negotiate and perform searches, and to practice daily to gain a familiarity with the online terminal and basic system commands.

As soon as the new searcher feels ready, she/he is encouraged to begin accepting appointments for actual searches. Experienced searchers are on call should problems develop during the search, and funding is provided by the library to cover the cost of any mistakes. This funding is regarded as a training expense and allows the searcher, at his/her discretion, to reduce the cost to the patron if the searcher feels that the search was not done as well as possible. This is an important factor in reducing a beginner's anxiety.

There are several reasons why this training program has been adopted:

- We feel that online vendors do a good job of explaining system capabilities, but they are not as successful at fully explaining search negotiation, search strategy preparation, search logic, file structures, or the importance of file documentation.
- New searchers tend to return from vendor training with a fear of not doing things correctly. We strongly emphasize that there is usually no "correct" way to do any given search.
- New searchers need the simple reassurance of a knowledgeable person that they are performing acceptably.
- The sample searches used as exercises allow us to passively illustrate pitfalls and problems that may be encountered.
- Discussions of searching methods allow us to correct any misconceptions that the new searcher might have acquired during the initial stages of training.
- Search strategy discussions provide an opportunity to judge subjectively the new searcher's ability and probability of success. They provide an opportunity to recommend additional training if it is deemed necessary.

This method, combining available vendor training with supplementary exercises, has worked quite well. The major problem with training of this type is that it is very labor intensive. Individualized instruction is not done without some cost, but it seems a necessity at the present time due to a lack of clear understanding of what is essential to online searching skills.

Dolan is an advocate of this "mentor method," although the program she describes at SUNY-Albany is handled differently. The common elements are:

- The new searcher works with an experienced searcher.
- Both searchers prepare strategies and compare their approaches to the same problem.
- The new searcher gains experience handling questions in a "real life situation with irate patrons, down time, and inappropriate searches."[20]

Dolan states that "searchers *not* trained in this way tend to be very dependent and panicky when a problem arises."[21] It would seem that correction and/or reassurance by an experienced searcher early in the training process is essential to the flexibility and self-confidence needed by proficient searchers.

The results of our program have been encouraging. Although the evaluation is purely subjective, searchers trained since the beginning of the mentor method display more self-confidence, are more likely to find creative solutions to difficult questions, are more willing, or even anxious, to search a greater number of databases with more subject variability, and are more comfortable in sharing their problems, failures, and successes. They are less likely to feel threatened or think that their problems are necessarily their fault. All of these improvements have led to greater staffing flexibility and efficiency, allowing a searcher who is available at a given time to do a search rather than requiring the user to return when the one person handling his subject will be available.

This mentor method is more difficult to achieve outside of the larger academic or public libraries, since other institutions tend not to have experienced searchers to act as mentors. Libraries and user groups should take the lead in providing internships or other methods of sharing knowledge with new searchers. It is currently one of the best ways to improve overall searcher quality.

CONCLUSION

It has been assumed for too long that a basic library education is the only important qualification for entry-level professional library jobs. Those additional factors that cannot be changed or corrected by education, such as cognitive style, must be used for employment decisions. Until this is done, quality control will remain difficult to achieve.

Reference librarians and online searchers play an important role in the image libraries project. They are the primary contact for the public in the "black box" of information. If we are to provide the best possible service to the public, more research must be done into what constitutes excellence in reference librarianship.

Footnotes

1. Carol H. Fenichel and Thomas H. Hogan, *Online Searching: A Primer* (Marlton, N.J.: Learned Information, 1981), p. 87.
2. William A. Katz, *Introduction to Reference Work*, vol. 1: *Basic Information Sources* (New York: McGraw-Hill, 1978), p. 6.
3. Donna R. Dolan and Michael C. Kremin, "The Quality Control of Search Analysts," *Online* 3 (April 1979):8.
4. Ann Van Camp, "Effective Search Analysts," *Online* 3 (April 1979):18.
5. Ibid., pp. 18-20.

6. Dolan and Kremin, "The Quality Control of Search Analysts," p. 9.
7. Harold Borko, "Teaching Online Retrieval Systems at the University of California, Los Angeles," *Information Processing and Management* 14 (1978): 477.
8. Ibid., p. 479.
9. Sue Kennedy, "Online Training: Pattern, Preferences, Predictions," paper presented at Online '81, Dallas, Texas, 2-4 November 1981, pp. 2-3.
10. "Online Training Sessions: Suggested Guidelines," *RQ* 20 (Summer 1981): 353-57.
11. Charles A. Bunge, "Approaches to the Evaluation of Reference Services," in *Evaluation and Scientific Management of Librareis and Information Centres*, eds. Frederick W. Lancaster and Cyril W. Cleverdon (Leiden, Netherlands: Noordhoff, 1977), pp. 41-71.
12. Samuel Rothstein, "The Measurement and Evaluation of Reference Service," *Library Trends* 12 (January 1964):464.
13. Richard H. Orr et al., "Development of Methodologic Tools for Planning and Managing Library Services: I. Project Goals and Approach," *Bulletin of the Medical Library Association* 56 (July 1968):237.
14. Elaine Caruso, "Hands Online in Multisystem Multidatabase Trainer," *Library Science with a Slant to Documentation* 15 (June 1978):83.
15. Charles T. Meadow and Pauline Atherton Cochrane, *Basics of Online Searching* (New York: Wiley, 1981).
16. Katz, *Introduction to Reference Work*, 1:126-28.
17. "Psychinfo," in *Guide to Dialog Databases* (Palo Alto, Calif.: Dialog Information Retrieval Service, 1981), file 11, pp. 1-37.
18. Frederick W. Lancaster and Julie N. Neway, "The Future of Indexing and Abstracting Services," *Journal of the American Society for Information Science* 33 (May 1982):185-88.
19. Donna R. Dolan, "Teaching Search Service Personnel," in *Aspects of Information Service and Management* (Proceedings of the Fall meeting of the New England Online Users Group, Tufts University, November 3, 1978), p. 3 (frame 40) (ED 180 453).
20. Ibid., p. 6 (frame 43).
21. Ibid., p. 6 (frame 43).

Search Analysts as Successful Reference Librarians

Mary M. Hammer

Reference librarians have always been challenged to satisfy patron needs. Now that online database searching has exploded the availability of information covering most areas of knowledge, many academic librarians are facing the need to successfully integrate traditional reference service with patron demand for computer-produced bibliographies of resources. With the tremendous growth of scientific technology, the question is no longer whether or not traditional reference service should be supplemented by online searching, but rather *how*, *when*, and *how much*.

In spite of patron demand, many reference librarians have not yet integrated online database searching with general reference service. Gardner[1] has found much conflict and diversity of opinion about the kind of reference service that many tax-supported libraries offer and the kind of reference service that has evolved for patrons who can pay for online bibliographic searches. Vickery[2] and Shera[3] have both documented the resistance and hostility which many librarians feel towards computers. According to James Kusack, "the actual use of online bibliographic searching systems is growing at a rapid rate but, regrettably, many librarians see them as a special and exotic service only tangentially related to the reference process."[4] However, attitudes are changing as online searching becomes more prevalent in libraries. For example, a poll in 1976 revealed that about 80% of the members of the Association of Research Libraries provided online computer based bibliographic searches for users.[5] Today, most academic libraries and a great many public and special libraries provide such services.

THE SEARCH ANALYST

The availability of online bibliographic searching has created demand for librarians with new skills and expertise. "In fact, an entirely new type

Reprinted with permission of Haworth Press from *Behavioral & Social Sciences Librarian* 2 (Winter 1981/Spring 1982):21-29.

of librarian is emerging: professionals who specialize in providing information services through machine-readable databases."[6] These librarians have various titles such as information specialist, data services librarian, online search consultant, or computer search analyst. This article will examine factors which are critical for successful functioning of search analysts as reference librarians: (a) professional training as online searchers, (b) training and experience as reference librarians, (c) interpersonal and communication skills, (d) assertive promotion, marketing, and staff education, and (e) patron evaluation, feedback, and postsearch assistance.

FORMAL AND INFORMAL TRAINING OF SEARCH ANALYSTS

Numerous publications have been written on the professional education, training, and continuing education needs of online searchers, especially in formal educational settings such as library schools. For example, Knapp and Gavryck provide a thorough account of their program at the School of Library and Information Science, SUNY, Albany.[7] Bellardo, Jackson, and Pikoff have recently published a useful bibliography.[8] Dolan and Kremin even advocate that search analysts be certified by library schools as part of a quality control program.[9] In addition, private consultants, database producers, and online system vendors (Lockheed, SDC, BRS, etc.) also provide valuable training on the mechanics of system language as well as techniques pertaining to specific databases.

Unfortunately, such training "leaves serious gaps because producers and vendors are usually unaware of one another's products. Combination sessions by both producer and vendor offer more in-depth education, but these are too little and too late for most new searchers."[10] In reality, formal training can only go so far. Search analysts are usually forced to learn a great deal about all aspects of online searching on their own through self-study of database guides, thesauri, newsletters from vendors, and search system manuals. In addition, new professional journals have recently emerged to satisfy the need of active online searchers to stay abreast of current developments.[11] Participating in online users' groups, attending professional library meetings and workshops, and seeking assistance from more experienced colleagues also contribute to the development of expertise.

KNOWLEDGE AND EXPERIENCE AS REFERENCE LIBRARIANS

After being formally trained in specific online searching skills, the search analyst needs a strong background of reference knowledge and working experience to provide individualized reference service tailored to patron needs. Ideally, the reference function and the online searching function should be integrated in libraries. This philosophy is strongly advocated by Kusack:

> Knowledgeable librarians who can work equally well in both modes of bibliographic retrieval induce a kind of synergetic symbiosis. The online service supplements and improves the reference service while the reference librarians, by explaining the capabilities and limitations of online searching, get the greatest advantage of that service.[12]

Integrating formal training with reference skills, the search analyst must use background knowledge of subject areas as well as familiarity with printed reference resources to determine whether or not an online search is necessary. Benefits and limitations need to be weighed according to the patron's need because "the manual search is still quite valid, sometimes better and more economical than a computer search."[13] According to Knapp:

> Very narrow subject searches may be easily accomplished in printed indexes which use KWIC title words for subject retrieval, such as the Permuterm Index of the *Social Sciences Citation Index*. Subjects which are described by a number of different synonyms and/or variant spellings of the same terms, however, are more easily searched by computer in such title-word indexes.[14]

Other types of subject searches which are more easily and efficiently done by computer include those which (a) involve newly coined terms or phrases which are not yet available through descriptors in printed indexes, (b) involve only the most recently published literature (not yet available through printed indexes), and (c) involve coordination between two or more topics. An example of this last type of search is described in the newest *Thesaurus of ERIC Descriptors*.[15] To retrieve a subject such as "Adult Education Programs," a searcher must look under two main topics: "Adult Education"*and* "Adult Programs." Obviously, an online search would greatly benefit the patron, considering the quantity of resources retrievable under both topics.

If online searching would best meet the patron's information needs, then the search analyst must determine the most appropriate database for a particular topic. Contrary to novice expectations, this is not always an easy task, as noted by Caldwell and Ellingson:

> The recent proliferation of databases that are complementary or overlapping in subject coverage creates a dilemma for searchers, especially those who work in the public sector where part or all of the costs of database searching

are borne by the end user. It is very appealing for the sake of comprehensiveness and ease of access to have so many different databases online; yet, . . . where does this multitude of databases leave the end user with limited financial resources? For how much duplication of references among databases is an end user willing to pay?[16]

In fact, there are no cut-and-dried, correct answers to the previous questions. The search analyst must make a decision considering the patron's needs and ability to pay as well as knowledge of database content, journal coverage, and database overlap. Unfortunately, this type of decision cannot be easily taught because it is based on prior training, reference experience, the unique characteristics of the search topic, and subjective online knowledge gained through trial-and-error.

COMMUNICATION AND INTERPERSONAL SKILLS

In addition to training, expertise, and reference skills, a good search analyst needs certain personality characteristics and unique interpersonal skills for successful online searching. Judith Wanger describes these skills as an undefinable "IT" which includes "the ability to relate to people, to listen, to read (and hear) between the lines, to make some fairly abstract connections, to feel confident about entering another person's world of interest and expertise, and *to begin relating a search problem to the world of information.*"[17]

According to Ann Van Camp, specific qualities which a search analyst must possess are self-confidence, a logical mind, people-oriented communication skills, knowledge in subject areas, good public relations skills, a retentive memory, training in the art of searching, efficient work habits, as well as perserverance, patience and a sense of humor.[18] Dolan and Kremin elaborate on other characteristics including the ability to analyze concepts, to think in synonyms, to anticipate variant word forms, and to look at a problem in more than one way at the same time, i.e., flexibility in thinking.[19] In summary, Atherton and Christian state their philosophy:

Information services librarians should be selected on the basis of their personality and intellectual power as well as their reference or subject matter backgrounds. . . . Particularly important is the ability to relate to and communicate well with other specialists. Searchers should also have a strong service orientation, for they should see themselves as *advocates* of clientele needing information, not as keepers of the keys to the terminal.[20]

It is not sufficient for a search analyst merely to possess these personality traits and interpersonal skills. "The search analyst's primary functions are analysis based on understanding and the reconstruction, in an abstracted form, of the essential parameters of the user's need."[21] In other words, the search analyst must now apply his/her skills, knowledge, and training by actively communicating with the patron so that the information need can be clearly understood and precisely defined. This process, usually accomplished during a reference interview, is critical for successful online searching.

Numerous publications stress the importance of the reference interview to patron service in libraries.[22] Arleen Somerville succinctly describes the interview process for search analysts in an academic library, including: determining if an online search is needed, explaining the overall process (techniques, logic, costs, time, etc.) to the patron, discussing and understanding the particular subject topic, determining the search strategy, planning alternative strategies and identifying potential problems, choosing the most appropriate databases, describing online procedures and print formats, executing the search at the terminal, and providing reference assistance at the conclusion.[23] Taking a slightly different approach, Knapp stresses the importance of actively involving the patron:

> User and analyst negotiate search strategy and the user's needs. . . . It is the feedback from both patron and system, combined with the patron-to-analyst interview prior to signing on but *continuing throughout the process*, which mitigates the disadvantages of the delegated search and takes advantage of the expertise of both search analyst and user.[24]

The success of the reference interview is the joint responsibility of both the search analyst and the patron. Empathy, rapport, open-ended questions, skillful listening, and perseverance are traits which search analysts find invaluable. According to W.L. Saunders, human factors must always be considered. "The sensitive handling and selection of what is appropriate for a particular purpose at a particular time will be a major criterion of operational effectiveness."[25]

PROMOTION AND MARKETING OF ONLINE SERVICES

Like any other product or service in our free-enterprise economy, searching will not be valued or utilized unless patrons are aware that it exists and that it can satisfy their information needs. Assertive promotion and marketing focuses on the needs of the buyers (the patrons) rather than on the needs of the search analysts or librarians. According to Douglas Ferguson, successful marketing strategy should consider five questions:

(1) Who am I trying to reach? (2) What are their interests? (3) What can I create to serve these interests? (4) Under what conditions can I offer services and products? and (5) How can I communicate with my natural audiences and how can they communicate their needs to me?[26]

Always keeping the patrons' needs foremost, Ferguson elaborates on specific products: brochures, leaflets, signs, radio-TV-newspaper advertising, posters, personalized letters, demonstrations, and regularly scheduled mass mailings to particular departments. Although a variety of advertising methods can be used, Van Camp emphasizes:

> One of the best methods of marketing the search service is to cultivate satisfied end-users. Explaining the capabilities and limitations of the system, producing high quality searches, and encouraging feedback from the users should help assure satisfied customers. These users will return then for additional searches and will recommend the service to their colleagues.[27]

Search analysts need assistance from other reference librarians and library staff to consistently provide this type of reference service. Ideally, "the entire reference staff should consider themselves to be online retrieval personnel, even though all may not perform online searches."[28] The search analyst needs to orient librarians not actually engaged in searching so that they can deal with patrons' initial requests for general information. These librarians should be aware of the capabilities or limitations of the service and alerted to new databases and other relevant developments. Other library staff may need training on related tasks such as referring phone requests, scheduling appointments, handling billing procedures, or collecting fees from patrons.

PATRON EVALUATION AND CONCLUSION

The entire online searching process is not completely finished when the patron picks up the computer printout or offline prints. Instead, the search analyst frequently provides further reference assistance in a postsearch conference:

> During these sessions the librarian also apprises the patron of what full-text materials are available in that library or elsewhere, and integrates the computer output with the other library resources. For example, it might be appropriate to pursue the topic further back in time through printed indexing and abstracting media, which might cover older material than that available online. Similarly, arrangements can be made during the interview to acquire full-text copies of the more important cited material, perhaps via photocopy or interlibrary loan.[29]

Although few research reports have been published, many search analysts informally request verbal feedback from the patron or seek brief written comments regarding the quality or usefulness of the online retrieval service. Searchers, being human beings, occasionally make mistakes or become aware that a different approach might have been more appropriate for the patron's information needs. Patron feedback is essential for the searcher's continuing professional development.

In conclusion, it should be obvious that online database searching has tremendous potential for meeting patrons' information needs. However, this potential can never be completely achieved because the search analyst must constantly strive to produce high-quality, cost-efficient, online searches. Each search is a unique challenge to meet the ultimate goal of patron satisfaction.

Footnotes

1. Trudy A. Gardner, "Effect of Online Databases on Reference Policy,"*RQ* 19 (Fall 1979):70-74.
2. A. Vickery, "The Clash of Interests in Computer Information Services," *Information Processing and Management* 14 (1978):37-43.
3. Jesse Shera, "Librarians Against Machines," *Science* 156 (May 1967):746-50.
4. James M. Kusack, "Integration of Online Reference Service," *RQ* 19 (Fall 1979): 64-69.
5. Jeffrey J. Gardner and David M. Wax, "Online Bibliographic Services," *Library Journal* 101 (15 September 1976):1827-32.
6. Pauline Atherton and Roger W. Christian, *Librarians and Online Services* (New York: Knowledge Industry Publications, 1977).
7. Sara D. Knapp and Jacquelyn A. Gavryck, "Computer Based Reference Service—A Course Taught by Practitioners," *Online* 2 (April 1978):65-76.
8. Trudi Bellardo, M. Virginia Jackson and Howard Pikoff, "Education and Training for Online Searching: A Bibliography," *RQ* 19 (Winter 1979):137-42.
9. Donna R. Dolan and Michael C. Kremin, "The Quality Control of Search Analysts," *Online* 3 (April 1979):8-16.
10. Ibid., p. 8
11. Consult the following article for a list of journals and addresses: Sara D. Knapp, "Online Searching in the Behavioral and Social Sciences," *Behavioral and Social Sciences Librarian* 1 (Fall 1979):23-36.
12. Kusack, "Integration of Online Reference Service," pp. 66-67.
13. Anne G. Lipow, "User Education and Publicity for Online Services," in *Online Bibliographic Services—Where We Are, Where We're Going*, ed. Peter G. Watson (Chicago: American Library Association, Reference and Adult Services Division, 1977), p.70.
14. Knapp, "Online Searching in the Behavioral and Social Sciences," p. 24.
15. *Thesaurus of ERIC Descriptors* (Phoenix: Oryx Press, 1980), p. xvii.

16. Jane Caldwell and Celia Ellingson, "A Comparison of Overlap: ERIC and Psychological Abstracts," *Database* 2 (June 1979):62-67.
17. Judith Wagner, "Multiple Database Use: The Challenge of the Database Selection Process," *Online* 1 (October 1977):35-41.
18. Ann Van Camp, "Effective Search Analysts," *Online* 3 (April 1979):18-20.
19. Dolan and Kremin, "The Quality Control of Search Analysts," p.9.
20. Atherton and Christian, *Librarians and Online Services*, pp. 46-47.
21. Sara D. Knapp, "The Reference Interview in the Computer Based Setting," *RQ* 17 (Summer 1978):320-24.
22. William A. Katz, *Introduction to Reference Work*, vol. 2 (New York: McGraw-Hill, 1978), pp. 61-80.
23. Arleen N. Somerville, "The Place of the Reference Interview in Computer Searching," *Online* 1 (October 1977):14-23.
24. Knapp, "The Reference Interview," pp. 320-21.
25. W.L. Saunders, " Human Resources," in *Information in the 1980's*, ed. L.J. Anthony (London: ASLIB, 1976), p. 55.
26. Douglas Ferguson, "Marketing Online Services in the University,"*Online* 1 (July 1977):15-23.
27. Van Camp, "Effective Search Analysts," p. 19.
28. Kusack, "Integration of Online Reference Service," p. 67.
29. Atherton and Christian, *Librarians and Online Services*, p.24.

Online Searching in Library Education

Stephen P. Harter and Carol H. Fenichel[1]

The last decade has witnessed a minor revolution in information systems and services, with sophisticated, publicly available online search systems accessing tens of millions of records in hundreds of bibliographic and other databases. Increasingly used by libraries and information centers, these services have created a growing need for the education and training of practicing librarians and other information specialists, as well as students, in the concepts, principles, and techniques of online searching. To partially fulfill this need, schools of library and information science offer, in a variety of formats, units in courses, entire courses, and even sequences of courses, in the use of this new technique, although at present, library schools account for only a small percentage of all online training received by librarians.[2] Is instruction in online searching an "adopted stepchild" to the library school curriculum, as one survey respondent put it? The present paper summarizes the major findings of a relatively in-depth survey, utilizing both an extensive questionnaire and interviews, of educational practices in the teaching of online searching in schools of library and information science.[3] Conclusions, recommendations, and implications for library and information science curriculi are then discussed.

The only previous broad survey of educational practices in online searching was conducted by Harter, who found that at least two-thirds of library schools accredited by the American Library Association provided some form of online education in 1977, although much diversity was reported among schools regarding the content and depth of the instruction provided and its place in the curriculum.[4] Several contributions to the professional literature have described the online searching course of instruction at the authors' schools.[5-11] With respect to instruction specifically in MEDLINE, a survey of 13 library schools that had been assigned educational codes by the National Library of Medicine was described by Berk and Davidson,[12] and Sewell,[13] and Rees *et al* [14] have

Reprinted with permission from the *Journal of Education for Librarianship* 23 (Summer 1982):3-22, a publication of the Association for Library and Information Education.

related their experiences in implementing MEDLINE modules within health sciences courses.

Vickery has reported on a project carried out in England and funded by the British Library Research and Development Department, in which ten schools experimented with online bibliographic instruction through inclusion of introductions to the technique in existing courses,[15] and Tedd and Keen[16] and Keenan[17] have described two of these introductory modules.

One of the most substantive contributions to the online education literature grew out of an institute for library educators on new techniques for teaching online searching, held at the University of Washington School of Librarianship in 1978. This was a position paper,[18] representing the collective judgment of the attendees, and including, in part, a set of proposed standards for online education in graduate degree programs in library and information science. Among the important contributions of this paper was the distinction made between consciousness raising instruction, which gives all (or most) students an awareness of the capabilities and potential of online searching, and operator training, which has the objective of qualifying students to be beginning professional searchers. We have borrowed this taxonomy and terminology in the present study.

With the exception of Harter's general survey, and Berk and Davidson's study of instruction in MEDLINE, both now badly out of date, the literature has concentrated on individual school and course curricula, and does not offer a general, in-depth picture of the status of instruction in online searching in schools of library and information science. We felt that such a picture is needed. Has online searching reached a stage in library education equivalent to, say cataloging or basic reference—in which it is regarded as a mandatory skill of the librarian or information specialist? How prevalent is an opposing view that instruction in the techniques of online searching is too technical to provide in academic institutions, and that it is more appropriately within the purview of vendors, database producers, and other sources? Are the invaluable reference functions of bibliographic utilities such as OCLC and RLIN being addressed in reference courses in the library science curriculum? Are students, especially those coming from a background in the humanities or social sciences, adjusting to using a computer terminal in addition to printed pages to retrieve needed information? Are library school faculty adjusting? Has online searching come to be viewed by non-information science faculty as we strongly believe it should be—as a powerful tool for the provision of reference service? And if so, have online searching concepts been integrated into general reference and specialized bibliography courses? How, and with what success? Are students gaining an overview and an understanding of the principles and importance of online searching (consciousness raising) but not acquiring specific technical search skills (operator training)? What is the content of a typical course of instruction that attempts to provide the former? The latter?

The over-all goal of the present study was to gather data sufficient to shed light on these and other questions. Our specific objectives were to document the current status of instruction in online searching in U.S. and Canadian schools of library and information science, in the following six areas:

1) Instruction in the use of systems designed primarily for technical processing, such as OCLC and RLIN, for reference service;

2) Consciousness-raising instruction, including course or unit content and the availability and nature of hands-on experience;

3) Operator training and education, including prerequisites, course content, amount and nature of practical experiences, and the type of courses in which the instruction is offered;

4) Continuing education offerings;

5) Physical facilities available for online searching and levels and sources of funding; and

6) Faculty options in regard to issues associated with online instruction, particularly the place of online instruction in the curriculum and the problems associated with its furthur development.

A questionnaire was constructed to elicit specific data relevant to the six objectives, and after critical reviews solicited from several faculty teaching online searching, was substantially revised. Questionnaires were mailed on April 21, 1980, to all library schools accredited by the American Library Association's Committee on Accreditation, to all associate institutional members of the Association of American Library Schools (referred to in this paper as nonaccredited schools), and to a few other schools indentified as having library science, school media, or information science programs. A cover letter accompanied the questionnaire, addressed to the head of each program, asking that the questionnaires be referred to the faculty member most involved in online education. Follow-up questionnaires were sent to non-respondents on June 13.[19] The over-all rate of response was 62 percent, with the highest response (76%) coming from the A.L.A.-accredited programs.

The survey was followed by ten in-person interviews, supplemented by later telephone conversations. For this portion of the study, we attempted to select schools following unusual approaches as well as schools that had followed more common patterns. The interviews are semi-structured, based on a formal interview schedule elaborating on answers from the questionnaire and also eliciting opinions more complex than could feasibly be obtained by a written instrument. The interviewers were not bound by the schedule and frequently followed up on interesting leads provided by the educators.

Reference Use of Technical Processing Systems. The first survey question asked respondents to discuss the extent to which bibliographic utilities such as OCLC and RLIN are taught as a tool for reference service. The responses indicated that this topic is addressed in one or more courses in 54 percent of the schools and at least mentioned somewhere in the curriculum in another 32 percent of the schools. However, the descriptions of reference use of these systems that were given as the final part of this question suggest that some of the respondents may have been providing information about the teaching of online technical processing systems in general, and not specifically the use of these systems for the provision of reference service. Thus, these percentages may be slightly inflated.

When the responses to the first question were analyzed by school category, we found, given the small numbers, that the distribution of responses among the three types of schools was relatively even. This was found to be generally true throughout the survey. That is, we found no major differences among accredited, non-accredited, and other schools of library and information science with respect to education and training provided in online searching. For this reason we have not in this paper broken down responses by school category.

Courses in which the reference use of technical processing systems is taught were categorized by type. Not surprisingly, reference cataloging courses were mentioned most frequently, although the topic is also found, in some schools, in courses in advanced cataloging, information systems, bibliography/resources, online searching, and several other courses.[20]

For the remainder of the survey, online searching was explicitly defined to include traditional online bibliographic search systems such as Lockheed, SDC, and BRS, as well as the use of numeric database systems, the Source, teletext, and similar systems. Specifically excluded were systems designed primarily for technical processing. We found that fully 68 of the 72 responding schools (94%) provide some type of instruction in online searching as part of their regular curricula. The four responding schools not teaching online concepts were from the non-accredited category. Two of the four stated that they planned to introduce instruction in online searching in the near future.

Consciousness Raising Instruction. Consciousness raising was defined in the questionnaire to be introductory instruction which helps students gain an awareness of the procedures and uses of online searching. According to this definition, all but one, or 98 percent, of the schools that provide some form of online instruction have courses in which only consciousness raising is provided. The most frequently mentioned courses containing a consciousness raising component were Introductory Information Science (38 respondents), Basic Reference (23 respondents), and Advanced Reference (21 respondents). Other courses listed three or more times, in decreasing order of frequency, were Literature of Science and Technology, Computerized Information Retrieval/Systems, Core Courses, Social Science Literature/Bibliography, Government Publications, Humanities Literature/Bibliography, and Research Methods. Thirty-one different courses were listed in all.[20] From written comments and interviews it seems probable that the distribution of consciousness raising instruction among such a wide variety of courses does not reflect purposeful planning so much as it reflects the interests and abilities of individual instructors. Several of the faculty interviewed felt that there should be an online component in the subject Literature/Bibliography/Resources courses in their schools, but believed that this was not likely to occur with the current instructors of these courses. courses.

"Hands-on" practice in online searching was a part of the consciousness raising experience in about two-thirds of the responding schools, with the amount of practice time provided per student ranging from 6 minutes to 10 hours with a median of .65 hours, a mean of 1.4, and a mode of .5 hours. Most schools (94%) used publicly available search systems for hands-on experience, although a surprising number (34%) utilized in-house systems. A few (15%) report the use of computer-assisted instruction.[20]

Instruction Beyond Consciousness Raising. All but nine of the responding schools and all but four of the accredited schools responding provide some form of online searching instruction beyond the consciousness raising level. Thirty-three of these schools offer more than one such course and 11 have five or more.

A full course entitled "Online Searching," or similarly, in which online searching topics comprise at least 84 percent of the course content, is offered by 28 of the responding schools, and three schools have more than one course in this category. The next most popular locations for instruction in online searching beyond the consciousness raising level are courses variously titled Information Storage and Retrieval, Analysis of Information Systems, Computer Based Retrieval and Information Systems (15 schools) and in courses in the literature of science and technology (15 schools). Instruction in online systems beyond the consciousness raising level also takes place in other advanced subject resources/bibliography courses, Reference, Introduction to Information Science, Advanced Reference, Library Automation, and many other courses. The full list is remarkably varied.[20] As we have already noted with respect to consciousness raising instruction, whether or not an advanced component in online searching is taught in a particular course not devoted entirely to the subject probably depends more on the instructor than any other factor.

Only one school presently has a course devoted entirely to non-bibliographic databases, but another school has been conducting a two-week workshop in numeric databases that reportedly will be expanded to a full course soon.

Courses in Which Fifty Percent or More Time Is Devoted to Online Searching. About two-thirds of the survey respondents (47 schools) offer at least one course in which at least half of the class time is devoted to online searching topics. Nine schools now offer two or three such courses. Faculty in five schools described more than one course in the questionnaires, so that the following data describe 53 courses in which 50 percent or more time is devoted to online searching topics.

Prerequisites most frequently named for these courses were reference courses and either Information Storage and Retrieval, Information Systems, or Information Science. A few schools required advanced reference or literature courses that may themselves have had pre-requisites.[20] The number of prerequisites required varied from none to four, most schools requiring a single course, usually Basic Reference. The school with four prerequisites listed three apparently basic courses and an Information Retrieval/Systems/Science course. One respondent, from a school with three online searching courses, stated that there were now no prerequisites, but that he was considering requiring a typing speed of 20 words per minute. In a one year program leading to a master's degree in which there is a group of basic, core courses that students must take first, it is difficult to schedule prerequisites, at least for full-time students. No doubt this has a considerable impact on the specification of prerequisites for online searching courses.

Topics covered in courses in which half or more class time is devoted to online searching are listed in Table 1. Nearly all of the courses covered the nature and types of machine-readable databases, although only about half currently deal in any way with nonbibliographic databases. Consistent with the idea that these courses are a start towards training and educating students to actually use online systems, 87 percent of the respondents stated that searching was a topic in their course. However, all of the persons who responded negatively when asked if they taught "searching" indicated that they taught either the "Conceptual Aspects of Search Strategy and Search Formulation" or "System Mechanics, System Commands," or both. Thus, at least some instruction on how to conduct an actual search is a topic in all the courses offered.

Database producers and vendors are treated in 89 and 87 percent of the courses respectively, while 81 percent of the courses cover user/librarian and user/system interaction. Finally, although they are all a

TABLE 1 Topics in Online Searching Courses

Topics	Number of Courses N=53		Percent	
Nature and Types of Machine-Readable Databases		49		92
File and Record Structure	49		92	
Databases Available	48		91	
Nonbibliographic Databases	30		57	
Searching		46		87
Conceptual Aspects of Search Strategy and Formulation	50		94	
System Mechanics, Commands	49		92	
Use of Equipment	45		85	
Structure of the Online Industry		44		83
Database Producers	47		89	
Database Vendors	46		87	
User/librarian, User/system Interaction		43		81
Reference Interview in a Computer-based Setting	43		81	
Management of an Online Search Service		43		81
Database Evaluation and Selection	43		81	
Costs and Charging Policies	41		77	
Evaluation	41		77	
Equipment and Other Start-up Considerations	38		72	
Document Delivery Systems	36		68	
User Education and Service Promotion	34		64	
Vendor Evaluation and Selection	34		64	
Service Organization, Procedures, and Staffing	30		57	

part of more than half of the courses, management topics were found least frequently.

Hands-on practice time is provided in 52 of the 53 courses. Students work in a variety of ways: alone at all times (in 20 courses), in groups of two (4 courses), in groups of three (4 courses), in groups of four (2 courses), or using a combination of these (22 courses). In some schools it was up to the students to choose to work alone or to form practice groups. In seven courses, the instructor or a laboratory assistant was reported to be present when students worked at the terminals.[20]

There is a considerable range in the amount of online practice time received by each student, from 0.4 hour to an average of 11-12 hours with no limits imposed. In one school, students practiced 28 hours using emulators of commercially available systems. The median number of practice hours reported was four, the mean 4.6, and the mode three hours.[20] The consensus of online educators present at the University of Washington Institute[21] was that the amount of online search practice time allotted to train a person qualified to perform searches for patrons— a novice searcher—be at least five hours. Based on this consensus, two-thirds of the schools are not providing enough time in these courses to bring their students to the level of novice searchers. Whether or not operator training is the goal of the instruction is not known; however, we can reasonably assume that students who take a full course in online searching are anxious to learn to search in order to improve their position in the job market, and that potential employers cannot be blamed for assuming that a recent graduate who has taken a course in online searching ought to be qualified as a beginning, novice searcher, at the very least.

Cost is an obvious factor affecting the amount of online practice time provided students. Even at a low educational rate of $15 per hour it can be expensive to train large numbers of students on commercial systems. However, courses that use an inhouse system or emulator are relieved of connect-time charges. Thus one might assume that the amount of practice time in such courses is likely to be a truer reflection of what the instructor feels is most appropriate to achieve the educational goals desired. Somewhat surprisingly, courses using in-house systems or emulators did not differ significantly in amount of online practice time as compared to courses using commercial systems. All but three of these courses scheduled five or more hours of practice time, but only one provided an unusually large amount (28 hours). The commercial systems on which students practice most frequently are the "big three"; Lockheed, SDC, and BRS, although a total of 14 other systems are being used as well.

There are two opposing philosophies in regard to the number of systems that should be taught in an online searching course. The most prevalent view is that students learn best the principles of online searching if they need only deal with the mechanics of one system, although exposure to additional systems may not be excluded. An opposing view is that students should learn several systems, proponents believing that this is more realistic and also more equitable to vendors. Table 3 [on page 102] shows that "one system" courses predominate, making up 57 percent of the total.

Among the databases, ERIC was by far the most utilized for student practice in online searching courses, used in twice as many courses as any other database. ERIC was also the most heavily used database within the individual courses; in 27 courses one database was used 50 percent or more of the time, and in 22 of these the database was ERIC. (See also Table 4.) Other frequently listed databases were PSYCINFO and

TABLE 2   Systems Used in Online Searching Courses

System	Number of Courses* N=52	Percent
Lockheed	37	71
SDC	22	42
BRS	15	29
National Library of Medicine	8	15
In-house	8	15
Emulator	3	6
New York Times	3	6
The Source	3	6
CAN/OLE	3	6
QL Systems	2	4
Dow Jones	2	4
Dartmouth	1	2
INDIRS	1	2
RLIN	1	2
OCLC	1	2
NASA/RECON	1	2
LEXIS	1	2

*Many courses reported the use of more than one system.

SOCIAL SCISEARCH, reflecting a predominance of social science databases.[20] We assume that instructors select social science databases because most students feel confident about searching topics in fields such as education. The choice of databases to be searched depends upon the interests of the students in some courses. And at some schools, students work with actual clients who have prepared search requests. The databases used then depend upon the subject of the request. We found that the tendency was for online searching courses to include instruction in more than one database, and fully half of the courses reported including practice on six or more databases.

TABLE 3   Distribution of Courses by Numbers of Systems Taught

Number of Systems	Number of Courses N=52	Percent
100% One System	20	38
80-99% One System	10	19
Two Systems but less than 80% One System	8	15
Three Systems but less than 80% One System	6	12
More than Three Systems but less than 80% One System	6	12
No responses	2	4

TABLE 4   Databases Used in Online Searching Courses

Databases*	Number of Courses** N=52	Percent
ERIC	33	63
PSYCINFO	14	27
Social Scisearch	13	25
NTIS	10	19
BIOSIS	9	17
MEDLINE	6	12
Magazine Index	6	12
AGRICOLA	5	10
CA Search	5	10
National Newspaper Index	4	8
INSPEC	4	8
COMPENDEX	3	6
CDI	3	6
ABI/INFORM	3	6
Scisearch	2	4
LIBCON	2	4
Predicasts	2	4
GPO Montly Catalog	2	4
Energyline	2	4
Other databases (mentioned once)	24	—

*Databases mentioned two or more times.
**Most courses used more than one database.

A variety of textbooks and manuals are used in online searching courses.[20] DIALOG publications were listed most often, no doubt reflecting the fact that DIALOG is the most used system. Materials published by the database producers were also frequently mentioned.

Most online searching courses are today taught by full-time faculty members. (Table 5.) This is a considerable departure from practice a few years ago, when most faculty for online courses were adjuncts, suggesting that online searching has achieved a respectability and permanence in the mainstream of librarianship that it did not then enjoy. It also implies an expertise among regular library school faculty not present a few years ago. A few schools utilize both full-time and adjunct faculty in this role.

TABLE 5   Status of Instructors

Status	Number of Courses N=53	Percent
Full-time Faculty	42	79
Adjunct Faculty	6	11
Both	3	6
No Response	2	4

Continuing Education. In addition to formal academic courses of instruction, slightly over half (53%) of the schools sponsor short courses or workshops in online searching. Twelve schools offer university credit for these workshops and short courses, 20 offer continuing education credits, and 11 offer no credit at all.[20]

Facilities, Equipment, and Funding. A room or laboratory in which terminals are available for student use is provided in 79 percent of the schools that offer online instruction, and in nearly half of these the laboratory is staffed with a qualified searcher. The number of hours per week the laboratory is staffed ranges from five to 90, with a mean of 26, a median of 20, and a mode of 20 hours.

The number of terminals dedicated to student use ranged from zero to 17; of the schools having terminals the mean number was four, the median three, and the mode two. We did not distinguish between terminals available only to students and faculty in the schools of library and information science and terminals available to the entire university community; nor between dial-up terminals and terminals hard-wired to inhouse systems.

Video monitors on which one can show taped and live demonstrations of searches have become an increasingly popular classroom instructional technique. Monitors are now reportedly utilized in 54 percent of the schools that provide some type of online instruction.

By far the major source of support for online searching instruction are the parent universities. Thirty-three of the 62 schools that provide for student practice on online systems derived all of their funds from this source. Student assessment is also frequently used to pay at least part of the connect time and communications costs (12 schools). In three schools, all of these costs were paid by the students. Two schools reported utilizing the sale of reference services to help finance the cost of online instruction. A few schools reported other sources of funding, including gifts, absorption by the university library, and grant monies.[20]

Faculty Opinions. In a recent article, Bourne and Robinson state: "In the long run, though, it is the library school that will be responsible for producing new librarians versed in computer-based search skills. First, we expect that courses in computer-based reference will enter the curricula of more library schools. Later, computer search techniques could be integrated into the regular reference courses."[22]

We asked for reaction to this scenario. Fifty-two (72%) of the respondents agreed with it, 13 did not, and there were seven "no responses." The scenario really contains two questions: (1) Should library schools be providing online instruction; and (2) If yes, in which courses in the curriculum should it be located? from the comments it was apparent that most of the negative responses addressed the second question, although two respondents felt that library schools had no business taking on online instruction:

Respondent 1:

Cost factors make this approach prohibitive. Vendors will have to provide practical training. Schools can only provide background information.

Respondent 2:

Our philosophy is that librarians are managers. Our newly-adopted curriculum strongly emphasizes management training. That must come first in a one-year curriculum. Searching skills, as with other technical skills, must take second priority.

A number of other respondents answering "No" commented variously that specialized courses are needed to give the students in-depth training; that searching should be integrated into other courses such as information storage and retrieval; that the specialized course step should be skipped; and that both the specialized and integrated courses are needed. Two schools reported that they had tried integrating online instruction into other courses and had found that a separate course was necessary.

Some of the "Yes" responses to this question mentioned the need for a separate, specialized course as well. Several faculty indicated that the scenario was being followed in their schools and a few reported that they had already achieved integration, some by skipping the specialized course step. A notable characteristic of some of the responses favoring integration was fervor—expressed in remarks such as "We feel strongly," and "the sooner—the better."[20]

In response to a question concerning barriers to the development of online instruction in schools of library and information science, cost was identified most often, implying that instructors are dissatisfied with the level of funding they are receiving. (Table 6.) Utilization of online services by students involves substantial costs above and beyond the typical course in the curriculum. As we have noted, a few schools pass the costs on to students, but most are reluctant to engage in what many feel is a discriminatory practice; or, they are simply not permitted by university rule to assess student fees. Alternative sources of funding are few and far between. Cost is clearly a major problem.

Obtaining adequately trained faculty, mentioned in 38 percent of the responses, is also a significant problem. Several comments on this subject, obtained both in the questionnaires and in the interviews, especially addressed the difficulty of obtaining adequately trained faculty in the subject-oriented reference courses, as well as the problems involved in training and educating faculty already teaching these courses. As one faculty member put it, "The reality is that this is a new

TABLE 6   Barriers to the Development of Online Instruction in Schools of Library and Information Science

Barriers	Number of Responses N = 72	Percent
Cost	53	74
Obtaining Adequately Trained Faculty	27	38
Faculty Opinion that It Does Not Belong	12	17
Other	2	3
No Significant Barriers	13	18

skill that some faculty do not want to learn." The reasons for this attitude are unclear—we did not interview faculty teaching subject-oriented reference courses—but questionnaire and interview data and our own experience suggest that some of the reasons might be: 1) a true lack of understanding regarding the power and usefulness to the provision of reference service of online systems; 2) fear of the unknown—computer technology being the foremost of the unknowns; 3) lack of confidence in one's ability to learn the skill; 4) the hope that one day it will all have gone away; 5) unwillingness to go to the effort of learning about online systems and 6) cost.

Faculty opinion that online instruction does not belong in the curriculum is an additional significant barrier, according to 17 percent of the respondents. In some cases faculty believe that online instruction does not belong because it is a technical skill and as such has no place in a graduate program. Other reasons for this opinion are not clear.

Other barriers listed were developing adequate teaching modules, faculty fear and ignorance, and finding time in an already crowded curriculum. Lack of student interest was also cited as a problem in two schools. On the other hand, many persons interviewed in conjunction with the survey volunteered that student interest in online instruction is extremely high, and that courses in online searching are among the most popular elective courses in the curriculum. Only 18 percent of persons answering the questionnaire felt that there were no significant barriers to instruction in online searching in schools of library and information science.[20]

Case Studies. In-person and telephone interviews conducted with respondents, selected on the basis of the diversity of their questionnaire responses, resulted in case studies of online education in ten accredited programs. The case studies, which are fully described in the OCLC report of this survey, attempt to provide a total picture of the role of online instruction in each of the individual schools. The only common theme identified is that the status of online instruction in the schools is constantly changing, so rapidly in some schools that we found the questionnaire results to be out of date by the time the interviews took place.

Discussion. The results of the survey confirm that instruction in online searching is well established in schools of library and information science in the United States and Canada. In some form, it is part of the curriculum of at least 76 percent of all programs accredited by the A.L.A. and in 39 percent of the non-accredited programs.

Although 54 percent of the schools responding reported teaching the use of systems like OCLC and RLIN for reference purposes, we have already noted that the question was probably misread by some respondents, who seemed to be reporting the teaching of these systems for the primary purposes for which they were designed—obtaining cataloging copy, etc. Lack of faculty knowledge and awareness undoubtedly prevents some extensive addressing of this need by library school faculty. Many, probably most, faculty teaching reference courses are not versed in online technical processing systems and know little about their reference potential. On the other hand, cataloging faculty may not be fully aware of the reference needs that these online systems can fulfill. The traditional distinction between public services and technical services is not helpful to an understanding of the potential to reference service of these systems. Continuing education could play an important role here, we believe.

One of our most interesting general findings, particularly in terms of its implications for the accreditation of new library school programs, is that the survey results showed essentially no difference between responding A.L.A.-accredited programs and responding non-accredited programs. The 18 non-accredited schools responding to the survey have made an instructional commitment to online searching and its applications to librarianship, surely an important step on the road to future A.L.A.-accreditation.

As we noted earlier in this paper, the variety of courses in which both consciousness raising instruction and more specialized online components are found is at least in part (in large part, we suspect) a reflection of the interest and expertise of individual faculty members. This visceral impression was born out in interviews and in written responses to several of the survey questions; there is still considerable library school faculty resistance to, or at least lack of knowledge concerning, the use of online systems in libraries. Continuing education can, and we believe, should, play an important role in helping non-information science faculty be brought at least to the consciousness raising level of understanding regarding online library systems.

In examining the questionnaire returns as a whole, it is possible to identify three educational patterns that have emerged in the past few years, although there are schools that do not quite yet fit any of the three. The first, most prevalent pattern we call the "Single Online Course." It is found in schools such as Kentucky, Illinois, and Columbia. There is one, and only one, course devoted entirely to online searching. Basic reference is likely to be a prerequisite and there may be an information science prerequisite as well. A single publicly-accessible system, probably DIALOG, is used for demonstration and student practice. The students begin their searching experience on one database, probably ERIC, and then move to other databases. There is considerable emphasis in the course on file structure, indexing languages, evaluation, the pre-search interview, and administrative aspects of searching as well as search strategy and the mechanics of searching. The course is taught by a full-time faculty member and the objective of at least some courses is to educate and train novice searchers. In the rest of the curriculum, online instruction is limited to a small consciousness raising component in basic reference and perhaps other courses.

The second pattern, typified by the University of Denver and the University of Mississippi, we refer to as "Large Component." Here online searching is a major part (40 to 60%) of another course; usually the other course is from the information science side of the curriculum, often information storage and retrieval, but it can also be an advanced reference course (Toronto). If the course is primarily concerned with information systems, an in-house system is likely to be used. A few schools offer a course of this type as well as a course devoted entirely to online searching; others have a "Large Component" information science course in parallel with the "Integrated Approach" described below.

Interview and questionnaire responses suggest that in both the "Single Online Course" and "Large Component" approaches, online searching is something like a neglected stepchild in many schools, tolerated but mostly ignored by the non-information science faculty. While there may be small consciousness raising components in courses in reference, advanced reference, subject bibliography, government documents, etc., online searching has not yet become a full fledged member of the family. Interestingly enough, faculty reactions to the Bourne scenario and comments made elsewhere in the questionnaires and interviews indicate that the majority of the educators responding to the survey feel that online searching is, and should be, headed in the direction of full integration.

By the "Integrated Approach" we mean full integration of substantial online instruction into all the general reference and subject bibliography courses; fully integrated schools might not have any courses devoted primarily to online searching. There are only a few schools (e.g.,

University of Texas, Rosary College, University of Michigan before a recent change) reportedly following an integrated approach. Even so, as we have already observed, there is a great deal of faculty support for the point of view that online searching is simply another reference tool—albeit an extremely valuable one—and that it should be taught in that context.

A legitimate question is why there exists such a large difference between what is being offered in the schools and what the majority of the educators responding to the survey believe to be the ideal—an integrated approach. First, a substantial minority of faculty members believe in integration but also believe that there should be a single course devoted entirely to online searching. The concepts, principles, and techniques are sufficiently complex, these educators say, that they cannot be taught properly within the context of another course. There are sound pedagogical reasons for this position as well. Without a prior course in online searching, integration of online topics into reference courses implies a great deal of repetition in the instruction provided in each course (operation of equipment, database and record structure, system commands, etc.) One solution to this repetition might be to offer a separate course, prior to or concurrent with advanced subject bibliography courses. However, prerequisites are already a thorny problem in one year library education programs. We found that most schools offering a separate course in online searching require one or more prerequisites for that course. The typical one-year library education program would find that creating prerequisites for prerequisites for courses would cause sequencing problems difficult or impossible to solve. This type of sequencing becomes really feasible only in a two-year curriculum.

A workable compromise, it seems to us, would be for substantial study of appropriate *databases* to become part of reference, advanced reference, subject bibliography, and other courses. Even a full semester course in online searching cannot examine in any depth more than a few databases commonly searched, such as ERIC, PSYCINFO, and Scisearch. Basic reference courses would seem to be an excellent place for students and faculty to compare and contrast the relative advantages and disadvantages of searching *Magazine Index* or other interdisciplinary databases as opposed to *Reader's Guide* in hard copy. In what way are the online versions of *Art Modern, MLA Bibliography,* and *Philosopher's Index* particularly useful (or not useful) reference tools in the humanities? DIALOG alone offered at last count 34 databases in business and economics; what are the characteristics and capabilities of the most important of these? How do the machine-readable versions compare with their hard-copy counterparts? Similar questions can easily be posed in government documents, sciences and applied sciences, and other fields.

We should note that actually performing online searches is not necessary for analyses of this nature to have great value, although occasional demonstrations might well play a useful role.

The school of library and information science cannot be and do everything, of course. But reference tools in machine readable form are here to stay, and with 40 odd class hours devoted to, say, Literature of Business and Economics, it seems to us that some class time could profitably be devoted to an analysis of information sources in machine readable form.

The cost of providing online instruction constitutes another barrier to integration. Even occasional demonstrations in courses such as Bibliography of the Social Sciences can be costly. Emulators are no solution to the cost problem, if kept up to date with the emulated system. One responding school that is maintaining such emulators employs a full-time programmer for this purpose!

The third major barrier to integration is the lack of adequately trained faculty. In some schools this many occur because faculty teaching subject bibliography and reference courses would prefer not to learn online searching, for a variety of personal and professional reasons. In other situations, the problem may simply be one of money. We believe that efforts should be made to aid this large group of library school faculty who teach reference and subject bibliography but do not have online education and training, to integrate concepts of online searching into their courses. This can be accomplished by providing continuing education opportunities and perhaps by creating teaching aids such as "canned" demonstrations, ready-made for use. A less desirable means of accomplishing integration is having online modules taught in these courses by faculty who already possess the online skills.

In some schools online education has become a focal point for arguments on the theoretical versus practical approach to education for librarianship. On the surface, one might suppose that the results of this survey show the theoreticians to be losing; online courses are being added to more and more of the curricula of schools. Pressure from students who feel that online skills will help them in the job market is almost certainly a factor that is contributing to this increase. While there is some truth to this assertion, there is more to the story than that. We do not believe that it is possible to be a good online searcher without an appreciation of the principles underlying online searching. Online searching is more than simply learning the commands of a language. Effective searching demands a knowledge of system design, file loading practices and their effect on retrieval, the effects of specificity, exhaustivity, stoplists, and other indexing practices on retrieval, Boolean logic, ability to read, interpret, and use abtruse database documentation, ability to conduct a good reference interview, to select appropriate databases and fields for searching, to design a search strategy likely to produce relevant output, to evaluate intermediate output and modify the search strategy accordingly, and much more. None of these are purely technical skills, like typing, for example. They involve intelligence, judgment, and knowledge of principles.

The question might be asked why specific system commands are studied in online searching courses if what is important are language-independent principles. There are at least two valid responses to this. First, practice in specifics can help students learn principles (just as traditional reference courses use practice search questions as instructional aids). Students can conceptualize the effect of, say, truncation or searching in abstract fields and then, virtually instantaneously, note the effect in a real system. The second reason that at least one specific system should, we believe, be studied in depth, is that, very simply, online searching is a marketable skill. One need only read the employment notices in professional journals to see the importance of this skill. In short, we see no problem in offering a course of this type in a professional program. However, what ultimately happens to the online searching component in library and information science curricula will result from a resolution of the over-all goals and orientation of the school, the needs of the marketplace, scheduling practicalities, the effects of well-designed continuing education programs, the interest and abilities of the available faculty, monetary considerations, and factors relating to further development of online searching technologies.

Footnotes

1. The authors wish to express their gratitude to OCLC, Inc., for its financial and moral support in the conduct of this study, especially to W. David Penniman, who has been enthusiastic in his encouragement since its inception. The full account of our findings is reported in Carol H. Fenichel and Stephen P. Harter, *Survey of Online Searching Instruction in Schools of Library and Information Science* (Columbus, Ohio:OCLC, Research Report #OCLC/DDRR-81/3, 1981). The present paper summarizes the major findings of the study and discusses implications for library and information science education.

2. M. Murphy, "Online Services in Some Academic, Public and Special Libraries: A State of the Art Report," occasional paper, Graduate School of Library and Information Science, University of Illinois, 1982.

3. In 1979 the User Group of Online Educators within the Special Interest Group on Education (SIG/ED) of the American Society for Information Science established a Curriculum Committee to develop ideas for improving education and training in online searching. Motivation for the present survey originated from this committee.

4. Stephen P. Harter, "Instruction Provided by Library Schools in Machine-

Readable Bibliographic Databases," in *Information Management in the 1980's: Proceedings of the ASIS Annual Meeting* (White Plains, N.Y.: Knowledge Industry Publications, 1977. In Microfiche, G10-G14, 1977).

5. Stephen P. Harter, "An Assessment of Instruction Provided by Library Schools in Online Searching," *Information Processing and Management* 15 (1979):71-75.

6. Thomas P. Slavens and Marc E. Ruby, "Teaching Library Science Students to do Bibliographic Searches of Automated Databases," *RQ* 18 (Fall 1978):39-41.

7. Charles P. Bourne and Jo Robinson, "Education and Training for Computer Based Reference Services: Review of Training Efforts to Date," *Journal of the American Society for Information Science* 31 (January 1980):25-35.

8. Sara D. Knapp and Jacquelyn Gavryck, "Computer Based Reference Service: A Course Taught by Practitioners," *Online* 2 (April 1978):65-76.

9. Harold Borko, "Teaching Online Retrieval Systems at the University of California, Los Angeles," *Information Processing and Management* 14 (1978):477-80.

10. Trudi Bellardo, Gail Kennedy and Gretchen Tremoulet, "Online Bibliographic System Instruction," *Journal of Education for Librarianship* 19 (Summer 1978):21-31.

11. Bert R. Boyce, "Instruction in Online Library Tools at the University of Missouri," *Journal of Education for Librarianship* 20 (Fall 1979):158-61.

12. Robert A. Berk and Rebecca W. Davidson, "MEDLINE Training within the Library School Curriculum: Quality Control and Future Trends," *Bulletin of the Medical Library Association* 66 (July 1978): 302-8.

13. Winifred Sewell, "Use of MEDLINE in a Medical Literature Course," *Journal of Education for Librarianship* 15 (Summer 1974):34-40.

14. Alan M. Rees, Lydia Holian, and Ann Schapp, "An Experiment in Teaching MEDLINE," *Bulletin of the Medical Library Association* 64 (April 1976):196-202.

15. Brian C. Vickery, "The Experimental Use of Online Services in Schools of Librarianship and Information Science," in *First International Online Information Meeting* (Oxford and New York: Learned Information, 1977), pp. 195-201.

16. Lucy A. Tedd and E. Michael Keen, "Methods of Teaching Online Bibliographic Searching: Experience at the College of Librarianship, Wales," *Information Processing and Management* 14 (1978):453-63.

17. Stella Keenan, *Final Report on Online Access to Bibliographic Databases for Teaching Purposes*, (n.p.: Department of Library and Information Science, Loughborough University of Technology, 1976).

18. Edmond Mignon, ed., *Position Paper Number 1: Proposed Standards for Education in Online Searching in the Professional Librarianship Curriculum* (n.p.: School of Librarianship, University of Washington, 1978).

19. The questionnaire, cover letter, case studies, and many other details can be found in Fenichel and Harter, *Survey of Online Searching Instruction in Schools of Library and Information Science*, (OCLC Research Report #OCLC/DDRR-81/3, 1981).

20. The full report of the study lists individual responses to this question (see reference 1).
21. E. Mignon, ed., *Position Paper Number 1: Proposed Standards for Education in Online Searching in Professional Librarianship Curriculum*, p. 7
22. Bourne and Robinson, "Teaching Online Retrieval Systems at the University of California, Los Angeles," p. 33.

Additional Readings—Staff Selection and Training

Atkinson, Hugh C. "Who Will Run and Use These Libraries? How?" *Library Journal* 109 (Oct. 15, 1984):1905-7.

Bourne, Charles P. and Robinson, J. "Education and Training for Computer-Based Reference Services: Review of Training Efforts to Date." *Journal of the American Society for Information Science* 31 (January 1980):29-35.

Caruso, Elaine. "Computer Aids to Learning Online Retrieval." In *Annual Review of Information Science and Technology* (Vol. 16), pp. 317-335. Edited by Martha E. Williams. White Plains, NY: Knowledge Industry Publications, 1981.

Dolan, Donna R. and Kremin, M.C. "The Quality Control of Search Analysts." *Online* 3 (April 1979):8-16.

Fenichel, Carol Hansen. "An Examination of the Relationship Between Searching Behavior and Searcher Background." *Online Review* 4 (December 1980): 341-347.

Howard, Helen. "Measures That Discriminate Among Online Searchers with Different Training and Experience." *Online Review* 6 (August 1982):315-327.

Jackson, William. "How to Train Experienced Users to Use Another System." *Online* 6 (May 1982):27-35.

Prentice, Ann. "Online Training: The Role of Schools of Library and Information Science." *Library Services and Use* 3 (August 1983):199-202.

Swanson, Rowena W. "An Assessment of Online Instruction Methodologies." *Online* 6 (January 1982):38-53.

Tedd, Lucy A. "Teaching Aids Developed and Used for Education and Training for Online Searching." *Online* 5 (June 1981): 205-216.

Tenopir, Carol. "An In-House Training Program for Online Searchers." *Online* 6 (May 1982):20-26.

Tenopir, Carol. "In-House Training and Staff Development." *Library Journal* 109 (May 1, 1984):870-871.

Van Camp, Ann. "Effective Search Analysts." *Online* 2 (April 1979):18-20.

In recent years, an increasing number of books and articles have been written for nonprofit organizations. Techniques and skills honed by successful companies have been adapted for organizations whose products are services. Hospitals, museums, and governments have been adept at distinguishing between those marketing approaches that are appropriate for their needs, those that must be substantially modified, and those that must be rejected as inappropriate. Libraries and information centers have been somewhat slower to adopt marketing approaches, and the literature relating marketing directly to online services is sparse indeed. Yet information managers are faced with shrinking budgets, changing user demands for services, and the increasing need to operate on a cost-recovery basis. All of these factors are clearly market-related and could undoubtedly benefit from techniques that have been developed to cope with just such problems.

Philip Kotler is perhaps the most noted proponent of marketing for nonprofit organizations. He defines marketing as follows:

> Marketing is the analysis, planning, implementation, and control of carefully formulated programs designed to bring about voluntary exchanges of values with target markets for the purpose of achieving organizational objectives. It relies heavily on designing the organization's offering in terms of the target markets' needs and desires, and on using effective pricing, communication, and distribution to inform, motivate, and service the markets.*

Viewed from this perspective, marketing is an integral component of the management function. It involves assessing user needs, developing appropriate means of meeting those needs, and ensuring that users are aware that these means are available. Transposed to the management of online services, it means that before a new service is undertaken, a user survey must be carried out and organizational objectives clarified. A service is then designed that is responsive to the expressed desires of the users. The costs of the service are determined, pricing policies formulated, and the new service promoted so that maximum levels of usage are obtained.

Each of the following articles treats marketing and promotion somewhat differently. Stanley J. Shapiro presents an overview of marketing and its relevance to the special librarian. He presents marketing as an attitude, an approach, and a set of tools, techniques, and concepts. The attitude he advocates is a willingness to allow user needs to determine organizational responses. Not all user needs will be similar, however, so the market must be segmented so that services can be more accurately targeted to relevant groups. A marketing plan is then devised which takes into account information-seeking behaviors, demographic changes, organizational constraints, and technological advances. A projection of increased usage over a specified period of time is made, and the variables of product, price, promotion, and place are studied to determine how they can be used to match the product with the market. At the manager's disposal are such tools as market research to identify user attitudes, likes, and needs; the findings of research on mass communication to increase the persuasiveness of the library's message; and that on forecasting to help predict the share of the target market that may be expected to become actual users. Shapiro advocates combined MBA-MLS training to provide information specialists with the in-depth education and training required to cope with the complex information environment.

Pauline Atherton and Roger Christian discuss marketing and promotion as they are related to online services. They, too, emphasize the importance of market research in identifying and locating potential user groups and stress the importance of user education in informing potential users of services available to them. And, they too advocate the tailoring of services to meet the needs of specific user groups. The main focus of their article, however, is a presentation of the advantages and disadvantages of using various promotional tactics to attract users. These range from persuading key personnel to use the service in the hope of creating a strong cadre of influential supporters to offering free searches as loss leaders. Fliers, publicity releases, brochures, price lists, posters, book marks, newsletters, reminders enclosed with payroll checks, and announcements are mentioned as possible means of promotion. The satisfied user who becomes the repeat user is recognized as one of the most effective sources for promoting the services. Effective promotion requires time, effort, and resources. It needs to be ongoing and coordinated and thus should be the responsibility of an individual who will prepare promotional copy, give demonstrations, and present the online service in its best light.

Alice Bahr is equally enthusiastic about the importance of promotional activities. She offers a set of guidelines that she feels should be observed by planners of promotional campaigns. They should ensure that the costs of promotion are included in the online budget. They should know what the system can do and be able to convey its capabilities clearly to others. They should involve those with the greatest knowledge about the system, the searchers, in promotional activities. They should provide for an increase in demand for traditional reference services generated as a result of promoting services. And, finally, planners should keep in mind resource limitations and not promote the online services beyond the capacity of the staff to handle searches. The remainder of her article is devoted to a discussion of promotional tactics. She discusses the relative merits of brochures, fliers, memoranda, letters, press releases, tours, meetings, audiovisual programs, free searches, demonstrations, and more personal approaches and suggests sources that may be approached to share ideas and materials. She illustrates her article with examples of some of the promotional aids she describes. Finally, she reminds the planner that promotion is a way of recognizing that the end user is the most important element of an online service.

the main aspects of marketing and promotion, managers responsible for these activities will want to explore each of these areas in greater depth and perhaps learn how specific types of libraries and information centers have carried out their campaigns and the results of their efforts. Additional Readings were selected with these purposes in mind.

Marketing and the Information Professional: Odd Couple or Meaningful Relationship?

Stanley J. Shapiro

While some doubt still exists as to the nature and importance of the relationship that will eventually evolve, marketing and the information professionals have recently "found" each other and, rather tentatively, embraced. What does marketing bring to this relationship?

The use of a marketing approach by a wide variety of not-for-profit organizations such as libraries, universities, churches, and health services, is a development of the last decade. We are just now beginning to learn what aspects of marketing can be used "as is" by the not-for-profit sector, what marketing techniques are appropriate but only after substantial modification, and what dimensions of commercial marketing have no real relevance to this sector.

PERSPECTIVES ON MARKETING

A surprisingly extensive literature already exists on "social marketing," the umbrella term often used to encompass the different types of not-for-profit marketing.[1] Some of this literature chronicles marketing triumphs or those marketing approaches which have failed in the not-for-profit sector. A number of other important lessons can be learned from a review of the relevant literature:

Lesson 1.—Many of those trained and employed in the so-called helping and learned professions harbor a deep-seated hostility toward marketing as a commercial activity. Such individuals turn livid when

---

Reprinted with permission of *Special Libraries* from Special Libraries 71 (November 1980): 469–474.

asked to accept the position that marketing has any real value to their area of special competence, be that area health, education, or librarianship.

Lesson 2.—The absence of objectives expressed in concrete, measurable terms and the lack of a "bottom line" profit or loss figure are other important barriers that prevent not-for-profit organizations from making the kind of far-reaching changes that a marketing approach usually requires and that corporations are prepared to make.

Lesson 3.—Churches, universities, hospitals, and libraries engage in labor-intensive activities that do not lend themselves to mass production or other cost-saving innovations as demand for their services increases. Marketing, therefore, has proven less useful to these not-for-profit institutions than it has to commercial organizations where increased sales generally facilitate mass production and a marked decline in per unit or per transaction labor costs.

Lesson 4.—Marketing talent for the not-for-profit sector is best "home grown." It is far easier for professionals from the government, health, education, and library science sectors to learn what they must about marketing than it is for marketers from the private sector to overcome the many barriers to their becoming effective in a new and strange environment.

Lesson 5.—Marketing is not an all-purpose cure for whatever ailment is troubling your library. However, marketing can make a meaningful contribution, since the kinds of services traditionally provided by libraries and the traditional ways of providing such services are viewed by marketers with a new, fresh, and different perspective.

It might be argued that intelligent and imaginative librarians have traditionally conducted programs that could be described as marketing activities. Library marketers, it could be maintained, are similar to the man Moliere wrote about who discovered at a relatively advanced age that he had been speaking prose all his life. But the librarian who leaves her desk to serve users rather than to silence them is not necessarily a marketing manager, and an eye-catching poster is no substitute for a marketing plan. If it were, Smokey the Bear would have extinguished the last carelessly lit forest fire decades ago.

Well then, what is marketing all about? What can it contribute to the world of special libraries and information science? One way to begin is to view marketing as essentially three things—as an attitude, as an approach, and as a set of tools, techniques, and concepts.

MARKETING AS AN ATTITUDE

A marketing attitude has a number of dimensions. Above all else, it starts with the recognition that one's organization must be responsive in helping its users solve their information gathering and processing needs.

What business do you think you are in? In a very real sense, are you not in the business of creating satisfied customers? Consequently, you should be prepared to take your marching orders from a market place consisting of those present and potential customers. The use of the word customer is a deliberate one: "patrons" are people we patronize; "customers" are people whose custom we seek.

What does it mean to be a responsive organization? The description Philip Kotler provides in his book, *Marketing for Nonprofit Organizations (2) says it all:*

- The highly responsive organization encourages its constituents to submit inquiries, complaints, suggestions, and opinions. Consistent with that objective, it utilizes suggestion boxes, comment cards, ombudsmen, and consumer committees.
- The highly responsive organization shows a keen interest in learning about the needs, perceptions, preferences, and relative satisfaction of its constituents. It relies on systematic information-collection procedures such as formal opinion surveys and consumer panels.
- The highly responsive organization systematically sifts all incoming information and takes positive steps, where called for, to adjust its products, services, organizational policies, and procedures.

Systematic information collection procedures, formal methods of encouraging inquiries, complaints and suggestions, and above all, a periodic adjustment of products and policies consistent with feedback obtained from the market place: if this is the kind of special library you are running, then you are half way toward being a marketing manager. If these phrases don't describe your library, then don't expect others to recognize your value or to defend your interests when budgets are being allocated, or when the need for staff services is being reassessed.

Finally, a marketing attitude requires that today's products and services be reassessed in terms of the user needs they are now satisfying. Nothing a special librarian does is an end in itself; it is but a means to an end. If consumer information needs can be better satisfied in some other fashion, no service has to be offered just because it has always been offered.

In summary, the three key dimensions of a marketing attitude are:

1) A willingness to take one's marching orders from the market.

2) A commitment to making the library a responsive organization.

3) A recognition that some products or services may have outlived their usefulness and should be substituted by new offerings.

MARKETING AS AN APPROACH

There are a great many prospective customers out there. A first step in marketing involves segmenting the potential market into smaller submarkets consisting of individuals who are essentially similar. Those segments can be similar in their needs, in their way of solving an information processing problem, or in many other significant ways. Grouping potential customers into fairly homogeneous segments enables you to do your marketing with a carefully targeted rifle rather than with a shotgun scattering pellets every which way.

Matching Services to Users

Next, think about the range of library products and services that are now being offered and match them to the needs of those groups you have identified and decided to cultivate. Matching products against target markets! A straightforward objective but what does it really mean? In the toothpaste market, this means identifying three distinct groups such as the "cavity conscious," the "shiny teeth set," and the "fresh breath fanatics." Once this has been done, one develops a different product—in this case a different brand of toothpaste—for each of these segments. Consumer surveys and small group interviews can be your starting points in developing new services to match the needs of the market group.

Developing a Plan

Assume, for purposes of illustration, that your library is serving three major market segments—R&D personnel, administrators, and commercial researchers—and is offering three services—acquisitions, reference, and bibliographical search. A marketing plan or program should be developed for each of these nine product-market segments, as well as for every new product that is developed. The plan can be as complex or as simple as you like; however, it must cover the following topics:

1) Relevant external factors providing a context for marketing. Such factors include organizational constraints, technological developments, and important demographic changes, such as a falling birthrate.

2) The information-processing problem that the particular market segment is trying to solve and the relative frequency with which its members rely on different sources of information, including the product or service you are offering, to find a solution to that problem.

3) A very specific statement, in quantitative and percentage terms, of how much you propose to increase usage during a twelve-month period.

Since increases in usage just don't happen, you must next spell out exactly what is going to be done to make that planned increase occur. Broadly speaking, a "larger share of the business" is obtained through making significant changes in one or more of the so-called "four P's of marketing"—product, price, promotion, and place. What changes, if any, are you making in the product offering? Is the price of that product, in terms of time, money or psychic energy, being reduced? Are you promoting the product through advertising (or personal selling) which stresses how users' needs will be satisfied or their problems solved? Is that product being promoted in a manner that makes your message stand out? (In other words, what are you doing to break "the boredom barrier" or to overcome "the ennui effect.") Finally, is your product or service going to be offered at a more appropriate time and place? Of course, your marketing plan will generate additional business only to the extent that users find these changes in the four P's more closely attuned to their needs.

MARKETING TOOLS, TECHNIQUES AND CONCEPTS

There are at least five areas of obvious relevance to special libraries:

1) A variety of marketing research techniques which can be employed to determine user attitudes, likes, and dislikes. The informal and inexpensive group interview has proven effective for librarians who are prepared to listen, to learn, and to adapt.

2) Literature on the new product innovation and diffusion process and the determinants of new product success or failure. This literature can prove helpful in determining the most effective manner in which to promote a new library service.

3) The concept of the product life cycle which suggests that each new library service goes through various stages in its development with each stage calling for different promotional approaches.

4) An extensive body of research findings on the theory and practice of mass communication. This literature can help increase the likelihood that the message about your library will be both perceived and persuasive.

5) A literature on forecasting and market potential which can help you predict the share of a target market that will actually use your library, the relative importance of "heavy users," and the amount of business you can expect to win away from competing suppliers of information.

In a nutshell, that's marketing: an appropriate attitude, an approach that matches products with market segment needs, and a set of tools, techniques, and concepts. The four P's—product, price, promotion, and place—are used as marketing variables in the plan developed for every important match of product with market. Of course, marketing is, in fact, a far more complex subject. If it weren't, marketing textbooks would not be 600 or 700 pages in length and even skilled corporate marketers would not so frequently launch products that fail in the market place. Nevertheless, you can learn all you need to know by taking a marketing course or two and then applying what you have learned in the market place served by your special library.

TRAINING LIBRARIANS TO BECOME
CORPORATE INFORMATION MANAGERS

Let us next turn to a somewhat different but related topic. Marketing is another one of the activities in which firms engage and about which business schools teach to become a concern of library administrators. That libraries are complex organizations and must be administered as such has long been recognized. The most recent volumes on library administration may say nothing about marketing. However, considerable attention is paid in such texts to budgeting and financial controls, to personnel and organizational behavior, and to certain "fundamental tasks" of management, such as planning, organizing, staffing, directing, and controlling.

But why must the flow of managerially-relevant material always be from other organizations to libraries rather than a two-way flow? Why have so few schools of library science developed joint MLS—MBA Programs? And finally, why isn't a librarian with an MBA recognized to be potentially much more than a better library administrator? He or she is also a logical candidate for corporate manager of information services. Who would be better qualified to direct the overall information gathering and information processing activities of the modern corporation? Information-oriented activities may account for as much as 5% of the total corporate budget. There could be a new professional job market out there for BLS or MLS graduates who also have degrees in Business Administration.

Librarians as managers of the overall corporate information function—is such a thought so outrageous? A joint MBA-MLS degree provides librarians with a knowledge of information science and computer capabilities, as well as with an awareness of marketing, personnel, production, and finance.

McGill University is going to experiment along these lines. The Graduate School of Library Science at McGill, though remaining a separate organizational entity, may soon be reporting to the Dean of the Faculty of Management. But whatever the reporting structure that eventually evolves, the Faculty of Management and the School of Library Science will soon be offering a joint MLS-MBA degree to a limited number of interested students. A special effort will be made to see if the resources of the Faculty of Management and the Schools of Computer

Science and Library Science can be harnessed within the joint degree-framework to train the same individuals as corporate information specialists and as library administrators. Hopefully, other institutions will begin experimenting along these lines over the next few years. SLA members are encouraged to monitor these efforts to see whether special librarians really can flourish as corporate information officers.

Footnotes

1. For the most useful review article in the area, see Christopher H. Lovelock and Charles B. Weinberg, "Public and Nonprofit Marketing Comes of Age," in *Review of Marketing*, ed. Gerald Zaltman and Thomas V. Bonoma (Chicago, American Marketing Association, 1978), pp. 413–52.
2. Philip Kotler, *Marketing for Nonprofit Organizations* (Englewood Cliffs, N.J.: Prentice-Hall, 1975), pp. 40–43.

Marketing and Promotion

Pauline Atherton and Roger W. Christian

With the possible exception of users' fees, no aspect of online bibliographic reference services is more alien to librarians than the need to actively promote and market these services. Nevertheless, experience invariably confirms that sustained and aggressive promotion is essential. Without it, the likelihood of attracting enough patronage to justify continuing the service approaches nil. Further, the service can only be of value if patrons take advantage of it; and, of course, they cannot take advantage of something they know nothing about.

The crux of the issue then, and the real objective of the promotional efforts that must be made is user education. Of course, educating library patrons with respect to the facilities and services available, is itself rather foreign to the traditions and practices of most libraries. Characteristically, libraries and librarians alike have been content to assume a passive, almost deferential, role with regard to library patrons, and to virtually ignore non-users, even though the result may be only limited and sporadic use of the libraries' resources.

This pattern is compounded by the predominantly formal atmosphere of the library itself, and by the cool and reserved posture of many librarians. The result creates in the minds of too many potential users an impression of the library as proprietary territory whose scope, dimensions, and promise are only dimly understood. However eager to serve and be helpful librarians may be (once a patron has taken the initiative and broken the ice) too many are content to rely on pamphlets and word of mouth among patrons to make the world aware of the full scope of services available.

NEED FOR PROMOTION OF ONLINE SERVICES

Particularly in the case of online reference services, however, which are comparatively new and a startling departure from traditional library offerings, potential users are not only understandably ignorant of the

Atherton, Pauline and Roger W. Christian, "Marketing and Promotion," in *Librarians and Online Services*. White Plains, NY: Knowledge Industry Publications, Inc., 1977, pp. 89–100. Reprinted with the permission of the publisher.

services, but in most cases have no reason to suspect that they might exist. Accordingly, the library must take the educational initiative. The effort can be restrained or flamboyant, narrowly focused or energetically broadcast, but it must be made. Moreover, it must be sustained more or less indefinitely.

The effort should begin with some basic market research and some strategic marketing decisions. The market research consists of specifically identifying and locating the potential user groups who can most benefit from the service and are most likely to be attracted to it. Without a fairly clear idea of who will be using the services, the library will be unable to relate its promotional literature and demonstrations to the perceived reference needs of potential users.

Fortunately, in any well thought out program the location, size, and general nature of the potential user population will have been identified during the exploratory stages leading up to the decision to institute online reference services. Thus, it remains only to isolate this clientele in more specific terms.

One marketing decision to be made early is whether to launch a broad-gauged publicity blitzkrieg at the outset, in hopes of attracting maximum attention and some vanguard users from each of the target populations, or whether to carefully restrict the initial promotion to a single user group with high potential. The advantage of the latter approach is that it is less costly, affords the library the opportunity to gain promotional experience from a limited effort before undertaking something more ambitious, and limits the incremental work load imposed on the library by the new online patrons.

The latter consideration is especially important for libraries that initiate online reference services without expanding the library staff. In addition, a controlled build-up of patronage permits the information services librarians to gain search experience and proficiency before they are required to cope with substantial demand for their services. Finally, a carefully focused appeal to a particular clientele permits a library with limited resources to initiate online searching with only one or a few databases. Subsequently, the library can expand both its offerings and the clientele it serves.

If this strategy is undertaken, of course, it is extremely important that the limited initial offerings be publicized only to those who can take advantage of them. Potential patrons who hear about the online reference services incidentally, and arrive at the library with search assignments that cannot be accommodated on the databases then available, are likely to feel disappointed and deprived—and to communicate their frustration to other potential users. Moreover, they may put the library under pressure to expand the scope of its online offerings more rapidly than is planned or advisable.

The alternative decision—to broadcast the availability of online reference services across a large variety of databases in the hope of quickly attracting a substantial cadre of early users—carries with it certain hazards of its own. One is that the effort might be too successful, inundating the service with demand levels that cannot be accommodated comfortably. Dallas Public Library triggered a related problem when it announced, with great public ballyhoo, that it had The New York Times Information Bank online. The public rushed in, convinced that NYTIB was some sort of electronic encyclopedia. Disillusioning them created a durable black eye for the library.

A second hazard is that unless adequate provision has been made in the start-up budget for the cost of promoting and demonstrating the new services, a library can find itself in a "Catch 22" situation: on the one hand, it is under the gun to attract the maximum number of new users, through demonstrations and publicity; on the other hand, it is unable to afford to sustain the effort necessary to do so.

A third hazard is that users who respond to the initial promotional efforts but cannot be promptly accommodated, owing to a logjam of demand, will be frustrated and disgruntled.[1] The risk of creating a core of disappointed potential users is very great, because word-of-mouth publicity is far and away the most powerful medium available. Too many dissatisfied customers can ultimately defeat even an expensive promotional campaign.

WHAT MARKET TO GO AFTER

Another strategic marketing decision that must be made early is that of market segmentation, that is, dividing the total, heterogeneous market for online reference services into homogenous segments with relatively common needs and interests. For example, a university library might partition its market along departmental lines (psychology, chemistry, biology, economics, etc.), or according to academic status (faculty, graduate students, undergraduates, offcampus users). Such differentiators can also be combined to produce, for instance, "life sciences faculty" as one market segment and "undergraduate physics students" as another.

A given market segment will be interested in access to certain databases while having no use for others. One market segment may require searches of a depth and chronological scope that would never be required by a member of a different one. To dramatize the point, consider the differing needs of a career medical researcher on the one hand, and, on the other, an undergraduate education major in the throes of preparing an overdue term paper.

The purpose of market segmentation, of course, is to permit the libraries' promotional efforts to be tailored exactly to the needs of each particular group being addressed. Another gross, but nonetheless functional, form of market segmentation is to divide the total community, or population, served by the library into two groups: those who do and those who do not take advantage of the traditional library facilities. Again, the marketing approach taken to the two groups would differ. The library will have established some rapport and credibility with the former group, so promotional efforts can build on this base with emphasis on the particular user benefits associated with the new online reference services.

The latter, and larger, group of potential users must be approached in a different way, with emphasis, perhaps, on the library itself as an intellectual resource to be called upon, and with online services being presented as only one of a number of other non-print holdings and services, including sound recording, films, and the like.

It may well be that many of the potential users within the non-patron category have been ignoring the library in the past because of dissatisfaction with the resources that they perceived of as being available. For these people, the speed, convenience, and personalized service available in connection with online reference services may provide what they found missing in the past.

With both groups, of course, the library must still demonstrate the ability of online services to meet specific needs of the patrons who try them.

MARKETING TACTICS

Once these strategic marketing decisions have been made—what services to offer initially, and for what groups—those concerned with promoting online reference services can address themselves to the tactical measures that might prove most effective. One useful ploy is to identify the few key personnel or "thought leaders" within a given user group, and to concentrate on persuading these individuals to try the online reference services. Commonly, such incentives as artificially low— or even no—fee searches are employed to make it easier for these bellwether accounts to agree to trial searches.[2]

Examples of such key personnel would include department heads, project leaders, prestigious scientists, and "information gatekeepers," members of the so-called invisible colleges that seem to exist in virtually all professional fields. These are the individuals to whom others in the field turn for information, and who play a central role in the sometimes elaborate but informal information and communications networks through which colleagues in an institution, or specialists within a particular field, exchange information—frequently by telephone.

The objective of inducing these leaders to utilize the new online reference services, of course, is both to create a record of successful searches for demanding individuals, resulting in at least their implied, if not actively expressed, endorsement of the service; and to make active users out of a cadre of individuals in a strong position to influence others.

Tactical alternatives range from offering free, or very low cost, sample searches to all comers, to pressing a vigorous publicity and educational campaign directed either at a target user group or at the client community at large. While some libraries have successfully used the telephone for this purpose, Betty Miller and David Mindel of Calspan Corp. caution that phone solicitors must be sure they are talking to key people. "Otherwise," they say, "you may spend a good hour fascinating a clerk, secretary etc." and never reach the decision makers.

Most library promotion relies instead, or at least primarily, on the various traditional print media available. Examples include:

- Flyers that are widely distributed to potential users, announcing the online search service and offering low cost trials;
- Publicity releases;
- Brochures describing the online services and the various databases available;
- Price lists;
- Posters and bulletin board announcements;
- Book marks and other favors and handouts;
- Formal advertisements, announcements, and articles in appropriate magazines, papers, and house organs;
- Printed collections of typical questions asked about the service, along with their answers;
- Newsletters;
- Direct mail pieces;
- Reminders to be enclosed with payroll checks, service invoices, and the like.

Most of these promotional materials can be generated at low cost on local copying or duplicating facilities; all that is required is the imagination to create them. One example is the fairly comprehensive handbook "Instructional Resources" distributed by the Center for Educational Development in the Walter Library at the University of Minnesota. An excerpt of this handbook, dealing specifically with computer based bibliographic search services, is shown on the following pages.

TABLE 1   Instructional Resources At The University of Minnesota

Excerpts from the Instructional Resources Handbook produced by the Center for Educational Development, 317 Walter Library, Minneapolis, MN 55455, James H. Werntz, Jr., Director (Third Edition).

*   *   *

LIBRARY SEARCH SERVICES

Beyond the regular reference services available in all library units, there is a specialized program which provides, on a fee basis, in-depth bibliographic searching:

INFORM, a service in Wilson Library (373-5938, Judy Wells) will provide information to any patron, on or off campus, to whatever depth is required. Examples of services available are compilations of bibliographies, extensive literature and information source surveys, publication of guides to the literature, compilation of statistics, preparation of reference guides or handbooks on particular industries or subjects, and current awareness programs.

Also available, on a fee basis, are a number of computer database search services. Currently available are the following:

In the Bio-Medical Library (373-7233, Gertrude Foreman):

MEDLINE or MEDLARS, a computer based service with direct telecommunications access to the Index Medicus bibliographic database, covers approximately 2,700 medical, nursing, dental, and life science journals indexed by the National Library of Medicine from 1966 to the present. In addition, there are other databases covering CANCER, EPILEPSY, CHEMLINE, and AV-LINE.

SDILINE, a current awareness service from the MEDLARS database, provides a monthly update of citations on a subject of choice. SDILINE covers the most recent indexing from the National Library of Medicine and is available one month before publication of the printed monthly Index Medicus.

TOXLINE is an extensive collection of computerized toxicology journal references, including toxicity studies, environmental studies, and drug reactions. The database contains: Chemical-Biological Activities, 1965 to date; Abstract of Health Effects of Environmental Pollutants, 1972 to date; International Pharmaceutical Abstracts, 1970 to date; Toxicity Bibliography, 1968 to date; and Health Aspects of Pesticides Abstract Bulletin, 1966 to date.

In the Business Reference Service (373-4109, Judy Wells):

Table 1 (continued)

INFORM, produced by Abstracted Business Information, Inc., provides comprehensive coverage of the literature in such areas as banking, finance, insurance, management, economics, statistics, business law, and marketing. Major feature articles are abstracted from more than 280 journals. Coverage is from 1971 to the present.

In the Chemistry Library (373-2375, Beverly Lee):

CHEMCON (Chemical Abstracts Condensates), produced by Chemical Abstracts Service, is a weekly current awareness service that provides information from the corresponding issues of Chemical Abstracts. Coverage is from 1970 to the present.

In the Education Library (373-3841, Celia Ellingson):

ERIC (Educational Resources Information Center), the educational data base maintained by the U.S. National Institute of Education, covers reports and periodical literature in education-related fields from 1966 to the present. Microfiche copies of the reports in the file are available at a nominal cost.

AIM/ARM (Abstracts of Instructional Material/Abstracts of Research Materials) lists 7000 abstracts of instructional and research materials, indexed by the Center for Vocational and Technical Education, Ohio State University.

EXCEPTIONAL CHILDREN ABSTRACTS includes 12,000 abstracts of material of particular interest in this field.

PSYCH ABSTRACTS lists more than 125,000 abstracts to journal articles in psychology dating from 1967 indexed by the American Psychological Association.

In the Engineering Library (373-2957, Crystal Clift):

COMPENDEX, produced by *Engineering Index*, is a database corresponding to the monthly issues of *Engineering Index Monthly*. AI examines over 3,500 journals and other types of publications, including proceedings of conferences, to provide world-wide coverage in all disciplines of engineering from 1970 to the present.

GEOREF (Geological Reference File), produced by the American Geological Institute, provides world-wide coverage of the geosciences including economic geology, geochemistry, marine geology, solid-earth geophysics, and engineering-environmental geology. The database includes 3,000 journals and coverage of conferences, symposia, and major monographs from 1967 to the present.

*   *   *

Another effective and very low cost tactic using print media is to make use of the various catalogs, guidebooks, handbooks, and the like that are prepared and distributed by the institution in any case. Each such publication can carry a descriptive paragraph or two announcing, and sketching in the general outlines of, the online reference services available through the library. Academic libraries find this promotional ploy especially useful in such documents as thesis-preparation booklets and the handbooks or guidebooks made available to help grant applicants. In this fashion, potential users become aware of the online services at a time when they are especially interested in learning about the resources available to them; and, in time to incorporate their cost into the proposed budget for the contemplated research project. A valuable promotional element can also be found in the efforts of some libraries to integrate online and conventional bibliographic search tools. For instance, the University of Kentucky tags appropriate printed indexes with a prominent question: "Do you know that this index can be searched online?" Similarly the State University of New York at Albany lists in its online services brochure the call numbers of printed counterparts of each available database.

Another very popular promotional gambit is the conduct of demonstration searches before groups of influential and interested potential users of the service. Acknowledging the convincing impact of such sample searches, the principal retrieval service vendors cooperate by making a limited number of such searches available at very low cost. Dartmouth typically offers one or two demonstrations in the Fall, and starting this year, graduate engineering students will be required to perform a literature search as part of their thesis or dissertation preparation. Many will very likely opt to have the search conducted online (the maximum charge is $15.00 per search). Particularly effective is the tactic of conducting an online search in an area of immediate interest to one of the witnesses of the demonstration. In fact, these are so intriguing and convincing that it's a good idea to fix some arbitrary limits —such as 10 citations printed online, or perhaps five input descriptors— in order to avoid inadvertent abuse of the demonstration privilege. The University of California at Berkeley, for one, suggests that 10 citations printed online is ample for a demonstration.

Other helpful promotional techniques include making announcements and presentations at important meetings such as graduate student orientations; brief seminars and speeches to appropriate groups; and direct, one-to-one contact with department chairmen, department librarians, and other important potential users of the online reference services.

A growing number of libraries, including that of Calspan Corp. (formerly Cornell Aeronautical Laboratory)—one of the few company libraries that offer online services to outsiders—have gone a step further, by commissioning or preparing audio-visual presentations that dramatize their marketing efforts. Kris Brooks of Oregon State University uses slides and a script for her one-hour presentations, each of which is tailored to suit the prospects she is addressing. She finds this much more productive than giving free demonstrations, and it's a great deal less expensive and more versatile. It would seem appropriate for the principal database and retrieval service vendors to prepare introductory audio-visual packages describing their services in general terms, but as of this writing none has seen fit to do so. This is probably because the bulk of their customers to date have been special and research libraries, which, with a "captive" and relatively stable clientele, are characteristically not faced with as intense and pervasive an educational task as are academic libraries.

This is not at all to say that special libraries can entirely avoid the need to promote online services, however. Several years ago Lawrence, Weil and Graham described their initial internal marketing effort as follows: "When we were ready, the first step in our full-fledged campaign was a series of demonstrations for research division managers. Each demonstration was introduced with a brief definition of online, interactive searching, a mention of available (and soon to be available) information bases, and an estimate of average costs. Then a single online search was made on an appropriate subject (pretested as being relevant and with 'good' answers). After that, we encouraged 'live' questions—which often produced useful results on the spot.

"The other two steps in our publicity effort were the publication of a feature article in the company newspaper and a word-of-mouth campaign both by the information staff and enthusiastic researchers. Whether people came to try the Library's new 'toy' or to get some of those good (and fast) search results, they usually went away pleased—and they told others. More than for almost any of our information programs, word-of-mouth publicity has been a major factor in the success of this program."

IMPORTANCE OF WORD-OF-MOUTH

This express recognition of the overriding importance of word-of-mouth publicity to the successful implementation and maintenance of online bibliographic reference services underlines one final, but extremely important, promotional consideration: the experiences and impressions that the users of online reference services have, and exchange with one another, can by themselves make or break the entire undertaking virtually regardless of any other factor in the equation. As Donald Hawkins of Bell Labs noted in an interview, "Word-of-mouth promotion is the best there is."

If the services performed are perceived as being successful and helpful, they will be talked up and demand for the continued service will grow. If the users are disappointed with the results achieved, or feel that the results are not cost effective, they will not only stop using the service, but will talk it down among their associates, and the service in time is doomed.

Accordingly, it is of the first importance that the searchers be well trained and that the searches themselves produce useful results, the value of which clearly exceeds their cost. Every member of the online searching staff who comes in direct contact with users and potential users must accept, as among his or her important responsibilities, the need to promote the use and benefits of these services.

Clearly, this orientation and responsibility are particularly important in the case of the information services librarians who function as the intermediaries between the patrons of the service and the system itself. They must be personable, enthusiastic, assertively helpful, and communicative, as well as merely competent. They must, in short, be market-oriented, and the market is the user they are serving.

RESPONSIBILITY FOR MARKETING AND PROMOTION

Beyond the general responsibility on the part of searchers to promote the service they are offering, it is probably advisable in most libraries to have someone specifically responsible for marketing and promotion. Since most search staffs are small, this task will often fall to the unit supervisor—as in Oregon State University or the Calspan Corp. Other libraries may have large enough staffs to be able to name someone as a promotion specialist. This is the person who will give talks or demonstrations, write promotional copy, and be able to field inquiries from potential users. Many, if not most, corporate libraries find that while initial promotion is important, the longer term problem is one of coping with spontaneous and sustained demand, without formal promotion. Academic and public libraries, however, experience a much heavier "turnover" of individual clients, so sustained promotion is imperative.

Having said all this, it would be naive to pretend that such activities will come easily, especially in a public or academic library setting. Vigorous marketing of a service for which the library is charging money smacks of commercialism, and many librarians will instinctively shy away from such endeavors. The head of the library, or the head of the reference department, must come to grips with this problem at the outset when online services are initiated. Because of the widespread feeling on the part of libraries engaged in online services that such services will not succeed without promotion, the library faces a difficult dilemma. It can offer a new service that can greatly improve the library's overall service to users—at the cost of mounting a commercial sort of promotional campaign. Or it can maintain its traditional posture of avoiding marketing and promotion—and by so doing prolong the length of time it takes for online services to "catch on" well enough to justify continuing them.

Next to the need to charge users, the promotional aspects of online services are the hardest for many libraries to swallow. Some would probably do well to recognize that, with present staff or present attitudes, they cannot effectively offer and promote such services themselves, and should simply refer patrons to other institutions. Others will recognize the obstacles, but decide that they should go ahead and work on changing the attitudes of their own professional staff members. In either case, administrators responsible for the decision must be clear in their own minds about what it entails, and able to spell out its ramifications for all concerned.

Footnotes

1. Soon after offering online services in 1973, SUNY at Albany had a backlog of 150 search requests.
2. The University of California at Berkeley has offered free trial searches to key faculty members, including demonstrating the system in their classes.
3. Barbara Lawrence, Ben H. Weil, Margaret H. Graham, "Making Online Search Available in an Industrial Environment," *Journal of the American Society for Information Science* 25 (November/December 1974):364.

Promotion of Online Services

Alice H. Bahr

The reluctance of some librarians to actively promote online services reflects a healthy concern that staff might be inundated with more work than it can handle, but it also reflects an unwillingness to accept the fact that such services redefine the nature of reference work. In 1977 Pauline Atherton reported that "no aspect of online bibliographic reference services is more alien to librarians than the need to actively promote and market these services."[1] Her conclusion is supported by the dearth of material on the subject. Comprehensive studies—such as those by Atherton,[2] Watson[3] and Wax[4]—mention promotion; these works and an article by Pensyl, Benenfeld and Marcus[5] describe general techniques for promoting online services. Most of the literature, however, emphasizes searching techniques far more than promotional activities.

A SPECIAL SERVICE

Effective promotion of online services begins with a clear perception of the product, an equally clear picture of the user and a sense of the best ways of yoking one to the other. Rather than a traditional reference service, online retrieval is a special one. While the goal of both is identical—helping patrons locate needed materials—the pattern of service that each establishes is vastly different.

To begin with, library users do not usually need to make appointments for traditional reference assistance. They merely approach the desk and ask a question. With online services, however, appointments are often standard. The service pattern at Drexel University Library is one exception. There, if a staff member is free, searches are done after brief consultations. Much more typical are the practices of the University of Pennsylvania Library at Philadelphia, for example, which schedules appointments for patrons—sometimes a week after the initial request— and of the State University of New York at Albany, where a section

Bahr, Alice H. "Promotion of Online Services" in *The Library and Information Manager's Guide to Online Services*. Edited by Ryan E. Hoover. White Plains, NY: Knowledge Industry Publications, Inc., 1980, pp. 161-179. Reprinted with the permission of the publisher.

secretary gives patrons a search request form to fill out and bring to a scheduled search session.[6]

The search request form further alters the nature of reference services. The majority of reference questions are general: Where can I find information on a Fitzgerald novel? What information is available on marketing theory? How much money does the U.S. government spend on welfare? Certainly, any of those questions could become online queries; nevertheless, they can be readily answered without recourse to the computer. Further, the patron does not have to do much preliminary research before formulating them.

Completing a search request form mandates both careful query formulation and prior research. The form that Princeton University uses requires a narrative description of the search topic, definitions of phrases with special meanings, research applications and names of two or three publishers, organizations and journals in the field. The Free Library of Philadelphia requests, when possible, a few citations relevant to the search topic.

In a traditional reference interview, the librarian directs the patron to potentially useful sources, briefly explains their use and sometimes locates a few relevant citations. The patron conducts the actual search, and the librarian is an intermediary. In online searching, the librarian is still an intermediary, but one who now conducts the actual search. The patron plays a number of roles. At Drexel University, for instance, he goes through thesauri and indexes to locate search terms and he may or may not be present during the actual search. At the State University of New York at Albany, patrons attend interviews, search formulations and online sessions. In contrast, during one phase of the University of California at San Diego's initiation of online services, users did not even meet the searchers.[7]

Another difference between traditional and online reference services—one of great consequence to library and patron alike—is cost. Most libraries charge a flat or hourly rate to collect either part or all of online service costs. In corporate libraries, the full costs are usually charged to the departments requesting the services. A 1975 Denver Research Institute investigation of 73 academic libraries with separate departmental or science libraries concluded that "the highest percentage [of them] charged the user for actual online costs, transmission costs and offline print charges, while the library paid the searcher's salary and the library overhead, including the lease or purchase of hardware."[8] Recouping all costs is ordinarily reserved for offcampus patrons.

Because online service constitutes a departure from the ordinary, most potential users are not only "understandably ignorant of the services, but in most cases have no reason to suspect that they might exist."[9] Telling patrons about them can be simple or complex, a matter of a few signs or of more elaborate methods such as radio and television interviews. Regardless of the tactics, planners of a promotional campaign should observe the following guidelines:

- Include promotion in the initial online budget.
- Know the system's capabilities before promoting.
- Involve searchers in promotion.
- Prepare for an upsurge in traditional reference services as a result of promoting online services.
- Keep staff limitations in mind.

An effective promotional program can increase the use of online services in the library.[10]

INCLUDING PROMOTION IN THE BUDGET

Few libraries include promotion in the online services budget. The notion is that the small outlays for fliers, posters, letters, articles and even demonstrations and instructional tours can be absorbed by the usual provisions for staff and supplies. Larger libraries often have separate public relations departments, whose budgets could encompass online promotion. For libraries without public relations departments, however, the decision not to schedule funds for promotion is unwise. Either it limits the extent and quality of the promotion that might be possible or it indicates that no thought was given to promotion.

Promotional costs are part of the real expense of providing online service. Putting brochures, price lists and fliers together is much easier when additional funds make overtime payments possible. Budgeting for promotion permits commercial production of inexpensive items like posters. It can also help to broaden a promotional campaign. By including connect time and telecommunications charges in promotional budgets, the library can offer more demonstrations, and perhaps, like the University of Missouri, offer them department by department. The university wrote $500 into the budget for promotion when it initiated online services late in 1977. Not only did the monies make department-by-department demonstrations possible, but they also covered costs of a commercially produced poster and other promotional activities.

KNOWING THE SYSTEM

A sure knowledge of system capability is essential. Only after the searcher knows precisely what the system can do and how much time it takes to do it can the library relay a clear message to users. Clarity is essential, as Atherton's description of the Dallas Public Library's energetic promotion of the New York Times Information Bank (NYTIB) proves: the public "rushed in" believing the computer a godsend and was subsequently disappointed to find it was a mere machine.[11] Free Library of Philadelphia Reference and Information Librarian Vilma M. Lieberman reports a comparable experience. After the NYTIB was promoted in the general media, she received a rash of inappropriate questions, such as "Can you help me find my grandmother?"

Even when the audience is narrower there can be problems. After one University of California at Berkeley library user received the results of an online search, he expressed his dissatisfaction as follows: "But there's nothing here that wasn't in the printed index!" Clearly, as Lipow points out, online service must be marketed so that "the users understand what they are getting . . ."[12]

There is little likelihood that promotional materials and activities will reflect system capability if staff members aren't given sufficient time to exploit the system. To allow staff to become comfortable with equipment, most libraries use a system for a few weeks or months before publicizing it. At the Free Library of Philadelphia, Computer Based Information Center Staff experimented with the New York Times Information Bank for three months before announcing the service. At Lehigh University a month lapsed between operation of SDC® Search Service and its promotion so that staff could become familiar with the system's operation, capability and cost. In October and November of 1977, the University of Mississippi began to use Bibliographic Retrieval Service (BRS) and DIALOG®, respectively, on an experimental basis; there was no promotion until use became established.

INVOLVING THE SEARCHERS

The period of experimental use is the best time for planning promotional tactics. They should be a natural outgrowth of the system's capabilities and should, in part, be directed by those with the greatest knowledge of the system or systems. Several experts agree that searchers should contribute to promotion, but perhaps Lipow sums it up best: "The job of publicizing should be done by reference librarians who know their clientele, who know the capability of the individual data bases, and who are in the best position to integrate computer searching with the manual."[13] At Drexel University and the University of Mississippi the job of publicizing online services is done by subject specialists who are also online searchers.

PREPARING FOR INCREASES IN TRADITIONAL SERVICES

Most libraries find that promotion of online services increases patrons' awareness not only of online, but also of other library services. The sophomore requesting a computer search for a term paper on marketing theory, for example, may be unaware of the *Index of Economic Journals, Business Periodicals Index* and interlibrary loan. After being directed to them, he's likely to use them again and to tell his friends about them. Many computer requests turn into manual searches. Staff members at the University of Mississippi make a distinction between questions suitable for manual or for online searching and often turn online queries back to the general reference department.

Promoting online services can afford the library a clearer picture of its clientele. It's generally assumed, for instance, that undergraduates are not as likely to benefit from online searching as graduates, faculty and administration. Nonetheless, undergraduates can make effective use of online searches. During a seven-month trial online searching period at the University of California at San Diego, 14% of all searches (160 out of 1166) were for undergraduates.[14] Many of the requests were highly sophisticated, such as the self-concept of Mexican Americans and the effects of toxoplasmosis on the fetus. It is likely that a lack of funds, rather than a lack of interest or applicability, prevents greater use of online services by undergraduates.

REMEMBERING STAFF LIMITATIONS

It is wise not to promote beyond the capacity to serve. Although experts advocate sustained promotional efforts, practical experience sometimes dictates the opposite. Atherton argues that "sustained promotion is imperative,"[15] and Wax suggests that, for academic libraries, "continuing effort will be required to accomodate new services, added data bases and additional potential users."[16] Nonetheless, after city-wide layoffs cut back staff in 1978, the Free Library of Philadelphia purposely avoided extensive publicizing of the NYTIB. Since inception of service in 1975, promotional efforts had already resulted in a steady community of users and further efforts might have overburdened the library's remaining staff. Similarly, when the Bethlehem Steel Corp.'s main library lost three staff members, a decision was made to promote online services selectively.

MARKETING STRATEGIES

One good way to assure that the library staff does not get more work than it can handle is to plan a promotional program using marketing concepts like market segmentation and product design. As the term implies, market segmentation means dividing users into groups on the basis of mutual interests or needs. One logical division is by department, either academic or corporate (e.g., biology, English, public affairs); another is by status (e.g., undergraduate, faculty, vice presidents, technicians). After so dividing, it is customary to decide which group to approach first, second and third, or to decide to approach all of the groups at once. Since the latter approach will hardly help to control staff workloads, it is wise to gauge each segment of the market in turn and then assess its impact on the workload.

Product design is a natural extension of market segmentation. The best way to reach an individual segment of a market is to speak its language, to devise materials and institute programs that focus on its precise needs. In essence, that's all product design means. The Free Library of Philadelphia began with a broad-based campaign to introduce the NYTIB to the public. A few years later—after discovering that the largest group of users (almost 50%) were businessmen and corporate libraries—the promotional focus was changed. Instead of placing articles in general circulation newspapers, the library prepared more specialized articles for the *Center City Office Weekly, Focus* and *Delaware Valley Business Fortnight*.

Advocating the application of marketing techniques to promotion of online library services, Ferguson suggests a number of creative promotional "search packages," or brochures, for special segments of the college or university market. "What about a Dissertation Search Package designed for the weary doctoral candidate struggling to get a proposal accepted by a faculty committee?" he asks.[17] Ferguson also suggests a package for college or university members holding research grants. The package would offer regular searches during the span of the grant. The usefulness of Ferguson's suggestions are, in part, the result of his familiarity with university operations and organization. Effective product design rests on knowing the audience.

PROMOTIONAL TACTICS

Regardless of marketing strategy, libraries have an array of promotional tactics from which to choose. Among the most popular are signs, posters, letters, announcements at meetings, brochures, company newsletters, memos to company department heads, newspaper and magazine articles, price lists, bookmarks, radio and television interviews, instructional tours, audiovisual packages, free searches and demonstrations. Wax suggests that signs be posted at service sites and comments further that "some success has also been achieved through the use of signs or posters at other locations in the library and other institution buildings."[18]

Brochures

Whether for mailing, distribution or display, brochures can document the history and range of the library's online services as well as the terms of its use—including cost, time factors, and staff and user responsibilities. Because they provide basic service statements, such brochures are as useful to staff as to patrons. To accommodate changes such as data-base availability and fee structures, brochures should be printed inexpensively. Most run between seven and 14 pages. Figures 1 and 2

FIGURE 1   Promotional Brochure from Gallaudet College Library

FIGURE 2   Promotional Brochure from the Free Library of Philadelphia

CITY OF PHILADELPHIA

THE FREE LIBRARY OF PHILADELPHIA
LOGAN SQUARE
PHILADELPHIA, PA. 19103

COMPUTERIZED LITERATURE SEARCHES

MERCANTILE LIBRARY
GOVERNMENT PUBLICATIONS DEPARTMENT
SOCIAL SCIENCE AND HISTORY DEPARTMENT
EDUCATION, PHILOSOPHY AND RELIGION DEPARTMENT
BUSINESS, SCIENCE AND INDUSTRY DEPARTMENT

represent the covers of brochures used at Gallaudet College (Washington, DC) and the Free Library of Philadelphia. Figure 3 shows a subject-specific brochure from the University of California, Los Angeles.

FIGURE 3   Subject-Specific Promotional Brochure from the University of California (4 pages)

Customized Bibliographies in the Current Literature of Education

Computer Searches
of
RESOURCES IN EDUCATION *and*
CURRENT INDEX TO JOURNALS IN EDUCATION

Here's an easy way for you to stay up to date on the literature in your field of education. Computerized Information Services (CIS) of the University of California can offer you an annual subscription to monthly searches of *Resources in Education (RIE)* and *Current Index to Journals in Education (CIJE)* prepared by the National Institute of Education, and published by the Educational Resources Information Center (ERIC). CIS automatically searches for you the computer tape versions of each issue of *RIE* and *CIJE*, which precede the printed issues by several weeks due to the time required to print, bind, and distribute the hard copy.

Resources in Education contains references to research and report literature in education, including all Office of Education-funded projects. *Current Index to Journals in Education* indexes over 600 key periodicals in education. Both indexes also include references to the literature of languages, library science, counseling and personnel service, etc.

How
CURRENT AWARENESS SEARCHING
works

This service which provides periodic searches of pertinent educational information to researchers with an on-going information need is called "current awareness" searching. Information analysts who are librarians and specialists in various subject disciplines are available throughout the CIS system to work with you in formulating search questions into a satisfactory "profile" of subject terms, codes, author names, journals, etc. Each time CIS receives a new issue of *RIE* or *CIJE*, the user's profile is matched against that issue to provide a tailor-made list of bibliographic citations which alert the user to current information in his/her area of interest.

Each computer search produces a bibliography, printed on 8½ x 11-inch paper, of retrieved citations or "alerts." Each alert contains standard bibliographic information, such as journal title, author, indexing terms, etc. In addition, *RIE* includes abstracts. For UC users the call number and UC library location of the journal in which the cited article appears will also be given.

University of California

CIS

Computerized Information Services

FIGURE 3,   Continued

A Sample CIS Search on Criterion - Referenced Tests

USER'S *SEARCH REQUEST* STATEMENT:

"We are primarily interested in references to particular tests that are criterion-referenced, in order that we may obtain copies of those tests from their publishers. Secondarily, we are interested in acquiring a comprehensive and up-to-date bibliography of contributions to the theory of criterion-referenced measurement or discussions of issues in the construction and evaluation of such tests."

SAMPLE SEARCH RESULTS FROM ONE ISSUE OF *CIJE*

```
002930 CURRENT INDEX TO JOURNALS IN EDUCATION - MAY 1976              PAGE 1

CRT SEARCH
        EJ128901.  THE CASE FOR CRITERION-REFERENCED MEASUREMENT.
   (ARTICLE)
        KRUMME, URSEL S.
        NURSING OUTLOOK, 23(12), 764-70.  DEC 75.
        CLEARINGHOUSE NO: CE504143.
        DESCRIPTORS:  *EVALUATION METHODS; *COMPARATIVE ANALYSIS;
   *CRITERION REFERENCED TESTS; *NORM REFERENCED TESTS; *NURSING:
   MEASUREMENT TECHNIQUES; PERFORMANCE BASED EDUCATION; EVALUATION
   CRITERIA.
        THE CASE FOR CRITERION-REFERENCED MEASUREMENT IS DISCUSSED
   VERSUS THE CONVENTIONAL NORM-REFERENCED GRADING METHODS.  (AUTHOR/BP).
   LOC:  CLU-M  (W1.NU739).
   SELECTED BY CRT_REFERENCE.  WEIGHT:  5
   ------------------------------------------------------------------
        EJ128937.  CRITERION-REFERENCED MEASUREMENT.  (ARTICLE)
        DAY, GERALD F.
        MAN/SOCIETY/TECHNOLOGY, 35(?), 84-6.  DEC 75.
        CLEARINGHOUSE NO: CE504199.
        DESCRIPTORS:  *CRITERION REFERENCED TESTS; *PERFORMANCE BASED
   EDUCATION; *TEST CONSTRUCTION; *MEASUREMENT TECHNIQUES; *NORM
   REFERENCED TESTS; TESTING PROBLEMS.
   SELECTED BY CRT_REFERENCE.  WEIGHT:  5
   ------------------------------------------------------------------
        EJ129727.  THE CONTENT ANALYSIS OF SUBJECT-MATTER:  THE COMPUTER
   AS AN AID IN THE DESIGN OF CRITERION-REFERENCED TESTS.  (ARTICLE)
        GAGNE, ROBERT M.; MERRILL, M. DAVID.
        INSTRUCTIONAL SCIENCE, 5(1), 1-28.  JAN 76.
        CLEARINGHOUSE NO: IR502625.
        DESCRIPTORS:  *COURSE CONTENT; *CONTENT ANALYSIS; *COMPUTER
   SCIENCE; *INSTRUCTIONAL DESIGN; *CRITERION REFERENCED TESTS.
   LOC:  CLU-E/P.
   SELECTED BY CRT_REFERENCE.  WEIGHT:  5
   ------------------------------------------------------------------
        EJ129839.  CRITERION-REFERENCED, DOMAIN-REFERENCED AND NORM-
   REFERENCED MEASUREMENT:  A PARALLAX VIEW.  (ARTICLE)
        DENHAM, CAROLYN H.
        EDUCATIONAL TECHNOLOGY, 15(12), 9-12.  DEC 75.
        CLEARINGHOUSE NO: IR 502737.
        DESCRIPTORS:  *MEASUREMENT TECHNIQUES; *CRITERION REFERENCED
   TESTS; *NORM REFERENCED TESTS; *EVALUATION CRITERIA; *TESTS.
   LOC:  CLU-E/P  (LB1043.E24); EMS  (LB1028.A1E24).
   SELECTED BY CRT_REFERENCE.  WEIGHT:  5
   ------------------------------------------------------------------
   CITATIONS SEARCHED:  1685   14 APR 1976
   ALERTS FOUND:        4
   ALERTS PRINTED:      4
```

FIGURE 3,   Continued

How do I get my own annual subscription?

IT'S EASY! YOU JUST

1) Fill out the enclosed *SEARCH REQUEST* form, excepting questions nos. 8 – 12.

2) Mail the form to CIS in the pre-addressed envelope provided. A CIS information specialist will then call you to confirm your interest and to further negotiate with you the specifics of your personalized profile.

3) Allow a maximum of 5 weeks for input into the system and processing before you begin to receive your RIE and/or CIJE bibliographies. You should thereafter receive your output every month for one year.

CONTINUAL PROFILE MONITORING AND REFINEMENT

The CIS information specialist or "profile analyst" will automatically monitor your first few searches and will contact you to revise the search as necessary. You are always welcome to inform your profile analyst of changes you would like to have made to the profile either to refine it or to reflect your changing research interests.

Diagram of an ERIC citation alert

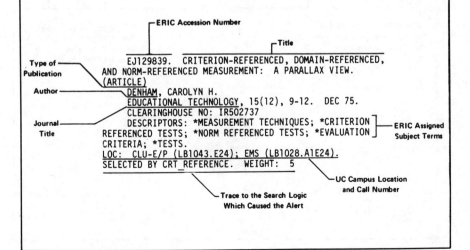

FIGURE 3, Continued

UNIVERSITY OF CALIFORNIA

RETROSPECTIVE SEARCHING

Users who have a short-term information need (such as a research paper), or who are just beginning in a field, have an immediate need for complete, state-of-the-art type information. Retrospective searching offers the user a one time search of back issues of both *Resources in Education* and *Current Index to Journals in Education* dating to September 1966. Most of the libraries of the University of California offer, or are in the process of developing, a retrospective search service covering the ERIC publications as well as a variety of other machine-readable indexes to the literature of many disciplines. Charges, user eligibility requirements, and staff time available for retrospective searching vary from campus to campus; however, information on the scope and costs of these services can be sought from CIS or from the Reference Department of one of the following UC libraries:

<table>
<tr><td>

Education Library
UC Berkeley
Berkeley, California 94720
415 – 642-4208

</td><td>

Shields Library
UC Davis
Davis, California 95616
916 – 752-1126

</td></tr>
<tr><td>

General Library
UC Irvine
Irvine, California 92664
714 – 833-6836

</td><td>

Education/Psychology Library
UC Los Angeles
Los Angeles, California 90024
213 – 825-4081

</td></tr>
<tr><td>

Bio-Agricultural Library
UC Riverside
Riverside, California 92502
714 – 787-3701

</td><td>

Library Systems Department
2519 Library
UC Santa Barbara
Santa Barbara, California 93106
805 – 961-3475

</td></tr>
<tr><td>

Library, Room 257 – S
UC San Francisco
San Francisco, California 94143
415 – 666-2334

</td><td>

Central University Library
UC San Diego
La Jolla, California 92037
714 – 452-3336

</td></tr>
</table>

FOR FURTHER INFORMATION
on any aspect of computerized
literature searching at the
University of California:

Computerized Information Services
32 Powell Library Building
University of California
Los Angeles, California 90024
213 – 825-1573

October 1976

Fliers, Memoranda and Letters

Fliers are abbreviated brochures. Their key word is selectivity. Cost, time operation and personnel are still listed, but data base information is restricted. Usually, only representative files are described. (See Figure 4.) Like bookmarks and price lists, fliers are good follow ups to but not substitutes for more detailed and comprehensive announcements.

Memoranda and letters announcing services are other good supportive efforts. According to Wax, however, "The general experience with institution-wide mailings . . . has been that the response has not appeared to justify the effort and cost."[19] It's best, therefore, to send brochures, letters, fliers and memoranda to select members of an audience and to use articles to reach a broader group.

Press Releases

In a broad-based campaign, it is preferable to send press releases to general, widely circulated publications or to popular radio and television programs. College papers and catalogs and general circulation newspapers are good bets. For example, *On the Green*, the weekly newspaper of Gallaudet College, includes an ongoing column of library activities with information about online services. When the Free Library of Philadelphia began publicizing the NYTIB, the public relations department sent press releases to major media. As a result, the service was publicized in the Philadelphia *Inquirer, Bulletin* and *Daily News*, as well as on television stations WPVI and KYW.

Tours, Meetings and Classes

One of the easiest ways to promote online service is through already existing communications channels and established library services. Most libraries include a brief discussion of online services in introductory tours as well as in advanced research classes. At the Air Products Library (Trexlertown, Pa.), for example, all new employees are given an online demonstration in addition to a general library tour. Other good places to mention computer searching are faculty and consortia meetings and

FIGURE 4 Promotional Flier from the University of Mississippi Library

COMPUTER ASSISTED RESEARCH

Research requires time -- time to locate information, time to read, time to digest and synthesize. Computerized literature searches, performed in the University of Mississippi Libraries, save you time and make your research easier. They help in the vital first stages of research by locating citations to books, articles, dissertations, and reports that may be relevant to your work. And computerized literature searches can locate these citations far more rapidly than you can locate them manually.

Many of the same indexes you would search manually -- Chemical Abstracts, ERIC, Index Medicus, Engineering Index, and others, are available in machine-readable form and can be accessed by trained literature searchers in the University Libraries.

You explain your topic to the searcher, listing key terms, concepts, and ideas important to your topic. The searcher translates this into a search program, and enters this program into the computer. The computer searches the data base and prints a list of articles which have been indexed under the key terms. In many data bases you even receive abstracts of the articles with your printout.

The real advantage of the computerized search over the manual search is flexibility. The searcher can combine and manipulate ideas on-line in order to create a unique search and bibliography for you. For example, two key-word terms in the ERIC data base are "Athletic Programs" and "Handicapped Students." If you were interested in studying athletic programs for handicapped students and had to do a manual search, you would have to look through all of the articles indexed under "Athletic Programs" to see which ones had to do with handicapped students and all of the articles indexed under "Handicapped Students" to see which dealt with athletic programs. This is very time-consuming to do manually, but the computer does it instantly through Boolean logic. The searcher programs the computer to retrieve only those articles that are about <u>both</u> "Athletic Programs" <u>and</u> ""Handicapped Students."

You can imagine how much time you could save on a thesis or dissertation by letting the computer help you compile your bibliography. But there must be a catch. The catch is that you must pay for computer time, and you pay a small charge for your printout. The computer time costs from 50¢ to $2 a minute, and the printout charge depends on the number of citations retrieved. Your overall charge depends on the subject and complexity of the search. We do many searches for less than $5 and many more for between $5 and $10.

If a search can help you -- and if you are starting a thesis or dissertation it probably can -- call Laura Harper, Coordinator of Information Retrieval, at 232-7091 or Nancy Fuller in the Pharmacy Library at 232-7381 or stop by the reference desk in the Main Library.

library instruction classes. At the University of California at San Diego, a class in library use included a discussion of online searching; a follow-up study showed that 18% of all undergraduates using computer information retrieval heard of the service through the class.[20]

Audiovisual Programs

Although Atherton lamented that no online vendors produce audiovisual promotion packages for subscribers, some libraries have produced their own—often for incorporation into bibliographic instructional sessions. A program called "The Saga of Susie Student or Graffiti on a Data Base" is an interesting case in point. This short slide and audio cassette program grew out of a Drexel University graduate library science audiovisual course. The presentation depicts young Susie in the midst of a dilemma—writing a term paper on graffiti. Susie goes through the usual processes. She checks the card catalog and consults several indexes and abstracts. Weary of consulting indexes year by year and finding little material, she learns of a better way: the computer search. The searcher introduces her to the basics of Boolean algebra, the need for thesauri to locate search terms and the differences between online and print indexes. In the last frame, Susie cheerfully pays a small fee and receives the citations that she needs to complete her paper.

Free Searches

At a few institutions, free searches entice users. Sometimes the free-search period is limited to a few months: when the University of California at San Diego first offered online services, there was no charge for the first seven months.[21] At other institutions the services have remained free. There is no charge for online bibliographic retrieval at either Gallaudet College or the University of Missouri.

The experience of four public libraries in Northern California indicates the difficulty of switching from a cost-free to a payment basis. During the first year, service was free. During the second, patrons paid half the costs. During the third year, full costs were collected. Interestingly, the change from the second to the third year had little effect, but going from a free to a partial payment resulted in "a large drop in demand. . . . "[22] In one month searches decreased 75%. The annual decrease was approximately 60%.

Demonstrations

According to Wax, "The most effective technique for user education and service promotion has been a live demonstration of the capabilities of online searching."[23] In and of themselves, however, demonstrations are not panaceas. They must be done carefully. First, the library should provide an overview of searching in general and specific mention of how the service is handled in the particular institution. Second, the relationship between an index and an online file should be clarified. Third, requests should be solicited ahead of time.

An effective approach is a visual presentation about online services used in the library or classroom at the University of Vermont, as reported by Crane and Pilachowski.[24] A live demonstration used in conjunction with the overhead projector in this presentation would really bring the message home.

Demonstrations are not always the most successful promotional tactic in nonacademic libraries. For instance, there was only minimal response to in-house demonstrations of the NYTIB at the Free Library of Philadelphia.

The Personal Approach

There is one tactic that receives universal endorsement: word of mouth. Wax is just one of many to suggest that, "in the final analysis, the most successful promotional strategy is the provision of effective convenient service to a core of users who will in turn favorably publicize the services by word of mouth."[25] Wax's comment is verified, in part, by the findings of a 1974 study conducted by four Northern California public libraries under the auspices of the National Science Foundation. Originally an investigation of the public library's suitability as a link between online data bases and the public, the study showed that "librarians and friends were responsible for almost one-half of the searches. . . . Participants were surprised that mailings and newspaper publicity had such low effectiveness."[26] A personal approach makes all the difference.

Any promotional tactic may be made personal. Signs and posters, for example, should not announce simply that the library now offers online bibliographic retrieval. Only a few library patrons will understand what that means. A series of simple statements or questions is preferable: "Will Twenty Articles Help?" "Congress is Now Next Door." "Looking for a Research Proposal?"

Even bookmarks and fliers can be made more personal. Instead of leaving bookmarks on the circulation desk, they can be handed to patrons as they check out their books. A few remarks about the service should be made at that time. Fliers and brochures can also be handed out during chats with library users or after reference librarians have answered reference questions. Why not place fliers, search request forms and price lists near the card catalog, by indexes or on bulletin boards?

A more direct way to make a promotional effort personal is to telephone key persons in the user community—those most likely to benefit from and to support online service. A particularly good time to call is after letters or memoranda have been mailed to all members of a particular group like faculty, the R&D department, administrators, the marketing department, friends of the library, etc. After meetings, key people can be invited personally to attend demonstrations. It's much more likely that faculty members who have never responded to requests for bibliographic instruction will change their minds if they are personally contacted and if the librarian offers to search a topic relevant to the professor's interests or classes.

A personal approach takes more time, but it reinforces one initial marketing goal—matching promotional tactic with users' needs (product design). Schmidt[27] reports that a well-rounded public relations program can be as effective in promoting online services as in promoting any other library service.

SOURCES OF PROMOTIONAL AIDS

Posters, brochures and press releases all take time. There are, however, a few shortcuts. For one, most libraries are more than willing to share their promotional ideas and materials. The latter are rarely copyrighted. Second, online service vendors supply some promotional materials and services.

Ordinarily, libraries will be flattered if their promotional materials are good enough to be borrowed. Schools such as the University of California at Berkeley and Lehigh University have designed posters and demonstration invitation forms. (See Figure 5 for a copy of the form used at Lehigh University.) Other institutions with good promotional materials are the University of Kentucky, Oregon State University, Massachusetts Institute of Technology and Stanford University. the Machine-Assisted Retrieval Service (MARS) of the American Library Association's Reference and Adult Services Division collects samples of publicity, forms and training for online services that are available through interlibrary loan.

Vendors will also supply some materials and services. Lockheed (DIALOG), SDC Search Service and BRS supply posters or other promotional pieces, such as ads. (See Figure 6.) DIALOG and SDC also provide demonstration data bases at reduced connect rates. Not as complete as full files, they cost substantially less to access. DIALOG's practice files—ONTAP CA SEARCH, ONTAP CHEMNAME and ONTAP ERIC—cost $15 per connect hour. To access SDC's practice

FIGURE 5   Invitation to Online Services Demonstration from Lehigh University Library

---

THE LEHIGH UNIVERSITY LIBRARY

ANNOUNCEMENT

Date: 18 September 1978

To: All Faculty

From: Library

Subject: Computer-generated Bibliographic Searches

The Reference Departments of Linderman and Mart are anxious to show off their new skill: computerized bibliographic searching. We'd like all of you to come to Mart for a show-and-tell during the weeks of October 2 to 6 and October 9 to 13.

We're soliciting sample questions from faculty to use for our free demonstrations. Please contact the relevant reference department for details.

Since attempting to schedule more than three people for any one time can be an all-consuming problem, we'd like you to indicate what time(s) would be convenient for you. If we have enough people with similar interests for the same time period, we will schedule our sample searches to reflect their interests. Otherwise, we will be varying searches and data bases throughout the two-week period.

Please return this form to S. Siegler, Mart Library:

Name: Extension:

Department:

Sample question (please be highly specific):

Time(s) convenient for demonstration:

---

files—DEMNTIS, CAS-ED, CDEX-ED and PESTDEM—users must acquire a temporary demonstration password. DIALOG supplies stick-on labels to place on the shelves holding abstract and index journals announcing that those sources may be searched online. DIALOG will also supply up to 49 copies of its *Database Catalog, Subject Guide to DIALOG Databases* and the general brochure DIALOG *Service* at no charge. All are suitable handouts for department heads and administrators. SDC Search Service will also supply copies of its brochure and catalog on request.

Find your information fast

Computerized information is here for you

Could you use help in . . .

Searching through the flood of journal articles, conference papers, government reports . . . to find just the information you need to prepare well-documented reports . . . papers . . . memos . . . dissertations . . . monographs . . .

Planning a scientific or technical research project, new business venture, marketing campaign, academic or professional paper . . .

Comparing statistics on economic data . . . industrial production . . . wages . . . prices . . . distribution trends . . . demographics . . .

The library now has access to **DIALOG**,* the largest, most powerful computerized information

system. With over 75 databases — covering science, technology, business and economics, social sciences, arts and the humanities — we can scan over 20 million articles, papers, and reports to **find what you want in minutes.** You can ask questions of a scope and complexity never before possible! The result: your assurance that, whatever your undertaking, you'll start with the most thoroughly researched information available.

To order a computer search, visit the library or call us at this number:

---

*Trademark Reg. U.S. Pat. & Trademark Office.
The DIALOG service is provided by Lockheed Missiles & Space Company, Palo Alto, CA.

SUMMARY

Promotion begins with a clear perception of how online services differ from traditional reference assistance. It exploits those differences to members of the user community most in need of online services, taking care to tailor the promotional product to the exact requirements of the audience.

While it is typical to appoint one staff member to oversee and direct promotional activities, it is mandatory that all of the searchers have some involvement in the promotional process and that reference librarians, who know the library's clientele best, conduct promotional activities.

With the exception of Wax's guidelines for academic libraries, there are no standards for publicizing online services. In the Association of Research Libraries' *Online Bibliographic Search Services*, Wax suggests that the minimum effort should be an inexpensive flier or brochure, which should be available at the service site as well as at the reference and circulation desks. It should include a general description of the service, a brief mention of the disciplines covered in the databases, charges, procedures for use and a telephone number and name of a staff member who may be contacted for additional information.

When choosing among the array of means to tell the library community about computer searching, one thought should remain uppermost: any tactic becomes twice as successful when it is personal. Make sure the audience realizes that it is more important than the service being offered, that the service exists for people.

Lastly, since, as Ferguson remarks, marketing is "an organized way of offering online services that includes user interests, databases, communication methods, imaginative design of services and products and feedback that improves what you are doing," it is wise to save time by borrowing materials from other libraries and by using vendor-supplied materials.[28]

An integral part of all planning for online service—one that should appear in the budget—promotion is a dedication to and a recognition of the importance of the end user of information. Resisting it is a resistance to the commitment to serve.

Footnotes

1. Pauline Atherton and Roger W. Christian, *Librarians and Online Services* (White Plains, NY.: Knowledge Industry Publications, 1977), p. 89.
2. Ibid.
3. Anne G. Lipow, "User Education and Publicity for Online Services," in P. G. Watson, *Online Bibliographic Services: Where We Are, Where We're Going* (Chicago: American Library Association, 1977), pp. 67–77.

4. David M. Wax, *A Handbook for the Introduction of Online Bibliographic Search Services into Academic Libraries*, Occasional Papers, no. 4 (Washington, D.C.: Association of Research Libraries, Office of University Library Management Studies, 1976).

5. Mary B. Pensyl, Alan R. Benenfeld, and Richard R. Marcus, "The Techniques Used to Promote Fee-for-Service Online Search Facility in a University Community," in *Proceedings of the 38th ASIS Annual Meeting* (Boston: American Society for Information Science, 1975), pp. 153–155.

6. Sara D. Knapp, "The Reference Interview in the Computer Based Setting," *RQ* 17 (Summer 1978):320.

7. William E. Maina, "Undergraduate Use of Online Bibliographic Retrieval Services: Experiences at the University of California, San Diego," *Online* 1 (April 1977):48.

8. Doris B. Marshall, "A Survey of the Users of Online Computer Based Scientific Search Services by Academic Libraries," *Journal of Chemical Information and the Computer Sciences* 15 (November 1975):248.

9. Atherton and Christian, *Librarians and Online Services*, p. 90.

10. Donald T. Hawkins, "Growth and Publicity of Online Information Retrieval in a Library Network," in *Proceedings of the 40th ASIS Annual Meeting* (Chicago: American Society for Information Science, 1977), p. 48.

11. Atherton and Christian, *Librarians and Online Services*, p. 91.

12. Lipow, "User Education and Publicity," p. 68.

13. Ibid., p. 70.

14. Maina, "Undergraduate Use of Online Bibliographic Retrieval Services," p. 45.

15. Atherton and Christian, *Librarians and Online Services*, p. 100.

16. Wax, *A Handbook,* 24.

17. Douglas Ferguson, "Marketing Online Services in the University," *Online* 1 (July 1977):17.

18. Wax, *A Handbook*, p. 26.

19. Ibid., p. 25.

20. Maina, "Undergraduate Use of Online Bibliographic Retrieval Services," p. 46.

21. Ibid., p. 45.

22. Roger K. Summit and Oscar Firschein, "Public Library Use of Online Bibliographic Retrieval Services," *Online* 1 (October 1977):59.

23. Wax, *A Handbook*, p. 26.

24. Nancy B. Crane and David M. Pilachowski, "Introducing Online Bibliographic Service to its Users: the Online Presentation," *Online* 2 (October 1978):20–29.

25. Wax, *A Handbook*, p. 27.

26. Summit and Firschein, "Public Library Use," p. 61.

27. Janet Schmidt, "Online for an Online Public Relations Program," *Online* 2 (October 1978):47–50.

28. Ferguson, "Marketing Online Services," p. 15.

Additional Readings --
Promotion and Marketing

Bauer, Charles K. "Managing Management." *Special Libraries* 71 (April 1980):204–16.

Crane, Nancy B. "Introducing Online Bibliographic Service to Its Users: The Online Presentation." *Online* 2 (October 1978):20–29.

Elias, Art. "Marketing for Online Bibliographic Services." *Online Review* 3 (March 1979):107–117.

Ferguson, Douglas. "Marketing Online Services in the University." *Online* 1 (July 1977):15–23.

Norman, O. Gene. "Marketing Libraries and Information Services: An Annotated Guide to the Literature." *Reference Service Review* 10 (Spring 1982):69-80.

Radway, Gerry and Steward, Connie. "Promoting Online Literature Searching." In *Library Management in Review*, pp. 67–71. Edited by Alice Bruemmer. New York: Special Libraries Association, 1981.

Schmidt, Janet. "How to Promote Online Services to the People Who Count the Most . . . Management . . . End Users." *Online* 1 (January 1977):32–38.

Smith, Patricia K. "Marketing Online Services, Part 1." *Online* 4 (Jan. 1980):60–62.

Smith, Patricia K. "Marketing Online Services, Part 2." *Online* 4 (April 1980):68–69.

Wolinsky, Carol Baker. "Marketing Secondary Information Services: How and to Whom." *Bulletin of the American Society for Information Science* 9 (April 1983):8–13.

Wood, Douglas. "Improving Your Image: How to Promote a Library or Information Service." Aslib *Proceedings* 36 (October 1984):401–408.

Accurately estimating the costs of providing online reference services and determining how these costs will be met is an important managerial function. Unfortunately, however, there are no uniform methods for determining costs and no standardized pricing structures that libraries and information centers favor. Rather, individual circumstances such as the vendor used, the databases accessed, the skill and experience of the searcher, the complexity of the search request, and other local demands combine to produce a cost configuration that is unique to the organization. As likely as not, the philosophical position of the host organization regarding services will play an important part in determining what proportion of the costs, if any, are to be recovered from the user.

The most common method of determining the cost of an online search is to include charges for computer connect time, communications, and offline prints. In fact, however, these represent only a portion of the actual costs incurred by the service provider. Other more indirect costs that must be considered are those for the leasing, renting, or depreciation of the terminal; overhead costs related to electrical, telephone, and janitorial services; secretarial or clerical help; promotional materials; forms for search requests, invoices, and recordkeeping; postage; office supplies including terminal paper; system and database manuals; subscription fees; photocopies of original documents; professional development and training costs; demonstrations; internal use of the service by staff; costs of failed, experimental, and practice searches; and the time of the professional searcher.

Whether or not the service manager decides to recover the costs from the user, an accurate assessment must be made of costs in order to budget for the expenditures of the service. The actual cost of an individual search is derived by determining the costs of each of the items mentioned and dividing the total by the estimated volume of searches expected over a year. Needless to say, the cost per search calculated in this way is quite high and most online services do not pass the full operational costs to the user.

User fees may be structured in a variety of ways. Probably the simplest and most frequently used approach passes on to the user the direct costs of the search—those pertaining to computer connect time, communications, and printing. In addition to these costs, services may charge a fee related to some portion of the ongoing operational costs. This indirect charge may be a flat fee pro-rated over the total volume of searches. The cost of searcher time may also be added to the total price of the search, either as a flat rate per search or calculated by time spent per search. Another pricing method involves charging a flat rate per search. This basic flat rate may increase according to the category of the users, whether they are internal or external to the organization, or, in the case of university libraries, whether they are undergraduate or graduate students or faculty. Yet another approach involves what amounts to a subscription service, whereby user departments of an organization cover the costs of the estimated volume of searches submitted by their staff over a given period of time.

Financial considerations involved in the provision of online services do not end with the determination of costs and the development of pricing structures. Equally important are the business procedures regarding billing, payment, and the handling of delinquent accounts. Finally, it must be remembered that technological advances will almost certainly affect the costs of providing online reference services. Increased printing speeds, downloading capabilities, and a highly competitive information industry can all decrease search costs, and the policies adopted by the service must remain flexible.

The articles that follow approach the financial considerations involved in the management of online reference service from quite different perspectives. Jean E. Koch reviews in considerable detail the costs involved in adding online searching to a library's services. She discusses costs related to a specific search (production costs), costs not related to a specific search (support costs), and overhead. She then compares online with manual costs, citing the advantages and disadvantages of each type of searching and suggests issues that must be resolved before changes are imposed. She concludes by examining probable changes in online searching and the benefits as well as additional costs these will bring to users.

The still problematic issue of fees for online searches is the topic of the article by James Rice, Jr. He summarizes the arguments for and against the imposition of user fees and presents alternatives for managers to consider. The arguments in favor of fees are essentially pragmatic. Those against claim that supporting online searches from existing library budgets means an unfair reduction in other services or resources; that online searching is merely an automation of the reference function and therefore should be supported in the same way as other computerized services; that user fees in publicly supported libraries constitute a form of double taxation; that charging is discriminatory and a violation of intellectual freedom. Rice urges managers to consider the effects of user fees and documents innovative approaches to the fees issue. He concludes by suggesting that as online searching becomes a fully integrated reference function it will become increasingly difficult to justify charging users and new financial and organizational options will have to become available.

Mary Jo Lynch presents the findings of a study carried out to determine how online services were financed in publicly supported libraries. Of the 985 responding libraries, 709 or 72 percent charged some type of fee. Most charged only for the direct costs of an individual search and absorbed all other costs. Over half the libraries had differential fee structures for primary and non-primary library clientele, but fee structures were so varied that they could not be analyzed in detail. The fee schedules are, however, included as a supplement to the complete published report.

Before deciding upon a new fee structure or revising an old one, the managers of online reference services will wish to be thoroughly familiar with the philosophical and practical options at their disposal. The Additional Readings are provided to help them in their deliberations.

A Review of the Costs and Cost-Effectiveness of Online Bibliographic Searching

Jean E. Koch

ONLINE COSTS

Online search service costs fall into three broad areas: support costs, all costs not tied directly to a specific search; production costs, all costs tied directly to production of a specific search; and overhead.[1]

Support Costs

One of the recurring support costs is the online terminal. Interactive terminals fall into two broad groups: a teleprinter and a display terminal. A teleprinter prints key-entered and/or computer processed data onto paper. A display terminal consists of a cathode-ray-tube (CRT) or other screen on which key-entered and/or computer processed data are presented. A paper printout will probably be preferred to review search strategies. For this reason and also to allow citations to be printed online, at least one teleprinter should be purchased. Many display terminals can be obtained with an auxiliary printer but the cost may be higher than a teleprinter. An important factor in the choice of a terminal is the communication speed. This is expressed in "bps" (the number of bits which can be transmitted or received in a given time period, usually one second) or "cps" (the number of characters transmitted or received per second) or "baud rate" (the number of signal elements transmitted each second). The number of characters which a terminal can type or display in one second is roughly one-tenth the baud rate; i.e., a 300-baud terminal is capable of 30 cps. A faster terminal will reduce the time and associated charges for that portion of an online search which consists of computer response. The older and less expensive printers which are limited to 110 bps (or 10 cps) will not support some communication facilities. The 300 bps terminal is commonly used. A 1,200 bps terminal can cost as much as 50 percent more than a 300 bps terminal but the increase may be justified if large numbers of citations must be printed online.

The print produced from a teleprinter is one of two types and the quality of print will vary between them. The less expensive type is formed by a "dot matrix" device. Characters are formed from a pattern of discrete dots which are printed onto paper. Teleprinters which produce typewriter-like output are slower and more expensive. Depending on the teleprinter equipment there will be the expense of paper, ribbons or thermal paper.

A decision must be made to purchase or lease a terminal. Purchasing requires a high initial capital investment. Leasing may be a better decision, since it minimizes the initial cash outlay and also offers better protection against equipment nonperformance and obsolescence. The monthly payment for a leased terminal will often include a charge for equipment maintenance. A good vendor will provide regular preventive maintenance. If a terminal is purchased, then an annual maintenance contract should also be purchased. To provide interface between the library's terminal and the telephone network it may be necessary to acquire a modem, if one is not already included as part of the terminal. Most libraries use the variant form of modem called an acoustic coupler which converts the terminal's electrical signal to audible tones suitable for telephone transmission. In addition to the purchase costs of this equipment, the library may have an initial equipment delivery charge.

Other start-up costs are related to site preparation. Electrical work may be required to provide a three-prong outlet which is needed by most terminals and acoustic couplers. Also, a telephone must be installed near the acoustic coupler. If simultaneous voice and data communications are required then separate phones and lines should be acquired. Typical phone installation charges will include a service charge, a wiring charge, if needed, and an equipment handling charge. If a modem is used the telephone company may require the installation of an additional interface called a Data Access Arrangement.

The basic furniture requirements for a search service are: a table or stand for the terminal and chairs for the searcher and patron. A surface for writing would be helpful, as well as shelf space for search aids. If microform search term lists are used, then a microform reader will be needed.

To aid the searcher the purchase of operator's manuals for all systems used will be necessary. Thesauri, subject classification lists, and other materials to aid in search formulation will be helpful acquisitions. Some of these aids are available online; however, it is probably cheaper to purchase printed copies, especially for the most used databases. To keep informed of changes in the field, the searcher will need to read vendors' newsletters, and commercial online journals and newsletters.

Other recurring costs directly related to online searching are: promotional materials and online charges of search service demonstrations; ledgers and forms for record keeping; miscellaneous supplies, such as postage, envelopes, and rubber stamps; reruns of searches due to searcher error or printouts lost in the mail; uncollectible debts (which may be avoided by advance payment or a sizeable advance deposit); and computer downtime.

Production Costs

Production costs are costs which can be directly traced to production of a specific search. These fall into four categories: communication charges, database charges, offline printing, and personnel time. Communication charges will be included in the library's monthly telephone bill. If long distance calls are placed they will be computed on the basis of elapsed time and distance. Direct dialing should be used only when the library is near the search service. To help reduce communication costs there is an alternative to conventional direct distance dialing. "Telenet," a service of General Telephone and Electronics, "Tymnet," a service of Tymshare, Inc., and recently, "UNINET," a service of United Telecommunications, Inc. provide computer-controlled networks consisting of leased telephone lines which link geographically dispersed time-sharing computer services with access nodes in major cities. (Note: BRS began offering UNINET service on a trial basis to users in selected areas in November, 1981.) Libraries in smaller cities and towns without a local node must access these telecommunications networks through a WATS number. Even with this additional charge it is probably cheaper than the direct distance dialing rate. Additional communication costs are calls to database vendors and suppliers for those without toll-free numbers, phone calls to search requesters, and telephone service charges.

The second category of costs which is search specific is the database charge. Lockheed/DIALOG and SDC/ORBIT charge on the basis of connect time alone. In 1979 the mean price per connect hour was $61.85 in DIALOG and $69.79 in ORBIT.[2] Government subsidized databases are the least expensive, while those produced by the private sector are the most expensive. When BRS entered the market it offered an annual subscription plan which has forced Lockheed and SDC to rethink their charging plans. They have begun to offer volume-based database usage discounts. For some databases there is also an hourly royalty fee charged.

Perhaps more meaningful than the cost differences of the various pay plans is the actual performance of a given database. This is illustrated in a study by James Bement.[3] The same search is performed on BRS, DIALOG and ORBIT and very different results are obtained. The reasons for this are that one database may update at a different time and each vendor processes the file differently. When they are loaded through their respective systems it results in three difference databases. When making cost comparisons it is probably more reliable to calculate the cost per relevant citation than to merely figure the total cost of the search.

The third production cost is offline printing. Because the cost of connect time is expensive, most retrieved citations should be printed offline, unless the number is very few or unless a high speed (1200 baud) printer makes it economical. Both DIALOG and ORBIT charge per record printed, while BRS charges by the page. Similar to online usage, certain databases are also subject to a royalty charge for offline printing.

The fourth charge is for personnel time. This time is both search specific and ongoing. Presently an average salary of an experienced searcher in an academic library is reported to be $16,200. The highest average salary for an experienced searcher in a corporate library, $21,000.[4] In computing the cost of a particular search it is necessary to include in addition to the search analyst's salary, fringe benefits paid, such as vacation, holiday and sick leave pay, workman's compensation, health insurance, life insurance and other paid benefits. It is estimated that these fringe benefits can be 15–25 percent of the direct payroll.[5] In totaling the personnel time spent on a search one should include requester interview time, formulation time, online time and printout edit time. Personnel time is also a recurring cost. A professional spends time teaching potential users about the search service and participates in continuing education sessions to update search techniques. New searchers must also be trained as a result of turnover. In addition to professional time, clerical support staff are utilized for record keeping, billing and receptionist activities.

The use of a professional librarian who acts as an intermediary between the client and a search service is somewhat controversial. Some people feel the end users would be the most effective persons to do the search. Others feel intermediaries are better equipped to search because they can keep abreast of the changes and developments in database structure and search system software. In a study of 159 clients surveyed by the NASA Industrial Application Center to examine user-identified dollar costs and benefits of an online computerized literature search, it was found that the interactive search technique was the most cost-effective. The client was either present during the computer search or in close communication, so that he/she was fully involved in the search process.

Without this communication, a searcher cannot determine what the client already knows, what he doesn't know, and what he doesn't need. With the client present, the searcher can redefine the search around these parameters. Searches were also conducted for clients who had made written or verbal requests but were not present during the actual search. Comparing this type of search technique to the interactive approach, it was found to take almost two times the number of searches to equal the benefits from the interactive searches.[6]

In the future a minicomputer or intelligent terminals may replace the need for an intermediary. Already there are systems designed for the mass market, such as the Source or Dow Jones News/Retrieval, which require less instruction than the large bibliographic systems. Some even use natural language and prompt the searcher with multiple choice questions.

Overhead Costs

Overhead costs related to online search services probably do not differ significantly from the overhead costs of manual systems. Included are costs of planning and administering the service and the facilities costs, i.e., the expense of providing heat, light and power.

Numerous studies have been conducted which try to justify the costs of online searching. The methodology used is as varied as are the results. In an early study published in 1975, Elman[7] computed the average cost of 48 manual literature searches at the Lockheed-California Company Library to be $250. The salary of a searcher was figured at $10 per hour and clerical help at $6 per hour. An average of 22 hours of professional time and a total of 4.2 hours of clerical time per search were needed. Reproduction costs were estimated at $5 per search. In comparison the average cost of 66 computer literature searches on DIALOG was $47.00. This total is found by multiplying the average time for a search (here, 45 minutes) by the cost per minute and adding to this the average offline printout cost. Included in the sum of all costs per minute of operation are the connect charges, the searcher's basic salary, the telephone charge and the cost of the equipment. The author concludes that DIALOG is efficient and cost effective to search online. No qualitative comparison of the two types of searches is made. This study is typical of many early studies because it fails to include the costs not tied directly to a specific search which were included under support costs and overhead in the previous section.

A later study conducted in 1978 by Dennis Elchesen[8] uses equivalent retrospective searches which are done both manually and online. Equivalent searcher skill levels were used for both search modes. Separate task times were measured for question analysis, searching, photocopying, shelving and output distribution. Component costs were calculated for labor, information, reproduction, equipment, physical space and telecommunications. Results show that approximately five online searches may be conducted in the two hours required to perform a single manual search. In this study an online search cost approximately $26.00 and a manual search about $30.00. The study shows a greater sophistication in that it included in the measure of cost-effectiveness the average number of citations retrieved per search, the average number of relevant citations retrieved per search, the recall ratio, a precision ratio and the cost per relevant citation. The author even suggests that for certain query/information-source combinations, manual searching may offer some advantage in precision and turn-around time, for example, when the topic is either extremely broad or extremely specific.

Another study, also published in 1978, compared 20 searches completed online and manually. The costs of both modes were determined and their effectiveness examined in terms of relevant references retrieved. The average computer-search cost was less than the average manual cost, while both modes were equally effective. The most significant variables in determining the relationship between manual and computer-search costs were user salary and the time required for a manual search. The costing models for each of the search modes illustrate an increasing awareness of detail in determining costs. The newer cost studies take into account for computer searching the costs of overhead, staff salary allocated on a per search basis, cost of the database(s), telecommunications and offline prints, and costs of the user in salary and transportation to come to the information center. For manual searches these studies take into account the cost of the bibliography per search (annual cost of purchasing, maintaining and storing divided by the number of uses per year, which is estimated), and the cost of user time: hourly salary multiplied by the time required for the manual search.[9]

In justifying the costs of online searching it is necessary to look closer at manual search costs. If the end product of the search is a list of bibliographic citations, then the cost of a typewriter and typewriter maintenance must be calculated. Other costs include a telephone (installation and rental) for receiving requests and giving replies, shelving for bound indexes and abstracts, floor space for these volumes, a desk, chair(s), subscription costs, technical processing and search aids. Even though many indexes are not available in machine readable form and are unaffected by online searching, there is a cost reduction potential for those with online equivalents. This is especially true for highly specialized printed indexes with limited audiences. The online equivalent may prove less expensive to search.

Many libraries will continue to have printed indexes, even when access is available to an online equivalent. Factors which affect this decision are the cost and acceptance of online searches, the hours of availability of the online system, and the usage of the manual index.

Some database producers offer printed index subscribers the incentive of lower connect time charges. In order to protect the printed indexes, a few database producers have limited online access to their printed subscribers. Other producers have made only a subset of bibliographic information available online. If a trend starts in cancelling printed subscriptions, then the possibility exists for higher online charges, so that producers can try to recover lost profits.

In comparing manual and online searching most studies emphasize the more efficient use of professional time. While online bibliographic searching is usually less labor intensive than manual searching, it is not invariably less expensive. In manual searching someone is involved at all times in the search activity. However, in academic libraries, it is not usually a professional who completes the manual search. In contrast, with online searching professional labor is involved in the formulation of a search strategy and its subsequent confirmation or modification. The computer performs the actual search. In addition to preparation time and online time there is time and effort invested to pull out from the retrieved citations the pertinent information. This is a greater factor with online searches. Either the searcher or the user must have the willingness to do this analysis and the knowledge of how to do it. Both factors are critical to the application of the information.

In a controversial article by Flynn, et al. it is shown quantitatively that online bibliographic literature retrieval is "considerably more cost-effective than traditional library manual searching, and online searching also offers many additional qualitative advantages."[10] In this study only one type of online search was found which was not cost-effective. These were very broad searches that required high numbers of offline prints such as searches covering whole business or technology areas.

Reaction to the Flynn article was strong in the form of several letters to the editor of the *Journal of Information Science*.[11] To some extent these reactions apply to many of the cost comparisons in the literature. Cost comparisons alone prove nothing unless the efficiency of the system is known. It is possible for an online user to look for the easiest way to search a topic and be unaware of what he/she failed to retrieve. In comparing online searching vs. manual searching the time "saved" by online searching may be spent in reading online search manuals or in attending training courses, for example, and cannot be claimed as a real cost saving.

Related to this point is the fact that in some libraries manual searches are not usually carried out primarily by professionals. This would eliminate the library's potential for cost reduction and the consequent prospects for cost justification with an online system. Nitecki[12] reports in a questionnaire sent to RASD members that respondents indicated the percentage of time spent doing literature searches was 21.8 percent and preparing state of the art literature reviews was 5.0 percent. Traditionally an academic librarian's argument for faculty status has been based on the ability to instruct the patron in the use of bibliographic sources rather than the actual performance of literature searches. Similarly, many school and public librarians view their roles as primarily instructional.

In concluding this section comparing manual and online searching I will summarize some of the advantages and disadvantages of online vs. manual searching.

Advantages: Several databases can be searched to give comprehensive coverage. Online searches have the added capability in some databases of being able to specify certain types of documents (e.g., review articles). Complex multiconcept searches, often impossible manually, are carried out easily online. Free text searching can yield results not easily attained with printed indexes. Large files can be searched quickly without handling heavy volumes or scanning tiny print. An online index is updated and cumulative, often long before a printed copy is received. A database may give access to a wider range of sources than a library can purchase in hard copy. There are unique databases that do not have a printed index counterpart. The output is relatively high quality without clerical effort. Online bibliographic databases offer greater flexibility in terms of physical access. They can be accessed from any compatible terminal in any physical location (this is especially true with the availability of portable terminal models).

Disadvantages: Generally only recent literature (about 10–15 years) is online. Certain subject areas are not well covered by existing databases (e.g., humanities). There is unavoidable duplication between databases.[13] Online charges are high, especially in non-government subsidized databases. A fee must be paid even if useful results are not obtained. Databases require a fee each time they are accessed, even though the same information is scanned over and over again. In contrast, a library pays for a hard copy once, and it can be used as many times as needed, without the user having to pay for leafing through the pages. An online system is not always available. Frustration can result from systems and telecommunication problems. Online searches can be done with one searcher at the terminal at a time, whereas printed indexes can have many users, depending on the number of volumes.

CHARGES RELATED TO COMPUTER SEARCHING

A frequently cited cost related impact of online searching is an increased demand for document delivery. The effect that this will have on interlibrary loan activity will depend on the size of a library's periodical collection and the ease of access to more extensive collections. Martin[14] suggests that in a special library, interlibrary loan requests may increase 50 percent after initiating computerized online search services. Even with adequate interlibrary loan resources, the time typically required to complete a loan transaction can negatively offset the speed advantage gained through online searching. An alternative to interlibrary loan has been offered by some database producers by developing various fee-based document delivery packages and services. These include document collections on microfiche or automated document ordering. Orders for these can be placed at the terminal and electronically transmitted. In some cases the requested documents are placed in the next day's mail.

If a library is unable to justify online searching on the basis of cancelled subscriptions or reduced labor or any other reason, then it may be necessary to pass on some or all of the costs to the user. Most academic and public libraries are probably unable to justify online search costs in this way. Saffady[15] cautions that the collection process itself can be a very costly procedure which can involve substantial amounts of paperwork, cash handling and accountability, and periodic audits.

Fee assessment for online services is a controversial issue. Gardner[16] sees the possibility in academic libraries of a kind of user elite developing, which consists of faculty and research staff whose fields of interest are currently receiving the attention of funding agencies. Price discrimination could also be used by libraries by charging some user groups differently than others. For example, professional users may be less sensitive to prices than students and would be charged more.[17] In 1977 the American Library Association Council adopted a policy of equal access to information. "The Association calls upon all concerned citizens to join in developing the kind of public support for libraries and information agencies which will insure the utilization of latest technological developments in information delivery without placing additional fees and levies upon the individual seeking access."[18]

King[19] believes that without any charge for online searches, some patrons might use the system unnecessarily. This is probably unlikely, since there is always the cost of a user's time, which would deter frivolous use. By asking users to pay only a trivial amount, such as for offline printing of results, many libraries will probably not even recover the cost of the fee collection process.

Before deciding to charge for online search services several issues should be resolved by the library offering the service: Will the fee cover all or part of the service? To what extent will individuals who need a search be deterred by the imposition of fees? Will charging a fee result in more efficient and/or better quality searching by library staff? Will library administrators be influenced in their resource allocation decisions by the fact that users are willing to pay for online searching? How will acceptable protocol be established for instituting a fee?[20]

FUTURE TRENDS

In concluding, it seems appropriate to suggest some probable changes in online searching in the future. These will, in turn, bring additional benefits (and, most likely costs) to the users. It is probable that online search service will develop stronger document delivery capabilities. This is already seen in some full-text systems. Durkin and others[21] describe a test database of full-text documents that has been established as a private database with BRS. The database consists of primary journal articles in full-text form from three years of the *Journal of Medicinal Chemistry*. Preliminary results show the database very useful but limited because of the small size. However, the test shows the BRS software very effective for online retrieval from full-text documents. Already some full-text reference databases exist, e.g., *Books in Print* and *American Men and Women of Science*. A full-text system requires a significant increase in online machine-readable storage space. The cost to convert such text is high. Likewise, the cost of transmitting it to the user requires costly online or offline time.

In the future online services will probably have a greater impact on printed subscriptions. Barlow, Kent, and Stern[22] report that revenues of printed abstract journals and indexes have not yet been seriously reduced by the growth of online retrieval. In this study database producers recovered only about 10 percent of their database creation costs from online and tape services. Over 90 percent still comes from subscriptions to the traditional indexing and abstracting journals. In the case of online services, 70–80 percent of the income is absorbed by telecommunications and computer operations. The main conclusion is that online services and royalties charged by the database producers are currently being subsidized by printed products. But, as online becomes established this policy will cease to be appropriate. There will most certainly be a gradual increase of online royalties in relation to print processes.

A second area which may affect online search charges is higher communication rates. Increased speed of data transmission causes reduced search time and, as a result, possibly reduces offline print usage. Even though increased speed of data transmission to the user will reduce his/her costs, it also reduces the contribution that the user is making to the construction of the database. The solution is probably found in a charging scheme not based on connect time.

King and Roderer[23] believe journal publishers will make increasing use of technology for editing and typesetting. It is possible now to receive manuscripts from authors in electronic form that can be edited online.

This will decrease costs and presumably decrease subscription prices. Some publishers may produce fewer subscription copies and instead provide masters to a national periodicals system for distribution.

Almost certainly the use of video discs will be more and more evident in the future. The discs are about the size and shape of phonograph records and cost about $50.00. The storage capacity is so great that a large database would fit on one disc. This opens up the possibility of performing retrieval operations on a local small computer. Discs could be mailed to receiving libraries periodically, similar to receiving a printed publication.[24]

Experiments are also being carried out using a micro-computer in the user's terminal to transform a non-Boolean search strategy into a sequence of Boolean search requests acceptable to one of the established online retrieval systems. This project, funded by the British Library, will implement and evaluate a technique known as "relevance weighting." It is hoped the result will be improved precision/recall over an existing Boolean system, or if that is not possible, equivalent retrieval at reduced user effort or cost.[25]

Other research is being done to create easy-to-use retrieval systems which, in some cases, may not require an intermediary. For the intermediary this means loss of control and for the user it usually means slower, less effective searching. What is likely to develop will be searching at two levels.[26] At this point, it is difficult to project the time frame within which any of these developments are likely to become widely available and accepted.

Footnotes

1. Sherrilynne Shirley, "A Survey of Computer Search Service Costs in the Academic Health Sciences Library," *Bulletin of the Medical Library Association* 66 (October 1978):390-6.
2. William Saffady, "The Economics of Online Bibliographic Searching: Costs and Cost Justifications," *Library Technology Reports* 15 (September/October 1979):591.
3. James H. Bement, "The New Prices: Some Comparisons" *Online* 1 (April 1977):9-20.
4. "Salary and Budget Survey," *Online* 3 (July 1979):52-53.
5. Shirley, "A Survey of Computer Search Service Costs," p. 391.
6. Rebecca J. Jensen, Herbert O. Ashbury, and Radford G. King, "Costs and Benefits to Industry of Online Literature Searches," *Special Libraries* 71 (July 1980):291-99.
7. Stanley A. Elman, "Cost Comparison of Manual and Online Computerized Literature Searching," *Special Libraries* 66 (January 1975):12-18.
8. Dennis R. Elchesen, "Cost Effectiveness Comparison of Manual and Online Retrospective Bibliographic Searching," *Journal of the American Society for Information Science* 29 (March 1978):56-66.

9. Brian E. Lantz, "Manual Versus Computerized Retrospective Reference Retrieval in an Academic Library," *Journal of Librarianship* 10 (April 1978):119-30.

10. T. Flynn, P. A. Holohan, M. S. Magson, and J. D. Munro, "Cost Effectiveness Comparison of Online and Manual Bibliographic Information Retrieval," *Journal of Information Science* 1 (May 1979):83.

11. "Letters to the Editor," *Journal of Information Science* 1 (October 1979):235-37.

12. Danuta A. Nitecki, "Attitudes toward Automated Information Retrieval Services among RASD Members," *RQ* 16 (Winter 1976):133-41.

13. It is possible to use an "Automatic Send-Receive" (ASR) terminal to obtain the results of an online search in machine readable form. The search results are recorded on a magnetic tape cassette for later editing and/or printout. With this device it is possible to perform searches on several databases and then reprocess the searches on an inhouse computer which will delete duplicate citations and print a customized bibliography.

14. Jean K. Martin, "Computer Based Literature Searching: Impact on Interlibrary Loan Service," *Special Libraries* 69 (January 1978):1-6.

15. Saffady, "The Economics of Online Bibliographic Searching," p. 625.

16. Jeffrey Gardner, "Online Searching in Academic Libraries," in *Buying New Technology* (New York: Library Journal, 1978) pp. 28-32.

17. Donald W. King, "Pricing Policies in Academic Libraries," *Library Trends* 28 (Summer 1979):47-62.

18. Allen Kent, "The Potential of Online Information Systems," in *Online Revolution in Libraries: Proceedings of the 1977 Conference in Pittsburgh, Pennsylvania*, ed. Allen Kent and Thomas J. Galvin (New York: Marcel Dekker, 1978), pp. 3-24.

19. King, "Pricing Policies in Academic Libraries."

20. Michael D. Cooper and Nancy A. DeWath, "The Effect of User Fees on the Cost of Online Searching in Libraries," *Journal of Library Automation* 10 (December 1977):304-319.

21. Kay Durkin, Janet England, Lorrin Garson, and Seldon W. Terrant, "An Experiment to Study the Use of a Full-Text Primary Journal Database," in *4th International Online Information Meeting*, London 9-11 December 1980 (New York: Learned Information, 1980), pp. 53-56.

22. D. H. Barlow, A. K. Kent, and B. T. Stern, "Information Costs in the Future," in *2nd International Online Information Meeting*, London 5-7 December 1978 (New York: Learned Information, 1978), pp. 103-106.

23. Donald W. King and Nancy K. Roderer, "The Electronic Alternative to Communication Through Paper Based Journals," *Proceedings of the American Society for Information Science* 15 (1978):180-82.

24. Carol H. Fenichel and Thomas H. Hogan, *Online Searching: A Primer* (Marlton, N.J.: Learned Information, 1981).

25. Stephen H. Jamieson and Robert N. Oddy, "Low-Cost Implementation of Experimental Retrieval Techniques for Online Users," in *4th International Online Information Meeting*, London 9-11 December 1980 (New York: Learned Information, 1980), pp. 201-209.

26. Fenichel and Hogan, *Online Searching: A Primer*.

Fees for Online Searches: A Review of the Issue and a Discussion of Alternatives

James Rice, Jr.

The practice of charging users fees to support online services has been a controversial issue for several years. It has assumed a prevalent place in the literature but this has not resulted in any consensus of opinion. This writer has encountered signficantly more articles opposing user fees than supporting them. However, as we shall see, most libraries that offer online searching have some form of cost recovery through user fees.

The purpose of this article is to summarize the literature on this topic and then to discuss the various alternatives. Library administrators may then have some additional basis for the decision they will make regarding the financial management of automated reference service.

THE PROS AND CONS

The arguments in favor of user fees tend to be pragmatic in nature. A frequently encountered statement on the subject goes something like this: "If we didn't charge some cost recovery fees, then we probably couldn't offer the services at all. If we tried to offer online searching at no cost, we would have to cancel other programs or services or reduce acquisitions." These people are arguing that to support online searching from the library budget would be robbing other users of services or resources they expect the library to have.

Another argument in favor of user fees is that only certain users actually need the services. They argue that online searches are not part of the traditional library role. Zella Shannon of The Minneapolis Public Library states that "When community diversity demands diversity in

Reprinted with permission of Haworth Press from the *Journal of Library Administration* 3 (Spring 1982):25-34.

funding . . . fees are a necessary evil to be monitored and controlled."[1] Although they are in a minority, users needing automated reference service should be given the choice of paying for the availability of online searching rather than not having the access at all.

Anyone who wants to become apprised of the arguments opposed to user fees might browse through the issues of *Library Journal* during the last several years. A considerable amount of space in that journal has been devoted to this topic. Some very persuasive and well written arguments are presented there.

One argument is that online searching is actually a part of reference service and should be integrated into the budgetary support for that function. "Skilled utilization of online searching tools may also save the librarian a great deal of valuable time required for searching a comparable manual index."[2]

This argument is very effectively developed by Jan Egeland:

First, why is this the only automated library service for which the patron is expected to pay? This is automation in the *reference* department. There are automated services everywhere else in the library, including circulation, cataloging, acquisitions—is there a charge for any of these services? Why, then, would libraries charge for automation in the reference department? The second question is this: direct cost recovery aside, is there any other library service for which we have even considered adding on overhead charges, space rental, lighting, staff time, etc.? Yet we have libraries that are doing precisely that right now with online reference services.[3]

An interesting expansion of this argument is that by James Capodagli:

While inflation has been especially devastating to book and journal budgets, libraries continue to provide these materials without a direct fee. On the other hand, online searching has decreased in cost since it was first introduced. It does not follow that one service, relatively stable in cost, should be selected for charging fees, while others are soaring in cost and yet remain free to the patron. This is not to suggest library fees on all services, but the logical budgetary support of computerized searching.[4]

These people are arguing that reference work *is* part of the traditional role of the library. Online searching provides new resources and new services to support that function. It therefore should be integrated into the library budget without having to charge fees to users.

Another argument in opposition to user fees is what has been called the double taxation argument. Put simply, this argument states that the library is a publicly funded institution and a citizen's tax payment should be the total payment for all library services. If we charge for online searching, we are making the user pay twice; once in taxes and once in the library.[5]

In 1977, the American Library Association approved a resolution which states that, "The charging of fees and levies for information services, including those services utilizing the latest information technology, is discriminatory in publicly supported institutions."[6] The philosophy inherent in this resolution was later reiterated in the White House Conference on Library and Information Services. One resolution contains the statement, "No citizen should be restricted from access to information by the imposition of fees." Another states that, "All persons should have free access, without charge or fee to the individual, to information in public and publicly supported libraries. . . . "[7]

It is interesting to note that some of the opponents to user fees admit that fees are probably inevitable in reality.[8] As Jan Egeland states, "The question has become, at least practically at this point, 'How much should we charge, rather than, should we charge?' "[9] But there are also those who stand firm and insist that user fees are not a necessary evil but should be avoided in all cases.

A major argument for these people is the intellectual freedom argument which grows out of the free and open access resolutions cited above. This argument states that,

> Having the right to express oneself without the information to substantiate the thinking, the decision-making, the judgment-making would be pretty short-sighted in a free society, because it would result in uninformed expressions. If you concede that the right of access to information is essential, then having fees levied which discriminate against those unable to pay creates barriers that negate that right. The fees amount to a form of censorship. . . . The ability to pay, not the need, or worth of the inquiry, then becomes the criterion for this reference service and thus, effectively discriminates against those who cannot afford the additional charge.[10]

Both the free and open access argument and the intellectual freedom argument represent a very emotional area of this issue. Unfortunately, they imply that there may be something fundamentally wrong or even unethical about charging fees for library services. It is for this reason that these two arguments (both based on the same concept) be more closely scrutinized.

Is it really fair to say that user fees are a form of censorship? If we do not charge user fees for online searching, then the money spent for these services must come from somewhere. This means that certain other materials or services will not be purchased. So, whether we charge for online searching or not, we have restricted or deprived someone the access to something. In fact, it could be said that a library violates intellectual freedom by making people come to the library for information. We are limiting access for the homebound or people who cannot, for some reason, travel to the library. Many libraries have cancelled manual indexes because of online searching (sometimes to avoid user fees). Does this not deprive some users of the type of access they need? Is that censorship?

The intellectual freedom argument as it is applied to online searching could be logically extended to a variety of library policies. Interlibrary loan and coin operated copy machines restrict access for people who have inadequate time or money. The decision not to select a book can be construed as censorship.

Steve Sherman a former librarian and the author of nine books argues that libraries in the U.S. are presently discriminating against authors. He proposes that writers be paid according to how often their books are checked out from libraries. He submits that current library practices rob writers of royalties they deserve. "This fundamental injustice . . . certainly shouldn't be dismissed as the essence of free public libraries."[11]

This writer submits that the charging of user fees is not necessarily a violation of intellectual freedom. Those administrators who have instituted fees have usually done so to realize open access, not to restrict it. They *don't* want to reduce materials or services elsewhere in the library but they *do* want automated reference service to be available. While user fees may impede access for some, free online searching may impede access to other materials which are just as important. User fees may be discriminatory, but the alternatives to them may be also.

In sorting through the user fee dilemma, the first thing we must do is view this issue in its proper perspective. The decision to charge or not to charge is a management issue. Most administrators on either side of the issue are trying to provide the broadest and most convenient access to the largest clientele. They are all trying to act in the interest of intellectual freedom and free and open access. The question that remains is how intellectual freedom can be maintained in the context of this new technology. It is this question that we must try to answer.

THE EFFECTS OF USER FEES

In attempting to decide whether or not to charge user fees, managers should consider the effects those fees might have. Mary Huston has found that in several well done studies, user demand for online searching is far greater when there are no fees. In some long term studies, demand decreased significantly when fees were imposed. This was even true for physicians who have an ability to pay.[12]

It is also interesting to note the possible effects of user fees on library costs. One study which yields data on this question is the DIALAB project completed by the Cooperative Information Network and Lock-heed. In this study, public library patrons in the San Francisco Bay area were offered online searching services. In the first year of this project, the searches were free to users because of a National Science Foundation grant. In subsequent years, fees were charged.

It was found in the DIALAB study that the free searches took more staff time than the searches with fees. Reference interview labor costs averaged $1.12 during the free period and $1.72 during the pay period. "Overall, there was a modest decrease in the average total cost of a search from $28.78 in the free period to $26.73 in the pay period, and a sharp decrease (44 percent) of 3.4 days in the number of days required to process a request."[13] It was also found that, during the pay period, the librarians spent more time in the reference interview and in preparing for searching and less time on the computer terminal itself. This is probably causally related to the $5.75 decrease in average connect charges that was discovered during the pay period. In general, when reference librarians plan better, the actual online searching time is less. In the DIALAB study, when users were paying, the librarians interviewed them more carefully and planned better. It was also discovered, however, that users requested more output from online searching when they had to pay for it. Offline print costs increased about $2.00 per search.[14] This tends to indicate that paying customers will want more tangible results from a search.

Studies of users' willingness to pay have presented conflicting evidence. One study surveyed students who were in the process of using a search service. Although 82 percent were satisfied with the results, only a third said they would be willing or able to pay the full cost.[15] Cogswell, however, reports that most users are willing and able to pay.[16] In both of these studies, researchers were attempting to study a variable which is very difficult to assess. User willingness to pay is probably best determined by the actual use of a fee-based service.

Surveys Assessing the User-Fee Issue

If libraries charge for online searching at all, there is a wide range of cost recovery possible. The cost of online searching in the library budget can be divided into two types; direct costs and indirect costs. Direct costs include connect time, offline print charges, and telecommunications costs. Indirect costs (or overhead) include staff time, equipment, supplies, utilities, furnishings, etc. Libraries may charge for any or all of these costs. Or they may charge a flat rate for searching intended to cover some or all of these costs. Furthermore they may charge varying rates for different types of users. In an academic library, for example, students may be charged and faculty not or vice versa. In a public library, patrons may receive free service while outsiders are charged. Or fees may be graduated based on an ability to pay. We shall now take a look at some data which indicates how libraries are currently handling this issue.

In a carefully designed and thorough survey conducted in the fall of 1979, Marcy Murphy gathered some evidence pertinent to this topic in a sample of over 200 academic, public and special libraries. The return rate of the survey was 92% or 192 libraries: 72 academic, 67 public, and 53 special. Of these, 53% of the total sample or 101 libraries had no online services in house but referred requests to other institutions. Broken down by type of library: 34 of the academic libraries (45%), sixteen of the public libraries (24%), and 40 of the special libraries (74%) had online services in house.

In Murphy's survey, of the libraries that had online capability, most of them "attempted to recover *some costs:* 21 academic, nine public and seventeen special. On the other hand, seventeen special libraries, a precisely equal number, recovered *no costs*. Only two academic and three public were in this group. Additionally, eight academic, two public and five special tried to recover *all costs* and 11 special libraries tried to make a *small profit*."[17]

These data indicate that cost recovery is not uncommon in any type of library. By manipulating the data gathered from these libraries, we find that 29 out of 34 academic libraries, 11 out of 16 public libraries, and 22 out of 40 special libraries attempted to recover *some* or *all* of their online searching costs. Certainly cost recovery appears most prevalent in academic libraries but over half of the reporting public and special libraries had fees.

In a 1980 survey of 47 academic libraries Connie Lamb discovered even a higher prevalence. Of these libraries, only one offers searches free to users, 32 fund searching entirely from fees, and 14 fund searching from fees and the library budget combined.[18]

In a survey completed in 1978, Mary Jo Lynch tried to assess the level of cost recovery in 930 public libraries. Of the 716 responding libraries only 109 reported that they had computer based reference services. Unfortunately, it was discovered that many of these were confused by the questionnaire and the actual number was well below 109. Lynch concluded that "Returns seem to indicate that the provision of computer-based reference service without user fees is possible in public libraries only if outside funding is available."[19]

The Alternatives

There are few prescriptive explanations published on how to go about charging fees. An exception to this is that by Helen Drinan of Charles River Associates, Inc. That firm introduced online services in 1976 and felt the need to charge fees to support the costs. She presents an excellent discussion of pricing methods, flat rate calculations, controlling costs, record keeping and forecasting. Those administrators who have decided to assess at least some fees will find this article helpful.[20]

At Lake Forest College, for example, searches are offered absolutely free to users as a routine reference service. Lake Forest serves 1,000 students and has a faculty of 100. Their beginning year's online searching budget totalled $4,963. However online searching clientele are limited "almost exclusively to those groups which receive classroom instruction in the use of the library, including the database searching."[21]

At California State College, Stanislaus, online searching is considered an alternative reference tool. "By not charging for searching, the librarian is free to provide the service to anyone who may need it. . . . The lack of flexibility caused by charging fees results in the librarian spending hours assisting some patrons in needless searches through manual indexes."[22] In this library, users may request searches online but the librarians determine whether a computer search is the most effective way to provide the information. If a librarian determines that manual indexes are the most effective way to fulfill a specific need, then the patron is instructed and directed accordingly. However, "some printed indexes have been cancelled due to the superiority and availability of online searching. The library does not feel obligated to acquire printed indexes if the same or better information is available online."[23]

Another noteworthy attempt to avoid fees is "the Westport Model". At Westport, librarians determine when online searching should be used in a specific situation. Then, they also determine how long it should be paid for by the library and when the patron should begin to pay. As with traditional reference work, a line is drawn with each patron as to how much individual service is justified or warranted. At Westport, this is usually about a half hour of online searching or traditional reference assistance. The time limit is a guideline, not a rigid rule. In the case of online costs further searching beyond this limit will be paid by the patron. The initial inquiry is free and librarians at Westport anticipate that most information needs can be met within the allotted time.[24]

Another interesting approach is that of voluntary charges for online searching. The Primate Research Center at the University of Washington/Seattle instituted such a policy in 1973 and it has worked very well. In this information center, a suggested fee is charged for searching but the user has a choice of whether or not to pay. The clients of this center range from high school students to corporate research managers. In the current awareness lists, users are notified of the suggested payment but the notice includes the sentence, "Service will not be denied clients unable to pay."[25] For retrospective bibliography searches, voluntary payments are requested for searches covering the last five years. Searches going back further require obligatory fees. It is interesting to note here that the use of both services has increased and the voluntary payments are made by many users.[26] This helps to support the service yet it does not deny access to anyone.

CONCLUSIONS AND RECOMMENDATIONS

Online searching has been developing for many years and has been commercially available since the late 60s. But the depth of information and service it now offers is relatively new. Its widespread use is so new in fact that it has taken most libraries somewhat by surprise. Additionally, it is a very different kind of resource and doesn't readily fit into the traditional patterns of collection development and public service. Computer based reference service has a high per unit cost and that unit is usually for the particular use of one patron and one specific need. Librarians have had difficulty integrating online searching into the ongoing budget without giving up very significant needs elsewhere in their program.

Furthermore, databases have been fairly concentrated in the science and technology subject areas and users are often viewed as a special group of our clientele, in many cases not the traditional student or public library user.

However, these tendencies are changing. More and more databases are being developed in the social sciences, humanities, and arts. Popular databases are becoming available. Non bibliographic information services will increase rapidly to offer statistical data, quick reference information, how-to-do-it sources, and news services. Games, recreational services and instructional programs will be available over television-based online services.

In all types of libraries, the users of online searching will become a broader cross-section of library users in general. Online catalogs and bibliographic networks will be more available on a public access basis. College students and public library users will be very comfortable with computer terminals and userfriendly time-sharing systems.

As online resources broaden and increase in number, librarians will become more accustomed to them as an integral part of library services and resources. It will be realized that online databases are not really very different from other information, they are just in a different format. In short, as this type of information evolves it will be increasingly difficult to distinguish it from other information.

This projected future is really not that speculative. In many ways, it is here. As far as the staffing of public service is concerned, it is very likely that online searching will *have* to be integrated into reference departments. As these new resources are relevant to a broader range of information needs, the total staff will have to become more involved in automated reference work. The point where fees begin and regular service ends will become more nebulous. Cost recovery fees will become much more difficult to justify or assess.

Nancy Kranich recommends that online searching become a shared resource supported at the state level. "There is no reason why libraries cannot adopt more advanced technological modes to provide much more effective services. New financial options and organizational formats merely need to be applied."[27]

Cost recovery fees have been necessary in many cases and it seems they will exist for some time. But, in all types of libraries, we will be faced with the realization that online information will be a necessary resource for general reference work. It is hoped that library administrators can evolve toward an ability to eliminate fees in making online services available.

Footnotes

1. Arthur Plotnik, "The Issues Revisited," *American Libraries* 9 (July/August 1978):432.
2. Nancy Kranich, "Fees for Library Service: They Are Not Inevitable," *Library Journal* 105 (May 1, 1980):1051.
3. Jan Egeland, "To Charge or Not to Charge—The Choices and the Implications," in *Charging for Computer Based Reference Services*, ed. Peter G. Watson, (Chicago: American Library Association Reference and Adult Services Division, September 1978), p. 30.
4. James Capodagli, "Online 'Free': How They Do It," *Library Journal* 104 (August 1979):1498.
5. John Berry, "Double Taxation," *Library Journal* 101 (November 15, 1976):2321.
6. "A.L.A. Policy Manual" in *A.L.A. Handbook of Organization 1979/80* (Chicago: American Library Association, 1979), p. 126.
7. James Rettig, "Rights, Resolutions, Fees and Reality," *Library Journal* 106 (February 1, 1981):303.
8. Ibid.
9. Egeland, "To Charge or Not to Charge," p. 30.
10. Zoia Horn, "Charging for Computer Based Reference Services: Some Issues of Intellectual Freedom," in *Charging for Computer Based Reference Services*, ed. Peter G. Watson, (Chicago: American Library Association Reference and Adult Services Division, September, 1978), p. 10-11.
11. Steve Sherman, "Pay Writers for Borrowing Their Books," *The Christian Science Monitor*, April 15, 1981, p. 23.
12. Mary M. Huston, "Fee or Free: The Effect of Charging on Information Demand," *Library Journal* 104 (September 15, 1979):1812-13.

13. Michael D. Cooper and Nancy A. DeWath, "The Effect of User Fees on the Cost of Online Searching in Libraries," *Journal of Library Automation* 10 (December 1977):317.
14. Ibid.
15. Pamela Kobelski and Jean Trumbore, "Student Use of Online Bibliographic Services," *The Journal of Academic Librarianship* (March 1978):15.
16. James Cogswell, "Online Search Services: Implications for Libraries and Library Users," *College and Research Libraries* (July 1978):276-77.
17. Marcy Murphy, "Online Services in Some Academic, Public and Special Libraries: A State of the Art Report," (Champaign: University of Illinois Graduate School of Library Science, 1981).
18. Connie Lamb, "Searching in Academia: Nearly 50 Libraries Tell What They're Doing," *Online* 5 (April 1981):78-81.
19. Mary Jo Lynch, "Confusion Twice Compounded: Report of a P.L.A. Survey on Fees Currently Charged in Public Libraries," *Public Libraries* 17 (Fall 1978):11.
20. Helen Drinan, "Financial Management of Online Services: A How to Guide," *Online* 3 (October 1979):14-21.
21. Joann H. Lee and Arthur H. Miller, Jr., "Introducing Online Database Searching in the Small Academic Library: A Model for Service Without Charge to Undergraduates," *The Journal of Academic Librarianship* 7 (March 1981):20-21.
22. Paula J. Crawford and Judith A. Thompson, "Free Online Searches Are Feasible," *Library Journal* 104 (April 1, 1979):794.
23. Ibid., p. 795.
24. John Berry, "The Westport Model," *Library Journal* 105 (May 1, 1980):1021.
25. Maryeva W. Terry, "Voluntary Charges: Experience on the Middle Road," in *American Society for Information Science, 1975* (Portland, Oreg.: Information Roundup, The Society, 1975), p. 172.
26. Ibid., p. 173-5.
27. Kranich, "Fees for Library Service," p. 1051.

Financing Online Services

Mary Jo Lynch

It would be hard to find a library in the United States today that isn't either offering online search services or thinking about doing so. Because these services provide dramatically improved access to information, many libraries are eager to make them available to the public. But adopting this technology forces a library to face economic issues that are essentially different from those libraries have faced in the past. Helen Drinan has explained the issue succinctly:

> The decision to offer online information services added an element of uncertainty to the financial management process. This is because online services generate not only predictable fixed costs (such as training fees, terminals and manuals), but also variable costs (such as online time and searcher time) which are difficult to forecast. These variable costs are demand-dependent; that is, costs incurred vary directly with the number of requests for service. Management of variable costs requires an ability to estimate demand, which is a very difficult task at the introductory stage of a new service.[1]

From a financial perspective, online services are quite unlike services most publicly supported libraries have previously offered. Therefore, the library wishing to make online services available faces a number of new questions. Among them are such questions as these: Should we charge users for online service? If so, what costs do we consider when calculating a fee? Should we provide a no-charge period? Should we differentiate our primary clientele from other users? How should we structure our fee schedule. How many searches can we expect in a year? What are the total direct costs we can expect in a year? What factors should we consider when deciding how to finance online services?

The librarian trying to answer these questions for his or her own institution will probably seek information about practices in other libraries. ALA has just published a report that provides that information

based on the responses of 985 publicly supported libraries to a questionnaire concerning the financing of online search services.

The survey was conducted by ALA's Office for Research with help
from the Council on Library Resources and three major vendors of online
search services—BRS, Lockheed, and SDC.[2] The vendors helped by
mailing ALA's questionnaire to their subscribers in the population of
interest. This methodology imposed unusual conditions on the survey
that are described in the published report and will not be repeated here.
Instead, we will summarize the major findings useful to libraries
planning to offer online services to the public. Most of the tables in this
article are expanded in the full report to show responses by type of
library. The report also contains additional findings and analysis, an
essay review of the literature, and a supplementary report on fee
schedules.

RESULTS

Because of the way the survey was conducted we are not justified in
claiming that results represent the entire library community. However,
our results do describe the financing of online search services in a
substantial number of publicly supported libraries ($N = 985$). Table 1
shows the type of libraries responding to the survey. Returns came from
all states of the U.S. Table 2 shows how long respondents had been
offering online search services. Table 3 shows how many searches
respondents had conducted in the last fiscal year.

TABLE 1 Libraries Responding to
Survey

| | | RESPONDENTS | |
TYPE OF LIBRARY	NO.	% ($N = 985$)
1. Public	53	5
2. 2-year College	28	3
3. 4-year College	137	14
4. University	445	45
5. School Library	6	*
6. Government Agency	166	17
7. Health Sciences	78	8
8. Library System	13	1
9. Other Library	59	6
Total	985	99%

*Less than 1%
Source: ALA, *Financing Online Services in Publicly Supported Libraries*, 1981. Table C.

The number of searches conducted ranged from a low of 0 (some
libraries were just beginning!) to a high of 50,000. When the respondent
reporting 50,000 is removed, the range is from 0 to 7,800, with a mean of
598 searches in the last fiscal year.

TABLE 2   **Length of Time Offering Online Services**

LENGTH OF TIME	NO.	% OF RESPONDENTS ($N = 985$)
No response to this question	4	*
0–2 years	301	31
2–5 years	444	45
6–10 years	209	21
Over 10 years	27	3
Total	985	100%

*Less than 1%
Source: ALA, *Financing Online Services in Publicly Supported Libraries*, 1981. Table D.

Table 4 shows responses to the major question of the survey: "Does your method of financing involve any fees to any user?" Table 5 cross tabulates the presence of a fee with the number of years a library has been offering the service. Clearly the longer the service has been offered, the more likely it is that a fee will be charged. Two hundred sixty-eight of the libraries charging fees (38 percent) reported that some or all searches begin with a no-charge period of online time, the costs of which are paid for by the library.

TABLE 3   **Number of Searches Last Fiscal Year**

NO. OF SEARCHES	NO.	LIBRARIES % ($N = 985$)
Up to 50	192	20
51–150	169	17
151–350	194	20
351–800	175	18
801–7,800	177	18
No responses or no searches yet	77	8
Total	984*	101%

*Plus one reporting 50,000 searches.
Source: ALA, *Financing Online Services in Publicly Supported Libraries*, 1981. Table E1.

Table 6 shows how many respondents indicated that a particular cost was included in calculating the fee. The eight components of cost identified in the questionnaire were based on the list in Saffady's "The Economics of Online Bibliographic Searching: Costs and Cost Justification."[3] It seems clear that most libraries charge only for direct costs related to a specific search and absorb other costs.

Since we suspected this would be true and wanted to know the amount of money involved, we asked respondents to indicate what the library was billed for direct costs in the last fiscal year. Responses ranged

TABLE 4   Libraries Charging Any Fees
to Any User

PRESENCE OF FEE	NO.	RESPONDENTS % (N = 985)
No Answer	1	*
No	258	26
Yes	709	72
Other	17	2
Total	985	100%

*Less than 1%.
Source: ALA, *Financing Online Services in Publicly Supported Libraries*, 1981. Table F1.

from a low of $32 to a high of $102,000. When the two libraries reporting direct costs of $100,000 and $102,000 respectively are removed, the range is from $32 to $54,000 with a mean of $6,816. Table 7 shows the amount billed in seven different dollar categories.

Respondents were asked "Does your fee structure differentiate between the primary clientele of the library and persons not in the primary clientele (e.g., for public libraries—non-residents of the area. For academic—non-students or non-faculty)?" Three hundred ninety-five of those charging fees (58 percent) do differentiate. Answers to the question "How is your fee system structured?" were impossible to analyze in any detail because of the great variety of fee structures reported. Responses to other questions revealed that few respondents collected data on the effect of a fee or the volume of use and most (82 percent) do not collect information on the characteristics of their users.

TABLE 5   Libraries Charging a Fee by
Length of Time Offering Search

LENGTH OF TIME OFFERING SEARCH	NO.	PRESENCE OF A FEE % (OF RESPONDENTS – THIS LENGTH OF TIME)
Less than 2 years (N = 301)	185	61
2–5 years (N = 444)	320	72
6–10 years (N = 209)	177	85
Over 10 years (N = 27)	25	92

Source: ALA, *Financing Online Services in Publicly Supported Libraries*, 1981. Table F2.

One surprising finding of the survey was the result of the following question: "In your opinion, how do users, searchers and library ad-

TABLE 6   Costs Included in Calculating
Fee

COST	NO.	RESPONDENTS INCLUDING % (N = 709)
Amortized Start-up Expenses	32	4
Annual General Operating Expenses	88	12
Communication Charges	537	76
Connect Time	629	89
Offline Printing Charges	616	87
Searcher's Time	103	14
Other Staff Time	17	2
Overhead	84	12
Other	78	11

Source: ALA, *Financing Online Services in Publicly Supported
Libraries*, 1981. Table H.

ministrators feel about the method of financing online services?"
Respondents were asked to indicate whether users, searchers, and
administrators were positive, neutral, or negative about the method
used. If "negative" was indicated the resondent was asked to explain.
Obviously answers to this question indicate only the opinion of the
respondent. However, an overwhelming majority of respondents believe
that all three groups have positive feelings about the financing method
used whether fees are involved or not.

TABLE 7   Amount Billed to Library for
Direct Costs

AMOUNT (IN DOLLARS)	NO.	RESPONDENTS % (N = 709)	CUM. %
Up to 750	77	11	11
751–1,500	75	11	21
1,501–3,000	101	14	36
3,001–5,000	79	11	47
5,001–7,500	59	8	55
7,501–15,000	119	17	72
15,001–54,000	64	9	81
No Response	133	19	100
Total	707*	100	

*Plus one at $100,000 and one at $102,000.
Source: ALA,*Financing Online Services in Publicly Supported Libraries*, 1981. Table K1.

Finally, the questionnaire asked "Which of the following factors
played a major role in your decision regarding a method of financing
online research services?" Nine factors were mentioned and space was
provided for additions. The factor most often chosen both by those
charging fees and by those not charging fees was the same: "Level of

funding available." The factor in second place was also the same whether or not fees were charged: "Need for a simple system."

CONCLUSION

In a recent article describing a survey similar to this one conducted in the state of California, Nancy Van House DeWath explains:

> Future innovations in information services will probably come from the application of technology to the storage, retrieval, and dissemination of information. They will have significant and identifiable costs. The products will be highly specific to the individual client's needs. And many will be aimed at making more effective use of the end-user's time. Libraries will have to decide what role (if any) they will play in making these services available, and who will bear the cost.
> In adopting online bibliographic searching, libraries have had to make decisions which have implications for these broader questions of fees and of innovative information services generally. What we have had is, in effect, a great natural experiment.[4]

The ALA survey documents important aspects of how that experiment was conducted in a large number of publicly supported libraries and provides solid information upon which decisions regarding future innovations can be based.

Footnotes

1. Helen B. Drinan, "Financial Management of Online Services: A How to Guide," *Online* 3 (October 1979):14-15.
2. The project was advised by an ad hoc subcommittee appointed by ALA's Committee on Research. Members of the subcommittee were: Sarah Knapp, Danuta Nitecki, Gary Shirk, Peter Watson and Douglas Zweizig.
3. William Saffady, "The Economics of Online Bibliographic Searching: Costs and Cost Justification," *Library Technology Reports* 15 (September/October 1979):567-653.
4. Nancy Van House DeWath, "Fees for Online Bibliographic Search Services in Publicly Supported Libraries," *Library Research* 3 (June 1981):31.

Additional Readings— Financial Considerations

Barker, Frances H. "Pricing of Information Products." Aslib *Proceedings* 36 (July/August 1984):289-297.

Beeler, Richard J., and Lueck, Antoinette L. "Pricing of Online Services for Nonprimary Clientele," *The Journal of Academic Librarianship* 10 (May 1984): 69-72.

Boyce, Bert R. "A Cost Accounting Model for Online Computerized Literature Searching." *Journal of Library Administration* 4 (Summer 1983):43-49.

Budd, John. "The Terminal and the Terminus: the Prospect of Free Online Bibliographic Searching." *RQ* 21 (Sept. 1982):373-378.

Cooper, Michael. "Charging Users for Library Service." *Information Processing and Management* 14 (1978):419-427.

DeWath, Nancy Van House. "Fees for Online Bibliographic Search Services in Publicly Supported Libraries." *Library Research* 3 (June 1981):29-45.

Drinan, Helen. "Financial Management of Online Services: A How to Guide." *Online* 3 (October 1979):14-21.

Dunn, Ronald G., and Boyle, Harvy F. "Online Searching: An Analysis of Marketing Issues." *Information Services & Use* 4 (June 1984):147-154.

Elchesen, Dennis R. "Cost-Effectiveness Comparison of Manual and Online Retrospective Searching." *Journal of the American Society for Information Science* 29 (March 1978):56-66.

Elman, Stanley A. "Cost Comparison of Manual and Online Computer Literature Searching." *Special Libraries* 66 (January.1975):12-18.

Flynn, T., et al. "Cost-Effectiveness Comparison of Online and Manual Bibliographic Information Retrieval." *Journal of Information Science* 1 (May 1979):77-84.

Hunter, Joane A. "What Price Information." *Information Services and Use* 4 (August 1984):217-223.

Kenton, David. "The Development of a More Equitable Method of Billing for Online Services." *Online* 8 (September 1984):13-17.

Kidd, J.S. "Towards Cost-Effective Procedures in Online Bibliographic Searches." *College & Research Libraries* 38 (March 1977):153-59. Comment July 1977:334-6.

Knapp, Sara D. and Schmidt, James C. "Budgeting to Provide Computer-Based Reference Services." *Journal of Academic Librarianship* 5 (March 1979):9-13.

Lynch, Mary Jo. *Financing Online Search Services in Publicly Supported Libraries: The Report of an ALA Survey.* Chicago: American Library Assn., 1981.

Saffady, William. "The Economics of Online Bibliographic Searching: Costs and Cost Justifications." *Library Technology Reports* 15 (September 1979):567-653.
Tenopir, Carol. "Pricing Policies." *Library Journal* 109 (July 1984):1300-1301.

Because of their very nature, online services readily lend themselves to quantitative measurement. Various aspects of the service may be measured, among them those factors related to the search, those that apply to the user, and those relevant to the searcher. Perhaps the simplest elements to measure are those involving aspects of the search. These may include the volume of searches performed, the databases and services used and the cost of each, the length of the search in minutes, the number and cost of online and offline prints, the topic and purpose of the search, how the search was paid for and by whom. Information pertaining to users includes a host of user profile characteristics including organizational affiliation and position, familiarity with database searching, and overall satisfaction. Data may also be gathered on the efficiency of the searcher; the conduct of the negotiation interview; the searching techniques, strategies, and tactics used; and the interaction with the system, database, terminal, and user.

Data on these and other aspects of the service may be collected using searcher logs, diaries, and appointment calendars; vendor invoices; search request forms; survey questionnaires; interviews and participant and nonparticipant observation methods. The difficulty then, does not lie so much in what may be measured but in determining the purpose for collecting the data. Why the data are needed and how they are to be used will determine what should be measured.

For the manager, the appropriate collection and use of service statistics are a prerequisite for an effective search operation. For example, high usage figures may indicate that an increase in staff is needed, or that additional vendor subscriptions should be considered, or that user fees are too low. Repeated use of one or two databases may show that further searcher training is necessary. A high volume of searches by one class of users may indicate that additional promotional efforts among other potential requester groups are called for.

The type of data collected, and the purpose and method of collecting it will vary, of course, to meet the individual needs of the organization. Attempts have been made, however, to introduce some uniformity into the data collection process. Recently, the Machine Assisted Reference Section Committee on Measurement and Evaluation of Service of the Reference and Adult Services Division of the American Library Association devised an online search evaluation form consisting of ten questions. In his article,

Richard W. Blood analyzes these questions, gives the rationale as to why each was included and the ways in which the data collected by it could be used and how it might be modified to meet local requirements. He also identifies those questions excluded from the evaluation form because they were deemed to elicit less meaningful responses in terms of the performance criteria felt to be indicative of user satisfaction or dissatisfaction with online services: recall, relevance, user effort, and response time. Also excluded were those questions that could be asked on other types of forms, especially the search request form. Those areas not probed for these reasons were user awareness of online services, previous use of online services, comparisons with manual searches, evaluation of the search intermediary, and format of document surrogates. An example of the search evaluation questionnaire is provided.

Eileen E. Hitchingham also approaches the evaluation of online searching from the manager's perspective. She ties the selection of evaluation measures to the objectives set for the service by the manager. These objectives are to provide searches that will meet user needs at the lowest possible cost and to ensure that the resources allocated by the service produce benefits that are equal to or greater than those that would have been achieved had the resources been committed to other uses. She charts and reviews the findings of eleven studies that attempt to determine the average cost of an online search and constructs a formula for arriving at the unit cost per relevant citation. This generalized expression of cost would allow the manager to assess whether the objective of providing the cheapest search had been met and would indicate which variables needed to be manipulated to achieve greater effectiveness.

Perhaps the most problematic aspect of the online search service to evaluate is the satisfaction of the user, for the first question that arises is satisfaction with what. Exposure to a search service usually involves the user in some form of interaction with a search analyst who negotiates and performs the search, at least one online system and database, online and/or offline prints, a pricing structure, and a billing procedure. Each of these elements is comprised of multidimensional facets each of which may be isolated and measured separately. A judicious correlation of the component elements comprising these interactions must be configured before a valid and reliable evaluation can be derived.

In her paper, Renata Tagliacozzo emphasizes the problems inherent in estimating the satisfaction of users. Her study was of a particular group of users of a specific database but the difficulties she encountered are by no means unique to her research nor an indication of faulty procedures. Rather, the contradictory and dissonant answers given to various items of her questionnaire suggest the varied and disparate factors that influence users' responses. She identifies factors related to the measuring instrument, perceptions and attitudes of users, and the search itself as contributing to response results. She cautions against taking users' judgments at face value or inferring users' satisfaction from single responses.

Even if methodological problems were resolved, at least one author suggests that the measurement and evaluation of search results is not always subject to purely rational processes. Marcia J. Bates argues that both the searchers and the user may make erroneous assumptions in arriving at their assessments. For the searcher this may stem from a mental model of a "perfect" search—one that consists of thirty items regardless of topic, user needs, or actual number of relevant documents in the database. The user, on the other hand, may be unaware of the trade-offs between precision and recall, the complexities of indexing, and the limits of Boolean logic. Dazzled by the sophistication of the technology, users may harbor greater expectations of the online system that it can in fact deliver. Bates explores the underlying causes of these fallacies and proposes techniques that can be employed to overcome or avoid them.

The measurement and evaluation of online reference services continue to be more impressionistic than scientific. The Additional Readings exemplify some of the attempts made at coming to grips with a baffling puzzle whose solution remains elusive.

Evaluation of Online Searches

Richard W. Blood

INTRODUCTION

Similarities exist between efforts to evaluate traditional reference and online services. For less than a decade, online services have been offered by libraries, and most key concerns relating to the provision of this service—hardware, database aids, training of search intermediaries, publicity, etc.—have been studied. As is the case with respect to traditional reference services, however, the evaluation of online services is generally nonexistent or suffers from ambiguous goals, questionable methodology, and poor survey instruments.

The surge of interest in online services in the 1970s caught most reference librarians unprepared to plan for and apply online technology to the delivery of information services. Reference librarians were eager to participate, however, in the Machine-Assisted Reference Services (MARS) Discussion Group formed in 1976 within the Reference and Adult Services Division (RASD) of the American Library Association. At the Annual Conference of ALA in 1977, Peter Watson presented a petition, with the required 250 signatures, for MARS section status within RASD to the RASD Board of Directors, which voted unanimously in favor.[1]

MARS members quickly identified measurement and evaluation as areas of key concern. As early as the third issue of *Messages from MARS*, the section newsletter, Sally Knapp, chair of the MARS Section, noted growing interest in: "What statistics are being kept on computer-based reference services? What should be counted? How do you analyze what you count? How could better statistics help you to manage your services better?"[2]

MARS COMMITTEE ON EVALUATION OF SERVICES

Achievement of section status for MARS permitted formation of committees to study issues in online searching of interest to the MARS

Reprinted by permission of the American Library Association from *RQ* 22(3):266-77 (Spring 1983); © 1983 by the American Library Association.

membership. At the 1978 Annual Conference of ALA an Ad Hoc Committee on Evaluation of Services was formed to study measurement and evaluation concerns. The preliminary statement of objectives indicated that the committee was "to develop criteria, instruments, and procedures to measure the quantity and evaluate the quality of computer based reference services provided by libraries."[3]

After the 1978 Annual Conference of ALA, the ad hoc committee was split into two separate committees: a Committee on Measurement of Services and a Committee on Evaluation of Services. The Measurement Committee was charged with studying quantitative measurements of service; the Evaluation Committee was charged with studying qualitative evaluations of service.

The specific charge made to the MARS Evaluation Committee was "to collect, analyze, and disseminate to the MARS membership information on qualitative evaluations of service and uses to which such evaluations can be put, to recommend criteria, instruments, and procedures for performing such evaluations."[4]

PROCESS OF EVALUATING ONLINE SERVICES

The recommended search evaluation form that appears as appendix A must be understood within the context of the total process for evaluating online services. This process consists of five sequential steps. First, the goals of evaluation must be identified, clearly stated, and measurable. The "why to evaluate" and the "what to evaluate" suggest operational aspects of the "how to evaluate"; that is, the goals of evaluation guide the design of the evaluation form and the procedures for the evaluation. Evaluation forms in general use in libraries suffer from ambiguity in evaluation goals.

Second, after the goals for evaluation are clearly stated, the evaluation form and methodology must be designed to collect, within cost constraints of the program, the evaluative feedback from users needed to assess progress toward the goals of the evaluation program.

Third, the actual evaluation program must be conducted. Evaluation must not be regarded as a one-time study, but rather as a continuing program for monitoring quality in the delivery of online services. Evaluation must be undertaken on a continuing basis to measure the effects of changes in service policies and procedures.

Fourth, evaluation results must be analyzed and interpreted to ascertain causes of poor search results and modifications that might be made in any aspect of the service to expedite attainment of evaluation goals.

Fifth, the modifications suggested by the analysis and interpretation of evaluation results must be implemented. The process of evaluating online service consists of not fewer than these five steps. The evaluation program is merely an intellectual exercise if it fails to implement modifications to improve the overall performance of online services.

GOALS FOR EVALUATING ONLINE SERVICES

Evaluation of online services should produce two types of data: "performance figures for a representative group of searches" *and* "examples of system failures to allow analysis of causes of failure."[5] F. W. Lancaster argues that evaluation

> involves analytical procedures whereby the major sources of system failure are identified, thus allowing corrective action to be taken to raise the performance level of the system. . . . Evaluation is essentially a diagnostic procedure which, like other forms of diagnosis, is intended to lead to *therapeutic* action. An evaluation program, hopefully, is not conducted merely as an intellectual exercise. Thorough evaluation tends to be expensive, and can only be justified if the evaluation program is likely to lead to significant improvement in the performance of the system.[6]

The Evaluation Committee feels that the primary goal of evaluating online services is to identify and analyze instances of poor search results and user dissatisfaction and to ascertain the modifications that can be made to improve the performance of online services. The committee also recognizes, however, that managers of online services might have other administrative goals for surveying users of online services; one of these administrative goals, for instance, might be the need to obtain data from users to justify budgetary and staffing resources committed to the online program. In the interest of keeping the recommended evaluation form as short and simple as possible to encourage good response rates from users, the questions included reflect only diagnostic goals for evaluation.

Managers of online services should include whatever other questions on their evaluation forms that are needed to attain other administrative goals for evaluating online services. Chapter three of Don Dillman's *Mail and Telephone Surveys* (New York: Wiley, 1978) discusses general principles for writing questions for survey questionnaires.

LEVELS OF EVALUATION

F.W. Lancaster defines three levels of evaluation: effectiveness, cost-effectiveness, and cost-benefits evaluation. *Effectiveness* is defined as "evaluation of system performance in terms of the degree to which it meets user requirements." *Cost-effectiveness* is defined as "evaluation in terms of how to satisfy user requirements in the most efficient and economical fashion." *Cost-benefits evaluation* is defined as "evaluation of the worth of the system (i.e., is the system worthwhile, does it justify its existence?)."[7] Owing to methodological problems in measuring costs in different library environments and benefits to users from online services, the committee's work emphasizes evaluation at the level of effectiveness.

PERFORMANCE CRITERIA FOR EVALUATION

Four major dimensions of the effectiveness of online searches are commonly identified: recall, precision or relevance, user effort, and response time.[8] These dimensions of evaluation constitute performance criteria that should be measured by users of online services. Most of the questions included on the recommended search evaluation form elicit feedback of diagnostic value regarding these four performance criteria.

DEFINITION OF THE ONLINE SEARCH

The MARS Measurement Committee defines the online search as "the interactive access by computer to as many databases as the searcher considers necessary to conclude the search."[9] In accord with this definition, "an online search accessing five databases to answer one query would be counted as one search, not five."[10] Since the MARS Evaluation Committee and the MARS Measurement Committee agreed to cooperate closely, not to duplicate each other's work, and to follow, wherever possible, each other's recommendations, the MARS Evaluation Committee accepts this definition of the online search for use with the search evaluation form.

If access to three databases is required to process a single search request, for example, the user would ordinarily receive a search output consisting of document surrogates (e.g. citations, abstracts) from three databases, but should be given only one evaluation form and be asked to evaluate overall the combined search output from the three databases, instead of being asked to evaluate separately the search results from each of the three databases.

USES OF EVALUATION FORM

The recommended evaluation form, however, cannot be used to evaluate all types of online searches consistent with the definition of the online search as recommended by the MARS Measurement Committee.

The recommended evaluation form should be used primarily to evaluate retrospective searches of document surrogate databases (e.g. ERIC, BIOSIS, etc.) performed by a search intermediary to satisfy a request for information involving unknown items.

Managers of online search services require systematic collection of information, using an integrated system of forms. The major forms used in the management of online search services are: search request form, search strategy work sheet, search log, and search evaluation form. Each form is designed to compile data for a particular use at a successive step in the progression of a search from the presentation of the request to the provision of evaluative data on the results of the search by the user.

The search evaluation form is generally the last form related to the processing of a search request. Since the goals of the search request, the search strategy work sheet, and the search log are clear and fairly similar from one library to another, the content of these forms is similar from library to library. In marked contrast to the goals for these three forms, the goals for evaluating searches are often ambiguous and not explicitly stated; the content of the evaluation form, therefore, predictably varies more from one library to another than in the case of the other forms. In relation to the great ambiguity and confusion in the goals for evaluating online searches, however, the search evaluation forms in common use are more similar than would be expected—probably the result of libraries copying or modeling their evaluation forms on those of other libraries.

DESIGN OF EVALUATION FORM

Unlike the other three major forms, the search evaluation form is rarely completed by or with the assistance of the search intermediary, but instead by the user following examination of search results consisting of document surrogates. Two major considerations for the design of the search evaluation form stem from its completion by the user, rather than by the search intermediary.

Motivating Users

First, users must be sufficiently motivated to take time to read, complete, and return the evaluation form. Motivating users to complete or assist in the completion of the search request form is not ordinarily a problem because this form is completed at a time when users still have an information need that is expected to be satisfied by the use of the online service. In other words, users regard completion of the request form as simply one of the necessary efforts to use the service. Motivating users to complete the evaluation form, however, is a major problem because the form is completed after the information need has been presumably satisfied; consequently, satisfaction of the information need is not affected by failure to complete the evaluation form.

Users can be motivated to read, complete, and return the evaluation form by keeping it as short and simple as possible. A long evaluation form intimidates users, reduces response rates, and increases the effort of users in using the service; this consideration is germane, for user effort is consistently identified as a major performance criterion in the evaluation of information services.

Since the evaluation form is only one form of an integrated set of forms used to collect different data at successive stages in a search, all the data required to analyze and interpret responses on the evaluation form and ascertain causes of failure in the service need not be collected on the evaluation form. A search number should be assigned to each search request form and used on all subsequent forms—search strategy work sheet, search log, and evaluation form—to link together the total data compiled on a search. If the evaluation form does not provide diagnostic data sufficient to analyze the cause of a poorly rated search, the search linkage number recorded on the evaluation form can be used to locate other search forms completed for the same search to allow examination of other data that may help ascertain the cause of poor performance and system failure. For this reason, most of the questions recommended for the search evaluation form focus on the user's evaluation of search results, especially in relation to the major performance criteria.

Users can also be motivated to complete and return the evaluation form by making its completion and return as convenient as possible. Fixed response categories are recommended for most questions, allowing users simply to check the category that best describes their response. The form should allow for easy return to the search service by including a pre-addressed envelope or by making the form self-mailing. If return of the evaluation form through the U.S. mail is required, the envelope or self-mailing form should be pre-stamped.

Phrasing of Questions

The second design consideration stemming from completion of the evaluation form by the user, rather than by the search intermediary, is the need to phrase questions appropriately, with special emphasis on using language understandable to most users. The search evaluation form must be free from the jargon of information science and online searching; terms such as *document surrogates, recall ratio,* and *false drops* are meaningless to most users and must not be used on the evaluation form.

COMMENTARY ON RECOMMENDED EVALUATION FORM

The search evaluation form recommended by the MARS Evaluation Committee appears as appendix A. Developing an evaluation form and presenting it as a recommendation, without accompanying commentary, would fall short of the committee's charge. This approach would also deprive others of the valuable discussions regarding the selection and phrasing of questions on the evaluation form. The following commentary does not record the full debate on each question, but it is sufficiently complete to reflect the consensus rationale used to select and phrase each question.

Purpose of the Survey

Users are more likely to complete and return a questionnaire when informed of the purpose of the survey; at the head of the evaluation form appears, therefore, the statement: "In order to evaluate and improve computerized literature search services, we would appreciate your taking a few moments to complete and return this questionnaire." The name or acronym of the online service may be substituted for "computerized literature search service." To this basic statement eliciting user co-operation, other statements may be added to encourage users to respond to the questionnaire or to provide local instructions on the return of the questionnaire.

Search Number

Staff of the online service must record the "search number" on the evaluation form before it is distributed to the user with search results. The search number must match the number assigned to the search on the corresponding request form and subsequently recorded on all additional forms completed for the search. The search number uniquely identifies each online search and links all search forms completed for a search, making available for analysis and interpretation the total data compiled on a search from the request to the evaluation stage. The search number is also used to eliminate anonymous respondents from the telephone follow-up of nonrespondents.

Anonymity of Respondents

If some users want to remain anonymous, they may be given the option of withholding their names on the evaluation form. Inclusion of a unique number on a questionnaire does not permit the respondent to remain completely anonymous, for the search number can be used to reveal identity by obtaining the respondent's name from the search request form bearing the same search number. Since each evaluation form must contain the search number, a statement needs to be added indicating that the search number is used to identify nonrespondents for subsequent follow-up by telephone and is not used to reveal the identity of respondents returning questionnaires completed anonymously. To encourage users to be completely frank in completing the evaluation form, a statement is also added that promises to keep responses "strictly confidential" whether or not respondents choose to remain anonymous.

User Identification Data

The next section on the evaluation form asks for user identification data: name, address, telephone number, and status. The telephone number is particularly important to permit telephone follow-up of users whose responses on the evaluation form are apparently contradictory, ambiguous, or otherwise difficult to analyze and interpret. Although the telephone number can be obtained from the corresponding request form, inclusion of the telephone number on the evaluation form permits telephone follow-up without referring to the corresponding request form.

Users are also asked to check a response category indicating their status. Since status categories of users vary by type of library, an online service should list categories that cover most potential users. The status of the user is included on the evaluation form, despite its frequent appearance on the request form, because of its diagnostic value in interpreting evaluation results. Some user identification data recorded on the search request form are repeated on the evaluation form to expedite analysis and interpretation of evaluation results by limiting the need to refer to the original request form.

The rest of the commentary discusses each of the ten queries included on the recommended evaluation form; question numbers correspond to those on the recommended evaluation form (see appendix A).

Question 1

What was your main purpose in requesting this search? In other words, at the time you submitted your search request, what had you planned to do with the results?

The evaluation form emphasizes evaluation at the level of effectiveness—that is, evaluation of search results by the user in the context of the purpose for which the search was requested. Consequently, a response to this question is essential to interpret responses to other questions.

A question regarding the purpose of the search is often included on the search request form to help formulate effective search strategy; this question is also appropriate for the evaluation form to expedite analysis of responses to the rest of the questions without having, in every instance, to refer to the original search request form through use of the search linkage number.

Another reason for including this question on the evaluation form is that it requires users to think about the purpose of the search before responding to any other questions. By asking this question first, the appropriate context is established for evaluation of search results—that is, this question encourages users to evaluate search results and answer the rest of the questions in the context of the purpose for which the search request was made.

Listing response categories appropriate for all types of libraries and users would needlessly extend the list of response categories. Response categories listed for this question should be locally phrased and include the purposes responsible for most of the search requests submitted to a specific online service. Response categories for the academic library might include: "research for an undergraduate term paper," "research for a graduate seminar paper," "research for an M.A. or M.S. thesis," "research for a doctoral dissertation," etc. Response categories for the public library would differ from those appropriate for an academic or special library. The response categories can be made as inclusive as possible, without forcing the user to respond by checking a related, but not entirely appropriate, category by including the category "Other? (specify)_____" as the last response option for this question.

Question 2

Was the purpose of this search to determine that no previous work had been done on this topic?

Most users submitting search requests want to retrieve document surrogates relevant to a purpose. Some users, however, submit search requests to determine that no previous work has been done on the topic of the request. Users investigating topics for doctoral dissertations, users investigating topics on the "research frontier" or at the "cutting edge of scientific knowledge," and users searching the existence of a patent often request searches in the expectation—and in the hope—of retrieving no published work. This question is included to avoid misinterpretation of apparently "negative" search results noted by the respondents.

Question 3

Does this search provide enough relevant citations for the purpose for which you submitted the search request?

This question asks whether or not the level of recall of the search results is adequate for the purpose for which the search request was made. Although a few users need a comprehensive search retrieving as many relevant citations as possible, most users need search results that provide enough relevant citations for the purpose for which the search request was made. Most users have an intuitive feeling for the number of relevant citations that they require to accomplish their purposes within their time and cost constraints.

The response category "No, but didn't expect to see anything" is included to expedite analysis of data from users submitting search requests to determine that no previously published work had been done. The "please comment" annotation is attached to the simple "No" response to encourage users to comment when not enough relevant citations are retrieved. It is anticipated that some users responding "No" to this question can provide commentary of diagnostic value that can be used to improve recall levels of future searches.

Question 4

Among the total citations provided by this search, what percentage appears relevant to the specific question or topic for which you submitted a search request?

A measure of recall by itself is meaningless without an accompanying measure of relevance or precision, for total recall can always be achieved by simply printing out the contents of the entire database. Questions regarding relevance or precision measure the filtering power of the search strategy—that is, the capability of the search strategy to retrieve enough relevant citations and simultaneously prevent retrieval of too many "false drops" or citations not relevant to the purpose of the search. Although "precision" terminology has replaced "relevance" terminology in discussions of relevance in information science, the term *relevant* is used, in this and other questions, because to users *relevant* is a more meaningful term than *precise*.

This question asks users to judge the relevance of the search results with respect "to the specific question or topic" for which the search request was made and *not* with respect to the overall information need. The output of any online search can be fairly evaluated only in terms of the specific question posed for retrieval.

Five response categories are included for this question. The first category (0 percent) is included to accommodate a specific response when search results do not provide any relevant citations. The remaining four response categories are ranges of uniform size, are mutually exclusive, and account for the entire range of possibilities. Inclusion of more than five response categories would increase users' efforts in responding to this question without adding much useful diagnostic data. Also, users may not be able to estimate the sufficiency of search results more precisely.

Question 5

Among the total citations provided by this search, what percentage appears relevant to your overall information need, rather than simply relevant to the specific question submitted as a search topic or question?

This question asks users to judge the relevance of the search results not just with respect to the specific topic of the search request, but in terms of their overall information need; it asks users to broaden their judgment of relevance. These two concepts of relevance—relevance to the specific search topic and to the overall information need—are quite distinct. Citations not relevant to the question posed in the search request may be relevant to the overall information need. Some users will probably fail to understand the distinction between this and the preceding question, a misunderstanding, which might, unfortunately, require telephone follow-up to clarify the distinction sufficiently to permit valid analysis.

As noted in the commentary on the previous question, relevance to the specific question posed for retrieval must be the basis for judging the performance of online searches, not relevance to the overall information need. Citations not directly relevant to the specific question posed for retrieval, but still relevant to the overall information need, nonetheless, contribute to the satisfaction of users; the response to this question may be useful, therefore, in analyzing and interpreting responses to other questions on the evaluation form.

The five identical response categories included for the previous question are included for this question to ensure comparability between responses to these two questions measuring two valid concepts of relevance. If users understand the distinction between this and the previous question, the response category checked for this question should be in a percentage range as high or higher than the percentage range checked as the response to the question concerning relevance to the specific topic of the search request, because relevance to the overall information need is a more inclusive concept than is relevance to the specific topic of the search request. In other words, citations relevant to the search topic are also relevant to the overall information need, but citations relevant to the overall information need may not be relevant to the specific question posed by the search request.

Question 6

Among the relevant citations provided by this search, what percentage is new to you, or, in other words, was unknown to you at the time you examined the search results?

This question asks users to judge the novelty of the relevant citations retrieved by the search by asking for the percentage of the relevant citations that were previously unknown. An online search cannot be fairly evaluated on the basis of whether or not the relevant citations retrieved were previously unknown, but the retrieval of relevant and previously unknown citations is of primary importance to users and is expected, therefore, to affect significantly their overall evaluation of search results. The five response categories included for this question are comparable to those included for the two previous questions, and the same comments regarding them pertain here in the context of this third measure of relevance that incorporates the concept of novelty.

Question 7

Do you feel that the citations that are both relevant and previously unknown to you are worth the cost that you paid for the search?

This question elicits a general "Yes" or "No" response as to whether or not the relevant and previously unknown citations are worth the cost paid for the search. F. W. Lancaster refers to this aspect of an online search as the "novelty-cost ratio."[11] Obtaining an adequate number of relevant and previously unknown citations at a reasonable cost is the goal of most users in submitting requests for online searches. Users that check "No" as the response to this question are further asked to "please comment" in the hope of eliciting comments of diagnostic value. If users are not charged for online searches, this question should be omitted from the evaluation form, or modified to read: "worth the time and effort you spent on the search."

Question 8

Was the time lapse between submitting your search request and receiving your search results reasonable?

This question elicits an overall "Yes" or "No" judgment as to whether or not the time lapse was reasonable between submission of the search request and the receipt of the search results. This question is germane to the evaluation of online services because the response time of information retrieval systems is consistently identified in the literature as a major performance criterion in evaluation. Users that check "No" as the response to this question are further asked to "please comment" in the hope of eliciting comments of diagnostic value regarding timeliness in the delivery of online services.

Question 9

Were the results of the search of value to you?

This broad question elicits a comprehensive judgment on the overall value of the search results. The response to this question is often of key value in analyzing and interpreting responses to more specific questions. Responses to more specific questions may seem to indicate a positive or negative evaluation in isolation, but that interpretation must be related to the overall evaluation of search results. Users that check "No" as the response to this question are further asked to "please comment," again in hope of eliciting comments of diagnostic value.

Question 10

The major reason for the Search Evaluation Questionnaire is to obtain your comments and suggestions for improving the computerized literature searching service. If you have suggestions as to how any aspect of the search services can be improved, please comment in detail.

While the nine preceding questions elicit comments regarding search results, this broad question elicits comments and suggestions regarding any aspect of the online service. Deliberately broad and non-suggestive, this question encourages users to comment on any aspect of the service needing improvement. In response to this question, users can comment on aspects as diverse as the pricing policy for online services, the value of the user's presence or absence during the online session, the desirability of offline versus online printing of search results, the assistance received from the search intermediary, etc. This question elicits comments from users that may be of diagnostic value to the criteria for evaluating online services.

QUESTIONS EXCLUDED FROM THE EVALUATION FORM

The standard for inclusion of a question on the recommended evaluation form is whether or not is is likely to elicit meaningful and useful responses indicative of the user's evaluation of search results in terms of four major performance criteria—recall, relevance, user effort, and response time—that would suggest user satisfaction or dissatisfaction with online services and, most importantly, identify instances of search failures. Poorly rated searches are then to be analyzed to determine whether or not modifications are needed in policies, procedures, hardware, search strategies, training of search intermediaries, etc., to increase overall performance levels of future searches. Another requirement for a question to be included on this evaluation form is whether or not it can better be asked on another search form, especially the search request form. The intent is to keep the evaluation form as short as possible to minimize the effort of users in complying with evaluation and to encourage a good return rate for the questionnaire.

Each type of question found on evaluation forms in general use in libraries was discussed as a potential candidate for inclusion on the recommended evaluation form. The following commentary explains why some questions found on evaluation forms in general use are excluded from the recommended evaluation form.

User Awareness of Online Services

A question excluded from the recommended evaluation form asks how the user found out about online services. This question is meaningful, for it provides data to evaluate alternate channels for publicizing the availability of online services. This question needs to be asked on the search request form, however, because users are more likely to remember the communications medium responsible for their finding out about online services at the time the search request is made, rather than at a later time when the search results are evaluated.

Previous Use of Online Services.

Another question excluded from the recommended evaluation form asks users about their previous use of online services. Since the expectations that users have of any information system are conditioned by their past experiences with the system, experienced users of online services are likely to set different standards of performance than new users. This question is meaningful, therefore, in interpreting evaluative feedback from users, but it can easily be asked on the search request form.

Comparisons with Manual Searches

Another question excluded from the recommended evaluation form asks users to compare one or more aspects of the online search to a hypothetical manual search done on the same topic. Most commonly, users are asked how the number of relevant citations produced by the online search would compare with the number produced by a manual search, or they are asked how much time was saved by having an online search made in lieu of their having done the search manually. These questions lack diagnostic value relative to the criteria for evaluating online services. Another reason for excluding these questions is that, in most instances, an online search obviates the need for a manual search on the topic, making these questions meaningless, for users lack any basis on which to answer them.

Evaluation of the Search Intermediary

Another question commonly asked on evaluation forms in general use, but excluded from the recommended evaluation form, asks users to evaluate one or more aspects of their interaction with the search intermediary; most commonly, this type of question asks users to evaluate the assistance received from the search intermediary. Many attributes of the search intermediary significantly affect the quality of search results and the level of satisfaction with online services; however, most users lack expertise to evaluate assistance received from the search intermediary. Search intermediaries are best evaluated by supervisors and peers as well as through use of self-evaluation techniques. The last question included on the recommended evaluation form is broad enough, however, to allow users to comment on the assistance received from the search intermediary.

Format of Document Surrogates

Another type of question excluded from the recommended evaluation form asks about some aspect of the format of the document surrogates retrieved by the online search; most commonly, this question asks users to evaluate the assistance provided by citations or abstracts in judging the relevance of published works to the purpose of the search. Responses to this question are of diagnostic value in instances of one database access to satisfy a search request, where users receive only citations or only citations with abstracts. With the increasing number of multiple database accesses made to satisfy a single search request, however, responses to questions regarding format of document surrogates are difficult to interpret owing to the different levels of information provided by document surrogates retrieved from accesses to multiple databases.

SOURCE OF ADDITIONAL INFORMATION

The focus of this article has been the online search evaluation form developed by the Machine-Assisted Reference Section Committee on Measurement and Evaluation of Service.[12] For additional information on the evaluation of online searches, consult the report by Richard W. Blood entitled "Evaluation of Online Searches," which will be available from the Educational Resources Information Center (ERIC) in 1983.

The ERIC report contains recommendations for sampling users of online search services and discusses sample size, sampling techniques, and the procedures for follow-up of survey respondents and non-respondents. The report also includes an extended discussion on the analysis and interpretation of the search evaluation form and the implementation of modifications to online services resulting from the evaluation process.

Footnotes

1. "MARS Achieves Section Status!" *Messages from Mars*, no. 3 (Sept. 1977), p. 1.
2. Sally Knapp, "From the Terminal of the Chair," *Messages from MARS*, no. 3 (Sept. 1977), p. 5.
3. "Committee on Evaluation of Services: Preliminary Statement of Objectives," *Messages from MARS*, no. 5 (March 1978), p. 3.
4. Machine-Assisted Reference Section Executive Committee, "Charge to the MARS Committee on Evaluation of Services," 1978. (Mimeographed.)
5. Frederick W. Lancaster, "Evaluation and Testing of Information Retrieval Systems," in *Encyclopedia of Library and Information Science*, vol. 8, eds. Allen Kent and Harold Lancour (New York: Marcel Dekker, 1972), p. 240.
6. Ibid., p. 234.
7. Ibid.
8. Frederick W. Lancaster, *The Measurement and Evaluation of Library Services* (Washington, D.C.: Information Resources Press, 1977), p. 146.
9. Donald T. Hawkins and Carolyn P. Brown, "What is an Online Search?" *Online* 4 (Jan. 1980):13.
10. Ibid., p. 14.
11. Lancaster, *Measurement and Evaluation*, p. 141.
12. After the MARS Committee on Evaluation of Services completed its recommended search evaluation form, it merged in 1982 with the MARS Committee on Measurement of Services to form the MARS Committee on Measurement and Evaluation of Service.

APPENDIX A: SEARCH EVALUATION QUESTIONNAIRE

Recommended by ALA/RASD/MARS Committee on
Measurement and Evaluation of Service

In order to evaluate and improve computerized literature search services, we would appreciate your taking a few moments to complete and return this questionnaire.

Search number _____

Since only a limited sample of users is asked to evaluate the results of their computerized literature searches, the validity of the sample results depends on subsequent follow-up of nonrespondents. The search number was entered by a member of the library staff in order to identify users who return their questionnaires and to eliminate them from a subsequent telephone follow-up of nonrespondents. If you prefer to complete and return this questionnaire without indicating your name in order to remain anonymous, the search number will *not* be used to identify your response. Whether or not you choose to remain anonymous, your response will be kept strictly confidential.

Name: _____

Address: _____

Telephone number(s): _____

Status: (Categories vary by type of library—local option phrasing)

    e.g. *Academic Library*:   Faculty _____   Graduate student _____

                          Undergraduate _____   Staff _____

                          Other (specify) _____

    e.g. *Special Library*:

                          Administrator _____ Salesman _____

                          Laboratory technician _____

                          Other (specify) _____

1. What was your main purpose in requesting this search? In other words, at the time you submitted your search request, what had you planned to do with the results?
   (Local option—provide list of possible responses, e.g. term paper, Ph.D. dissertation, faculty research, grant proposal, etc.)
2. Was the purpose of this search to determine that no previous work had been done on this topic?
   Yes _____   No _____
3. Does this search provide enough *relevant* citations for the purpose for which you submitted the search request?
   Yes _____
   No, but didn't expect to see anything _____
   No (please comment) _____
4. Among the total citations provided by this search, what percentage appears *relevant* to the specific question or topic for which you submitted a search request?
   0% _____
   1 to 25% _____
   26 to 50% _____
   51 to 75% _____
   76 to 100% _____
5. Among the total citations provided by this search, what percentage appears *relevant* to your overall information need, rather than simply relevant to the specific question submitted as a search topic or question?
   0% _____
   1 to 25% _____
   26 to 50% _____
   51 to 75% _____
   76 to 100% _____
6. Among the *relevant* citations provided by this search, what percentage is new to you, or, in other words, was unknown to you at the time you examined the search results?
   0% of the *relevant* citations are new to me _____
   1 to 25% of the *relevant* citations are new to me _____
   26 to 50% of the *relevant* citations are new to me _____

      51 to 75% of the *relevant* citations are new to me _____

      76 to 100% of the *relevant* citations are new to me _____

7. Do you feel that the citations that are both *relevant* and previously *unknown* to you are worth the cost that you paid for the search?

      Yes _____   No _____

      If "No," please comment:

      (Optional question—may be omitted if library does not charge)

8. Was the time lapse between submitting your search request and receiving your search results reasonable?

      Yes _____   No _____

      If "No," please comment:

9. Were the results of the search of value to you?

      Yes _____   No _____

      If "No," please comment:

10. The major reason for the Search Evaluation Questionnaire is to obtain your comments and suggestions for improving the computerized literature searching service. If you have suggestions as to how *any aspect* of the search service can be improved, please comment *in detail*:

Selecting Measures Applicable to Evaluation of Online Literature Searching

Eileen E. Hitchingham

INTRODUCTION

Advances in online computer technology, the expansion of time-sharing networks, and the advent of commercial vendors of bibliographic databases have made it increasingly possible, in both a technical and an economic sense, for libraries and information centers to consider an additional option for service. This service is the provision of machine-generated bibliographies tailored to the specific information needs of individual users. The bibliographies are the product of online, interactive searches of one or more databases. Libraries can now search several million bibliographic citations in a relatively short time with the installation of a terminal and communication linkage. Subject fields available for searching range from the physical and social sciences to the humanities.

Interest in providing online search services is high. The Reference and Adult Services Division of The American Library Association has formed a special discussion group on Machine-Assisted Reference Services (MARS).[1] System Development Corporation, one of the online database vendors, has published the results of a study of the impact of online database use. Their survey questionnaire drew responses from 472 user institutions. Categorized by type, libraries responding included those in academic (30.7 percent), business (32.2 percent), government (21.3 percent), and other (15.7 percent) sectors.[2] While public libraries are less likely to be current users of online search systems, there are indications that expansion of this service to public libraries would be welcomed by users. Seventy percent of responding users in the Lockheed DIALOG

Reprinted with permission of the author from *Drexel Library Quarterly* 13 (July 1977): 52-67.

public library experiment found the searches they received to be of major or considerable value.[3]

For some libraries provision of bibliographies for individual users is not a new service, only the mode of searching (online rather than manual) has changed. This is particularly true for a number of special libraries which have established a long history of individualized services to users. In most libraries, however, the product of online searching—bibliographies for an individual consumer—represents an additional rather than a replacement service. Libraries, especially academic and public, have heretofore perceived their role to be one of helping the user to help himself in doing bibliographic searches. In offering online search services librarians have been thrust into a direct production role rather than that of the provision of auxiliary services. This production analogy may prove useful in considering measures applicable to the evaluation of online literature searching.

THE NEED FOR MEASURES

Measurement pursued for its own sake is a purposeless activity. In initiating a measurement program we imply that there are questions to be answered and decisions to be made. If there are no questions concerning the provision of online services there is no point in measuring service activities. However, the absence of questions concerning online services is unlikely.

One question—whether an online searching service should be initiated by a library—falls outside the scope of this paper. The decision to implement online search services appears to rest more upon philosophical foundations than upon demonstrated evidence from a user population that there is a need for such a service. In fact, one of the commitments that should be recognized in initiating online services is the need for active promotion of system capabilities. Capital Systems Group, studying the feasibility of marketing bibliographic database products, indicated that "research administrators and active researchers showed themselves almost totally unaware of computerized databases in their major fields of interest."[4]

Once an online search service is initiated by a library it is assumed that objectives, even if vaguely articulated, exist for the service. Clarification of these objectives is a necessary first step in selecting measures for evaluating the online search operation. Two factors affect the formulation of objectives: the economic base which supports the online search system, and the viewpoint from which the objectives are formulated (manager, manager/user, user). We can consider at least five configurations by which online searching might be financed:

1. The searching operation is partially or totally subsidized by an agency external to the library.
2. The library absorbs all costs of the search service.
3. Costs of online searching are shared by the library and the user.
4. Total searching costs are borne by the user.
5. The searching institution recovers all costs from the user and seeks a profit from the search operation.

While examples of online operations financed by each mode may be located, and several libraries may have passed through developmental stages in which a number of modes have supported their service, the majority of libraries today appear to operate under the third configuration: costs are shared by the library and the user. Costs most often assumed by the user are the direct costs associated with searching—offline printing, computer connect time, and communication costs.[5] If this is an accurate reflection of current online search operations, it seems that two viewpoints must be represented in system objectives, the manager's viewpoint and the user's viewpoint. Modifying Miles definition of value,[6] it is possible to formulate one encompassing objective for online search systems appropriate to both managers and users: To provide online searches at the lowest cost consistent with those qualities and specifications that the user wants.

However, since the library providing the online search service is supporting certain costs—staff time, terminal rental or purchase, overhead—the manager of the library has made a decision to allocate resources to a particular service function. He or she chooses this function over the many possible competing library functions to which these resources might be directed (collection building, support staff for reshelving of materials, etc.). From the manager's viewpoint then, we can consider an additional objective for the online search system: To provide a service with benefits equal to or greater than those benefits that would be achieved by allocating the resources committed to online search operations to other service functions.

If we accept these objectives, albeit broadly stated, as appropriate for libraries providing online services, we are led to those measures outlined by King and Bryant for determining the extent to which system objectives are met—cost, effectiveness, and benefits.[7] Returning to the production analogy mentioned previously, it is possible to frame several questions applicable to measurement activities:

1. What is the cost of the product? (Cost)
2. What is the quality of the product? (Effectiveness)
3. Can the level of production be improved? (Cost-Effectiveness)
4. Should production be continued? (Benefits)

Measures responsive to these questions will be discussed in the following sections.

COST

Cuadra indicates that one of the preliminary questions raised prior to contracting for online services is "Can I afford it?"[8] Where costs are shared the question of cost is important to both managers and users. In considering average cost per online search as reported in the literature (Table 1), several components of the cost question become apparent. Determination of average cost (and credibility of reported figures) depends upon the extent to which all constituent factors have been isolated. Recognition of salary cost—time spent in preparation, interviewing, online searching, and reviewing of results—is an important part of cost determination since this is an area that may merit further investigation when the question of improvement of operations is considered. The four reports discussed below, from the eleven outlined in Table 1, reflect a substantial number of searches (100 or more) and a recognition of salary as a component cost. However, each differs in the situation for which cost is being measured, so that direct comparison is not possible.

Standera reports costs associated with one month of online searching for SDI purposes.[9] It appears that all other costs reported in Table 1 were for retrospective searches. Costs indicated by Standera include salaries for profiling, training, screening, mailing, handling, and typing; network costs; computer connect time; terminal depreciation; communication lines; and offline prints. This is the only report indicating cost per "hit," i.e., for each item retrieved, at $0.39, as well as average cost per search.

Jestes's figures reflect four months of involvement with a single online system (CAIN): one month for start-up costs (planning) and three months of actual searching.[21] Planning costs include time spent investigating terminals, ordering a phone and terminal, developing data and evaluation forms, developing promotional materials, and learning search procedures. Salary costs in this first planning month are based upon approximately 90 hours spent in these activities. Costs associated with the second through fourth months include those for personnel time (management of service, training searchers, searching time, clerical time for mailing and other functions), equipment and supplies (phone installation, monthly phone bill, terminal rental, terminal paper, printing of announcements); and actual computer searching costs (connect time for searches, demonstration connect time, and offline prints). The value reported in Table 1 is based upon all of the preceding costs. Jestes indicates that average cash flow per completed search was $14.

Cooper and DeWath investigated costs associated with online searching in four public libraries participating in the NSF-Lockheed

TABLE 1   Average Search Costs—Online

Average Cost	No. of Searches	Data Base(s) Searched	Costs Included						Source (chronological by publication date)
			Salaries	Computer Connect Time	Terminal	Communication (time-sharing and/or phone)	Off-line prints	Indirect costs	
$13.00	?	F		X	X	X	X		Wanger[10]
9.50	100	?	X	X	X	X	X	X	Standera[11]
31.00	237	C	X	X	X	X	X	X	Jestes[12]
12.00-33.00	164	D,F,K		X	X	X	X		Lawrence[13]
47.00	66	?	X	X	X	X	X	X	Elman[14]
74.55	111	C-F, H-K, N-P	X	X	X	X	X	X	Benenfeld[15]
12.00	?	F		X	X	?	X		Hock[16]
6.44	56	D		X			X		Linepensel[17]
36.29	82	A-G, I-P		X		X	X		Atwood[18]
28.41	411	A, C-G, I-K, M-N, P	X	X			X		Cooper[19]
44.04	604*	B-F, H-P +others		X		X	X		Hawkins[20]

*604 sessions at 2 sessions/search

A AIM - ARM
B BIOSIS
C CAIN
D CHEMCON
E COMPENDEX
F ERIC
G EXCEPT. CHILD ABSTRACTS
H GEOREF
I INFORM
J INSPEC
K NTIS
L POL. ABSTRACTS
M PREDICASTS
N PSYCH. ABSTRACTS
O SCI. SEARCH
P SOCIAL SCI. SEARCH

DIALIB project.[22] Costs identified are based upon personnel time involved from the point of initial user contact through follow-up of the search with the user, plus costs for computer connect time and offline prints. Seven tasks were identified as constituents of the salary component, although all tasks were not necessarily carried out for each search conducted. Tasks included the reference interview, originating library preparation (applicable for several branch libraries which sent searches to a main library for search processing), preparation time at actual searching library, search time, follow-up time at library conducting the search, originating library follow-up (once again applicable in branch libraries with no terminal), and follow-up with the patron requesting the search. Terminal rental, physical space charges, and indirect costs of overhead, administration and supplies were not computed for this study. Across the four libraries significant differences were noted for the time involved with three tasks, the reference interview, the online search, and the search follow-up. Online searching times (connect time) reported in this study may reflect a lesser pressure concerning cost than that which exists in other searching operations. Each participating library was given 16 hours per month of free searching time and 16 hours per month of free demonstration time.

In the MIT-NASIC study results are reported for 111 searches (non-MEDLINE) conducted over a year.[23] Three cost components are noted: a direct computer search cost (the sum of the cost from the suppliers plus administrative costs), cost of the time spent by the information specialist, and the cost of the offline printouts. An earlier report of the initial MIT-NASIC activities defines administrative costs as those related to providing central personnel, telephones, terminals and materials necessary for service.[24] It is assumed that these cost areas are also reflected in total costs reported in Table 1. Substantially higher average search costs reported in the year-long study ($74.55 vs. $50.47) appear to be a function of increased supplier charges for connect time and offline prints, as well as greater use of the more expensive scientific databases during this time.

Reviewing these four reports, we find a wide range of average costs per search ($9.50 to $74.55). A lower cost for SDI searches is expected. This type of search would involve little personnel time once the initial profile is constructed, and minimal printout costs for the limited segment of the database searched. Yet, even if this report is excluded, the range is still substantial—$28.41 to $74.55. A similar spread is noted in those cost determinations which exclude salary—$6.44 to $44.04. In considering the range of costs reported, it seems that either cost is a sufficient measure for online searching, in which case the "cheapest" searches are the "best" searches; or, another measurement parameter must be introduced. The second case appears to be true. To evaluate whether the first objective of online searching—lowest cost with qualities and specifications that the user wants—is being met, we must consider a user dependent measure of quality.

QUALITY

How do we measure the quality of searching? User satisfaction might be considered an appropriate yardstick for measuring search quality. A simple measure could be used—for example, determining whether, having once used the search service, the user returns for additional searches. With more effort an evaluation form for the user could be developed. This form might ask for an indication of the perceived value of the search, whether the search has saved time over that which would have been spent in a traditional manual search, and other similar questions.

A difficulty arises if we depend upon these methods for assessing quality. Repeated usage and expressions of satisfaction have no relationship to the cost factors mentioned in the previous section. In general, reports of the introduction of online search services appear to be coupled with indications that users of these services are satisfied. If all users of online services are indeed satisfied, then we are forced to return to the supposition that the cheapest searches are the best searches. Intuitively we can see a number of objections to this assumption. For example, current users may be satisfied because of a novelty effect, or users may be satisfied because any searching service is better than the condition of no service which previously existed. As a measurement of quality, satisfaction or nonsatisfaction gives us no information to address the question of cost. We need measures that can demonstrate quality in relation to cost. Two measures commonly applied to the evaluation of information systems—precision and recall—offer a means for more concrete determination of search quality in relation to cost.

Precision is a measure of the relevancy of the citations retrieved in a search; that is, of the total number of citations retrieved by a search, the number which were identified as relevant to the user's information request. Recall is a measure of the completeness of the search; that is, the relationship of the number of relevant citations retrieved to the number of relevant citations present in the data base(s) searched. Precision and recall are commonly expressed as ratios.[25]

$$\text{Precision} = \frac{\text{Number of relevant records retrieved}}{\text{Total number of records retrieved}}$$

$$\text{Recall} = \frac{\text{Number of relevant records retrieved}}{\text{Number of relevant records in the file(s)}}$$

Of the two measures, precision is the more easily determined. Precision values can be computed with the cooperation of the user. The user receives an evaluation form indicating the number of citations sent and is asked to indicate the number of citations in the total which are relevant to the request. The choice presented to the user may be dichotomous (Relevant, Not Relevant),[26] or multiple (Relevant, Peripherally Relevant, Irrelevant).[27]

Jestes presents a composite indicator or precision for 87 CAIN searches evaluated by users.[28] For a total of 10,333 citations sent to users, 36 percent were determined to be directly pertinent to the research needs of the user, 25 percent were considered interesting but not directly pertinent and 37 percent were considered not useful. Two percent of the citations were not accounted for. Of the ten reports of retrospective searching noted in Table 1, this is the only one which includes an evaluation of the number of relevant citations.

Recall determinations present a more formidable obstacle in the assessment of searching performance than precision. Some justification for suggesting recall as a measure applicable to online systems may be appropriate since its importance has been played down elsewhere.[29,30] Several studies suggest that a desire for high recall is important to users of information systems. Twenty-six of the 48 searches studied in the AIM-TWX investigation were tagged by the requesters as needing all possible relevant citations.[31] Users evaluating information retrieval services in a study conducted at the University of Georgia-Athens and UCLA ranked lack of a recall measure at the top of their list of least liked characteristics of the systems.[32] Lynch and Smith, comparing a manual search of the literature with the performance of a profile constructed for a search of the *Chemical Titles* database, indicate, "To us, as potential users of the service for our everyday needs . . . accuracy and completeness of retrieval were paramount considerations."[33]

Many institutions providing online searches imply to their users that a high recall search is possible. For example, on the search request form or during the search interview varying forms of questions concerning recall may be asked: "Do you want all possible references?" "Do you want a broad search?" Asking such questions suggests some confidence on the part of the searching institution in the ability to provide high recall results. For cases in which the user responds affirmatively to these questions, recall measures appear to be a necessary component of evaluation.

For searches of large databases, recall can, at best, be determined as an estimated value only, since absolute recall determination would require the evaluation of every nonretrieved item in the database searched, to determine whether it was relevant or nonrelevant. Miller outlines seven methods which have been used for estimated recall determinations.[34] The recall-base method appears to provide the most practical solution for evaluation in online searching institutions. A recall-base is formed from relevant references already known to the user and additional relevant references located by a limited manual literature search conducted by a librarian. The percentage of these references found in the machine search is understood to be an estimate of recall performance.

IMPROVEMENT

Considering the previous measures discussed it is now possible to propose two measures for performance evaluation of online searching— unit cost in dollars per relevant citation and recall. Application of one or both of these measures is dependent upon user expressed needs for *some* relevant citations (unit cost measure) or *all possible* relevant citations (unit cost and recall measures).

Unit cost determination as discussed here differs from that suggested by Lancaster and Fayen[35] in its inclusion of four additional factors—total time spent by the search intermediary, offline printing costs, database being searched, and system used (e.g., SDC or Lockheed). Lancaster and Fayen's suggestion of unit cost—minutes of terminal time used per relevant citation retrieved—appears to be based on the supposition that most online use will be for situations in which a few citations are needed in a short time; that is, no citations are printed offline. This does not appear to be true for respondents in the SDC *Impact* study. A combination of printing modes (online, offline) was used. Under certain conditions, for some of the higher priced databases (equal to or greater than $40 per hour), offline printing is more economical than online printing.[36] It seems, then, that the decision to continue a search online (added online costs with the possibility of increasing precision) must be weighed against the alternate choice—to print offline (added printing costs with the possibility that a percentage of the unexamined items so printed will be irrelevant). The same rationale applies to recognition of total searcher time (preplanning, interviewing, online time). Time spent other than online may be an influential factor in the speed with which the online search is accomplished.[37] For some databases offered by both of the commercial vendors there is a substantial difference in cost per hour for the database.[38] A unit cost determination should consider whether the lower cost per hour for the database is supported by comparable time spent online, or, whether the economic advantage of lower database charges is offset by the need to spend more time online to achieve comparable results with a particular vendor.

For comparative purposes (internal and external), an expression of unit cost which recognizes variables common to most online search operations is preferred. Such a measure is applied so that the effect of changes in these variables can be weighed against effectiveness of the operation. To the extent that less costly alternatives (e.g., decreased searcher time for preplanning, use of graduate students for searching) might be used to bring about equal search effectiveness, it is possible to improve the cost/effectiveness of the operation. Unit cost per relevant citation would be determined in the following manner:

$$C_R = \frac{C_1(X_1 + X_2 + X_3) + C_2(X_3) + C_3(X_4)}{R}$$

where C_R = Unit cost per relevant citation
C_1 = Costs per minute of searcher time
X_1 = Minutes of pre- and post-search activities (exclusive of interview time and online time) spent by the searcher
X_2 = Minutes of interview time
X_3 = Minutes online
C_2 = Cost per minute for the database
C_3 = Cost per offline print
X_4 = Number of offline prints
R = Number of relevant citations retrieved

Although they represent very real costs to individual institutions, start-up costs—vendor training, purchase of terminal, phone installation, office equipment, searching manuals, etc.—and continuing costs—terminal lease, monthly base charge for a phone, overhead, etc.— are not included since different configurations are to be found in each institution. For the same reason, time-sharing costs are not included— some libraries must make a long-distance call to access the time-sharing node, other libraries have direct access to the vendor system. A case could be made for including a cost for user time (interview time, online time if the user is present during searching, time for reviewing search results) if this variable appears to weigh heavily in the cost-effectiveness consideration. For some search operations the objective will be to achieve a low value for C_R, or low C_R with high recall, within a certain dollar limitation imposed by a particular user.

CONTINUING THE SERVICE

The question of whether the service is to be continued is the most difficult area to address. In isolation, if we consider only the online operation itself, criteria for determining benefits of the system might include those five suggested by Lancaster and Fayen:

1. Cost savings in using this system as compared with the costs of finding needed information elsewhere.
2. Avoidance of loss of productivity (of engineers, for example), that would result if information sources were not readily available.
3. Improved decision making or reduction in the level of personnel required to make decisions.
4. Avoidance of duplication or waste of engineering or research effort that has either been done before or that has been proved infeasible by earlier investigations.
5. Stimulation of invention (a serendipity factor). . . . [39]

Even if benefits can be shown for each of these five areas, or if other benefits can be demonstrated for the online system, we have not yet determined whether the second objective of online searching—benefits equal to or greater than those achievable by a different allocation of library resources—has been met. Measures for this consideration require a greater knowledge of costs, cost-effectiveness, and benefits from each library operation. This analysis would appear worthwhile for determining the value of online searching in the context of total library services; it may lead to a reassessment of priorities in libraries.

Footnotes

1. "Librarians on MARS: Session Probes New Machine-Assisted Reference Services," *American Libraries* 7 (September 1976):504.
2. Judith Wanger, Carlos A. Cuadra, and Mary Fishburn, *Impact of Online Retrieval Services: A Survey of Users, 1974-75* (Santa Monica, Calif.: System Development Corporation, 1976).
3. Roger K. Summit and Oscar Firschein, "Online Reference Retrieval in a Public Library," *Special Libraries* 67 (February 1976):91-96.
4. Capital Systems Group, *A Study of the Feasibility of Marketing Bibliographic and Census Database Products and Services Via the Northeast Academic Science Information Centre*, Appendix C of the NASIC Phase 1 Report (Wellesley, Mass.: New England Board of Higher Education, January 1974), p. 2.
5. Wanger, Cuadra, and Fishburn, pp. 154-55, 159.
6. Lawrence D. Miles, *Techniques of Value Analysis and Engineering*, 2d ed., quoted in Rowena Weiss Swanson, "Performing Evaluation Studies in Information Science," *Journal of the American Society for Information Science* 26 (May-June 1975):146.
7. Donald W. King and Edward C. Bryant, *The Evaluation of Information Services and Products* (Washington, D.C.: Information Resources Press, 1971), p. 16.
8. Carlos Cuadra, "SDC Experiences With Large Data Bases," *Journal of Chemical Information and Computer Sciences* 15 (February 1975):48-51.

9. Oldrich R. Standera, "Cost and Effectiveness in the Evaluation of an Information System: A Case Study," *Journal of the American Society for Information Science* 25 (May-June 1974):203-7.
10. Judith Wanger, "A View from the Middle: The SDC/ERIC Search Service," *ERIC Database Users Interchange*, Attachment No. 4 (March 1974):1-6. Cost data from 6 months of online searching of ERIC at the Texas Information Service.
11. Standera, p. 206.
12. Edward C. Jestes, "CAIN Online Project Report for the Period October-December 1973," unpublished report (Davis: University Library, University of California, June 1974), p. 8.
13. Barbara Lawrence, Ben H. Wei, and Margaret H. Graham, "Making Online Search Available in an Industrial Research Environment," *Journal of the American Society for Information Science* 25 (November-Decmeber 1974): 364-69.
14. Stanley Elman, "Cost Comparison of Manual and Online Computerized Literature Searching," *Special Libraries* 66 (January 1975):12-18.
15. Alan R. Benenfield et al., *NASIC at MIT, Final Report, March 1 1974– February 28, 1975*, Report ESL-FR-587 (Cambridge: Electronic Systems Laboratory, MIT, February 1975), p. G-13.
16. Randolph Hock, "Providing Access to Externally Available Bibliographic Databases in an Academic Library," *College and Research Libraries* 36 (May 1975):208-15.
17. Kenneth C. Linepensel, "Online Literature Searching in the Small-to-Medium-Sized Research Library, A Comparison of Results in 1973 and 1974 Periods," Presented at a Contributed Paper Session of the 66th Annual Conference, June 8-12, 1975, Special Libraries Association, Chicago, Ill., p. 5. (ED 121295).
18. Ruth Atwood, letter (Louisville: Louisville Information Retrieval Centre, December 1, 1975).
19. Michael D. Cooper and Nancy A. DeWath, *The Cost of Online Bibliographic Searching*, Technical Report 003-75-01 (Stanford: Applied Communication Research, December 1975), p. 31. (ED 118087).
20. Donald T. Hawkins, "Impact of Online Systems on a Literature Searching Service," *Special Libraries* 67 (December 1976):559-67.
21. Jestes, pp. 6-8.
22. Cooper and DeWath, pp. 6-7, 27-32.
23. Benefeld et al., p. 402.
24. Alan R. Benenfeld et al., *NASIC at MIT, Phase I Report 16 July 1973-28 February 1974*. Report ESL-R-543 (Cambridge: Electronics Systems Laboratory, MIT March 1974), p. 21.
25. Charles T. Meadow, *The Analysis of Information Systems*, 2d ed. (Los Angeles: Melville, 1973), p. 163.
26. King and Bryant, p. 22.
27. Frederick W. Lancaster, *Evaluation of Online Searching in MEDLARS (AIM-TWX) by Biomedical Practitioners*, Occasional Papers No. 101 (Champaign: University of Illinois, Graduate School of Library Science, 1972), p. 2.

28. Jestes, p. 10.
29. Frederick W. Lancaster and Emily G. Fayen, *Information Retrieval Online* (Los Angeles: Melville, 1973), p. 130.
30. William S. Cooper, "On Selecting a Measure of Retrieval Effectiveness. Part I. The Subjective Philosophy of Evaluation." *Journal of the American Society for Information Science* 24 (March-April 1973):87-100.
31. Lancaster, *Evaluation of Online Searching*, p. 5.
32. James L. Carmon, *Final Report to the National Science Foundation on Grant GN-41236 to Model the User Interface for a Multidisciplinary Bibliographic Network* (Athens: University of Georgia, Office of Computing Activities, May 1975), p. 14.
33. J. T. Lynch and G. D. W. Smith, "Scientific Information by Computer," *Nature* 230 (March 19, 1971):153-56.
34. William I. Miller, "The Extension of User's Literature Awareness as a Measure of Retrieval Performance, and Its Application to MEDLARS," *Journal of Documentation*, 27 (June 1971):125-35.
35. Lancaster and Fayen, pp. 130-2.
36. Wanger et al., *Impact of Online Retrieval*, pp. 137, 140-2.
37. Charles P. Bourne, Jo Robinson and Judy Todd, *Analysis of ERIC Online File Searching Procedures and Guidelines for Searching*, Report ILR-74-005 (Berkeley: Institute of Library Research, University of California, November 1974), p. 11.
38. Irvin Weiss, "Evaluation of ORBIT and DIALOG Using Six Data Bases," *Special Libraries* 67 (December 1976):547-81.
39. Lancaster and Fayen, p. 370.

Estimating the Satisfaction
of Information Users

Renata Tagliacozzo

Two different lines of research are commonly followed in order to
evaluate the satisfaction of the users of an information retrieval system.
One of them consists in measuring the effectiveness of the information
system and taking that measure as an indicator of how successful the
system was in satisfying the information needs of its users. The other
type of research consists of directly asking the users for their opinion of
the service provided by the information system.

System effectiveness may be measured in various ways.[1] Among the
most frequently used methods for measuring the performance of an
information retrieval system are the recall and precision ratios.[2] The
performance of an information system, however, should not be confused
with the value of the system to the individual user, as perceived by the
user himself.[3] Any method that tests how well the system is performing
will tell much about the system but probably very little about the degree
of satisfaction of the users. Especially when the system is based on a
technological innovation, the user's reaction and his degree of acceptance
may be influenced by factors other than the performance of the
system.

The second type of research is based on eliciting the users' opinions by
way of questionnaires or interviews. This approach also is not exempt
from criticism. Some investigators are reluctant to take the word of the
user as to whether the service provided by the information system has
satisfied his information needs. It is not an uncommon observation that
the judgment of some users reflects their general opinion of the potential
usefulness of the system rather than the specific appraisal of the service
rendered to them. Many users do not want to discourage a new service,
even if it has not helped them, in view of possible future advantages they
might derive from it. A more general and fundamental objection is that
the user himself may not have known with perfect accuracy which
information he needed to retrieve. If that is so, how could he know if the

Reprinted with permission of the Medical Library Association from the *Bulletin of the
Medical Library Association*, v. 65, pp. 243-249.

retrieved information satisfied all, or part of, his needs for information? And finally, it may happen that the user's response is an expression of his general attitude toward technological innovations, rather than an appraisal of realistic and relevant factors, such as the extent to which the outcome of the search has met his needs for information.

In response to these objections, one can argue that, even if the users are influenced by their idiosyncratic perceptions of, and attitudes toward, the information system, their responses provide a valid estimate of the degree of acceptance of the system by the particular community of users of which they are part. From a practical point of view, "users' acceptance" may be an adequate substitute for "users' need satisfaction." Perhaps we will never be able to determine what the *real* information needs of the users are, and should therefore content ourselves with what the users believe—and tell us—that they are.

In view of the objections outlined above, however, one should be wary in taking the data of a single rating scale to assess the value that an information system has for its users. In particular, if the rating scale measures a global judgment of the service (such as "helpfulness," "success," "worthiness," "value") rather than the appraisal of specific search results, a single response may be inadequate to assess the extent to which a user's information needs were satisfied by the search. A questionnaire therefore should not be limited to eliciting an overall judgment, but should tap several aspects of the user's reaction to the outcome of his request for information.

THE QUESTIONNAIRE

In the course of a survey on the use of MEDLINE bibliographic service at seven information centers, we sent a follow-up questionnaire to the people who had used the service during the period April-September 1973, asking for their judgment on the value of the search or searches and on the relevance and usefulness of the obtained references.[4] Of the 1,017 questionnaires that reached the addressees, 904 were filled out and sent back, for an overall return of 88.9%.[5]

The first question asked the users to evaluate the results of their MEDLINE search by checking one of four categories: "not helpful," "moderately helpful," "helpful," and "very helpful" (see Appendix 1). The distribution of the responses is shown in Table 1. The data from the four major centers contributing to the survey (A, B, C, and D) are presented separately, while the data from the three minor contributors have been pooled.

If we assume that the searches that fall into the category of "helpful" or "very helpful" produced higher satisfaction in the requesters than

TABLE 1 Users' Judgment of Helpfulness of MEDLINE Search

	MEDLINE centers*					
	A N = 243	B N = 294	C N = 182	D N = 113	E-F-G N = 63	Total N = 895
Not helpful	10.7%	7.5%	12.6%	8.8%	9.5%	9.7%
Moderately helpful	28.8%	27.6%	34.1%	28.3%	28.6%	29.4%
Helpful	34.2%	40.5%	23.6%	33.6%	42.9%	34.6%
Very helpful	26.3%	24.5%	29.7%	29.2%	19.0%	26.3%

*A: University of Illinois at the Medical Center-Chicago; B: Indiana University; C: University of Chicago; D: University of Illinois at Urbana; E: Cleveland Health Sciences Library; F: Mayo Clinic; G: Wayne State University.

those which were judged "not helpful" or "moderately helpful" then we can say that all the MEDLINE centers we investigated exhibited a preponderance of satisfied users. The data show, in fact, that over 60% of the users expressed a positive reaction toward the outcome of the search.

We are not sure, however, that all the users' responses expressed a judgment closely related to the outcome of the search that they had requested. Some users, for instance, may have manifested a high opinion of the value of the MEDLINE service in spite of the fact that their needs for information were not satisfied by the results of the search. On the other hand, users who had a preconceived, poor opinion of the system—or of information systems in general—may have expressed an unfavorable judgment, even if the service that they had obtained was, in their particular case, valuable. For these reasons, we thought it would be useful to compare the "helpful" response to subsequent responses.

Item 5 of the questionnaire required a more precise judgment than item 1. The response consisted of marking a point on a line having as extremes the qualification "completely useless" at the left and "very useful" at the right. The judgment concerned the *results* of the search,

TABLE 2 Users' Judgment of Usefulness of MEDLINE Search

	MEDLINE centers*					
Intervals on line	A N = 217	B N = 288	C N = 162	D N = 112	E-F-G N = 47	Total N = 826
−3	8.8%	4.2%	9.9%	8.0%	10.6%	7.4%
−2	6.9%	5.9%	8.6%	5.4%	10.6%	6.9%
−1	5.5%	6.6%	4.3%	5.4%	8.5%	5.8%
0	10.1%	9.0%	10.5%	14.3%	6.4%	10.2%
+1	13.4%	12.4%	13.0%	20.5%	12.8%	13.9%
+2	25.8%	31.3%	23.5%	17.9%	31.9%	26.5%
+3	29.5%	30.6%	30.2%	28.6%	19.1%	29.3%

*A: University of Illinois at the Medical Center-Chicago; B: Indiana University; C: University of Chicago; D: University of Illinois at Urbana; E: Cleveland Health Sciences Library; F: Mayo Clinic; G: Wayne State University.

rather than the search in general. Table 2 shows the frequency distribution of the responses, obtained by dividing the line in seven equal intervals (from -3 to +3) and calculating the percentage of the responses falling into each interval.[6] Even in this distribution we find a preponderance of favorable judgments (intervals +1, +2, and +3) against those expressing unfavorable judgments (intervals -1, -2, and -3).

ANALYSIS OF RESPONSES

In Table 3 we have plotted the judgment of *helpfulness* against the judgment of *usefulness*. The numbers in the cells of the matrix are the raw frequency figures. They say that, for instance, fifty-three of the respondents who judged the search "not helpful" marked the line on the interval to the extreme left, seventeen marked the line on the second interval from the left, and so on. Of the respondents who judged the search "very helpful," 165 marked the line on the interval to the extreme right, forty-nine on the second interval from the right, and so on.

As could be expected, a strong positive correlation is evident between the two judgments. Almost all the responses carrying a "not helpful" judgment lie at the left of the middle interval on the line, and all the "very helpful" responses are on the right (see also Fig. 1). But the two middle categories ("moderately helpful" and "helpful") present a distribution pattern that is somewhat ambiguous. In the left part of the "helpful" row we find six responses which may be considered deviant. These responses in fact say that a search that was judged "helpful" produced useless—or nearly useless—results. In one of the six cases a reasonable explanation for the contradiction was offered by the user himself. He wrote a note explaining that he had called the search "helpful," in spite of the fact that it had not turned up any references, because it had saved time and effort and had eliminated the need for searching other sources. The other five cases of discrepant responses were less extreme but they also supported the conclusion that a search can be

TABLE 3   Judgment of Helpfulness of the Search vs. Judgment of Usefulness

	Intervals on line							Total
	-3	-2	-1	0	+1	+2	+3	
Not helpful	53	17	4	4	—	—		78
Moderately helpful	7	38	41	55	44	37	9	231
Helpful	1	2	3	25	66	131	66	294
Very helpful	—	—	—	—	4	49	165	218
Total	61	57	48	84	114	217	240	821

judged helpful, in terms of convenience, labor saving, and supporting evidence, and at the same time may not produce useful results.

The frequency distribution of the "moderately helpful" responses on the "usefulness" dimension spreads out in almost identical fashion to the right and to the left of the middle interval, approaching a normal distribution curve (see Fig. 1). This suggests that the qualifier "moderately" (helpful) was perceived differently by different users: for those who marked the line at the right of the middle interval (about 40% of the respondents) it had apparently positive connotations, while for an almost equal number of respondents, those who marked the left, it implied some degree of dissatisfaction. But a different interpretation could also be given to the data. Perhaps the users who checked the answer "moderately helpful" were those who did not have—or were unwilling to express—a strong opinion on the MEDLINE service. If this was the case, it is not surprising that the question concerning the usefulness of the search results, a more precise and more direct question, was given widely disparate answers by this category of users.

The above results stress the importance of not trusting an overall single response by the user to represent his degree of satisfaction. Before

FIGURE 1   Distribution of Judgment of Usefulness by a Group of Users

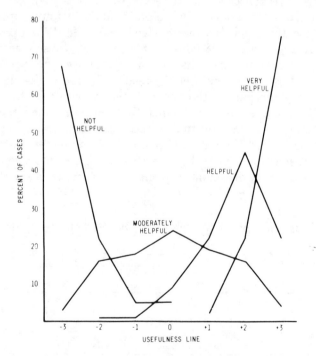

inferring that the information needs of the users were satisfied by the service, one should assess and compare their responses to various aspects of the search outcome.

To further test the validity and reliability of the users' overall evaluation of the service, we looked at the degree of association between the judgment of helpfulness and the number of retrieved references that the user found useful, as stated in the answer to question 6 of the questionnaire. We expected a high probability that the user's judgment would be favorable when the search produced a large number of references. We were not sure that the reverse would be true: depending on the type of search, one or two references may be sufficient at times to satisfy the information needs of a user as well as numerous references would. Table 4 shows the distribution of users divided according to number of useful references (five or less in the upper row, six or more in the lower) and to judgment of helpfulness ("not helpful" or "moderately helpful" in the left column; "helpful" and "very helpful" in the right column).

A strong association is evident between number of useful references and judgment of helpfulness. More than 80% of the users who received a high number of useful references (290 of 352) gave a favorable estimate of the helpfulness of the search, as compared to 40% of the users who received a lower number of useful references (142 of 354). A chi-square value of 131 was obtained, indicating that the difference between the two proportions is statistically significant at the 0.001 level of confidence. One may wonder, however, about the meaning of that part of the distribution in which the association does not hold, that is, the 142 cases where the number of useful references was lower but the judgment of

TABLE 4 Judgment of Helpfulness vs Number of Useful References

No. useful refs.	Helpfulness		
	Lower	Higher	
0 5	212	142	354
6 or more	62	290	352
	274	432	706

$$\chi^2 = 131; p < 0.001$$

helpfulness was higher, and the 62 cases in which the number of useful references was higher but the judgment of helpfulness was lower.

The first group is not hard to explain. One can envisage situations in which a small number of references are as helpful, or more helpful, than a large number of them. Even a single reference—especially if it is the crucial one—can make a user happy. There are searches, as we have seen earlier, that produce zero references and are still judged helpful.

The second type of discrepancy (cases of searches judged less helpful, although they had produced a higher number of useful references) is more difficult to interpret. One can only speculate about the factors which may have induced a negative or tepid judgment in users who had received a large number of "useful" references. For instance:

1. The user interpreted the word "useful" to mean "good, valuable articles" and therefore rated the articles high on the usefulness scale, even if they were not useful *to him;*
2. The references were potentially useful, but the material could not be located; therefore the search turned out to be less helpful than it could have been;
3. The references judged useful were already known to the user; consequently he did not gain any additional information;
4. The user knew, or suspected, that the search had missed some useful references, and therefore felt less inclined to give a favorable judgment of the service.

While we cannot support the arguments advanced in 1, 2, and 3 above, we have data that suggest some relationship between the user's knowledge that the search had missed some references and his judgment of lower helpfulness. Table 5 shows that if we divide the users in two groups: one that stated that no references had been missed (see question 3 of questionnaire), and the other that mentioned that one or more references had been missed, we notice a larger percentage of favorable judgments in the first group than in the second (70.0% versus 48.4%). Even in this case the difference is statistically significant at the 0.001 level of confidence.

These data, however, do not necessarily imply a causal relationship between the user's knowledge that the search had failed to produce some relevant references and his lower satisfaction. The association between the two may simply signify that the users who noticed that some references were missing were those who had greater expertise and familiarity with the area of the search, and consequently were more demanding and less easily satisfied customers. The hypothesis that the level of satisfaction of the user is inversely related to his knowledge of what is being published in the area of the search cannot be tested with the present data, but seems interesting.

TABLE 5   Judgment of Helpfulness vs Missed References

Missed refs.	Helpfulness		
	Lower	Higher	
None	150	347	497
1 or more	152	146	298
	302	493	795

$$\chi^2 = 33.87; p < 0.001$$

CONCLUSIONS

The investigation reported in this paper shows the difficulty of estimating the extent to which the bibliographic service provided by an information retrieval system satisfies the information needs of its users. When a questionnaire has been used as the basis for the estimate, one is puzzled by the contradictory and dissonant responses given to its various items. The picture which emerges from the data that we analyzed suggests that a great variety of factors, some related and some unrelated to the performance of the information retrieval system, influence the users' responses. Factors related to the measuring instrument, such as the different interpretation of questions, the tendency to avoid extreme positions on rating scales, and the questionable reliability of memory in reporting past events certainly affect the users' responses. More directly related to the service provided by the information retrieval system are the users' attitudes and perceptions, their knowledge and expertise in the area of the search, their previous acquaintance with the literature. Finally, the type of search requested by the users may be responsible for some of the variance in their judgments: certain searches by their very nature have a higher probability than other searches of producing results that satisfy the users (for example, generic searches versus specific searches).

Caution should therefore be used in taking the users' judgments at face value, and in inferring from single responses that their information needs were, or were not, satisfied by the service. Especially those questions which elicit general, overall judgments of the service provided by the system should be looked at suspiciously. Comparing these responses to other, more specific responses can provide a good indication of the validity and reliability of the users' evaluation of the system, and can be suggestive of the various factors affecting their responses.

In our survey of the use of the MEDLINE bibliographic service, we found a strong, but not complete, agreement between a global judgment of "helpfulness" of the MEDLINE search, and more specific and detailed appraisals of the results of the search, such as the usefulness of the search results, the number of useful references retrieved, and the number of references known to have been missed by the search. MEDLINE was perceived as "helpful" by respondents who, in other parts of the questionnaire, showed that they had *not* found it particularly useful. On the other hand, some users, while admitting that the search had produced a number of useful references, gave less than enthusiastic total appraisal of the service. We tried to explain the dissonant responses in terms of the shift of the respondents' attention from one to another aspect of their search for information. The reason for using the service as well as the type of information needed may also provide clues to the users' reactions to the outcome of the searches.

Footnotes

1. Rowena Weiss Swanson, "Performing Evaluation Studies in Information Science," *Journal of the American Society for Information Science* 26 (May-June 1975):140-56.
2. Frederick W. Lancaster and Emily G. Fayen, *Information Retrieval Online* (Los Angeles, Calif.: Melville Publishing Co., 1973); Jason Farradane, "The Evaluation of Information Retrieval Systems," *Journal of Documentation* 30 (June 1974):195-209; Cyril H. Cleverdon, "User Evaluation of Information Retrieval Systems," *Journal of Documentation* 30 (June 1974):170-80.
3. Ibid.,; William S. Cooper, "On Selecting a Measure of Retrieval Effectiveness," *Journal of the American Society for Information Science* 24 (March-April 1973):87-100.
4. Renata Tagliacozzo, "The Consumers of New Information Technology: A Survey of the Utilization of MEDLINE," *Journal of the American Society for Information Science* 26 (September-October 1975):294-304.
5. This return, quite high if compared with other surveys (see, for instance, footnotes 7 and 8), was obtained by following the questionnaire with one or two reminders.
6. The total of this distribution (N=826) is lower than that of Table 1 because a technical error in typing a batch of questionnaires forced us to discard a number of responses.
7. Wilhelm Moll, "MEDLINE Evaluation Study," *Bulletin of the Medical Library Association* 62 (January 1974):1-5.
8. Susan E. McCarthy, Shirley S. Maccabee, and Cyril C. H. Feng, "Evaluation of MEDLINE Service by User Survey," *Bulletin of the Medical Library Association* 62 (October 1974):367-73.

ESTIMATING SATISFACTION OF INFORMATION USERS

APPENDIX 1

FOLLOW-UP QUESTIONNAIRE

1. Was the MEDLINE search
   not helpful □; moderately helpful □; helpful □; very helpful □?

2. If helpful, in what way?
   (If more than one applies, mark P for primary, S for secondary.)
   (a) saved time and/or effort _____
   (b) provided references that might have been missed _____
   (c) uncovered obscure or not easily accessible references _____
   (d) helped in getting acquainted with a new field _____
   (e) gave a feeling of security _____
   (f) other _____
   (please specify)

3. Did the search miss references which you found through other sources?
   (Keep in mind that MEDLINE covers the biomedical literature from January
   1970 to the present.) Yes □ No □
   If yes, how many? _____ references

4. Was the MEDLINE search of value to the particular information need for
   which you requested it? Yes □ No □
   To some other information needed? Yes □ No □

5. Please mark on the line below a point indicating your judgment of the search
   results from *completely useless* at the extreme left to *very useful* at the
   extreme right:
   completely useless _____ very useful

6. How many references, out of the total, appeared to be relevant? _____
   Of the *relevant* references, how many turned out to be *useful*? _____

7. Do you plan to use the MEDLINE service in the future? Yes □ No □
   If yes, within 3 months □; 6 months □; 1 year □; at some indefinite time □

The Fallacy of the Perfect Thirty-Item Online Search

Marcia J. Bates

INTRODUCTION

Imagine the following situation: Sitting at an online terminal, a searcher inputs a carefully worked out search formulation for a client's query, then sits back and awaits the results. There are 1,282 postings. What happens now? Most likely, the searcher groans and says, "I've got to cut that down—1,282 is far too many." Where does this response come from? What, in fact, constitutes "too many"?

One source of that response is the client's limitation of the search either to a certain maximum number of references or to a maximum price. The latter restriction is common in academic libraries where the client pays for the search. Even where the client does not impose restrictions, the searcher is likely to try to reduce the search output to a "manageable" number. As a teacher of online searchers, I have noticed what is apparently a spontaneous tendency on the part of students, in the absence of any stated maximum, to consider search output "too large"if it is much in excess of seventy-five or one hundred items. Conversations with more experienced searchers suggest that they feel more flexibility than this; they key search size to a combination of factors, but often still find the need to alter initial search output sizes, particularly in the direction of reducing the output.

There is more to the question of what constitutes a good output size than first meets the eye. This matter will be explored here by means of examining a fallacy in thinking about searching and search modification. Taking a figure comfortably under the seventy-five to one-hundred item limit mentioned earlier, we shall call it the fallacy of the perfect thirty-item online search. Beginning searchers may find this discussion particularly instructive, and experienced searchers may also find it useful to consider the various nuances of determining good output size.

Reprinted by permission of the American Library Association from *RQ* 24 (1):43-50 (Fall 1984); copyright © 1984 by the American Library Association.

"Search formulation" is defined as a search statement or series of statements expressing the search topic of a request. A "search strategy," on the other hand, is a plan or approach for the whole search and operates at a level above specific term choice and command use. (See also discussion in Bates.[1])

In the next selection the fallacy is described, in the succeeding section the ways in which the fallacy may arise are discussed, and in the final section solutions are proposed.

WHAT IS THE FALLACY?

The fallacy lies in assuming that somewhere in the database one is searching there exists a high-quality thirty-item (or n-item, whatever n is for the searcher) set and that if one is just clever enough, one can produce a response set of the desired size for the client. To put it differently, the fallacy lies in gearing the search to the size of the output desired instead of to the topic to be searched. It may simply be that the relevant documents available in a database on a given topic are not the same number as the searcher or client would like.

The fallacy can occur in two ways. First, the output of a search may be the "wrong" size, and the searcher goes to great and clever lengths to modify the search formulation until the output is the "right" size. Most commonly, the output is "too large," so this form of the fallacy will be called the "overcutting" version.

In this case, cutting down the output drastically for a query may yield a final set that is an unrepresentative and atypical subset of the whole set of documents relevant to the query. Its prime virtue may be that it contains only thirty items, not that it is a good or complete response. Thus, in trying to get an output of a certain size, the searcher may violate the topic itself.

But, it may be argued, clients frequently limit the output to a certain number, either by preference or because they do not want to pay for any more. The search *has* to be limited. I am not suggesting that clients be swamped with citations they do not want. But first it is important that we be clear on just what the thinking is on the part of client and searcher. It may be possible to come to a solution that produces searches of a higher quality than is likely when the fallacy is operating in their thinking. The latter part of this article will suggest ways of producing such higher quality sets.

An output set of the "wrong" size can also be too small. It is possible, figuratively, to "scrape the bottom of the barrel" to try to increase a small set up to a desired size. The dangers of producing a poor output set are less here. Because the searcher tries many variant search formulations to identify relevant citations, this approach is not likely to overlook valuable citations, and searchers are unlikely to give clients a response set full of irrelevant items. (The one real danger here is that the searcher may use up too much of the client's money searching for nonexistent citations. There comes a time when the searcher must have the confidence to declare that there is nothing on the topic in the database.) Consequently, efforts to increase the output set up to thirty will be disregarded in the following discussion of the fallacy.

The second way that the fallacy may occur is that the initial search output is the "right" size, and the searcher stops immediately, without determining whether the initial search formulation is indeed the best one for the query. It may be that in such a case, to do a thorough, careful search on the query, the searcher should OR in related terms and try variant terms either in addition to or instead of the terms used the first time. Searchers often cannot be certain to have found the best search formulation for a given query without such experimentation. But that experimentation may produce larger response sets. So the searcher operating under the fallacy stops after the first response that lists the desired output size. This form is called the "quick and dirty" version of the fallacy.

Fenichel noted a tendency on the part of many searchers to make little use of the feedback and search modification capabilities of online systems.[2] Such searchers go in with just the terms asked for by the client in simple, brief search formulations. There are times when such quick searches are just what the client needs, but other times they constitute an expression of the quick and dirty form of the fallacy. This tendency to "anchor" on the initial search formulation is reminiscent of the anchoring problem discussed in Blair, in which online searchers are reluctant to alter the initial terms of their search formulations.[3]

The above is not to suggest that every effort to modify the search is overcutting, or that failure to modify a search always means the searcher has not developed the best search formulation for a query. Clearly, judgment and experience are involved here. But if the searcher falls into one or the other forms of the fallacy, there is danger that the quality of the search output will be less than it might be.

HOW DOES THE FALLACY ARISE?

There are a number of possible causes for the development of this fallacy in the thinking of searcher and client. It is worth going into these causes in detail because they point to ways of avoiding the fallacy.

What the Client (and Sometimes the Searcher) Does Not Know

There are a lot of things about information retrieval that the typical client does not know and probably has not even thought about. The simplistic assumptions brought to the presearch interview may be presumed to have a strong influence on the demands and expectations placed on the searcher. The searcher, on the other hand, in trying to be helpful, may attempt to meet inappropriate demands that arise out of the client's limited knowledge of the system.

There are three points in particular where misunderstandings are likely to arise:

- Complexity of indexing
- Limits of Boolean logic
- The trade-off between recall and precision.

Let us take them one at a time. There is both research and anecdotal evidence that most people do not realize that any given topic may appear in an information system under many different descriptors.[4] They have little awareness of the complex problems involved in subject indexing and the variety of ways in which any given topic is likely to be described. In its simplest form, their mental model is likely to be that a topic that interests them is to be found under a single term; all documents found under that term will be relevant to their query, and no documents relevant to the query will be found elsewhere in the system. Thus, they expect that in principle it should be possible to get a response set with 100 percent precision (percentage of relevant documents retrieved out of all documents retrieved) and 100 percent recall (percentage of relevant documents retrieved out of all relevant documents in the collection).

When clients demand high precision for their search output, as they often do, they may be basing this demand on such a naive model of online systems. They may assume that any request on their topic—especially in an automated system, which is usually thought to be much more sophisticated than manual information retrieval systems—will automatically produce a set of documents, all of which are relevant to their query.

In fact, not only is subject indexing much more problematic than most clients realize, but the online systems themselves are not as sophisticated as clients may assume. Boolean logic is simpler than natural-language syntax—and also rides roughshod over many grammatical distinctions that make a difference in the relevance of a document to a request. Consequently, false drops are endemic in online searching.

Furthermore, it has long been argued that Boolean logic is not ideally suited to be the basis of term combination in information retrieval. The

OR is too weak and brings in too many documents and the AND is too stringent and cuts down output sets too severely. My purpose here is not to argue the value of using Boolean logic—only to point out that the actual conceptual system embedded in the fancy-looking technology may not be as sophisticated as the client assumes.

Above all, clients are not likely to understand the trade-off between recall and precision. Searchers are generally aware of it, but some may not recognize its full practical implications for online searching.

Let us therefore look at the trade-off more closely. It is one of the best-established results of information science research that, in general, high precision is gained at the price of low recall and vice versa. Consequently, the tricks one uses in search modification to improve precision tend to lower recall and vice versa. Lancaster has an excellent discussion of this in chapters eleven and twelve of his *Information Retrieval Systems.*[5]

Let us use one of Lancaster's examples to demonstrate this pattern. Suppose an aeronautical engineer wants a search on "slender delta wings." This is exactly what interests the engineer, not other types of wings. The chances are that a search on this term will produce a high precision output set.

But it may be that for all sorts of reasons there are documents of relevance to this request under other terms as well. Mention of slender delta wings may appear in documents on delta wings in general (and indexed under "delta wings") or even in documents on wings in general. Good material may also be found under synonymous terms such as "narrow delta wings," or even under closely related terms. These other terms may reflect a necessary variety in the information retrieval system or may be used because of sloppy vocabulary control, changes in terminology over time, or other reasons.

In order to improve recall and retrieve relevant documents indexed under these other terms, it is necessary to search under them as well. But in doing so, it is likely that a higher proportion of the documents indexed under these more distant terms will be irrelevant to the request than is the case with the initial highly precise term. In other words, in casting a wider net to improve recall, one also pulls in *disproportionately* more junk. Consequently, when recall goes up, precision goes down. The same thing happens, of course, in reverse: if one reduces the search formulation to only the most precise terms, percision will be improved, but recall will fall.

The practical, and virtually unavoidable, result of the recall-precision trade-off for online searching is that where recall is important to the client, there will usually be a substantial proportion of irrelevant citations retrieved in even the best-designed search. Where cost is an important factor, it may be particularly puzzling and irksome to the client to get an output set with dozens of irrelevant citations. In response to the client's dissatisfaction, the searcher may retreat to the overcutting version of the fallacy—producing high-precision searches for clients who really want high recall.

Differences Between Manual and Online Searching

Habits and expectations formed with manual searching may carry over inappropriately to online searching. Let us compare these two forms of searching and note two important respects in which they differ.

First, the number-of-postings output from an online system in response to any query is likely to be far larger—often by an order of magnitude or more—than the output of a manual search on the same topic. This comes about for two reasons:

First, the typical manual search segments the output into yearly or biannual chunks, corresponding to the published volumes of the abstracting and indexing (A & I) service, whereas the typical online database covers many years and produces postings for all the years covered at once. The total base number of citations is the same, of course, but, psychologically, getting them all at once makes the searcher feel that the output of the online search is larger.

Second, the number of postings reported to a searcher in an online search is the number of citations indexed by a term before the searcher has had a chance to select out the potentially relevant items. In a manual search we record only the most promising citations, not all the citations listed under the term. In an online search, on the other hand, a well-stated, carefully worked-out search formulation still produces the set from which the client or researcher selects the desired items, not the final selected set.

The client, however, still wants the same low number of citations gotten previously from manual searches, and/or wants the online output especially low in number because of the cost. The poor searcher is thus squeezed between two contrary pressures: the output from any given online search is going to be quite large on the average, and the client has as much or more desire for small output sets as ever.

Now to the second point of difference between manual and online searches: In an online search, because of high print costs (on- or offline), the searcher usually must find a way to select out the most promising subset of the database, while looking at no more than a tiny sample of the citations matching any given search formulation. In other words, the searcher must select the final output set virtually sight unseen.

Probably because the online search thus involves a lot of decision making without full knowledge, Standera found the development and the modification of the search formulation (what he calls "strategy") to be the two points of greatest stress out of seventeen identifiable phases of online searching.[6]

It may be argued, however, that it is much easier with online systems than I have made out, because they have many capabilities not available in manual sources. These capabilities can be used to design initially precise search formulations, or to cut down (or increase) the size of the response set and get the thirty-item output the client wants and expects. Let us note some of the more common devices available in online search systems:

- Search terms may be combined according to Boolean logic.
- Search terms may be truncated, so that all variations on a root are automatically searched.
- Searching can be done on terms or strings other than assigned descriptors, often throughout the record, including the abstract.
- Searching can be done conjointly on descriptors, free-text words, classification codes, and other subject elements.

The above devices all deal with subject or topic access. In addition:

- The search can be limited by date or accession number.
- Depending on the database, the search can be limited by other characteristics, such as language, country of origin, document type, presence of literature reviews, etc.

Let us call the first set of devices "searching by subject characteristics," and, for lack of a better name, the second set of devices "searching by secondary characteristics." We will use these terms in the next section.

These are powerful capabilities; they allow many options for clever search design and modification. Use of them may indeed lead to drastic modification of the size of output sets. But the fact remains that in practice they are mostly carried out "blind." Through design and modification of the search formulation, the searcher selects the potentially relevant citations and rejects the probably irrelevant ones for the client without seeing the overwhelming majority of those citations.

The nature of searching and search modification is thus quite different for online and manual searching. In both cases the client may set a comparatively low limit on the number of citations wanted, but the danger of unwittingly rejecting large numbers of highly relevant documents is much higher in online searching. Since the client asks for a small set, and may have to pay for the output on a per citation basis in an online search, the searcher may determinedly find ways to reduce the output—and thus slip into the fallacy. We will consider ways to deal with this problem in the next section.

WHAT STRATEGIES CAN THE SEARCHER USE TO DEAL WITH THE FALLACY?

In order to identify strategies it will be helpful first to distinguish common types of search. Based on ideas developed originally by Charles Bourne, Markey and Cochrane describe three types of search: high recall search, high precision search, and brief search.[7] The first two types emphasize those retrieval values, while a brief search "is done in response to the need for retrieving a few items either to lessen expenses or to perform a rapid survey of the file before a more comprehensive and lengthy strategy."[8]

The purpose of a recall search is very clear; the client needs everything that can be found on the topic for, say, a dissertation or review paper. With respect to precision searches, many researchers take a casual attitude toward the literature searches they do for articles they are writing. Those of us with a library background may assume recall is important; people in other fields often do not. They see the background survey that they must write at the beginning of articles as a tiresome, if necessary, task. They feel the purpose of the survey is to mention some typical articles on the topic of their research, not all the articles. They show where their work fits into the stream of research; they do not attempt to show everything that has been done. If this is the attitude taken by the client, then a precision search is indeed called for. In this case, the client's insistence that the size of the output be limited and irrelevant documents be minimized makes sense.

But there is another possibility here—that the client who is apparently asking for a precision search really wants a recall search. This can come about for reasons discussed in the previous section. Ignorant of the recall-precision trade-off, the client may think that, of course, irrelevant documents are not wanted; the output should be limited to relevant items only. It is assumed that the fancy automated system can easily produce such a result. The client may even assume—this is common—that when the search is limited to thirty items the system will produce the thirty most relevant items, i.e., a ranked output. Thus why waste money on more citations?

Furthermore, the client may make the same carryover from manual to online searches that was discussed above for searchers. Manual searches done as a student may have produced only a few items—after scanning and selecting. The output of those earlier searches may have been especially low if the client was ignorant of the complexity of indexing and the variety of bibliographic sources available in most fields. This client, in other words, may actually want high recall and assumes that the most references there could possibly be on the subject is thirty.

So if a limit is set there, the search output will contain all the relevant items that exist anyway.

How can one tell whether the client really wants a precision search or recall search? What is really at issue here is how important recall is. We may presume that everyone would like to minimize irrelevant citations retrieved. So the crucial question of the client is, "Do you want everything we can find on this topic or just some examples, some typical references?"

Now, assuming that the searcher is able to identify true recall and true precision searches in the interview with the client, what strategies should be used to avoid the fallacy?

I suggest that different strategies should be used for recall and precision searches. In both cases, modification by subject characteristics (described in the previous section) is often necessary initially in order to home in on a search formulation that is both a good representation of the query and a good match with available terms in the database. But after these initial changes, emphasis should be on modification by secondary characteristics (limitation by date, bibliographic form, etc.) for recall searches and by subject characteristics for precision searches.

Why suggest these different approaches for the two types of search? As noted earlier, a good recall search will often have an extensive search formulation with many marginal terms included. It will generally produce a large output with a comparatively large number of irrelevant documents. It is thus particularly tempting to use modification by subject characteristics to reduce both the output size of a recall search and the percentage of irrelevant documents. For example, one might drop marginal subject terms, drop truncation if already used, drop broader terms, and so on. Once one is confident, however, that the search formulation is a good one for the query and for that database, the use of extensive subject modification later in the search, solely to reduce output size, simply introduces covert precision searching when a recall search is wanted. A good recall search requires those marginal terms, broader terms, etc. To drop them is to convert the recall search into a precision search.

But how then is one to deal with the client who insists on limiting the size of the output for a recall search? There are two main options: (1) Work out a fallback narrower topic with the client in the presearch interview, and/or (2) arrange as a fallback option to cut down the postings by using modification by secondary characteristics; i.e., limit by date, bibliographic form, language, etc.

Either of these approaches is preferable on recall searches to running the risk of overcutting through subject modification and missing many relevant citations. When a recall search is restricted by date or other secondary characteristic, the client knows that nothing will be retrieved prior to the stated date or outside the limit. Most importantly, the client knows that the searcher has gotten the highest recall possible within the stated limits. On the contrary, when extensive subject modification is used to cut down the output of a recall search, especially considering that the modification is mostly done blind, there is no way to know just what sort of relevant documents have been cut out as well. Thus, in such a case, what is ostensibly a recall search may, in fact, have poor recall.

In a precision search, on the other hand, by the trade-off rule of precision and recall, we expect to lose some relevant documents in order to maximize precision. (If the client cannot bear to lose those relevant items, then a recall search is what is really wanted.) With a precision search, there is less danger of overcutting, so the searcher can pull out all the stops to modify the search formulation by subject characteristics. As noted earlier, the possibilities for modification by subject are many and various, and the clever searcher can reduce the output set size considerably through ingenious exercise of these options. By using subject modification the searcher gives the client a set of references on the precise topic desired, and across all years, languages, bibliographic forms, etc. Of course, if the client wants the search limited by date or other secondary characteristic, the limit should be used.

When there is heavy subject modification, there is still some possibility of overcutting with precision searches, however, and care should be exercised. Consider the case where a searcher gets an initial output in the high hundreds or thousands of postings. In modifying this down to a small requested set, such as thirty, the modification may be so drastic that it cuts out whole subareas or branches within the stated topic. Thus, the searcher may want to arrange a fallback narrower topic in such cases as well.

Adams [9] takes a different view on the question of how to narrow searches. He says:

> Restricting a search to several recent years—or printing just the first fifty or so items retrieved in a search—are two other frequently used techniques. It is strongly recommended that they not be used. It is very likely that useful material will be eliminated if they are. Knowledge of the other search refinement methods makes these techniques unnecessary.[10]

He highlights four other search refinement techniques for narrowing searches:

- Restricting to English
- Using NOT
- Restricting a term to fields such as title or descriptor
- Using AND.[11]

In the terminology of the present article, the first of Adams' techniques is a form of modification by secondary characteristics, and the remaining three techniques are forms of modification by subject characteristics. Adams' recommendations are well taken if the searcher habitually makes no modification whatever of the initial search formulation. As noted earlier, some initial subject modification is frequently needed on all types of searches to home in on terms used in a given database. But beyond that first step, I would split out Adams' four techniques, and recommend that the first generally be used on recall searches and the others on precision searches.

So far in this section the emphasis has been on avoiding the overcutting version of the fallacy. What about the quick and dirty version? Here the problem is one of accepting as final the output of a simple, off-the-top-of-the-head search formulation because it produces the desired small number of citations. In cases where the client actually wants a very quick search, i.e., a "brief search," and the searcher is confident that good terms are being used, this approach is adequate. Otherwise, some initial experimentation with subject modification is always advisable to be sure the best term combination has been found.

Here are summary recommendations for avoiding the fallacy of the perfect thirty-item online search:

Presearch interview: Probe carefully to determine what kind of search the client really wants. In the case of recall searches explain that it is in principle a contradiction in terms to limit in advance the number of items desired in a recall search. If practical exigencies still require limiting the search, then arrange a fallback narrower topic, and/or limitation by secondary characteristics.

In the case of precision or brief searches it is less essential to arrange fallback options, since by definition, these types of searches allow for dropping (or failing to pick up) some relevant documents. With topics that are very broad, however, because of the difficulty of narrowing them enough to get small output sizes, it is a good idea to arrange one or both of the fallback options mentioned in the previous paragraph.

The search itself: For searches of all types, use modification by subject characteristics (listed in section titled "How Does the Fallacy Arise?") to home in on the proper description of the topic. If the initial search formulation proves to be off center and retrieves large numbers of false drops or irrelevant citations, revise the formulation by these various subject techniques until one is confident that the topic is well described in the terms used by the database. This first step prevents the quick and dirty version of the fallacy. An exception may be made to this rule in the case of brief searches where the experienced searcher is confident that the initial search formulation will lead to a good match with the terms used in the database.

For brief and true precision searches, after the initial homing in on a good description of the topic in the terms used in the database, subject modification techniques may continue to be used in order to get the output set down to the desired size. (Note that these techniques may also be used in the other direction to increase output size; for reasons discussed earlier, that case is not being covered here.) Some loss of relevant documents is to be expected with these types of searches, so subject modification techniques (which often drop relevant documents) may be used extensively in order to maximize precision. The searcher is cautioned, however, to be careful about reducing initial postings sets too drastically—say, to one-tenth or less of the initial postings size—for fear of losing whole areas or classes of documents within the topic. In order to avoid the overcutting version of the fallacy, the searcher should consider using prearranged fallback options instead.

For recall searches, modification by subject characteristics should generally only be used to home in on a good description of the query, not to cut postings down to a desirable size, for fear of losing relevant documents. If the size of the output set must be limited, then to avoid the overcutting version of the fallacy, the search formulation should be modified by secondary characteristics, or a narrower topic should be used, as arranged in the presearch interview. If the client is present during the search, final selection of fallback options can be made during the search.

Use of these techniques should enable the searcher to satisfy the needs of clients without falling into the fallacy of the perfect thirty-item online search.

Footnotes

1. Marcia J. Bates, "Search Techniques," *Annual Review of Information Science and Technology* 16 (1981):139-169.
2. Carol Hansen Fenichel, "Online Searching: Measures That Discriminate Among Users With Different Types of Experiences," *Journal of the American Society for Information Science* 32 (Jan. 1981):23-32.
3. David C. Blair, "Searching Biases in Large Interactive Document Retrieval Systems," *Journal of the American Society for Information Science* 31 (July 1980):271-277.
4. Marcia J. Bates, "Factors. Affecting Subject Catalog Search Success," *Journal of the American Society for Information Science* 28 (May 1977): 161-69.
5. F. Wilfrid Lancaster, *Information Retrieval Systems: Characteristics, Testing and Evaluation*, 2d ed. (New York: Wiley, 1979), pp. 154-91.
6. O.R. Standera, "Some Thoughts on Online Systems: The Searcher's Part and Plight," in *The Information Age in Perspective: Proceedings of the American Society for Information Science 41st Annual Meeting*, v. 15,

comp. Everett H. Brenner (White Plains, N.Y.: Knowledge Industry Publications, 1978), p. 322-25.

7. Karen Markey and Pauline A. Cochrane, *ONTAP: Online Training and Practice Manual for ERIC Data Base Searchers*, 2d ed. (Syracuse, N.Y.: ERIC Clearinghouse on Information Resources, 1981), pp. 7-8.

8. Ibid., p. 8.

9. Arthur L. Adams, "Planning Search Strategies for Maximum Retrieval from Bibliographic Databases," *Online Review* 3 (Dec. 1979):373-79.

10. Ibid., p. 376.

11. Ibid.

Additional Readings—
Measurement and Evaluation

Auster, Ethel, and Lawton, Stephen B. "Search Interview Techniques and Information Gain as Antecedents of User Satisfaction with Online Bibliographic Retrieval." *Journal of the American Society for Information Science* 35 (March 1984):90-103.

Cleverdon, Cyril. "Optimizing Convenient Online Access to Bibliographic Databases." *Information Services and Use* 4 (April 1984):37-47.

Cooper, William S. "A Perspective on the Measurement of Retrieval Effectiveness." *Drexel Library Quarterly* 14 (April 1978):25-39.

Glunz, Diane, and Wakiji, Eileen. "Maximizing Search Quality Through a Program of Peer Review." *Online* 7 (Sept. 1983):100.

Hoover, Ryan E. "Patron Appraisal of Computer-Aided Online Bibliographic Retrieval Services." *Journal of Library Automation* 9 (December 1976): 335-350.

Lawton, Stephen B.; Auster, Ethel and To, David. "A Systems Evaluation of the Educational Information System for Ontario." *Journal of the American Society for Information Science* 35 (Jan. 1979):33-40.

Mick, Colin K., Lindsey, Georg N., Callahan, Daniel. "Toward Usable User Studies." *Journal of the American Society for Information Science* 31 (Sept. 1980):347-356.

Penniman, W.D. and Dominick, W.D. "Monitoring and Evaluation of Online Information System Usage." *Information Processing and Management* 16 (1980):17-35.

Roderer, N.K., et al. *Evaluation of Online Bibliographic Systems*. Report prepared for National Science Foundation. Rockville, Md.: King Research, Inc., July 1981.

Swanson, Rowena W. "Performing Evaluation Studies in Information Science." Reprinted from *Journal of the American Society for Information Science* (May-June 1975). In *Key Papers in the Design and Evaluation of Information Systems*. Donald W. King, ed. White Plains, N.Y., Knowledge Industry Publications, Inc., 1978, pp. 58-74.

Tessier, Judith A.; Crouch, Wayne W. and Atherton, Pauline. "New Measures of User Satisfaction with Computer Based Literature Searches." *Special Libraries* 68 (Nov. 1977):383-389.

Wanger, Judith; McDonald, Dennis; and Berger, Mary C. *Evaluation of the Online Search Process: A Final Report*. Santa Monica, Calif.: Cuadra Associates and Rockville, Md.: King Reasearch Inc., January 1980.

The advent of the microcomputer onto the library scene is a phenomenon of the 1980s. While little was seen in the library literature previously, the past five years have witnessed an explosion of workshops, conferences, and journal articles devoted to the topic. This is hardly surprising. Micros are relatively inexpensive, easy to use, and adaptable. Software is improving all the time. In short, micros are part of the new computer literacy sweeping society at large.

The new improved generation of micros can perform a variety of library-related functions. Tasks for which they are especially suited are those areas that rely on the creation and maintenance of files such as for acquisitions or circulation; tasks that are essentially clerical such as the generation of accounts, mailing lists, and maintenance of employee records; tasks that require the manipulation of data such as budgets and other decision-support systems; and tasks that require repetition and patience such as computer-assisted instruction.

Of primary concern here, of course, is the microcomputer's place in the performance and management of online searching. In the last five years it has been responsible for the introduction of a whole set of hitherto unforeseen issues and impacts. The mushrooming presence of micros in private homes, in business, and on campus has meant, among other things, that many more end users have the potential capability of performing their own searches. This increased access by untrained users has spawned a whole new emphasis on the design and implementation of intelligent front-ends that mediate, augment, and enhance the search process. These user interfaces not only simplify searching but improve cost effectiveness by logical multiplexing, managing access protocols, storing search strategies and responses, providing user helps, and logging search activity. They can not only allow novice users to perform their own searches but teach them how to do so and remediate their errors as well. Reduced after-hours rates also encourage home-based end users to do their own searching. Not only is more searching being done, but it is being done cheaper.

These technological improvements have clearly changed the face of online searching. Their implications for the types of services offered by libraries and the role of the online searcher have not yet become fully felt. At the very least, it can be anticipated that users to whom micros are commonplace will have different and undoubtedly higher expectations for library services and searcher performance. Expertise will have to be current and in-depth to satisfy the more sophisticated user.

With the increased use of micros for searching, other issues will have to be confronted and resolved as well. The ability to tailor the output of searches to individual requirements is not a totally unmitigated benefit. For that same manipulation of the information on the database raises questions about breach of copyright, the ownership of machine-readable data, and the rights of the end user. Downloading in its worst form may in fact be a type of piracy—the spectre of lawsuits looms for librarians.

While interest in microcomputers for online searching is intense, as yet few libraries are actually using them for that purpose. Currently, they appear to be most prevalent in special and corporate libraries, due perhaps to their close affinity with industry. Many librarians are still reluctant to join the micro revolution because of the proliferation of hardware products, the lack of standardization, and the incompatibility of software packages. The articles that follow are intended to clarify some of the confusion by providing practical guidelines for the evaluation and choice of suitable machines and programs.

For those libraries or information centers either embarking on the use of microcomputers for the first time or contemplating upgrading the devices they already own, the choices available in video display terminals (VDTs) can be bewildering. Rapid changes and improvements in recent years have rendered terminals cheaper, lighter, and sturdier. Features that formerly were costly options are now standard and terminals purchased as recently as 1980 may very well be obsolete when compared with what is currently on the market.

Recognizing that increased choice can lead to greater confusion, Walt Crawford has compiled a checklist of factors that will help potential purchasers determine what equipment best meets their particular needs on behalf of TESLA, the Technical Standards for Library Automation Committee of the Library and Information Technology Association (LITA) of the American Library Association. While his main focus is on cathode ray tubes (CRTs) and VDTs, the information is also relevant to personal computers as keyboard and display devices.

Before selecting a VDT, Crawford urges readers to evaluate their own needs, uses, and budget; to survey the market against the criteria they have set down; to try out lively choices; to talk to users of the machines being considered. He then describes specific VDT characteristics that should be considered before any purchase is made. He divides these into those that are related to the screen (such as number of characters per line and number of lines on the screen, character definition, graphics, flicker, instability, distortion, noise, glare, contrast, focus, and display enhancements) and those that are relevant to the keyboard (such as detachability, profile and design, repeating and special keys, tabs, rollover, feel, and other aspects). For each of these areas, and others, Crawford suggests standards to be met and concludes by reminding the reader of the importance of site preparation and handling.

While the selection of hardware is not easy, it is only half the problem. The appropriate software must also be identified and evaluated. The articles by Carol Tenopir and Louise R. Levy discuss criteria that should be applied in selecting packages for microcomputers.

Carol Tenopir starts off by discussing the drawbacks and benefits of buying pre-written software packages, leasing or purchasing a turnkey system, or creating customized programs. She goes on to list sources of software targeted to information applications. But the core of her piece is the formulation of guidelines for evaluating library software. She poses a series of questions that should be asked and answered before any decisions are arrived at and provides a checklist of major areas that should be examined and rated. Tenopir leaves the reader in no doubt that the evaluation process is difficult and time-consuming and requires a significant commitment on the part of the prospective user and manager if rational decisions are to be made. She concludes by identifying journals and recent monographs that have descriptions and reviews of microcomputer software packages for inhouse databases.

Louise R. Levy discusses software packages that have been designed specifically to act as interfaces between users and the online bibliographic retrieval systems they search. These packages take search statements expressed in plain English and translate them into the command language of the system thereby providing easier access to users with limited knowledge. Additional enhancements, such as automatic log-on, downloading capabilities, text processing, and other features may also be included. Levy describes and compares four such programs: In-Search, the Universal Online Searcher, microDISCLOSURE, and SEARCH HELPER. It should be noted that since the recent appearance of her article, further product development has taken place. For example, In-Search has been expanded to permit searching of all BRS databases and is fully compatible with Dialog II. Because of the rapidity with which changes occur in this area, the reader is urged to contact the software companies for the most current information about their products.

Paralleling the availability of enhanced software has been the emergence of new storage technologies that have profoundly affected the ways in which microcomputers can be used. Currently, searchers can, and do, obtain information from mainframe-based databases, download it to their own micro-computers, manipulate and reuse it to suit their needs and convenience. With the development of the microdiskette which can store nearly a million characters on a 3¼-inch plastic platter and the optical disk, this practice will be accelerated and become commonplace. This capability of storing and reusing information not only allows the searcher to avoid paying database producers, vendors, and services for accessing their information by obviating the necessity of performing additional searches, but raises complex issues regarding copyright liability.

Thomas S. Warrick, an attorney with a special interest in the fields of copyright and computer law, examines the legal dilemma of downloading. He begins by defining current copyright law, examining "fair use," and in view of the fact that at present no court has yet ruled on whether copyright has been infringed when data are downloaded for future use, provides informed specu-lation as to how a court would likely resolve the downloading question. Warrick offers five possible solutions to the legal uncertainties surrounding downloading and ends by cautioning the reader against relying on any predictions as to how the issues will be resolved.

The Additional Readings list some of the recent monographs that provide overviews of microcomputer applications in libraries, articles that give advice to those contemplating the use of a micro for online searching, examples of front-ends developed for searching on micros, and discussions of some of the issues that arise from the application of this new technology to bibliographic retrieval.

VDT Checklist: Another Look at Terminals

Walt Crawford

INTRODUCTION

Visual display terminals (VDTs) are nothing new in library automation; for several years, a keyboard and visual display have been the standard communications device for people to direct computers and for computers to respond. As library automation grows and diversifies, keyboard/screen combinations become more common in more library settings, in public areas as well as technical processing areas. If you're selecting new devices or replacing old ones, you need to consider a number of factors; this checklist should help you identify factors and determine which ones are most important for your needs.

This checklist is loosely based on the *CRT Terminal Checklist* prepared in 1979 on behalf of ALA LITA TESLA, the Technical Standards for Library Automation Committee of the Library and Information Technology Association. That checklist appeared in the March 1980 *Journal of Library Automation*[1]. A more recent article, prepared by R. Bruce Miller on TESLA's behalf and considering health and ergonomic aspects of VDT use, appeared in the June 1983 *Information Technology and Libraries*[2]

As in 1979, this checklist is prepared on TESLA's behalf but represents my own viewpoints and not necessarily those of the committee. The checklist focuses on displays and keyboards for general use; while specifically related to cathode ray tube (CRT) and other VDTs, much of the information also applies to personal computers as keyboard and display devices. Some points also apply to the specialized terminals used for OCLC, RLIN, WLN, and other technical processing and information retrieval systems.

Reprinted with permission of the American Library Association from *Information Technology and Libraries* 3 (4):343-53 (Dec. 1984); copyright © 1984 by the American Library Association.

Changes in VDTs

Since 1980, terminals have gotten better and cheaper, lighter and more rugged. Most terminals now incorporate microprocessors (dedicated computers), and many microcomputers make good terminals. Features which used to be expensive options are now standard; most older terminal designs are now either obsolete or obsolescent, even as newer terminals face possible replacement by powerful personal computers at moderate prices, produced on a mass scale (a phenomenon that did not exist in 1979).

Compromises made for economic reasons in 1980 should not be necessary in 1984: technology has made them unnecessary, and knowledge of ergonomics has made them undesirable. If you are using terminals purchased in 1980 or before, you should be considering replacements; with rare exceptions, your existing terminals should have been amortized and are probably a burden on those using them. See what's available now and how much more pleasant your working environment could be; while there are still no perfect terminals, today's low-priced models tend to be far better than those of 1979.

This checklist takes up selection steps and considers each aspect of a terminal. If you have not already done so, read the article by R. Bruce Miller in the June 1983 issue; [2] it includes an excellent discussion of health hazards, ergonomic guidelines, and a brief annotated bibliography. This checklist generally does not repeat information and suggestions appearing in Miller's article.

SELECTING A VDT: FOUR STEPS

There are hundreds of VDTs on the market and dozens of personal computers in the same general price range as the most expensive VDTs. You may well consider several dozen devices even in a brief search; you should take at least the first three of the four steps toward selection.

Step One: Evaluate Your Needs

There is no perfect terminal, just as there is no perfect computer; what's best for you depends on your intended uses and your budget. Before you start looking at terminals and computers, you should develop your own criteria and weighting system. Know your real uses and needs; desirable features for some situations may be drawbacks for others. Don't try to plan for too long a term; if a device serves you well for five to seven years, you should be more than satisfied. Go through this article and the

Miller article, consider your situation, and make sure you know what you want before you start looking.

Before proceeding to the second step, you should have established your own selection worksheet: a set of criteria with weighting for each one, allowing you to make comparisons between models. You should have a budget range and know the number of devices you require; you should already be planning sites, so that you'll be able to use the terminals once they're acquired. If you have a budget range or some flexibility in the number of terminals acquired, your selection worksheet should be set up to help you use your flexibility. For each criterion and for the full set of criteria, you should have a minimum acceptable score and a level for complete acceptability (that is, the point beyond which further improvement would not be worth any additional cost under any circumstances). Your worksheet should include subjective measures and will almost certainly include many items that can't be answered as simple yes/no criteria (though objective yes/no criteria are the fastest and most conclusive way to narrow the field of choices). On the other hand, you should establish levels of minimal acceptability for each criterion and recognize that failure to meet any such criterion should immediately rule out a VDT: a "great" VDT that, for instance, only displays upper-case letters or emits a 65 dB, 15.7 kHz tone should be ruled out regardless of its other virtues.

Your worksheet should yield a set of numbers for each terminal considered; this will allow you to make relative judgements, particularly if you've established the guidelines in advance. That is, if your minimum total point score is fifty out of a complete acceptability level of ninety, and your budget allows a range of $500 to $900 per terminal, you should establish the relationship of price to points: in this case, you may be able to simply establish $10 per point as a break-even point. (Thus, if a $600 terminal scores sixty and a $750 terminal scores seventy-eight, the $750 terminal is a better bargain by your pre-established guidelines.)

Step Two: Survey the Market

Once you've got a basic set of criteria, weighting factors, and a budget, you should get a rough idea of what's available, so that you can refine your criteria and budget and narrow your choices. Common sources of information include trade magazines and journals such as *Computerworld* and *Datamation*, the microcomputer magazines such as *Byte* and *Infoworld*, information services such as Datapro and Auerbach, and trade shows, including the National Computer Conference and various business-oriented shows. Some computer stores also handle terminals, as do some larger business-supply stores.

Terminals are not as glamorous now as they were ten years ago; personal computers have taken over the spotlight and most of the press. You may well consider a computer as a terminal replacement, particularly if you only expect to use the terminal part-time; all the sources above, and many more computer stores, will serve to inform you on personal computers through advertisements, reviews, and articles.

A few hours spent looking through journals and information services should give you a feel for the range of prices and devices available. Find out what special institutional arrangements you can make (or, in some cases, are required to make), then go to the most critical step.

Step Three: Observation and Use

You should now have your own criteria well defined and should have already started using your worksheet to establish the range of possibilities. With luck, you will have narrowed your search to a modest number of terminals or computers. Now you need to try them out; literature can't substitute for hands-on experience.

If you're buying VDTs for staff use, get the staff involved in the process: have them look at the literature, and bring one or more of them along to try out the terminals. Try to have at least one expert typist along; a staff member with bifocals or trifocals can provide critical judgement, as can a staff member with acute high-frequency hearing (most likely a woman or a young man). If you're making a large purchase, you may be able to do in-house comparisons of terminals, with all the staff members who will use terminals judging them; otherwise, you'll need to go to shops and user sites to try out terminals.

You may be able to look at a variety of newer terminals and computers by visiting other libraries, colleges and universities, and businesses; you can combine step three with step four in this process. If you can't think of at least a dozen nearby sites where terminals are being used, you probably live in an unusually isolated area. Site visits can easily be overdone; terminal purchases are small items unless dozens or hundreds of terminals are involved, and you can easily spend too much of your time and the time of your staff and the staffs of other institutions.

After you've narrowed the field and tried out the final group of terminals or computers, you may have a clear choice from a company you already know. If you're down to a difficult final decision, you should try to take the extra step below.

Step Four: Talking to Users

If possible, talk to people who use the terminals you are considering. If you can find libraries that use the same model, so much the better. If you're buying personal computers rather than terminals, or if you're buying several terminals at once, the store or manufacturer should provide you with names and numbers of customers.

When you're talking to present users, find out how long they've had the equipment: new purchasers tend to be more positive than those who have had more experience, particularly if the users you talk to helped to select the device. Stress the negative: every terminal and computer has flaws and weaknesses, and users are the only reliable source of negative information (other than the rare critical review). If a library uses more than one type of terminal, ask the staff to compare the models. If the user has no problems at all with the terminal or the company, you may be talking to an uncritical user.

VDT CHARACTERISTICS: THE SCREEN

Most VDT screens look alike at first glance: a CRT measuring twelve inches diagonally, displaying 80 characters on each of twenty-four lines, commonly with a twenty-fifth line at the bottom of the screen that carries status information. A number of VDTs, particularly those which are part of microcomputers, vary from this common form; in addition, there are many detailed differences among "standard" CRTs. Your worksheet should include basic and ideal levels for most of the following items.

Numbers of Characters Per Line

Many inexpensive microcomputers display fewer than 80 characters per line (particularly when televisions are used as VDTs): the most common smaller number is 40 characters, but 20-, 32-, and 56- character lines are not unknown. Many programs will not work properly with lines narrower than 80 characters, and most uses will be severely hampered by narrower lines.

Some VDTs and microcomputers can display more characters per line, usually 132 (the line width of traditional computer listings). Such displays are useful for spreadsheet work and program listings; unless the terminal can be switched back to 80 characters, however, the smaller characters may be undesirable, as they will generally be harder to read.

Suggested standards: For nearly all library uses, 80-character lines should be the minimal acceptance level. If you expect the terminal to be used for financial work or programming, a switchable 132-character capability may be ranked higher; otherwise, 80 characters should be a simple yes/no criterion.

Number of Lines on the Screen

Most displays with 80-character lines have twenty-four text lines on the screen, yielding sufficient display capability for most purposes. Except for portable microcomputers, very few 80-character displays have fewer text lines. Screens that can display more lines are rare except in word processing uses, where a "full page" display (from fifty to sixty-six lines) is sometimes available. Full-page displays tend to be expensive and may or may not be desirable: to some eyes, the screen simply has too much information. Most library applications and most packaged programs are oriented to the twenty-four-line screen; such applications will look very odd on a taller screen.

Suggested standards: For normal use within a library, a twenty-four-line screen is a yes/no criterion. Note that the twenty-fifth line on the bottom of many VDTs is not a text line. That line is dealt with below.

Status Line

VDTs increasingly feature status lines at the bottom of the screen; such lines, always present on IBM 3270-class terminals, have spread to many of the least expensive devices. Whether you need a status line depends on the software to be used. In most cases, an optional status line (one not required by your software) serves no useful function.

You're likely to find a status line whether you want it or not; in this case, there is a crucial question: can the status line be turned off? Some high-quality, low-cost terminals display a set of terminal status codes in inverse video (black on green) on the status line; many users find the bright but meaningless line to be annoying and tiring. There should be a switch or a simple character sequence, which can be keyed in at the terminal or sent to the terminal by software and which will turn the status line off, not leaving it black (not inverse).

Suggested standards: If your software uses a status line, its presence is mandatory. If not, a status line should carry no weighting by itself; a non-defeatable status line (or one which is difficult to defeat) should carry a negative weighting, possibly even an absolute negative weighting.

Screen Size

Most VDTs use rectangular screens measuring 300mm diagonally (12 inches), with the characters displayed over an area about 150mm (6 inches) high and 215mm (8.5 inches) wide. (While the screen is typically about 19mm high and 25mm wide at extremes, the outer portions are usually illsuited to text display: the status line is not included in the

150mm height.) This yields a character cell size of 6.25mm high by 2.7mm wide, or about 1/4 inch high by 1/10 inch wide.

Miller proposes 3mm as a minimum acceptable height for characters; this means that a screen as little as 74mm high (3 inches) can be considered adequate. Most operators would disagree with this minimum; for terminals which will be used for any length of time, a minimum of 4mm is about the smallest acceptable size. This means a display height of 100mm, the height usually found in a "9-inch" (225cm) screen. Such screens are not uncommon, particularly as monitors for microcomputers; their chief drawback is the narrowness of the characters: almost exactly 2mm wide, or less than 1/12 inch.

Some recent devices use a different screen shape, much wider than it is tall. Since the chief objection to 3mm characters is not their height but their very narrow width, such displays may well be worth considering. A 5-by-9-inch (roughly 125-by-225mm) screen has proportions similar to those of twenty-four single-spaced lines of typing, with a character cell as much as 4.5mm high by 2.8mm wide; such characters can be very legible, possibly even easier to read than the overly tall characters on a normal CRT screen.

At the other extreme, a number of CRT's have 14-inch diagonal measure (about 250mm); if the characters have enough elements (see below), such screens can be unusually legible. For the same number of character elements, however, a 12-inch screen will usually have clearer characters than a 14-inch screen.

Suggested standards: Minimum acceptable for extended work: cell size at least 2mm wide and 4mm high. Beyond that, this measurement is a subjective one that must be taken in combination with the measurement below.

Character Definition

Nearly all VDTs use matrices of dots or small lines to define characters. Typically, each character is made up of a certain number of dots within a defined cell (the "character cell"); the cell includes spacing between lines.

In 1979, the most common character was defined as a five-by-seven matrix in a six-by-eight cell. By 1984 standards, such a display is crude and may not be considered acceptable; a seven-by-nine display within a nine-by-twelve matrix is common, and higher densities are not all that rare. Dedicated technical processing terminals tend to have significantly higher densities. Higher-density characters are easier to read because they are more clearly defined, more distinctive, and look more like regular type.

Legibility has several components: character definition density, actual character design, size of screen, colors, and others. An overall legibility rating is necessarily subjective, but character definition density is one objective aspect of legibility. Two different seven-by-nine matrices may yield sharply differing legibility, but a poorly designed seven-by-nine matrix will probably be more legible than a well-designed five-by-seven matrix.

Suggested standards: Minimum acceptability: seven-by-nine character matrix within an eight-by-ten cell. Optimum density: include as part of the subjective legibility rating.

Character Set and Graphics

Odd as it may seem, there are still some terminals and micro-computers that display "full sixty-four-character ASCII"—upper case only—rather than the standard ninety-six-character ASCII set. Many terminals have graphics characters or alternate character sets; some terminals and microcomputers allow full graphics, using "bit-mapped graphics" (where an image of the entire screen, dot by dot, is stored in the computer).

If you need graphics or special characters, your choice of terminals will probably be constrained: your terminal must meet the requirements of your system. Otherwise, character set is basically a yes/no decision: anything less than ninety-six-character ASCII, including upper case only, is unacceptable in 1984. The full ALA character set, which is not standard ASCII, may well become available in future terminals (it is now available, but not in any known ASCII terminals that cost less than $1700); if full ALA Extended ASCII is available at a competitive price, it will serve you well in library processing.

Suggested standards: Minimum and optimum: full ninety-six-character ASCII.

Character Legibility

The previous two characteristics can be used to disqualify terminals without even inspecting them. Legibility is more subjective; it requires actual inspection, preferably by the people who will be using the system. Don't judge a terminal by its legibility for eight people at once; terminals aren't designed for groups, and what serves a group may not serve an individual user nearly as well.

Character legibility is only one aspect of screen legibility, but it is an important one. In judging legibility, you are really judging whether the character set is clear, but also whether it is pleasant. A clear but annoying character font is fine for quick lookup, but is not as good for long sessions.

Some basic judgements of character legibility may be yes/no decisions. Do the lowercase letters *y, g, p* have true descenders, that is, go below the line of other lowercase letters? Do the letters have normal height relationships? Are the lowercase letters actually lowercase, or are they smaller capital letters? Finally, can you tell the close pairs of characters apart instantly, regardless of context?

The close pairs and sets include:

1,l
Ø, 0
m,n
u,v,w,
[,(,<,{
],),>,}
I,T

The last "close pair" was not regarded as a close pair in 1979. Oddly, design changes that have led to generally greater legibility have also (in certain cases) compromised the legibility of such an apparently clear case.

Other judgements of character legibility are wholly subjective. Most people will find a slightly serifed font more legible than a fully sans serif font, even though the sans serif font may appear "cleaner" at first glance. Any display on which the characters appear fully formed at 18 inches, or half a meter (the typical distance from operator to screen, assuming a detachable keyboard), will be more desirable than one, even a larger one, in which the dots or lines are distinctly visible.

Suggested standards: Minimum acceptable: true descenders, actual lower case letters, some serifs, and all character groups above easily distinguished. Optimum: subjective rating, depends on staff.

Screen Color and Polarity

In 1979, most visual display devices showed white characters on black or dark gray backgrounds. White-on-black displays are still common, but most users will find other alternatives more appealing. Basically, VDTs come with four color combinations and two polarities.

The colors normally available are black and white, black and green, black and amber, and full color. The polarities are positive and negative. Perhaps most common among current VDTs is black and green with negative polarity (green characters on a black background).

Europeans argue that amber displays are more ergonomically sound than green displays; most users agree that green and amber are both much easier on the eyes than white-on-black displays. Amber displays have had problems with flicker and with durability, but these appear to be on the road to resolution; meanwhile, while it is clear that amber-on-black is a sharper contrast than green-on-black, quite a few users are reporting preference for the green-on-black.

Positive polarity may appear more "natural" but does not, in general, seem to work very well. Some noted microcomputer manufacturers are claiming otherwise, introducing very high-definition, black-on-gray displays; such displays have not been in use long enough for objective long-term judgement. In most cases, dark letters on a light background appear well-suited to reflective light (ink on paper) but ill-suited to transmitted light (VDTs), where the light is directly in the user's face.

Full-color terminals are very attractive on an exhibition floor and can be sold on the basis of improved user efficiency. The results aren't in. A full-color display is much more expensive than a single-color display for the same clarity; some full-color displays compromise character definition. In any case, a full-color display makes no sense unless the software makes use of color.

Suggested standards: Minimum acceptable: reverse polarity (or selectable polarity), green-on-black or amber-on-black; color only if character clarity is not compromised. Optimum: subjective test.

Flicker, Instability, Distortion, and Noise

Terminals are still imperfect; while most of these characteristics will not turn up in a showroom, they are worth checking with other users. There is no excuse for flicker. Some microcomputers only refresh the monitor image thirty times per second; this can, under some conditions, lead to flicker. "Non-interlaced" images, which are refreshed fifty or sixty times per second, should be flicker free. If a terminal brags about "fast phosphors," look carefully at its performance under various lighting conditions including fluorescent light, the most difficult condition: fast phosphors, while very desirable for some special applications, can increase flicker.

Instability or distortion of any sort is simply unacceptable in any contemporary terminal or display, under any reasonably normal operating conditions.

Noise is a bit trickier. A display should be silent (unless, for some fairly unusual reason, it requires a fan). Most men and many women find all displays to be silent; many women, and a few men with acute hearing, can become very upset after working with some terminals and may not realize why.

Terminals can emit audible whine in the 15.5-15.7 kHz range for at least two different reasons: cheaply made or badly shielded flyback transformers, or poor filtering of video control signals in terminals with audio output. Most men can't hear anything at 15 kHz or above; those who can will tend to sense rather than hear the noise, and may even think that it is in their heads.

Many contemporary terminals have eliminated the 15.7 kHz noise problem, but many still have it. If a young woman with superlative hearing is not available for your test sessions, it may be worth creating a sound measurement system that will respond in the 15 kHz region. Requiring a person with superb hearing to use a terminal with significant emissions in the 15 kHz region ("significant" possibly being measured as fifty-five decibels or higher at an 18-inch distance from the screen) is a form of slow, subtle torture; no library caring about its staff would buy such a terminal.

Suggested standards: Minimum acceptable: no visible distortion or instability; refresh rate of at least 50 Hz; no emission in the range of 20 Hz to 24 kHz (with particular attention to the range of 15.5-15.7 kHz) in excess of fifty decibels. Optimum: even quieter, and with a refresh rate high enough that flicker can never be detected.

Glare, Contrast, and Focus

Glare is a problem with many VDTs, including some very good ones. Some newer VDTs contain anti-glare filters; such filters can be added at a cost of $50 or less to other VDTs. Proper siting is an aspect of protection against glare, as is proper lighting; at the same time, an anti-glare VDT is more desirable than one which is heavily subject to glare.

Any VDT should have crystal-clear focus; cheap televisions used as monitors have no place in a professional library operation. Contrast should be crisp. Brightness should be adjustable; on many monitors, brightness is the only adjustable characteristic.

Suggested standards: Minimum acceptable: accessible brightness control. Optimum: glare protection, contrast control.

Cursor, Display Enhancements, and Features

Just because a screen doesn't show colors doesn't mean you can't draw attention to text. Many, perhaps most, current VDTs allow for a variety of display enhancements, typically two levels of intensity, inverse video (dark on light), and blinking; some VDTs also allow for underlines. Such enhancements can increase the usefulness of a display.

The cursor should have optional characteristics; for those sitting at a terminal for half an hour or more, a blinking cursor is a continuing annoyance. Some terminals allow choice of solid cursor, solid blinking cursor, underline cursor, or underline blinking cursor. Such a choice allows you to tailor each terminal to existing needs.

Other features tend to be operation-specific. Is "block move capability" worth anything extra to you? Probably not. A slave printer port may be useful, and is quite common.

Suggested standards: Minimum acceptable: cursor constant or selectable; at least one enhancement available under character-by-character software control (either blinking, dual intensity, or inverse video: any one will do nicely for special messages). Optimum: depends on application.

VDT Display Characteristics: Summing Up

These points cover the display. Don't let a salesman attempt to sell you a display by showing how wonderful it is very close up, or how good it is at a great distance. Most work will be done at distances of 450 to 700mm from the screen, roughly 18 to 27 inches; a terminal should be judged on the basis of its intended use.

Some issues that were relevant in 1979 are less so in 1984. Any terminal should automatically "wrap" any line that is too long: a one-hundred-character line should take up two display lines; if the last twenty characters disappear, the terminal should be removed from consideration. Virtually all contemporary terminals scroll (roll up existing lines when a new line is entered at the bottom); the differences in 1984 are between "jump scrolling" (where the display moves one full line at a time, jumping up) and "smooth scrolling" (where the display moves up one dot at a time, smoothly rolling the screen up). Some people prefer smooth scrolling, while some find that it is disconcerting; for most applications, most people probably don't care one way or the other. Scrolling is a subjective criterion.

The final suggested standard for display, then, is simply "niceness": how does it feel to use the screen; how does it look (can the display be tilted and rotated, does the frame surrounding the screen seem appropriate, etc.); how easy is it to read? These may be major considerations; frequently, a tiltable/rotatable display may be much more useful than one which is fixed.

VDT CHARACTERISTICS: THE KEYBOARD

Display quality is a blend of several objective and subjective characteristics. Keyboard quality is nearly all subjective, though a few objective measures can filter out unacceptable keyboards. An expert touch typist is the fastest and best judge of a keyboard; the qualities that make a keyboard pleasant for the expert will also help the novice.

Detachability

Most terminals and microcomputers introduced since 1981 have detached or detachable keyboards, usually sleek, low-profile keyboards attached to the display or computer by a coiled cable. If the terminals your're buying are for public use and security is a problem, you'll probably rule out terminals with detachable keyboards. In most other cases, you may end up requiring detachable keyboards. The virtues of a movable keyboard are subtle, but important for those using terminals for extended periods. You don't really get a detachable keyboard so you can put it in your lap—while some writers do this, most experienced typists would not find such a position useful. A detachable keyboard simply allows flexibility and control; sometimes, just moving the keyboard an inch forward and slanting it a bit makes typing more pleasurable.

Suggested standard: Strong weighting for detachable keyboard. For terminals intended for heavy use, detachable keyboards should be considered essential.

Profile and Design

Newer keyboards tend to be thin: usually less than 1.5 inches (or 40mm) at home row. A thin keyboard allows an operator to rest palms on the work surface; alternatively, a thicker keyboard can have a palm rest built in. Built-in palm rests are a mixed blessing; they make the keyboard so deep that good placement is difficult (rightly or wrongly, many skilled typists prefer to work close to the keyboard). A thin keyboard is usually preferable to a thick keyboard, all else being equal. The crucial point regarding height of keyboard has to do with the work station: the keyboard should be placed so that the keyer's arms form a right or oblique angle, that is, the home row should be lower than the elbow.

Design criteria for a good keyboard are well-known, though often ignored, and are largely embodied in the IBM Selectric keyboard. Briefly, those criteria include:

- Concave keys: each keytop should be hollowed out slightly, improving user confidence and accuracy;
- Full-stroke keys: keys should actually move, and there must be a recognizable feedback (touch, sound, or both) when the keystroke is complete;
- Horizontal keytops: each key should be level or nearly so at its outer edges (but concave within those edges);
- Sloping keyboards: the keyboard as a whole should slope, having a "stairstep" effect of several horizontal rows, each at a lower height than the one above;

- Matte finish and neutral color: keys should not cause glare, and should not have bright or interesting colors;
- Clear labels: keys should be clearly labeled, to assist those who are not expert typists and those who must move from keyboard to keyboard.
- Familiar layout and size: keys should be the same size and spacing as on a good electric typewriter and should generally be in the same positions. This generally implies a "Qwerty" keyboard (so named for the characters on the first alphabetic row); a "Dvorak" keyboard is theoretically more efficent, but should only be considered if those planning to use the terminal like the idea.

Most of these points should seem obvious as you read them; surprisingly, they are apparently not obvious to microcomputer manufacturers and some terminal manufacturers. The final point may be the most controversial. Supporters of the Dvorak keyboard (which has an entirely different layout based on letter frequency) correctly state that the Qwerty keyboard was designed to slow typists down and claim that the Dvorak keyboard allows for much greater efficiency. These claims are still open to question; the ease of retraining from Qwerty to Dvorak has not been demonstrated. At this point, the Dvorak keyboard may have the same difficulties in the United States that left-side driving would, even if it was proven safer: most people learn Qwerty, and most people don't want to relearn something that basic.

Suggested standards: Most points above should be absolute criteria: a keyboard that lacks concave keys in flat staggered rows, matte finish, neutral colors, and clear labeling, is simply not a good keyboard. Some form of feedback is required, but the desirable form is subjective; most experienced typists want some tactile feedback and minimal auditory feedback—if clicks are involved, the clicks should be controllable.

Repeating Keys

Most modern keyboards have delayed repeat on all keys, a feature usually called "auto-repeat" or "Typeomatic": any key held down for more than a second will begin repeating. Deliberate auto-repeat, with a suitable delay, is a desirable feature; a keyboard with a separate "repeat" key is far less desirable, and a keyboard with selective repeat is archaic. At the other extreme, some keyboards develop "bounce": characters repeat when no repeat was intended. Bounce is usually a sign of wear, and is unlikely to show up except when talking to other users; any keyboard with significant bounce problems should be rejected immediately.

Suggested standard: Minimal acceptability: auto-repeat on all keys (except control keys) with a one-second (or so) delay. No bounce after heavy use.

Special Keys

Several special keys are required for terminal operations. The rule for most special keys is that they should be easy to find when you need them, and hard to hit accidentally. The [ENTER] or [RETURN] key should be much larger than other keys, as should both [SHIFT] keys; the [ENTER] or [RETURN] key should usually be distinctly shaped and placed. A terminal must have a [BREAK] key for most telecommunications systems, and the [BREAK] function cannot usually be generated by other keystrokes; the [BREAK] key should always be in a position where it won't be hit accidentally.

Microcomputers usually have some form of [RESET] key, button, or key combination. A [RESET] key on the main keyboard is an invitation to disaster: well-designed systems either have a button in a very special position on the disk drive, or use a multi-key combination for [RESET].

If a terminal will be used for computation or other heavy numeric entry, it should have a separate numeric keypad; the best pads will include decimal point, [ENTER], and sometimes basic arithmetic functions such as -, +, *, and /. If a terminal will be used with screen-oriented software (text editors, for instance), cursor movement keys will prove useful. There are many different opinions on the best placement for such keys, but the best placements are easy to recognize and remember and do not share keys with numeric keypads. "Diamond" placements are possibly the best, but also take up the most space; four keys in a square are nearly as good, and four cursor keys in a horizontal row appear to make a reasonable compromise between ease of use and size of keyboard.

Other special keys depend on the application. A keyboard with too many keys, particularly if they are not well laid out and clearly distinguished, is intimidating; a keyboard with too few keys is frustrating. Many terminals include function keys, which can be very helpful if the software supports them; otherwise, they may simply contribute to keyboard clutter.

Suggested standard: Large, clearly placed [RETURN] key; numeric keypad if terminal is to be used for multiple purposes; separate cursor keys. Optimal special key placement is a subjective decision.

Tabs, Rollover, and Other Aspects

Some older terminals don't have tabulation functions (and thus don't have a TAB key). If you're just using a terminal to search databases, you may not care; if your're using it for text editing and the like, a TAB key is essential—as is a clear method for setting tabs, which requires co-ordination of the computer and the terminal.

Some terminals and microcomputers allow rollover, storing key-strokes until the software can deal with them. "N key rollover," as it is usually called, provides a safeguard for fast and erratic typists; novice typists may actually be able to test roll-over better than experienced ones, as experts usually maintain smooth rhythms.

Suggested standards: Minimal acceptability: TAB key with clear method for setting tabs. Roll-over sufficient to handle occasional bursts of speed without losing characters.

Feel

The most subjective aspect of keyboards is also the single most important for heavily used terminals and microcomputers: *feel*. Some keyboards are soft and springy; some clatter but are reassuringly firm. No standard exists for keyboard touch and overall noise; different people have different tastes. Those who will use a terminal should be the judges of the keyboard's feel. This subjective aspect of keyboards cannot be overemphasized: keyboard feel may well be 30-40 percent of the overall weighting in judging a terminal and should probably be the primary (perhaps sole) criterion for judging acceptable keyboards. Other keyboard criteria may be distinct yes/no judgements; feel will always be subjective.

VDTs: OTHER ASPECTS

Most modern terminals are sturdy, but almost any terminal will eventually need servicing. You should be sure that servicing is available in some form that meets your needs. If you will be heavily dependent on terminals, service contracts with guaranteed turnaround times may be warranted; in other cases, you may prefer to rely on available carry-in service on a time and materials basis. If you are buying a large number of terminals, and intend to replace them after a few years, you might find it more economical to buy one or two more than you need, rather than paying for a service contract on all your terminals. Many terminals will go through a three or four-year useful life without requiring servicing.

You should ask about servicing before making a purchase. Can the dealer or manufacturer cite a mean time between failures (MTF) based on actual experience? How easy is the terminal to service? Can the service agency give you a mean time to repair (MTTR) or guarantee a repair or replacement time? If you choose carry-in service, how convenient is the service depot?

If you are considering a microcomputer to be used as a terminal part-time or full-time, you will need to consider the software. Most probably, you will be able to choose from a number of different programs. Some terminal programs turn your computer into a "dumb terminal," with no special features. Better programs allow you to save information on disk or send information from disk to the remote computer; some also allow direct file transfer, though this requires compatible software in the remote computer. Your software must also work properly with your modem, and should give you enough flexibility to handle present and future telecommunications needs.

Other aspects of VDT selection and installation, covered in the *CRT Terminal Checklist* or R. Bruce Miller's article, involve locating a terminal and providing proper power. Site preparation is important and is covered in the earlier papers; by and large, all terminals will need similar site preparation and handling.

CONCLUSION

There are still no perfect terminals, but the medium-priced terminals of 1984 are much better than most high-priced terminals of 1980. Most of the good-quality terminals of 1980 are now obsolescent; few of them live up to today's nominal standards for VDTs. Many of the ergonomic issues raised with regard to VDTs are equally valid for typewriters; with VDTs, however, it is possible to do better.

VDTs can be an imposition in a library, causing distress and lowered morale. With care, involvement, but little or no additional cost, VDTs can make work easier and more pleasant. In today's market, library managers have no excuse for buying unpleasant, inadequate VDTs. A clear set of criteria and a clear procurement strategy, with extensive involvement of the users should yield VDTs that will be a pleasure to use even after better ones appear on the market.

Footnotes

1. Walt Crawford, "CRT Terminal Checklist," *Journal of Library Automation* 13 (March 1980):36-44.
2. R. Bruce Miller, "Radiation, Ergonomics, Ion Depletion and VDTs: Healthful Use of Visual Display Terminals," *Information Technology and Libraries* 2 (June 1983):151-58.

Identification and Evaluation of Software for Microcomputer-Based In-House Databases

Carol Tenopir

INTRODUCTION

In-house online databases, created by a library or information center to meet the special information retrieval needs of its clientele, are becoming increasingly popular. These databases serve many purposes. They can replace print versions of such locally created tools as referral directories, indexes to verticle file materials, or abstracts of literature on a specific topic. They can be indexes to special types of materials or collections (e.g., audiovisuals, engineering drawings); full text or abstracts of internal corporate reports; or a central access system for all of the information resources in the information center. What in-house databases have in common is that they are all created with the library's own unique constituency in mind. The databases are created for a given situation and thus tend to be narrowly focused and very patron-oriented. They offer online retrieval to materials that are sometimes accessible nowhere else; allow easy updating of often rapidly changing information; and provide increased control over all information resources.

Until recently, however, the high costs of hardware made in-house databases out of reach for the small information center. The proliferation of small, powerful, but relatively inexpensive microcomputers since the late 1970s is changing this, and many managers of small libraries or information centers are now creating (or considering) online information retrieval systems for in-house materials.

The creation of an in-house database is not merely a matter of identifying the application and purchasing a microcomputer. Many decisions and plans must be made to create a successful database system, both in conjunction with and independent from the hardware choice. Some of the most important of these decisions relate to software, for poor software can cost information managers and end users more than the cost of the hardware in terms of wasted time, extensive modifications, and frustration. Without good software that is suited to the application, the system will never perform as it should. Appropriate software is so important that many experts urge potential microcomputer users to first shop for software to meet their needs, then purchase hardware that can run this software.[1]

Information managers must decide whether to purchase a prewritten, off-the-shelf software package, lease or purchase a hardware/software turnkey package, write their own programs, or have custom programs written for them. They must be familiar with existing packages in order to see all options open to them. Finally, they must feel comfortable with their ability to evaluate the many choices in order to develop or select the software that best meets their needs.

Unfortunately, no definitive formula for choice of microcomputer software for in-house databases is possible because software choice is ultimately dependent on each individual situation. The literature on the topic is sparse and uneven in quality, and "most reports deal with isolated techniques and system features."[2] There is a growing body of literature, however, that can provide help in choosing software for the creation of a microcomputer-based in-house database in the information center. This article will review and evaluate that literature, including sections on purchasing versus programming; directories of software; evaluation of software; and sources for software descriptions or reviews. It will not discuss literature that deals only with microcomputer characteristics or choice of hardware, nor will it include most descriptions of specific in-house database applications. Literature from related fields will be included only as it supplements the library literature.

PURCHASE OR PROGRAM

One of the first software decisions that must be made is whether to purchase a pre-written software package, lease or purchase a turnkey system, or create custom programs. Custom-created programs may either be written by the library or data processing department staff or by consultants hired for that purpose.

The debate over whether to purchase or program is not unique to microcomputer systems, but it surfaces repeatedly with microcomputers because they have been sold as "personal computers" that are especially easy to program and because commercially available microcomputer software has the reputation of being poor.

Until very recently, little microcomputer software for library applications was available, so programming in-house may have been the only alternative. As recently a 1980, the fact that there was little software for libraries and information centers was a real problem in the use of microcomputers in libraries. Pratt said in that year, "There does not seem to be anything presently on the market aimed at libraries. Thus it is necessary for libraries to write, or have written, their own programs for their own purposes."[3]

Lundeen noted in 1980 that "much of the applications software being marketed for micros is of mediocre quality, and is often very poorly documented. The librarian eager to use a micro in a library application will usually have to write (or have written) the software to do the job."[4] Lundeen went on to point out, however, that "the librarian who is contemplating using micros to automate should realize that the programming is not likely to be a trivial task. Software may well cost much more than the system hardware."[5]

Pratt also realized that the complexity of many library applications complicates in-house programming. He believed "it is unlikely that any library would have sufficient in-house capability to develop an adequate system. To have one custom-designed by outside consultants will probably prove more costly than acquiring one of the already available commercial turnkey systems."[6]

In the last year, a growing recognition of the complexity of the in-house database programming task, together with an increase in the number of available software packages and turnkey systems, has led to a swing away from recommending customized programming. In spite of Rowat's fear that "packages suitable for use in libraries will not be developed by the commercial sector until the library and information market is perceived to be one of sufficient coherence and size to warrant the considerable investment needed,"[7] more and more writers are realizing that "an astonishing number of companies . . . are now competing frenetically to anticipate and fulfill all conceivable needs of consumers of software," including libraries.[8] The number of packages suitable for creating in-house databases has grown tremendously in the last year. The introduction of the de facto standard operating system CP/M, together with the availability of standard higher-level languages on microcomputers, has allowed the proliferation of prewritten software packages.[9]

Programs for in-house databases are complex and expensive to develop, making it less advantageous to do in-house development when something good is available commercially. Complicated "total library systems" are compared to home building in *Small Computers in Libraries.*

> These total systems are much too elaborate and complex to consider writing them "in-house," at least for libraries that do not have NLM-style budgets. This is not to imply, as some think, that computer programming "is too complicated for librarians". . . . It's not that librarians can't write complex programs, it's that doing so is not their job.
> You could build your own home, but hardly anybody does. It's simpler, and probably cheaper, to have somebody else build it.[10]

The *Library Systems Newsletter* estimates that programming costs more than 80 percent of the total cost of developing a new system.[11] This article cites another disadvantage of doing your own programming or having it written for you—"the customer pays directly for the developer's mistakes. In contrast, when one purchases a software package from an established firm, one normally gets a working product that has already been installed and which can be investigated before purchase."[12]

Rorvig, in his 1982 book *Microcomputers and Libraries,* takes exception to the trend away from in-house programming when he states that "the best way for librarians to get the software they need is to learn BASIC or other languages and then to program functions for themselves. . . . In the final analysis librarians will not receive the applications software of greatest benefit to their institutions unless they themselves learn to program microcomputers. This is not as formidable a task as it might first seem."[13] These statements are not in tune with the growing current consensus and were met with an outcry of dissension.

In a review of Rorvig's book, Gordon says that for librarians to write their own application programs is "neither a practical nor financially feasible approach." She points out that "major computer manufacturers . . . spend two thirds of their engineering dollars on software development; and typically 30 percent of a large corporation's total data processing budget is spent on software."[14] Clearly, small libraries cannot afford such an investment.

Schuyler advises that the "expertise needed to program a sophisticated application is quite substantial; the time necessary is considerable." He goes on to warn that "information such as this, written with a tone of authority, may set the reader on the wrong path from which it may be time consuming (and therefore costly) to recover."[15]

Even favorable reviews of Rorvig's book by Grosch and by Pratt take exception to his opinion on programming. Grosch advises, "It still is true that a certain class of serious professional users will find that they must do some software development; however many librarians will find an assortment of software to enable them to use their micro as a professional support tool."[16]

Pratt warns:

Except under unusual circumstances this [writing your own program] is not a good idea. The writing of a fully debugged and operational system to perform any library task is not something to be undertaken without a strong commitment of resources and time. It is difficult to do, especially by inexperienced programmers. Librarians simply do not have the time to become good programmers in addition to their normal duties.[17]

The consensus in the library literature seems to have changed in two years to favor the purchase of existing microcomputer software or turnkey systems rather than developing programs from scratch. This may not always meet every need in all situations, however. Turnkey systems especially allow no local modifications, and the application must be tailored to meet the constraints of the software. A middle ground that combines both options is often desirable.

Modifying an existing software package to meet individual needs may provide the best of both options. Kelley recommends purchase of "modular software" for applications that are "fairly complex and unique." Modular software is defined as a "program that acts as a tool, enabling someone with very limited programming skills to develop useful programs which are somewhat specific to the user's situation."[18] Database management systems (DBMS) are well-known examples of modular software.

The literature contains many descriptions of DBMS software, including examples of libraries or information centers that have adapted different DBMS programs for the creation of in-house databases. (See, for example, *Small Computers in Libraries*.) The DBMS literature is too extensive to be covered completely in this article, but the adaptation of DBMS for use in libraries is addressed, as DBMS software allows information managers to create customized database systems without having to do extensive programming. There are many commercially available DBMS programs suitable for library/information retrieval applications to varying degrees. Kelley believes a "DBMS program is the most important piece of software one can purchase."[19]

Another, more difficult, way to combine prewritten software and customized programming is to purchase a package written in a known programming language and to write additional routines "to layer over the preprogrammed ones."[20] The problems with this approach are that the information center must then also be responsible for programming and that modification of an existing program may affect other parts of the program in unexpected ways. Plans for any such modifications should be made cautiously.

If prewritten software is the best option for the creation of microcomputer-based in-house databases, how can information managers find out what is available? Vickery and Brooks saw the need for a directory of available software for use in libraries in 1980.[21] Even in January 1982, there was "no easy way of discovering what software was available."[22] Garoogian calls this a "variation on the familiar library problem of bibliographic control."[23] In the last year, several publications have appeared that help to meet this problem.

SOFTWARE SOURCES

Until 1982 there were no microcomputer software directories targeted to library or information applications, although there were directories of microcomputer software applicable to other special interest areas (notably education and business). Several general microcomputer software directories have had to serve the information manager's needs. Myer's 1982 book includes an annotated list of software directories of all types. Garoogian covers sources for identification of software (pre-1982) in her article in the premiere (February) issue of *Software Review*.

Datapro Directory of Microcomputer Software began publication in 1981. In its section on "Data Management and Database Management," it includes information about DBMS, file management, storage and retrieval, and specialized storage and retrieval software packages. *Small Systems Software and Services Sourcebook* describes more than thirteen hundred small-computer software packages. *International Microcomputer Database* is available online via DIALOG. It is a combined online file that includes the *International Minicomputer Software Directory* and the *International Microcomputer Software Directory* and describes more than ten thousand commercially available software packages. Management Information Corporation, Cherry Hill, New Jersey, publishes an annual survey on small business computers, peripherals, and software.

Many other microcomputer software directories include only programs for a specific type of computer or operating system. (See, for example, *The IBM Personal Computer Software Directory*, Farmingham, Mass., International Management Services, second quarter, 1983.)

Database management system software for microcomputers is included in general DBMS directories, notably *A Buyer's Guide to Database Management Systems* (Delran, N.J.: Datapro Research Corp.) and *Datamation* magazine's regular DBMS software surveys. Appendix A lists some general microcomputer software sources.

These general directories include more software packages that are inappropriate for library applications than are appropriate. They therefore provide an information glut and can be frustrating to use. Recently published directories that are limited to library applications software are briefly reviewed by Tenopir.[24] These directories are a welcome addition to the field and will be examined more closely here. Publication information for each is given in appendix A.

Online Micro-Software Guide and Directory: 1983-84 includes descriptions of more than seven hundred microcomputer software packages, ninety of which are database management systems. A chart compares the major features of the most popular DBMS packages, although not enough information is given to allow real evaluation.

Information for each package includes:

- name, address, phone number of company
- contact person
- software name and version and date released
- cost
- applications
- operating environment
- hardware requirements
- documentation (a list and prices but nonevaluative)
- product description (several descriptive sentences)
- where purchased

The arrangement of the *Online Micro-Software Guide* is alphabetical by company, with indexes by software name and producer. An addendum provides a much needed index by applications, but an index by operating systems or hardware would be another useful addition.

The arrangement of this directory is straightforward and easy to follow. Four packages are listed on each page with a reduced typescript that keeps the size of the total directory manageable but causes some eyestrain.

A large number of microcomputer software packages are added to the market each month. Supplements to the directory in October 1983 and 1984 include hundreds of these new packages. The microcomputer software market changes so rapidly, however, that a printed publication can never be up-to-date. The *Online Micro-Software Guide and Directory* is also available online in a BRS as "File Soft."

A nice feature of this directory is the inclusion of nontechnical articles on various aspects of software use and a bibliography of articles on microcomputer software. These additions make this directory more than just a listing of hundreds of packages.

Micro Software Report: Library Edition (Jeanne Nolan) came out in July 1982. This directory contains almost three hundred software packages, approximately sixty of which are DBMS. It does not claim to be selective, so it is difficult to explain why there are four hundred fewer packages in it than in the Online, Inc., directoy. One explanation is that the Nolan directory is more focused on the library market; the Online directory contains many general-purpose software packages that might be used in information work. Another reason is that information on packages in the Nolan directory was gathered from printed sources, while Online contacted software vendors directly.

Micro Software Report is arranged alphabetically by software-package name with an index by application. Information for each package includes:

- package name
- producer
- description (one to two sentences)
- equipment requirements
- source of reviews if any
- whether or not the review was favorable
- installations (this element is usually missing)
- price
- address.

Citations for reviews is a nice idea that was expanded in the fall of 1983 with the publication of *Microsoftware Evaluations.* (See "Software Description and Reviews," in this article.) No articles or guides to evaluation are included in this directory.

A 1983 edition of *Micro Software Report* includes many new software packages, additional review citations, an index to software by producer, an index to producers, and an index to software by type of equipment. The new edition is better than the first, since the first seems to have suffered from the hurry to get it out. Three pages of addenda and errata arrived with the 1982 edition.

The Online and Nolan directories are limited to microcomputer software for information work, but other directories of library/information software also include some microcomputer software. *Directory of Information Management Software: For Libraries, Information Centers, Records Centers* covers only commercially available software packages for the creation of in-house databases. Detailed information on more than fifty packages includes:

- software name
- address and phone number of vendor
- contact person
- hardware and operating system environment
- capabilities and components of the package

- total price based on several typical library scenarios
- sample installations
- evaluative comments.

The information is more comprehensive than that given in the two microcomputer software directories because the scope of this directory is limited to in-house database software. A hardware index allows ready identification of the microcomputer packages. Additional lists of special application software and general-purpose DBMS suitable for information work include only name of package and address and phone number of vendor.

The *UNESCO Inventory of Software Packages*, to be published soon, will contain descriptive and comparative information about many software packages for information work. It will not be limited to microcomputer software, nor will it be limited to software for one type of library application, but it will attempt to be a comprehensive international summary of all software for information work.

Information on software for this directory was solicited from libraries and information centers around the world. Information managers were asked to notify the National Center of Scientific and Technological Information about computer applications in their centers. The information about the software used in their applications was then verified with the software vendors. Locally developed software, as well as commercially available packages, will be included.

In addition to these directories, several journals have published listings of library applications software. Results of the second annual survey of the library automation market by J. Matthews in the March 15, 1983, *Library Journal* include a directory of all active systems, including microcomputer systems. The October 1982 *Software Review* includes descriptions of five microcomputer packages for library applications. The July 1982 issue of *Program* profiled several British software packages for in-house databases. *Monitor* surveyed interactive online software in April and May 1982. An early issue of the new periodical *Electronic Library* will contain an international directory of mini-and microcomputer software for library and information applications.

Appendix A lists all of these directories and periodicals that will help the information manager identify software packages for the creation of microcomputer-based in-house databases. Other new directories can be expected now that the microcomputer software market is growing so rapidly.

EVALUATION OF SOFTWARE

Software directories allow available packages to be located, but they as yet provide little help in the evaluation of these packages. This is in part because of the lack of critical or evaluative information in the directories, but it is also because, as mentioned earlier, software evaluation is so dependent on individual situations. There is no one best microcomputer software package for every library's in-house database system because "best" will vary with varying needs. However, some general guidelines for software evaluation are applicable to every in-house database.

The literature on evaluation of software for library applications is still sparse, unlike the extensive literature on educational software evaluation. Library and general computing literature does contain enough information to allow formulation of guidelines, however. In many cases, these guidelines are not unique to microcomputer software selection. Many general principles of selection of automated systems or software evaluation for libraries are applicable to evaluation of software for microcomputer-based databases.

The first step in any software evaluation should be analysis of needs and preparation of general specifications. Tenopir advocates the preparation of formal, written specifications whether or not they are required by the parent organization.

> The exercise of identifying the library's needs and determining specifications to meet these needs is the best way to formulate specific questions to be asked, to communicate needs to the vendor, and to ensure that a software package will be able to deliver all the things expected.[25]

She goes on to outline the things that must be included in the specifications. These include both general and specific library and data processing requirements.

Matthews stresses that each information manager must identify and emphasize "my needs" before thinking about purchasing microcomputer software.[26] "These requirements should be written and reviewed by various shareholders in the selection process."[27]

Emard cautions that the "first, and maybe the most important, thing to remember when you set out on your quest for software is to have your applications (or your problems if you like) firmly in mind—and preferably on paper."[28]

Blair echoes these feelings when he advocates that "you sit down with your staff and outline several major needs before reading the computer journals or visiting a computer store."[29] The questions he suggests answering in the initial phase are:

1. Is there any reason to store retrieval from online database searches?

2. Will editing of reports and other documents be attempted?

3. Are there records that need cross-indexing for retrieval via several keys?

4. Would exchanging files with several other companies be advantageous?

5. To what degree would online accounting and budgeting enhance operations?

6. Do statistics and graphs play a significant role in your reporting procedures?

7. Who will be in charge of the application?

General guides to needs analysis and specification writing for library automation projects are also applicable to the purchase of microcomputer software. Matthews' *Choosing an Automated Library System*, Corbin's *Developing Computer-Based Library Systems*, and Boss' *Library Manager's Guide to Automation* are mentioned by Tenopir as some of the sources that can help in this phase.[30]

When the needs assessment is completed and preliminary specifications have been written, it is time to evaluate how individual software packages meet these needs. Suggested evaluation strategy varies in the literature from the extremely simple to an involved process. Because the requirements of software for in-house databases are complex, the prices are usually higher than other microcomputer software, and because so much staff time is involved in implementing a database system, the evaluation of software for in-house databases should not be overly simplified.

Matthews summarizes possible evaluation techniques for choosing any automated library system. He outlines five possible ways to approach evaluation: subjective judgment, cost-only technique, weighted-scoring technique, cost-effectiveness ratio, and least total cost.[31]

Subjective judgment follows no strategy or set procedure and is not recommended. The cost-only technique also should not be used as it considers only which system has the lowest cost and does not draw distinctions based on priorities of system features. Weighted-scoring allows distinction to be made as to the relative importance of different features, but according to Matthews, "This approach suffers because there is no way to establish a meaningful and understandable relative value among the desired items, and, in addition, there is no way to incorporate the system-life costs for each vendor."[32] In an attempt to solve this perceived deficiency, cost-effectiveness ratio divides the total systems cost of each vendor by the sum of the weighted-scoring score. The least total cost technique looks at all present and ongoing costs of each system and assigns a dollar value to each feature, allowing dollar comparison of all components. No one of these evaluation methodologies is clearly the best way to evaluate software packages. Evaluation should incorporate all of them.

Garoogian includes a lengthy discussion on evaluation with many practical examples.[33] Before the product and the vendor are evaluated, she advises examining possible hardware or software constraints. The software must be compatible with the computer and peripherals in use, and possible software contraints such as operating system and programming language must be identified. If these things do not pose a problem in the individual situation, the software characteristics can then be evaluated.

Among the characteristics of the software that should be evaluated are the following:

- How easy is it for users to interact with the program?
- Instruction manuals should allow interaction with the program. If not, will the vendor provide training?
- Do modifications need to be made, and, if so, do they require a programmer?
- Will you receive new versions (releases) of the program as they become available?
- Does the system have expansion capabilities (e.g., modules)?
- Is complete and accurate documentation included?[34]

Evaluation of the vendor is also important. Garoogian recommends answering the following questions about the vendor in the evaluation process:

- How long has the vendor been in the software business?
- Does the vendor maintain a research and development program directed at the constant enhancement of the product you are considering?
- Does the vendor have an active user group?
- Can the vendor provide references for the companies who use the software you contemplate using?
- Can the vendor offer other packages that interface with the one you want?
- Does the vendor provide technical support?
- Can the software be purchased "on approval"?
- Is there a warranty or some sort of maintenance agreement?[35]

Tenopir advises formalizing the evaluation process by using some sort of form or checklist to ensure consistency with the weighted-scoring technique. Major areas that should be examined and rated in the evaluation include:

- vendor or producer
- software contraints and flexibility
- query language

- security
- output capabilities
- input capabilities and procedures
- documentation
- training
- hardware constraints
- costs

Specific concerns to be considered in the evaluation are discussed under each area.[36]

Datapro Research Corporation includes information on general evaluation of application software in their *Applications Software Solutions*. They too urge use of a standard questionnaire and rating form to ensure consistent evaluation. They break evaluation into a two-stage process—first evaluation on a technique basis, then comparing the "survivors" on a "management basis, including cost, timetable and risk."[37]

Datapro recommends paying close attention in the evaluation to the following considerations:

1. comparison of the capabilities of the package with the user requirements;

2. hardware constraints that may affect use of the package;

3. software constraints such as operating system, compiler;

4. throughout timing, ease of installation, ease of operating, clarity of operating instructions;

5. ease-of-use;

6. maintainability (including documentation, programming language);

7. flexibility of the package in meeting changing needs and growth.[38]

Site visits and benchmark tests or demonstrations are emphasized.

Other authors give hints to help with evaluation of microcomputer software without providing the level of detail in Garoogian, Tenopir, and Datapro. Kelley urges evaluators to preview the software if possible, look for reviews in computer magazines, and tap the experience of both vendors and professional colleagues.[39] *MIS Week* advises securing modification rights and paying careful attention to negotiating performance guarantees.[40]

Blair emphasizes the vendor-user relationship. He says to look for such things as the ability to get software updates, a vendor hotline for customer questions, or a company newsletter. He recommends seeing the package run on a hardware configuration identical to yours if possible (with at least a demonstration) and buying a copy of the documentation before buying the software.[41]

Emard stresses building a relationship with the computer store that sells software and evaluating the store just as you would a software package. (This approach will work with general-purpose software, but library-specific packages are generally not sold through the computer stores.) He also discusses at length the importance of documentation, suggesting the following evaluation criteria:

- Is the manual of appreciable length?
- Are there any illustrations and detailed examples?
- Is the documentation organized in a coherent fashion?
- Is there an index?
- Are "cheat sheets" enclosed (i.e., cards that summarize system commands)?
- Is there a glossary?[42]

Boss also stresses the importance of complete documentation, even with inexpensive packages. He concludes that modifications are difficult to make without good documentation, and new employees can be trained more rapidly if the documentation is good.[43]

Matthews gives suggestions to help librarians become wise microcomputer-software shoppers. He advises reading the microcomputer literature, but be sure to insist that all jargon be explained by vendors and ask them to show you how desired features work rather than just asking if it can be done. Reading and comparing vendors' literature and software manuals will also help in the evaluation process.[44]

Dowlin believes that "service is the most important element in selecting a system. This service should not only cover hardware repair and maintenance, but should include software assistance and hand-holding. It is extremely important to have a reliable, *and interested*, local dealer,"[45]

Norris and Marincola's "Guidelines for Developing an Online In-house Database through a Commercial Vendor" are also applicable to evaluation of prewritten software or turnkey systems. Under "Selecting a Vendor," they advise comparing:

- cost
- system/software capability
- support mechanisms
- responsiveness
- organizational features
- customer satisfaction[46]

All of these authors emphasize the importance of the vendor and the documentation—two things that are often overlooked in practice. They also recognize the importance of the opinions of colleagues and users of the packages. Personal contacts at conferences, user groups, and vendor lists of installations are all essential to the evaluation process.

Other recommended evaluation criteria vary but usually include such things as hardware constraints, how the various features of the software meet your needs, expandability, and the opinions expressed in reviews or by colleagues.

Evaluation is not a simple process. It involves time and rigorous application of consistent criteria. Datapro summarizes the problems with evaluation of applications software:

> Package evaluation is hard—each package has hundreds, even thousands of features. No two packages are alike, or even close. Each has its strengths and weaknesses. It becomes mind-boggling to compare packages in a rational way.[47]

Rational evaluation is not impossible, however, and can be done successfully if the proper commitment of time is made. If evaluation seems too difficult or time-consuming, it is also possible to get help in this phase. Hayes emphasizes that the "consultant's advice will be of even greater value than ever before, since the array of alternatives will be vastly increased and the complexity of effect upon the library deeper."[48]

There are a growing number of both library and software consultants who can aid in software evaluation. Also, there are now many workshops being offered by SLA, ASIS, graduate library schools, and others on the identification and evaluation of software for in-house databases.

SOFTWARE DESCRIPTIONS AND REVIEWS

Printed descriptions and reviews of specific software packages help in the evaluation process. Several new journals now feature reviews of microcomputer software for in-house databases. (These journals are reviewed by Tenopir and Beisner.)[49] Two periodicals that are dedicated to microcomputers in libraries often contain descriptions and reviews of software. *Small Computers in Libraries (SCIL)* has been published monthly since 1981. It is in a newsletter format with short software reviews often written by librarians who are using the packages for their own applications. SCIL is up-to-date and easy to read and is especially strong in descriptions of DBMS software adapted to library use. It is a valuable tool in the evaluation of microcomputer software for library applications. *ACCESS: Microcomputers in Libraries* is a quarterly journal that includes articles on software and library applications among its longer subject-oriented articles. Unlike SCIL, it publishes programs as well as software reviews.

Other journals include information about software for database and other library applications for all types and sizes of computers. *Software Review* (v.1, no.1, Feb. 1982) "seeks to provide an overview of software products and the way they can be used in library and educational settings."[50] Software reviews are lengthy and intermixed with substantive articles on all aspects of library and education software management. The two Online, Inc., magazines, *Online* and *Database*, now often contain descriptive information about microcomputer software. Blair's "Micro Magic" column often features information on database applications development and software. His columns and articles are consistently well written and easy to understand. Online, Inc., is actively expanding its coverage of microcomputer applications. *Library Hi Tech*, first published in the summer of 1983, includes a column on library software.

Three recent monographs include information about specific software packages for microcomputer-based in-house databases. Grosch's *Minicomputers in Libraries* and Rorvig's *Microcomputers and Libraries* both describe Warner-Eddison's Inmagic software, Cuadra Associates' STAR, and the Cooperative Library Agency for Systems and Services' (CLASS) Golden Retriever. (Rorvig's description of Golden Retriever is actually a description of the CLASS serials control package, Checkmate, one of many errors in his text.) Grosch's book is about minicomputer systems but includes these micro packages. Woods and Pope's *Librarian's Guide to Microcomputer Technology and Applications* has information on all types of library applications of microcomputers, including software used in more than four hundred libraries. It includes users' opinions of commercially available microcomputer software. It is also a good source for identifying locally developed software that a library will share with other libraries.

Appendix B lists some of the major microcomputer software packages for the creation of in-house databases as of spring 1983. DBMS not specifically aimed at the information center market are excluded.

Proceedings of the International Online Meeting, National Online Meeting, Online, Inc., yearly meetings, Aslib conferences, and the American Society for Information Science twice-yearly meetings are other fruitful sources for microcomputer software descriptions. Increasingly, traditional library journals such as *Special Libraries* and *Library Journal* carry descriptions of microcomputer database applications.

A publication from Nolan Information Management Services is devoted to evaluations of microcomputer software for information work. *Microsoftware Evaluations* is a compendium of evaluations solicited from current users of the software. Sample screen displays and printouts highlight the narrative reviews. This new publication should be of great help in the evaluation process.

Two new online databases, BRS/DISC (Data Processing and Information Science Contents) and DIALOG's Microcomputer Index, help with the location of general microcomputer software reviews that have been published in the microcomputer journal literature. Both cover more than thirty microcomputer periodicals.

In addition, there are a growing number of business-oriented services that scan and summarize the microcomputer literature. PrimeStar, for example, offers a monthly printed SDI service that scans most of the micro magazines, in addition to general business sources such as the *Wall Street Journal, Business Week, Fortune*, etc. *Business Systems Update* includes abstracts and citations to articles about microcomputer business systems, general software solutions, specific business solutions, turnkey systems, outside services, specific business topics, hardware news, and systems software. Articles cover all types of special applications on microcomputers, not just business applications.

Microcomputer Software Letter is another of a growing number of new publications aimed at the microcomputers-in-business market. It provides information on new business-oriented software packages, how to modify prewritten programs, and evaluations of different packages for the same application. Like PrimeStar's service, *Microcomputer Software Letter* is a synthesis of longer articles found in the microcomputer and business literature.

CONCLUSION

Microcomputers are allowing even small special libraries and information centers to create in-house databases, but the success of the system is very dependent on the software chosen. Thanks to standardization of operating systems, availability of higher-level languages, and a growing software market, many prewritten or turnkey software packages are now available for microcomputer-based in-house database systems. These programs are complex and often more expensive than other microcomputer software. Identification of all possibilities and careful evaluation are thus important steps. Luckily, there are a growing number of consultants, directories, and reviews that can help with both of these steps.

No publication or consultant, however, can create a magic formula to allow information managers to choose the best microcomputer software package. The various new directories can be used to identify software possibilities, but a clear understanding of each situation together with a written set of specifications are necessary in order to use the tools and to evaluate the software packages. Software choice is ultimately a personal and somewhat subject process, but there are an increasing number of guidelines and aids that can assist in this important decision-making process.

Footnotes

1. Jeff Pemberton, "Should Your Next Terminal Be a Computer?" *Database* 4 (September 1981):4-6; _____, "The Spread of Microcompters—Fast and Wide," *Database* 5 (August 1982):6-7; John B. Gordon, "Microcomputer Applications in a Corporate Headquarters Staff Environment," in *Online Micro-Software Guide and Directory 1983-84* (Weston, Conn.: Online, 1983), p. 8-15; John C. Blair, Jr., "Decision Support Systems Software: The Key to Library Microcomputer Operations," in Helen A. Gordon, ed., *Online MicroSoftware Guide and Directory, 1983-84* (Weston, Conn.: Online, 1983), p. 3-7; Joseph R. Matthews, "The Automated Library System Marketplace, 1982: Change and More Change!" *Library Journal* 108 (March 15, 1983):547-53.
2. Beatrice Marron and Dennis Fife, "Online Systems—Techniques and Services," *Annual Review of Information Science and Technology* 11 (1976):169.
3. Allan D. Pratt, "The Use of Microcomputers in Libraries," *Journal of Library Automation* 13 (March 1980):13.
4. Gerald Lundeen, "The Role of Microcomputers in Libraries," *Wilson Library Bulletin* 55 (November 1980):184.
5. Ibid.
6. Allan D. Pratt, "Microcomputers as Information Dissemination Tools," in *Communicating Information: Proceedings of the 43rd Annual ASIS Meeting*, ed. Allen R. Benenfield and Edward John Kazlauskas (White Plains, N.Y.: Knowledge Industry Publications, 1980), p. 316.
7. M.J. Rowat, "Microcomputers in Libraries and Information Departments," *Aslib Proceedings* 34 (January 1982):29.
8. Don R. Swanson, "Miracles, Microcomputers, and Librarians," *Library Journal* 107 (June 1, 1982):1057.
9. Rhoda Garoogian, "Prewritten Software: Identification, Evaluation, and Selection," *Software Review* 1 (February 1982):12.
10. "Turnkey Trends," *Small Computers in Libraries* 2 (February 1982):5.
11. "Software for Micros and Minis," *Library Systems Newsletter* 1 (August 1981):14.
12. Ibid.
13. Mark E. Rorvig, *Microcomputers and Libraries: A Guide to Technology, Products and Applications* (White Plains, N.Y.: Knowledge Industry Publications, 1982), p. 41, 101.
14. Helen A. Gordon, review of *Microcomputers and Libraries*, by Mark E. Rorvig, *Online* 6 (May 1982):44.
15. Michael R. Schuyler, review of *Microcomputers and Libraries*, by Mark E.

Rorvig, *Information Technology and Libraries* 1 (September 1982):308, with a reply from Rorvig:308-9.

16. Audrey N. Grosch, review of *Microcomputers and Libraries*, by Mark E. Rorvig, *Special Libraries* 74 (January 1983):102.

17. Allan D. Pratt, review of *Microcomputers and Libraries*, by Mark E. Rorvig, *Small Computers in Libraries* 2 (February 1982):6.

18. David Kelley, "Software—What's Available," in Ching-chih Chen and Stacy E. Bressler, ed., *Microcomputers in Libraries* (New York: Neal-Schuman, 1982), p. 66.

19. Ibid., p. 67.

20. John C. Blair, Jr., "Micros, Minis and Mainframes . . . A Newcomer's Guide to the World of Computers—Especially Micros," *Online* 5 (January 1982):20.

21. A. Vickery and H. Brooks, "Microcomputer, Liberator or Enslaver," *Proceedings of the Fourth International Online Information Meeting* (Oxford, England: Learned Information, 1980), p. 394.

22. Rowat, "Microcomputers in Libraries," p. 32.

23. Garoogian, "Prewritten Software," p. 13.

24. Carol Tenopir, "Software for In-House Databases: Part I, Software Sources," *Library Journal* 108 (April 1, 1983):639-41.

25. _____. "Evaluation of Library Retrieval Software," in *Communicating Information: Proceedings of the 43rd ASIS Annual Meeting*, ed. Allen R. Benenfield and Edward John Kazlauskas (White Plains, N.Y.: Knowledge Industry Publications, 1980), p. 64.

26. Joseph R. Matthews, "Introduction to Micros" (talk given at the Online '82 Conference, Oct. 1982).

27. Matthews, "The Automated Library System Marketplace," p. 550.

28. Jean-Paul Emard, "Software Hang-Ups and Glitches: Problems to Be Faced and Overcome," *Online* 6 (January 1983):18.

29. John C. Blair, Jr., "Software Applications Packages and the Role of the Computer Applications Specialist," *Online* 5 (March 1982):65.

30. Carol Tenopir, "Software for In-House Databases: Part II, Evaluation and Choice," *Library Journal* 108 (May 1, 1983):88.

31. Joseph R. Matthews, *Choosing an Automated Library System: A Planning Guide* (Chicago: American Library Association, 1980), p. 49.

32. Ibid., p. 50.

33. Garoogian, "Prewritten Software."

34. Ibid., p. 18-20.

35. Ibid., p. 20-21.

36. Tenopir, "Software for In-House Databases: Part II."

37. *Datapro Applications Software Solutions* (Delran, N.J.: Datapro Research Corp.), p. 106.

38. Ibid., p. 105-6.

39. Kelley, "Software," p. 71.

40. "Step by Step Method for Software Purchasing," *MIS Week* (October 20, 1982).

41. Blair, "Software Applications Packages," p. 69.

42. Emard, "Software Hang-Ups and Glitches," p. 20.

43. Richard W. Boss, "Software Documentation," *Software Review* 1 (October 1982):167.
44. Matthews, "The Automated Library System Marketplace," p. 550.
45. Kenneth E. Dowlin, "Micro Mag," *Library Journal* 107 (February 1, 1982):237.
46. Carole L. Norris and Diana A. Marincola, "Guidelines for Developing an Online In-House Database through a Commercial Vendor," in *Proceedings of the Third National Online Meeting*, ed. Martha E. Williams and Thomas H. Hogan (Medford, N.J.: Learned Information, 1982), p. 437-38.
47. Datapro Applications, p. 103.
48. Robert M. Hayes, "Consulting in Computer Applications to Libraries," *Library Trends* 28 (Winter 1980):396.
49. Tenopir, "Software for In-House Databases: Part I," p. 639-41; Karl Beisner, "Microcomputer Periodicals for Libraries," *American Libraries* 14 (January 1983):46.
50. Beisner, p. 46.

APPENDIX A SOFTWARE SOURCES

Directories Specific to Library/Information Applications

The Aslib library maintains a continuously updated list of commercially available software packages for library and information applications. Write to: The Librarian, Aslib, 3 Belgrave Square, London SWiX 8PL, England.

Cibbarelli, Pamela; Tenopir, Carol; and Kazlauskas, Edward, eds. *Directory of Information Management Software: For Libraries, Information Centers, Record Centers*. Studio City, Calif.: Cibbarelli and Associates, Inc., 1983. $45.
Information on commercially available software for in-house databases.
Gordon, Helen, ed. *Online Micro-Software Guide and Directory*. Wesport, Conn.: Online, Inc., 1983. $40.
Directory and guide to more than seven hundred software packages for all types of information center applications.
Nolan, Jeanne, ed. *Micro Software Report: Library Edition*. Torrance, Calif.: Nolan Management Information Services, 1982. $49.95. 2d ed., 1983.
Includes descriptions of nearly three hundred microcomputer programs of interest to libraries.
UNESCO Inventory of Software Packages. Tel-Aviv, Israel: National Center of Scientific and Technological Information, 1983. (P.O. Box 20215)
International software directory for information work.

General Directories: A Selected List

Auerbach Software Reports. Auerbach Publishers, 2 v. Updated monthly, looseleaf. $475/year.
A Buyer's Guide to Data Base Management Systems. Delran, N.J.: Datapro Research Corp., 1974-. Updated anually. Selected from *Datapro 70*.
Datamation regularly surveys software packages. Of special interest to information center applications are: May 1982 "Application Software Survey," December 1981 "System Software Survey," and September 1981 "The DBMS Market Is Booming."
Datapro Directory of Microcomputer Software. Delran, N.J.: Datapro Research Corp., 1981-.
Datapro Directory of Software. Delran, N.J.: Datapro Research Corp., 1975-. Updated monthly, looseleaf.
Datapro 70. Delran, N.J.: Datapro Research Corp. 3 v. $755/year. Updated monthly, looseleaf. Guide to hardware and software.
ICP Software Directory. Indianapolis, Ind.: International Computer Programs. Semiannual. 5 v. $65 per volume.
Minicomputer Software Quarterly. Wayland, Mass.: Applied International Management Services. Quarterly. $48/year.
Small Systems Software and Services Sourcebook. Available from J. Koolish, Information Sources, Inc., 1807 Glenview Rd., Glenview, IL 60025. $135; $125 if prepaid.
Describes thirteen hundred packages.

Available Online

International Software Database. DIALOG, file 232.
File Soft, BRS.

Other Useful Sources

Access: Microcomputers in Libraries. P.O. Box 764, Oakridge, OR 97463. Quarterly, $11/year.
The Electronic Library will devote one issue to a directory of mini-and microcomputer software. Learned Information Ltd., Besselsleigh Rd., Abington, Oxon OX13 6LG, England.
Library Hi Tech. Pierian Press, P.O. Box 1808. Ann Arbor, MI 48106.
  Began summer 1983 and includes information on software.
Monitor surveyed interactive online software in April and May 1982. Learned Information, Box 550, Marlton, N.J. 08053.
Nolan, Jeanne. *Microsoftware Evaluations*. Torrance, Calif.: Nolan Management Information Services, 1983.
  Evaluations of library-oriented microcomputer software by users.
Small Computers in Libraries. Graduate Library School, College of Education, University of Arizona, 1515 E. First St., Tucson, AZ 85721. $20/year.
Software Review reviews information applications software. Meckler Publishing, 520 Riverside Ave., Westport, CT 06880.
Available online: BRS/DISC (Data Processing and Information Science).
Microcomputer Index, DIALOG, file 233.

APPENDIX B   SOFTWARE PACKAGES

GOLDEN RETRIEVER
  CLASS, 1415 Koll Circle, Suite 101, San Jose, CA 95112, (408) 289-1756; or Capital Systems Group, Inc., 11301 Rockville Ave., Kensington, MD 20795, (301) 881-9400; or Gaylord, P.O. Box 4901, Syracuse, N.Y. 13221, (800) 448-6160.
  Operates on a TRS-80 Model II with three floppy disk drives or a Winchester hard disk and 64K memory. This package has been widely reviewed in the literature and is in use in many libraries. A demonstration disk can be obtained from CLASS for $50. Software costs for a database of up to forty-five hundred records are under $2,000.
STAR
  Cuadra Associates, Inc., 2001 Wilshire Blvd., Suite 305, Santa Monica, CA 90403,(213) 829-9972.
  Operates on an Alpha Micro with a hard disk. It has been described in the library literature and is a powerful and highly regarded software package. It incorporates sophisticated searching features of the large commerical systems and can accommodate large or small databases. Software price is approximately $20,000.

BRS/Search for Micros
  BRS Software Group, 1200 Rte. 7, Latham, NY 12100, (800) 833-4707.
  Introduced late last year, this package is a micro/mini version of the powerful
BRS/Search software. It runs under the UNIX operating system and currently
runs on the Onyx and WICAT microcomputers as well as PDP/11 and VAX
minicomputers. Software costs vary with the hardware configuration but are in
the $5,000-$30,000 range.
INMAGIC
  Warner-Eddison Associates, Inc., 186 Alewife Brook Pky., Cambridge, MA
02138, (617) 661-8124.
  A new CP/M micro version of the popular minicomputer software, Version 1 of
Inmagic for micros was first available in April of 1983. Version 2 runs on
Televideo, Superbrain, and DEC Rainbow micros; a version for the IBM Personal
Computer was introduced in the fall of 1983. Cost for version 1 is under $1,000,
plus $250 for a separate report generator.

Other microcomputer software (mostly in the $2,000-$3,000 range) for in-house
databases include:

CARD DATALOG
  DTI Data Trek, 121 W. E St., 2d floor, Encinitas, CA 92024, (714) 436-5055.
  For any microcomputer with CP/M operating system, it is based on the dBase II
database management system (DBMS). Also includes acquisitions, circulation,
and series modules.
COMPUTER CAT
  3005 W. 74th Ave., Westminster, CO 80030, (303) 426-5880.
  For Apple II Plus or Bell and Howell computers.
GAYLORD System
  Gaylord, P.O.Box 4901, Syracuse, NY 13221, (800) 448-6160.
  For Apple II Plus computers; includes acquisitions, circulation, film booking,
and the CLASS Checkmate serials system modules.
SCI-MATE
  Institute For Scientific Information, 3501 Market St., University City Science
Center, Philadelphia, PA 19104, (215) 386-0100.
  Personal data management software for IBM-PC, Vector 3 and 4, Apple II, TRS-
80 Model II with CP/M-80, $540. (Universal Online Searcher software $440, or
both for $880.)

Gateway Software:
Is It For You?

Louise R. Levy

INTRODUCTION

Gateway software, a term coined by Fran Spigai (4), refers to the new microcomputer software packages which act as interfaces between the users and the bibliographic retrieval systems they are searching. These interfaces effectively translate a search statement formulated in plain English into the command language of the system being searched, thus simplifying the search process. By taking advantage of the micro's capabilities, these packages sometimes offer additional enhancements such as auto-dial, automatic logon, downloading, offline search strategy formulation, text processing, and search strategy save features. Gateway software fulfills, therefore, a value-adding role in the growing information utility market.

What makes gateway software especially worthy of attention is not what they do but how they are being marketed. The first commercial product in the United States was developed by the Institute for Scientific Information (ISI). ISI's Universal Online Searcher, purchased alone or with a data management program, was targeted at the scientific community—end users who search ISI's own databases, as well as other systems' databases. In the interim, new gateway software have been developed by database producers in order to provide for easier and enhanced searching of their databases. In this category are Disclosure's microDISCLOSURE and Information Access's SEARCH HELPER™. Their goal, an enlarged end user and intermediary audience, is being met by increasingly aggressive marketing campaigns.

The most recent entrant into the gateway software market is In-Search, developed by Menlo Corporation. Unlike the aforementioned programs, In-Search has been developed not by a member of the information industry but by a new start-up software development firm

Reprinted with permission of Online, Inc. from *Online* 8 (Nov. 1984): 67-79.

located in California's Silicon Valley. Menlo's well-planned marketing campaign is aimed not only at intermediaries, but at the largely untapped end user population. In-Search will be sold throughout the U.S. by computer chain stores who will receive training in the program's use by Menlo's sales force. The commercialization of gateway software on such a large scale is an historically noteworthy step in the evolution of online services. This may be the first time when the general public will be the target of a marketing campaign designed to convince individuals of the merits of bibliographic services, which until recently were primarily in the domain of information professionals.

It is worth questioning whether or not these products are useful for the experienced searcher. Many of the features, such as auto-dial, automatic logon, and downloading, are available in less expensive communications programs. The primary selling point of these products is their interface, which simplifies the search process by attempting to eliminate the need for the user to learn the online system's command language. The user of gateway software has paid for this interface, the communication features mentioned above and, perhaps, auxiliary software which perform word processing or database management tasks. As an experienced searcher you want to provide less expensive, and more enhanced services, but you may see little need for an interface.

Not seeing the need for gateway software's essence—the interface— you may be wondering why you need to know about these packages. First, gateway software may be worthy of your attention because it can ease the occasional searching of unfamiliar systems. Second, you can use these programs to train inexperienced searchers to use a particular system or database. Third, the interface and its companion features may actually allow you to perform less costly and less time consuming searches. Fourth, as nonintermediaries become retrieval system end users through the use of these programs, you may be called upon to provide training, consultation and evaluation of these programs. Finally, the success of gateway software will bring more sophisticated programs worthy of the most clever searchers.

Having convinced you of the need to know about gateway software, this article will now address the current state of such software, including communication, interface and auxiliary features, as well as their searching capabilities. Four programs, In-Search, the Universal Online Searcher, microDISCLOSURE, and SEARCH HELPER, are described and compared. This comparison will emphasize how these programs benefit and limit both intermediary and end user searchers. In order to understand the benefits of these programs, general features and capabilities are described first.

FEATURES

Available features can be divided into three categories—communication, interface, and auxiliary program features. While communication features are the most standard, the interface and auxiliary programs vary from program to program. Below is a brief description of some currently available features. Please refer to Chart 3 for a detailed comparison of the features belonging to the four programs under consideration [on page 305].

Communication Features

Auto-dial enables the microcomputer to automatically dial and redial the telecommunication networks until a connection is made. A modem with a capacity to support this feature is needed. Saves time and aggravation.

Automatic logon eliminates the need for manual protocol insertion. A modem capable of supporting this feature is needed. This is a time and headache saver.

Interface Features

The interface, at the heart of gateway software, is the focus of all the fuss. Below is a description of some salient features.

Format: Two different types of formats exist—menu-driven and graphically represented search forms. In the former case, the user's responses to a series of easy-to-understand queries form the search strategy. The responses are then translated into the language of the databank's computer. Menu-driven formats tend to be easy to use, but tedious. See Figure 1 [on page 300] for an example of a screen from a menu-driven program. A graphic search form, on the other hand, presents the user with sections to input terms and selected indexes. Graphic techniques such as windows appearing on the search form are used to prompt the user. A more flexible format, search forms may be initially harder to use. See Figure 2 for an example of a graphic search form [on page 301].

Offline search strategy formulation: The user inputs the search strategy into the micro without being connected to the retrieval system. Satisfied with the strategy, the user can automatically dial-up, log on to the retrieval system, and send the search strategy with one command or key stroke. An essential cost-saving feature, it allows for an iterative search process which consists of offline strategy input, quickly connecting to the retrieval system, receiving results, logging off, and restrategizing.

FIGURE 1 Example of Menu-Driven Interface Format Screen is from the Universal Online Searcher.

SCI-MATE SEARCH MENU   Sets exist

--$$-------------

Do you want to:

1. BROWSE the Search term index
·2. SEARCH and retrieve

3. DISPLAY and/or offload
4. LIST current sets and queries

5. Use the SAVE STRATEGY subsystem
6. Set current awareness parameters (SDI)

7. Return to the Online Search menu

Select a Number: 7

Downloading: Allows retrieved records to be saved to the user's floppy or hard disk for later manipulation.

Strategy save feature: Save main frame storage costs by creating your own SDI service with this feature. Successful strategies can be saved to disk and later used when performing an update.

Online Help: Decreases reliance on the user manual and also helps eliminate the run to the bookshelf while online. Different in each program, the user may access help either by a command or help may be available on each screen.

Auxiliary Program Features

The availability of the auxiliary programs, those which are either included with the software package or purchased separately is what makes gateway software fall under the "integrated software" category. Not always stated in the promotional literature, gateway software may be compatible with other programs developed for use with the same hardware. Three main features of auxiliary programs are listed below.

Word Processing allows for text manipulation of downloaded records. Particular fields may be eliminated or enhanced, and errors corrected. Needed for report generation, bibliography creation, and formatting.

Database management software lets the user create and search a database of downloaded or input records.

FIGURE 2   Example of a Graphic Search Form From IN-SEARCH.

Set #	MEDLINE (1988-) DI-154 Search Keywords and Phrases	Index Selected	Refs Found
S1	caffeine		1427
S2	sleep		5866
S3	s1 and s2		28
S4	caffeine or coffee		1684
S5	sleep		5866
S6	insomnia		583
S7	sleeplessness		14
S8	s4 and s6		8
S9	s4 and s7		0
S10			
S11			
S12			
S13			
S14			

Enter keywords and phrases to search the selected database. To retrieve references press the command key, F9, and then the ⏎ key. For help press the help key, F1.

Phone = Online

Spreadsheet analysis programs turn any bibliographic database containing numeric data into a mini I.P. Sharp. Simplistic and sophisticated manipulation of the data contained in downloaded records can be performed. Output is in the form of charts, graphs or reports.

PROGRAM CAPABILITIES

An interface functions as an intermediary between the searcher and the host computer. If it is a good intermediary it will, like a good reference librarian, offer the searcher the capabilities of the information system it is searching. It is unfortunate that some interfaces now on the market offer limited host capabilities. The user pays a price for the pleasure of simplified searching—the more simple the software is to use, the fewer number of system capabilities available. Creative approaches to interface design will hopefully solve this problem.

When shopping for gateway software, one is advised to become aware of the software's ability to perform all the functions of the system it is accessing. Based solely on gateway software designed for searching DIALOG databases, this review found that some programs did not offer all search operators, expansion, access to online thesauri, field and index selection, limiting, sorting, or display format options. In regards to DIALOG's utilities, some programs did not allow for explain commands, cost displays, document ordering, SDI, display sets, or purge (see Charts 1 and 2).

FOUR PROGRAMS: A COMPARISON

Four programs have been chosen for analysis and comparison. At the time of the project's inception, these were the only programs available to the public for searching bibliographic databases. Each program is reviewed on the basis of its ability to meet the needs of both intermediaries and end users. Readers should refer to Charts 4 and 5 for general information such as cost and hardware compatibility [on pages 306 and 307].

In-Search is the first product of Menlo Corporation, and it is also the first product to use a graphic search form as the interface—a development that may change the face of future gateway software. Menlo's active campaign to sell In-Search to the growing audience of home and office micro users may well be successful.

In-Search is designed to access all databases on DIALOG. Experienced searchers will find satisfaction in that its interface is in no way limiting. All of DIALOG's capabilities are available—a statement which cannot be applied to the other programs' interfaces. End users and

CHART 1

CAPABILITIES	IN-SEARCH	SCI-MATE'S UNIVERSAL ONLINE SEARCHER	IAC'S SEARCH HELPER	microDISCLOSURE
LOGIC	Same capabilities as System	Each search statement can contain only one type of operator In Version 1.2 operator can be mixed within the same search statement.	"and" only -Others forthcoming	"and" "or" only
VARIABLE CHARACTER OPERATORS	Same capabilities as System	Same capabilities as System	Same capabilities as System	Same capabilities as System
PROXIMITY OPERATORS	Automatically inserts (W) between words on search line or (1W) between phrase containing a stopword	Automatically inserts (W) between words in a phrase	Automatically inserts (2W) between words in a phrase	Not applicable
EXPANSION	Same capabilities as System	Same capabilities as System	No	No
THESAURUS	Same capabilities as System	No	Not applicable	Not applicable
INDEX SELECTION	Same capabilities as System	Same capabilities as System	Basic & author index only (documentation mentions certain additional indexes can be searched)	Same capabilities as System but program simplifies searching the plethora of Disclosure indexes
LIMIT	Same capabilities as System	Only useable w/SDI feature	No	Not applicable
SORT	Same capabilities as System	No	No	Same capabilities
OTHER SEARCH OPERATORS ("L", "F", "C")	Same capabilities as System	No	Automatically inserts (F) between 2 words in a name	No
DISPLAY FORMAT OPTIONS	Same options as System	Same options as System	One display format option available (#4)	Same options as System

[1] Based on DIALOG
[2] Based on Sci-Mate Search Mode

CHART 2

UTILITIES[1]	IN-SEARCH	SCI-MATE'S UNIVERSAL ONLINE SEARCHER[2]	IAC'S SEARCH HELPER	microDISCLOSURE
EXPLAIN COMMAND	YES	NO	NO	NO
COST DISPLAY	YES	At logoff only	N/A	At logoff only
DOCUMENT ORDERING	YES	NO	NO	NO
SDI	YES	NO	NO	NO
DISPLAY SETS	YES	YES	NO	Can view search status (this is not DIALOG's "Display sets")
PURGE	YES	YES	NO	NO

[1]Based on DIALOG utilities
[2]Based on Sci-Mate Search Mode

CHART 3

FEATURES	IN-SEARCH	SCI-MATE'S UNIVERSAL ONLINE SEARCHER	IAC'S SEARCH HELPER	microDISCLOSURE
COMMUNICATION FEATURES	-Auto-dial -Automatic logon	-Auto-dial -Automatic logon -Passive Terminal Mode allows manual dial-up. logon/off	-Auto-dial -Automatic logon	-Auto-dial -Automatic logon
SEARCH SEQUENCE	Search terms entered offline or online	Search terms entered online Version 1.2 will offer offline search formulation for Sci-mate Search Mode only.	Search terms entered offline	Search terms entered online
ABILITY TO USE THE SYSTEM'S OWN LANGUAGE	May use much of DIA-LOG's command language	Native Search Mode allows complete use of host language Sci-Mate Search Mode	Limited Usage	No
FORMAT	Graphic search form	Menu-driven	Menu-driven	Menu-driven
ONLINE HELP	Yes	Yes	Yes	No
STRATEGY SAVE FEATURE	Yes	Yes	Forthcoming	No
DOWNLOADING CAPABILITIES	Records may be downloaded to disk and loaded into separate word processing program for text manipulation	Records may be downloaded to Scimate's Personal Data Manager	No	Records can be downloaded to "Database Disk" included w/package
AUXILIARY PROGRAM FEATURES	None	-Downloading records into Personal Data Manager -Create free-text searchable custom databases and report generation	None	Spreadsheet analysis software which allows basic and sophisticated analysis of downloaded or input data, as well as report generation

INTERFACE FEATURES

CHART 4

GENERAL CONSIDERATIONS	IN-SEARCH	SCI-MATE'S UNIVERSAL ONLINE SEARCHER	IAC'S SEARCH HELPER	microDISCLOSURE
LEVEL OF INTERFACE	System DIALOG	System: DIALOG, BRS, NLM, SDC. Other systems searchable in natural language only	DIALOG databases: Magazine Index, National Newspaper Index, Legal Resource Index, Trade and Industry Index, Management Contents, Newsearch	DIALOG database: Disclosure II
TARGET AUDIENCE	-Intermediaries -End users	-Intermediaries -End users	-Primarily end users -Intermediaries	-Intermediaries -End users
COST	$399.00	$440 Universal Online Searcher $540 Personal Data Manager $880 Both Programs	$200 yearly subscription includes search aids -$1750 for 700 prepaid searches consisting of 20 citations each	$250.00
HARDWARE COMPATIBILITY	-IBM PC or IBM compatible (192KB) -Texas Instruments Professional Computers -2 disk drives -Dos 2.0 -Modem (Hayes Smartmodem or Novation 113/212 Smart Cat) -Printer color/graphics monitor (optional)	-IBM PC (128KB) -Apple II, IIE, II+ -TRS-80 Models 11 or 12 (64KB, 80KB) -CP/M 80 systems for Z80 processor -2 disk drives -Hayes Smartmodem -Printer	-Eagle IIE -Apple II, II+, IIE, 1 disk drive -IBM PC or XT, 2 disk drives, DOS 1.1 or 2.0 or above -1200 baud modem (Bizcomp, Hayes, U.S. Robotics) -Printer	-IBM PC (64KB) -Dos 1.00 or 1.10 -2 disk drives -300 or 1200 baud modem -Printer
DISK REVISION POLICY	-Updated disks sent at no charge -Downloading updates to users is forthcoming	-Revised disks for a nominal fee	-Revisions included in yearly subscription fee	-Updated disks provided free -Small updating fee being planned

CHART 5

USER SUPPORT	IN-SEARCH	SCI-MATE'S UNIVERSAL ONLINE SEARCHER	IAC'S SEARCH HELPER	microDISCLOSURE
DEMONSTRATION DISK	-yes -cost: $5.00	-Planned	-yes -no charge	Planned
TUTORIALS	-Extensive tutorial on disk	-Searching instruction provided online	-Yes, included with User Manual	No
DOCUMENTATION	-User Manual -DIALOG Blue Sheets on disk	-User Manual -newsletter	-User Manual -newsletter	-User Manual -newsletter
PERSONAL ASSISTANCE	Phone: 408/986-1200	Phone: 800/523-4902	Phone: 800/227-8431 Ask for Search Helper Customer Service	Phone: 800/638-8076
OVERALL QUALITY				
SCREEN DESIGN	-Color graphics -Commands on screen or accessible by key stroke	-Standard monochrome screen -Major commands visible	-Standard monochrome screen	-Standard Monochrome screen -Major commands visible
KNOWLEDGE OF RETRIEVAL SYSTEM OR DATABASE NEEDED	-Previous knowledge of DIALOG and databases would facilitate program use	No prior knowlede of system needed -Database familiarity would be useful	-No knowledge needed	-No knowledge needed but would be helpful
FLEXIBILITY	-Ability to easily stop strategy formulation and perform other functions	-Exit out of menu easily	-Search statement display for review & revision before going online	-Exit out of menu possible
EASE OF USE	medium to hard	medium to somewhat hard	very easy	easy

intermediaries will find delight in that they do not have to recall DIALOG's commands. A listing of commands flashes at the bottom of the screen—the searcher places the cursor over the command function for the desired action. Experienced searchers will find that they may actually use many of DIALOG's commands including search operators not listed in In-Search's user manual. An interface which can offer all of a retrieval system's capabilities plus simplify the search process must have its trade-off. In this case, it is one of the more difficult programs to master in comparison to the other programs under review. It could be that the more complex nature of this program will make it a more satisfying and challenging program to use.

However, much of the initial difficulty can be resolved by using In-Search's excellent tutorial available on disk and included with the software package. Two criticisms only can be said of this tutorial: (1) the graphic windows move too fast and (2) there is no ability to page back through a lesson. This tutorial, offering an innovative approach to online instruction, is helpful to end users and intermediaries, as well as to supervisors responsible for training employees or to instructors of online retrieval classes.

In-Search's online documentation is especially helpful to end users, although experienced searchers accustomed to dragging around bulky user manuals may not find this feature a strong selling point. In addition to command descriptions available via the interface disk, In-Search supplies the user with disks containing DIALOG Bluesheets categorized by broad subjects. The category disks are available for viewing at any time during the search process. In-Search's user manual offers clearly written instructions on configuration, searching basics, and use of the interface. The inclusion of database descriptions, a guide to purchasing DIALOG documentation, and a list of SIC codes make for a reasonable starter package for end users. Knowing that end users may resist turning to the plethora of documentation necessary for searching, Menlo has put together a friendly and more compact documentation package.

Two other In-Search features—offline search strategy formulation and downloading—will please end users and intermediaries with their ability to save costs and time. With In-Search, searching becomes an iterative process; the search strategy can be formulated and input offline, checked for errors, and can be sent to DIALOG after quickly logging on with the automatic communication features. After receiving the results, the user can either continue online or can save costs by logging off and restrategizing offline. Search results can be viewed printed or down-loaded—a feature Menlo refers to as "disk capture." After being retrieved, records are stored on disk and can be reviewed at some future time, when they can be loaded into a word processing program to be edited or formatted.

In sum, it can be said that In-Search offers the best of all possible online experiences to end users and intermediaries. However, it is not flawless; its flashy graphics flash too fast at times, plus it must be remembered that it is a costly program—$400 buys enhanced access to only one retrieval system. The more cautious intermediaries and end users may feel the need to wait for interfaces which can search many systems as effectively as In-Search searches DIALOG. However, for those information services only accessing DIALOG or end users who are just getting involved with bibliographic retrieval and find their needs met by DIALOG, this is an ideal program.

The *Universal Online Searcher*, the other half of ISI's Sci-Mate software package, offers considerably different features and capabilities than In-Search. Initially conceived as a sister component to the Personal Data Manager, it allowed ISI to offer scientists and librarians a means to search five retrieval systems (DIALOG, BRS, SDC, ISI, NLM) without learning the service's language and to create databases of downloaded and input references. Since its introduction in the Spring of 1983, the programs have been primarily marketed to scientists and information professionals.

The Universal Online Searcher's interface, known as Sci-Mate Search Mode, is menu-driven. It is relatively easy to use and master, but tedious, timeconsuming, costly and limiting. Its ease lies in its step-by-step menu approach to strategy input. However, users will still perform best if they have some conceptual understanding of online terminology and record structure. It is tedious because of the many queries to which the user must respond—an especially boring task once the program is mastered. It is timeconsuming because of the number of menus to which the user must respond. Figure 3 [on page 310] compares a screen from a search using natural language with one from the same search using Sci-Mate Search Mode. It is costly because the user is online with the services while interacting with the menu. (ISI's Universal Online Searcher's new version 1.2 addresses the cost issue by offering offline search strategy formulation for its Sci-Mate Search Mode.) Finally, the interface is limiting because it does not support all of the service's searching and utility capabilities. Although many intermediaries may be dissatisfied with incomplete access, being able to access highly desired databases on unfamiliar systems may more then compensate.

Two additional search modes ameliorate the disadvantages of the interface mode. Figure 4 [on page 311] is a Sci-Mate menu of search mode choices. First, the Native Search Mode allows users who are familiar with the service's language to search without an interface. End users and beginning intermediaries can "graduate" to this mode. Where there are multiple users of a micro searching system, this program supports various levels of searching ability. Second, the Passive Terminal

FIGURE 3   Screen from a Search of ERIC Using DIALOG's Command Language.

TERMINAL =

@ 415 20

415 20 CONNECTED

ENTER YOUR DIALOG PASSWORD
■■■■■■■■ RECONNECT File7 Sat 7apr84 13:50:14 Port054

** SORTS ARE NOT WORKING IN FILE 117 **
** FILES 73,63,241,86,33 ARE UNAVAILABLE
**

7 bi
    7apr84 13:52:06 User 7064
    $0.44 0.029 Hrs File1* 3 Descriptors

File*:ERIC – 66-84/Mar
    Set Items Description

? $ microcomputer?
    1 2147 MICROCOMPUTER?
? $ learning(w)disabilit?
    2 5741 LEARNING(W)DISABILIT?
? c 1 and 2
    3   23 1 AND 2
? 3/5/1-3
3/5/1
EJ289902 EC160587
  Microcomputers and Learning Disabled Adolescents.
  Rude-Parking, Carolyn
  Pointer, v27 n4 p14-19 Sum   1983
  Available from: UMI
  Language: English
  Document Type: JOURNAL ARTICLE (080): TEACHING GUIDE (052)
  The paper discusses the major topics of software, examines research on
the effectiveness of computer assisted instruction (CAI) for learning
disabled adolescents, and suggests specific and creative uses of
microcomputers in academic and cognitive skill development. (Author/CL)
  Descriptors: Academic Achievement; Adolescents; Cognitive Development;
*Computer Assisted Instruction; *Computer Programs; *Learning Disabilities;
Microcomputers; Secondary Education

? logoff
    7apr84 13:54:44 User 7064
    $0.68 0.045 Hrs File1*3 Descriptors

LOGOFF 13:54:47

415 20 DISCONNECTED 00 00

FIGURE 3, **Continued**

2 SCREENS FROM THE SAME SEARCH USING SCI-MATE SEARCH MODE
THIS SEARCH INVOLVES CONSIDERABLY MORE STEPS

SEARCH   B=Browse   D=Display/Offload   L=List   F=Full Menu
--$$

What do you want to SEARCH?

1. Set Number
2. Subject Term or Phrase
3. Author
4. Specific Field

Select a Letter or Number: 2

Enter Subject Term or Phrase: microcomputer?

SEARCH   ESC=Cancel Query
--$$

QUERY: microcomputer?

Do you want to:

1. Submit Query
2. Refine Query with AND Logic
3. Extend Query with OR Logic
4. Limit Query with NOT Logic
5. Specify Proximity to Another Term

Select a Number: 2

FIGURE 4   Screen from the Universal Online Searcher Illustrating Access
to its Three Search Modes.

ONLINE SEARCH

You are connected to the 1 data base.

The WORK file does not exist.

Search modes available are:

   1. SCI-MATE Search Mode (menu-driven)
   2. Native Search Mode (DIALOG command language)

   3. Leave the 1 data base (return to Online menu)

Select a Number: 3
Select Option 3 to leave 1

Mode literally opens up the world of online databases by allowing the user to access systems not available through the other two modes. This access is accomplished via manual dial-up, logon, and use of natural language searching.

Sci-Mate offers other value-adding features. First, is the optional purchase of the Personal Data Manager which allows for fairly easy creation of custom free-text searchable databases from downloaded or input records. This is an auxiliary program best left to serious end users and information professionals; the cost of the two programs is considerable. Second, is the availability of both online help and documentation. Commands are displayed on most screens and a short program instructing users in the basics of searching is on the interface disk. Third, is the ability to save strategies to disk—a cost saver for intermediaries operating SDI services. Fourth, is an active customer support service offering a toll-free line, a newsletter, and user support groups. It should be noted that the user manual, due to its bulk, is awkward to use.

The Universal Online Searcher's major flaws are (1) its inability to provide access to each systems' command capabilities in the Sci-Mate Search Mode and (2) its lack of offline search strategy formulation in the Passive and Native Search Mode. An expensive program, many unknowledgeable users may be sold on its ability to access so many systems in plain English. The price for that ease has been the high cost of operating the menu while online. The introduction of Version 1.2 provides an excellent means for users of gateway software to reduce the connect-time costs as well as enjoy the ease of the menu-driven mode. The Universal Online Searcher may be a good choice for those intermediaries and end users who use the interface only for searching infrequently accessed databases while performing most searches with the Native Search Mode or for those users who find the downloading/database management package useful.

The following two programs, SEARCH HELPER and microDIS-CLOSURE, differ from those previously discussed in that these are database specific packages. Their utility must be measured against the amount of need one has to search a specific database or databases. The need for simplified access or the functions of an auxiliary program may or may not outweigh the limitations of the interface.

IAC's *Search Helper* is clearly an example of a database producer attempting to capture a wider audience for is information products. IAC's databases, providing access to a broad spectrum of current and retrospective information, have only been used directly by library patrons on COM. This program enables end users to easily perform their own searches of both IAC's bibliographic databases and the Management Contents database on DIALOG.

SEARCH HELPER performs well because of its ease of use and simplicity. The user is literally guided thorough each search with the optimum amount of help. Having responded to a menu which defines the topic, the user then receives brief, but thorough instructions on how to enter terms or names (see Figure 5). Not overburdened with lengthy menus or wordy instructions, the new or seasoned user can quickly and without anxiety formulate a search strategy while not connected to the service. It is SEARCH HELPER's simplicity which accounts for this ease. It does not allow the user the full capabilities of DIALOG including Boolean "not" and "or," expansion, limiting, sorting, display format choices, and DIALOG utilities. Further, although all indexes may be searched, the documentation does not make this clearly known. Downloading, or saving retrieved records to disk, is not possible at this time.

Although SEARCH HELPER's promotional literature is aimed at both end users and intermediaries, its unique purchase arrangement is what makes this interface most appropriate for public and academic libraries. In addition to a required annual license fee, the purchaser must prepay for 700 searches each consisting of 20 citations. Libraries are then able to offer an end user search service with a fixed cost of $2.50 for each search which retrieves 20 or less references. IAC expects the library patron to be satisfied with a "quick and dirty" search of their databases. The patron, it is thought, will not want, need, or miss the DIALOG features its interface lacks. SEARCH HELPER does perform well for end users, but the intermediary who lacks online skills should be aware of SEARCH HELPER's limitations. The lack of a downloading feature,

FIGURE 5 Example of SEARCH HELPER's Online Instruction

*** SPECIFYING A PERSON ***

Enter the first AND last name, separated by a blank.
Example: 'GROUCHO MARX'
  (Single names are allowed, but you may get
  spurious references.)

Avoid initials. If you must use them, leave out the '.'
Examples: 'E T'

Do not use ANY punctuation. Leave spaces instead.
Example: 'SANDRA O CONNOR'

If you are not sure of the spelling, or there is more
  than one variation, give the first part of the
  name, then type a '?'.
Example: 'MENA? BEGIN'

ENTER FIRST AND LAST NAME:
  george orwell

DIALOG capabilities, and the drawbacks of the purchase agreement must be considered.

SEARCH HELPER's ability to provide easier access to current information has the potential to satisfy end users and libraries, as well as increase revenues for IAC's and Management Contents' online products. A no frills program, SEARCH HELPER fills a gap in library services and, if successful, will lead the way for other database producers to follow.

microDISCLOSURE is designed to simplify searching the Disclosure II database on DIALOG, as well as capture, store, manipulate, and format the data found in Disclosure's records of publicly owned companies. By simplifying access and allowing manipulation of its data, Disclosure is seeking a wider and more satisfied audience for its online product. Not only a cumbersome database to search, the users of its records have had to perform much of the data manipulation manually or have had to access the database on other systems capable of data manipulation and report generation.

Although microDISCLOSURE offers numerous enhancements, it has several limitations. Like ISI's interface, the user interacts with the menu-driven format while online with DIALOG. Already an expensive database to access, microDISCLOSURE's lack of an offline search strategy formulation feature does not help decrease connect time costs. The ability to save strategies to disk, another cost-saver, is also missing. Experienced searchers preferring to use the language of the online system will find there is no provision for bypassing the menu. microDIS-CLOSURE is capable of searching all of Disclosure's indexes, but does not allow for expansion, Boolean "not,"or most of DIALOG's utilities. Despite these limitations, microDISCLOSURE has effectively simplified access to an otherwise complex database. Even end users with little online experience or intermediaries with no knowledge of the database can quickly perform good searches. (See Figure 6)

The auxiliary programs included with this reasonably priced package are what make it outstanding. Like the Universal Online Searcher, microDISCLOSURE allows the creation of inhouse databases (which, in this case, contains public-company records accessible by company name only). The information analyst or business end user will appreciate the ability to save or download company financial data onto a database disk and perform basic and sophisticated analysis, including customized reporting and ratio analysis. microDISCLOSURE's spreadsheet analysis program attempts to approximate those capabilities found only on number-crunching systems such as I.P. Sharp. For those intermediaries and end users with an IBM PC and a high priority for searching and analyzing the data found in the Disclosure II database, this program is excellent. Serious users, however, may need to consider whether their

FIGURE 6   Screen from a Search Using microDISCLOSURE as a DIALOG Interface Illustrates how Interface Simplifies Searching Disclosure's Many Fields.

Which criteria do you want to search . . .

1 – Type of Business
2 – Geographic
3 – Income Statement Information (eg. Net Sales, Net Income)
4 – Balance Sheet Assets Information (eg. Cash, Total Assets)
5 – Balance Sheet Liabilities Information (eg. Notes Payable)
6 – Officers or Directors
7 – Shares/Employees
8 – Miscellaneous (eg. Auditor, Exchange)

Choice? 1

needs can be best met by using the microDISCLOSURE package or by accessing the Disclosure II database on I.P. Sharp. Sharp's software may be more powerful and flexible, but the user lacks the convenience of offline manipulation provided by microDISCLOSURE.

A truly useful example of gateway software designed for enhanced searching of one database, microDISCLOSURE could be substantially improved. The addition of offline search strategy formulation and the ability to perform natural language searches in addition to the menu-driven format would make this program more attractive to cost conscious users and might entice more experienced searchers.

CONCLUSION

The major features and capabilities of gateway software have been discussed. Four programs were reviewed on the basis of their utility to both end users and intermediaries. For interfaces designed to search whole systems or particular databases, it was found that ease of use, the existence of cost and time saving features, access to the system's capabilities, and the utility of auxiliary programs are important criteria on which to judge a gateway software package. The potential user should carefully assess his or her needs and measure them against the program's abilities. Programs which can offer the user both simple and more sophisticated levels of searching, in addition to optional or included auxiliary programs, may be the most useful.

Although the number of microcomputer owners with modems is expected to mushroom in the coming years, it may be some time before the average person becomes a serious segment of the bibliographic interface market. In the meantime, software developers will have to be content with intermediaries and micro-happy end users who require retrieval system access for their professional work. Already familiar with online searching, the intermediary is in a unique position to assess and effectively use these interfaces, suggest improvements to their developers, and provide training and consultation to end user searchers. No doubt there will be many new interfaces on the market offering a wide array of features and enhancements designed to add value to traditional information products. Hopefully, intermediaries, researchers and other information professionals will accept the challenge of contributing to the development of new and better gateway software.

For more information about the products reviewed contact the addresses below.

Sci-Mate Universal Online Searcher
Institute for Scientific
Information
3501 Market Street
University City Science Center
Philadelphia, PA 19104
(800) 523-4092.

In-Search
Menlo Corporation
4633 Old Ironsides Drive
Suite 400
Santa Clara, CA 95050
(408) 986-1200.

microDISCLOSURE
Disclosure
5161 River Road
Bethesda, MD 20816
(800) 638-8076.

SEARCH HELPER
Information Access Company
11 Davis Drive
Belmont, CA 94025
(800) 227-8431.

References

1. Susan Casbon, "Online Searching with a Microcomputer—Getting Started." *Online* 7 (November 1983):42-46.
2. Virginia W. Eager, "microDISCLOSURE—Software for the IBM PC/XT Enduser." *Database* 7 (June 1984):79-84.

3. Doran Howitt, "Customizing Software: New Programs Make it Easier to Use On-Line Services." *InfoWorld* 6 (June 1984):32-33.
4. Fran Spigai, "Gateway Software: A Path to the End-User Market?" *Information Today* 1 (February 1984):6-7.
5. Catheryne Stout, "Sci-Mate: A Menu-Driven Universal Online Searcher and Personal Data Manager." *Online* 7 (September 1983):112-116.
6. P.W. Williams, "Microprocessor Assisted Terminals for Online Information Systems." *Third International Online Information Meeting* (London 4-6) Oxford: Learned Information, 1979. pp. 139-146.

Acknowledgements

The author wishes to express appreciation to David Powell of Information Access, Laura Lyon of Menlo Corp., and the customer service staff of Disclosure and ISI. A special thanks to Barb Settel of the SU School of Information Studies for her support and advice. Also, a thanks to the Central NY Library Resource Council for the use of their hardware.

Large Databases, Small Computers and Fast Modems . . . An Attorney Looks at the Legal Ramifications of Downloading

Thomas S. Warrick

Recent technological improvements in mass storage devices and high-speed modems for inexpensive small computers have made feasible the large-scale downloading of data from the many online databases that serve the members of the information science community and their patrons. This capability, however, may put those who would use these innovations at legal risk because the downloading of information could infringe the rights of the database proprietors who have brought online information to the public, often at great cost. Those who would take advantage of these technological advances must keep in mind the legal ramifications of downloading.

THE TECHNOLOGY

We are now seeing the emergence of several new mass storage technologies which will have a profound effect on the capabilities of microcomputers. The first, which is just now becoming available, is the microdiskette, which can store almost a million characters on a 3 1/4-inch platter of flexible plastic. At the same time, hard disks, which retail for about $1,000 apiece and up until now could store five or more millions of characters, can now store hundreds of millions of characters for very low prices.[1]

The next stage of mass storage technology is the optical disk.[2] Rather than using the magnetic technology in use over the last two decades, optical disks usually use laser light to record data. While the full potential of this technology is not yet certain, it is not unreasonable to expect that in two years or less it will be possible to store five million characters on a plastic card the size of a credit card. The reader for such a device could cost in the hundreds, not thousands, of dollars.

The effect of inexpensive mass storage technology will be to give individuals the physical capabilities necessary to operate their own databases. While the cost of the equipment necessary to allow others to go into competition with mainframe-based databases will likely continue to be out of reach of most users, the cost of obtaining information once and saving it for reuse on one's own computer or computers will become quite low.

Until recently, modems were quite expensive, but in the last year several companies have begun marketing modems priced under $100. Additionally, until recently most inexpensive modems transmitted and received data at 30 characters a second, a speed that is slower than reading speed. Modems capable of transmitting characters at the rate of 120 characters a second were priced until a few years ago at about $1,000. In the last few months, however, one manufacturer of 120-character per second modems has been offering them at discounted retail prices of $250. Other manufacturers will undoubtedly follow suit.

This price revolution will make modems an inexpensive addition to most microcomputer systems, thereby giving more people access to online databases. More importantly, however, low-cost, high-speed modems will make it feasible to receive large volumes of information for later processing.

Downloading and the Legal Dilemma

The downloading of data from databases using the equipment described above is a simple procedure. By using downloaded data, an online searcher will be able to avoid paying the database proprietor for additional searches of the same information. Additionally, he or she may be able to perform certain types of searches more quickly and efficiently on the microcomputer than on the database.

But by downloading this information, has our hypothetical user become subject to liability under the copyright laws? This question admits of no simple, universally-applicable answer, as this article will show.

In addition to potential copyright liability, a downloader may be subject to liability for violating explicit contractual undertakings not to engage in the copying of data on the database. Some databases are beginning to place specific restrictions on the rights of the user to copy downloaded information in machine-readable form. Many database proprietors, however, have not addressed in their contracts the issue of contractual restrictions on downloading data. One large database that deals with sophisticated users says in its contract:

> The subscriber will use the [proprietor's] library for research purposes only and will not publish, broadcast, or sell any materials in the . . . library in any manner whatsoever, nor will the subscriber use such materials in any other fashion that may infringe [the proprietor's] copyrights or proprietary interests in such materials.

Truly a "non-provision," as it says that the subscriber has only those rights that the law says he has, which would of course be the case if this provision was not in the contract.

An additional aspect of the attempt to control downloading by contract is that at least insofar as *copying* is concerned, the federal copyright law pre-empts state law to the contrary, including the law of contracts, which is assigned to "state law" in the American legal system. Thus even contractual provisions regarding downloading might in some circumstances be held to be superseded by copyright law. Further discussion of this complex topic is outside the scope of this article.

THE PRESENT LEGAL REGIME

In order to appreciate copyright law, it is necessary to adopt a perspective on the law that, while not novel, may seem somewhat unorthodox. United States Supreme Court Associate Justice Oliver Wendell Holmes, Jr., stated this philosophy as, "The prophecies of what the courts will do in fact, and nothing more pretentious, are what I mean by the law."[3] Justice Holmes is saying that the law is not and does not attempt to define precisely what is "legal" and what is not, nor does any one law control absolutely how judges must decide specific cases before them. Justice Holmes is saying further that the usefulness of law is that it allows people to *predict* how judges would decide specific questions of liability or nonliability. The law, under this theory of jurisprudence, is merely a predictive tool that can be used to make a probabilistic assessment as to how a court will ultimately decide a particular case.[4]

This attitude toward the law is essential when analyzing copyright law. Unlike some areas of the law, cases construing copyright law often reach results totally inconsistent or irreconcilable with other cases. Copyright cases often depend on the specific facts and parties involved, rather than the acts that are the subject of the copyright infringement suit before a court.

The utility of this approach is that it recognizes that it is impossible to predict with certainty how a court will rule as to whether specific acts by particular persons will be found to infringe a copyright. The best that can be hoped for, especially in the gray area of copyright law explored by this paper is to make informed estimates as to the *likelihood* that particular conduct is or is not immune from liability. The question is not "Is this conduct an infringement of copyright?" but rather "What is the probability that this conduct will eventually be determined to be an infringement of copyright?"

A Functional Definition of Copyright

What is copyright? In practical terms, copyright *regulates* the *copying* of *original* works of *authors* who give *notice* of their copyright.[5] Each of the italicized words requires some elucidation.

First, copyright only regulates the copying of copyrighted works; it does not prohibit all copying. Second, works protected by copyright must embody originality. As will be discussed below, some courts seem to have ignored this requirement and granted copyright protection to non-original works.

Third, a copyrighted work must be the sort of thing associated with "authorship." This is usually interpreted to mean that in order for the creater of a work to copyright it, he or she must have used some amount of creative effort. The actual amount of creative effort required is, however, very slight.

Fourth, in order to protect fully the rights of the copyright holder, notice must be placed on the work so as to inform the public that the work is copyrighted, as well as the date and holder of the copyright.[6] Failure to give proper notice will not necessarily invalidate the copyright, and may relieve an infringer of any liability for his or her infringing acts.[7]

Finally, the copyrighted work must be "fixed in any tangible medium of expression."[8] Data in databases is almost always fixed on the magnetic disks or tapes that, while not directly perceptible to the human eye, "can be perceived . . . with the aid of a machine or device."[9]

As section 102(b) of the copyright law makes clear, copyright is not intended to protect facts apart from the way in which those facts are expressed. Notwithstanding this principle, courts have in many cases extended copyright protection to facts on the ground that to allow the copying of facts that were obtained only by considerable effort would be to allow copyists to appropriate the labor of the original researcher. This point will be discussed in detail later.

No Court Has Yet Ruled on Whether Downloading Data for Later Use Is a Copyright Infringement

Based on research done—appropriately enough—on a computerized database, it appears that no court has yet ruled on the question of whether and to what extent downloading data for later use is a copyright infringement. Yet, while there is no legal authority directly discussing the subject, there are several statements by copyright scholars that give some clues as to how a court would address the question. The Final Report of the National Commission on New Technological Uses of Copyrighted Works,[10] which devoted six pages to copyright aspects of computer databases, said:

> There is little doubt that one who obtained access to a copyrighted database by . . . paying the proprietor . . . for the right to search the database . . . would infringe an existing copyright by retrieving the entire database and marketing an exact duplicate in competition with the copyright proprietor. Such activity beyond question would be unauthorized copying in violation of a valid copyright.[11]

But while statements such as these state clearly the rule in an "easy" case, it is somewhat less clear what the rule is or should be in other cases where the copying is less than complete or where the downloader uses the data for a purpose other than direct competition with the proprietor of the original database. The more likely case is not the downloading of an entire database by one who plans to compete with the original proprietor, but is rather one where the downloader is collecting a number of related records for later use, whether personal or for his business. Here, as will be seen momentarily, the CONTU report is less clear.

In the absence of a clear and unequivocal rule, it is necessary to apply more traditional forms of legal analysis by examining in stages the copyright questions raised by downloading. First, however, it should be noted that the one feature of online databases that makes them particularly useful—the fact that they are computerized—is one that should have no effect on the legal analysis. The close analogy between online databases and "hardcopy" databases such as encyclopedias and almanacs, which are clearly entitled to copyright albeit in a limited way, strongly suggests that online databases would be treated in an identical manner. This was clearly the view of the Judiciary Committee of the

House of Representatives, which said that "[t]he term 'literary works' ... includes catalogs, directories, and similar factual, reference, or instructional works and compilations of data. It also includes computer databases ... ".[12]

There are only two passing shadows cast by computers over the copyrightability question. The first is that one of the requirements of copyrightable material is that it be "fixed in any tangible medium of expression,"[13] which would indicate fixation on a disk but would not include presence in the random-access memory of a computer.[14] Thus, if the database was entitled to copyright protection only as regards to the arrangement of data rather than the data itself,[15] and if the data existed in one form on the database proprietor's mass storage devices and in an entirely different form when stored in the memory of his computer, the arrangement in memory would not be a "fixation" according to the House Report. As a practical matter, however, this is not likely to cause courts significant problems, because the new arrangement would become fixed as soon as it was saved to disk or printed out by the downloading user.

The second possible difficulty relating to computers as such arises because online databases are updated continually with new information, whereas the Constitution requires that copyright protection be available for only a limited time.[16] It is possible that old material could fall into the public domain upon the expiration of the copyright term at the same time that new material was still entitled to protection. It would be difficult for both the database proprietor and the user to know which specific data were protected and which were not. But this too is not likely to cause significant concern. First, the term of copyright is now the life of the author plus 50 years,[17] so this problem is likely to be theoretical rather than real for some time. CONTU said that this problem did not need to cause serious concern, as the same issue has already arisen in connection with telephone directories and the like, without deleterious effects on the copyrightability of phone books.[18]

Original Works Written for a Database Are Protected by Copyright but May Be Copied if a "Fair Use"

Just as original works in print media can be copyrighted, so too original works written for databases can be copyrighted. The legality of downloading such works would be governed by considerations of fair use,[19] as would the copying of printed works. As noted above, the fact that the work may be accessed by a computer should not give a downloader any greater or lesser rights.

Works Written for other Media and Entered Into a Database Are Protected by the Underlying Copyright

Many databases offer online versions of journals and other publications that are copyrighted in their hardcopy format. Downloading this type of data, except for a fair use, is almost certainly copyright infringement.

Data originally written for another medium is separately copyrightable as a "derivative" work, because it is based on one or more preceeding works.[20] Common examples of derivative works include translations, motion pictures based on books, books based on movies, and articles based on speeches. In order to qualify as a derivative work, "something" must be added to the original work, but that "something" can include the effort and skill required to convert a printed work into computer-readable form.

In addition to being copyrighted in their derivative form, the holder of the copyright on the original form of derivative works is entitled to bring infringement actions to protect his or her rights in the underlying works. Thus even if the effort and skill required to convert a printed work into computer-readable form would not be sufficient to qualify for a separate copyright, the copyright on the underlying work will protect it from copying by someone downloading that work.

Databases That Contain Works Gathered from Many Sources May Be Copyrighted as a "Collective Work" or as a "Compilation"

An online database would be virtually useless if it did not contain a large amount of data. In addition to any copyright that may be obtained on any one datum, the copyright laws also allow the entire collection to be copyrighted.

Two such categories of copyright exist. A work may be copyrighted as a "collective work," which is defined in section 101 as "a work, such as a periodical issue, anthology, or encyclopedia, in which a number of contributions, constituting separate and independent works in themselves, are assembled into a collective whole." The second category, "compilations," embraces the first, and is defined as "a work formed by the collection and assembling of preexisting materials or of data that are selected, coordinated, or arranged in such a way that the resulting work as a whole constitutes an original work of authorship. The term 'compilation' includes collective works."[21] For purposes of this discussion, there is no reason to distinguish between these two categories.

Copyright in a compilation extends only to the form and arrangement that brings the separate elements together. It does not, except as discussed below, go so far as to give the copyright holder a copyright on the individual elements themselves. Copyright in a compilation therefore extends only to the compiler's original effort, the making of the compilation.[22] Section 103(b) says, "The copyright in a compilation or derivative work extends only to the material contributed by the author of such work, as distinguished from the preexisting material employed in the work, and does not imply any exclusive right in the preexisting material."

Of course, the original elements themselves may be covered by copyright, and, if so, the downloading of those elements would be infringement except where a use was deemed "fair." The more interesting case is where the individual elements are not copyrighted, but rather are in the public domain. The largest category of such works is works made by employees of the United States Government.

The United States Government may not hold a copyright on any of its works. Section 105 provides, "Copyright protection under this title is not available for any work of the United States Government, but the United States Government is not precluded from receiving and holding copyrights transferred to it by assignment, bequest, or otherwise." A work of the United States Government is defined in section 101 as "a work prepared by an officer or employee of the United States Government as part of that person's official duties." In addition, works made by contractors or consultants may under some circumstances qualify as "works made for hire,"[23] thereby making them ineligible for copyright.

This section means, for example, that if a United States Government agency set up a database made up of original material, information on that database could be downloaded without fear of copyright infringement.[24]

What makes the question of copyrightability of public domain material so important is that much data on computerized databases originates from government statistics, students and reports. In addition, data on databases often includes material that is a matter of public record, such as court opinions and historical documents. Aside from abstracts of scholarly articles and current publications, perhaps the most useful aspect of online databases is the ability to draw upon statistical information or the large body of public records.

Assuming that much data is not copyrighted before it is entered into a computer, does collecting the data and entering it into a computer allow the database proprietor to claim a copyright on the specific data collected? The existence of a category of compilations in copyright indicates that the answer is clearly yes as to the collection, organization and arrangement of the data, but, as noted above, a copyright on a compilation extends only to the compilation, not the specific data therein.

Sound policy considerations underlie the limited scope of copyright for a compilation. Granting private individuals copyright protection for works created by the government amounts, in the eyes of many, to allowing those persons the right to appropriate public property.

Additionally, no "originality," in the sense that originality is a requirement of the copyright law, is required to enter data into a computer. Indeed, database operators usually strive to follow the original source as closely as possible. How much originality is required to re-format or abstract public domain material?

Many court cases have addressed the question of how much originality is required in order to qualify a work for copyrightability. The standard is not high, but neither does it allow the bringing-together of any disparate facts into a copyrightable whole. In one case, 40,000 changes in spelling, punctuation and correction of typographical errors were found to be merely trivial and not copyrightable.[25] In another case, changing the language in a form agreement was also held to be non-original and therefore non-copyrightable.[26] Publishing a public domain work with a new pagination with decorative borders on each page has been held insufficient to qualify for copyright as to the public domain text.[27]

On the other hand, what might appear to be changes too trivial to merit copyright protection have in some instances been found to be copyrightable nevertheless. In *American Greetings Corp. v. Kleinfab Corp.*,[28] the insertion of the non-copyrightable phrase "Put on a Happy Face" was sufficient to grant the author a derivative copyright. Adapting a public domain design to fabric has been held to be copyrightable.[29]

Some of these decisions seem inconsistent, or at least difficult to reconcile with anything more than arbitrary distinctions. One often sees judges using phrases like "distinguishable variation,"[30] but these beg the question as to what it takes to qualify as "distinguishable." Because copyright law is not amenable to simple, decisive rules, inconsistencies abound.

An unanswered question—indeed, it may be *the* critical question—is whether a downloader can avoid copyright infringement by selecting only limited data and altering the arrangement of data as it is received so as to avoid the charge of having copied the original effort added by the compiler of the database. This question raises two interrelated secondary questions. First, to what extent does the copyright of a compilation cover the individual data elements therein? Second, at what point in the continuum from copying no part of a work to copying the entire work does the copying of elements of a compilation constitute infringement?[31] For purposes of the present analysis, it is sufficient to treat the two questions as substitutes for the other, since an answer to one will lead to a particular answer to the other. Courts may use either of the two secondary questions as a means of analyzing whether to find copyright infringement, but the result does not seem to depend on the analytical tools employed.

No court has yet decided this issue in the context of downloading of information from a database. Courts have, however, decided similar questions in other contexts, but they have reached inconsistent conclusions.

The classic situation in which these questions arise is where someone copies only the non-copyrightable elements in a copyrighted compilation such as a directory containing names and other data. The inconsistency in decisions involving copyright law, and the need to avoid thinking of copyright law as a coherent, consistent whole, is nowhere more apparent than in these two conflicting lines of cases. Nevertheless, these cases do illustrate the way courts analyze those who copy only limited data and alter the arrangement of that data in contexts other than the downloading of data from computer databases.

The most famous of the line of cases holding the copying of otherwise non-copyrightable elements in a compilation to be an infringement is probably *Leon v. Pacific Telephone and Telegraph Co.*, [32] in which the plaintiff's telephone directory, containing names listed in alphabetical order along with the corresponding telephone number, was used as a basis for the defendant's telephone directory, which contained telephone numbers listed in numerical order along with the corresponding name. The court said that the individual names and numbers as such were not copyrightable, and the only originality in the plaintiff's directory was in the arrangement of the names. The court nevertheless found that the defendant's "reverse directory" had infringed the plaintiff's directory.

The reasoning used in this and similar cases has always focused on the fact that the infringer has taken advantage of work done by another, thereby gaining financial advantage because the infringer did not have to go to the expense of doing the original research and work done by the first party. Professor Arthur Miller of Harvard has called this rule the "sweat" theory of copyright law.

Other courts and commentators have criticized this notion. In *Triangle Publications, Inc. v. Sports Eye, Inc.*, [33] a publisher of horse race handicapping forms sued a competitor who used factual data on prior horse races taken from the plaintiff's "Daily Racing Form." The court held that the copying of raw data and defendant's expression of that data in a different format was sufficient to render the defendant's work noninfringing, notwithstanding the fact that defendant was able to save large sums of money by relying on the plaintiff's publication rather than doing the work itself.[34]

Professor Nimmer has stated this view succinctly: "One who explores obscure archives and who finds and brings to the light of public knowledge little known facts or other public domain materials has undoubtedly performed a socially useful service, but such service in itself does not render the finder an 'author.'"[35]

In determining whether a database proprietor can claim copyright on public domain materials by virtue of his efforts in making that public domain information available online, a court could seize upon either of the two lines of judicial reasoning.

Whether a particular judge would find the downloading of a large number of public domain facts to be an infringement becomes a test almost of the individual preferences of the judge as to which of two lines of reasoning and authority he or she chooses to follow. It is in situations such as this one that "probabilistic jurisprudence" comes into play, as persons attempting to take full advantage of downloading technology while remaining within the law must take into account that there is no certainty that until a number of these cases are decided, downloading of public domain data might or might not be found to be an infringement of the copyright of the database proprietor.

Of course, even in this area of ambiguity there are some clear boundaries, such as the ones cited in the CONTU Final Report, where the copying of an entire database for commercial gain was described as infringing[36] and the copying of small parts of the database was described as non-infringing.[37] As for the all-important middle ground, CONTU said:

> Similar also to a telephone directory, copyright in a dynamic database protects no individual datum, but only the systematized form in which the data are presented. The use of one item retrieved from such a work—be it an address, a chemical formula, or a citation to an article—would not under reasonable circumstances merit the attention of the copyright proprietor. Nor would it conceivably constitute infringement of copyright. The retrieval and re-duplication of any substantial portion of a database, whether or not the individual data are in the public domain, would likely constitute a duplication of the copyrighted element of a database and would be an infringement. . . .
>
> The unauthorized taking of substantial segments of a copyrighted database should be considered infringing, consistent with the case law developed from infringement of copyright in various forms of directories.[38]

The use of the word "substantial" is sufficiently imprecise as to give little guidance to database users, since it could easily be argued that, almost by definition, the real advantages of downloading data begin only when the amount of information becomes "substantial." More importantly, reference to the "case law developed from infringement of copyright in various forms of directories" is of no real assistance to users and proprietors of databases, because, as has been described, the case law is sufficiently muddled so that there is no single rule of law clearly applicable to infringement of directories.[39]

"Fair Use": A Defense to Copyright Infringement

Even in the face of what would otherwise be copyright infringement, courts will sometimes not hold a person who copies liable for damages for copyright infringement if the copying was for a "fair use." The doctrine of fair use was originally developed by judges as part of the judiciary's broad equitable powers, without direct statutory authority. In the new copyright law, this judge-made doctrine has been codified in section 107:

> Notwithstanding the provisions of section 106 [which says that only the copyright holder may authorize the making of copies of the copyrighted work], the fair use of a copyrighted work . . . for purposes such as criticism, comment, news reporting, teaching (including multiple copies for classroom use), scholarship, or research, is not an infringement of copyright. In determining whether the use made of a work in any particular case is a fair use the factors to be considered shall include:
> (1) the purpose and character of the use, including whether such use is of a commercial nature or is for non-profit educational purposes;
> (2) the nature of the copyrighted work;
> (3) the amount and substantiality of the portion used in relation to the copyrighted work as a whole; and
> (4) the effect of the use upon the potential market for or value of the copyrighted work.

The doctrine of a fair use is thus only a defense to copyright infringement, and does not affect the validity of the underlying copyright. Because of this, what is found by one judge in one case to constitute fair use rather than copyright infringement may not necessarily be found to be a fair use in another, similar case. Thus each copyist must defend his or her own acts, as the focus in fair use is on the acts of the copyist as well as on the work allegedly infringed. As a result of this, downloading might or might not be found to constitute copyright infringement. Immunity from liability would inhere not in the literal act of downloading, but would inhere, if at all, in the purpose and scope of the downloading.

The first of the four tests focuses on the purpose of the use. Courts have been particularly sensitive to the "worthiness" of a particular use, and have made the purpose of the use perhaps the most important of the four factors.

Generally, courts will react very favorably to non-commercial uses such as teaching, scholarship, research, criticism or comment. Other "worthy" uses, such as in news reporting, are also looked upon favorably.

If someone whose conduct would otherwise be regarded as an infringement can persuade a judge that he fits under one of these "worthy"
categories, the conduct generally will be found noninfringing, and the
court will even try to stretch one or more of the other factors so that the
defendant's conduct is found noninfringing under those tests as well.

The CONTU Final Report discussed the "worthiness" test in the
downloading context:

> The example of a copyrighted work placed in a computer memory solely
> to facilitate an individual's scholarly research has been cited as a possible
> fair use. The Commission agrees that such a use, restricted to individual
> research, should be considered fair. To prevent abuse of fair use principles,
> any copy created in a machine memory should be erased after completion of
> the particular research project for which it was made.[40]

And elsewhere in the report, CONTU said:

> Principles of fair use would be applicable in limited instances to excuse
> an unauthorized input of a work into computer memory. Exemplifying such
> fair uses could be the creation of a copy in a computer memory to prepare a
> concordance of a work or to perform a syntactical analysis of a work, which
> but for the use of a computer would require a prohibitive amount of human
> time an effort. To satisfy the criteria of fair use, any copies created for such
> research purposes should be destroyed upon completion of the research
> project for which they were created.[41]

The downloading of data from a database could be fair use, although
the prudent downloader would take to heart the repeated suggestion that
the downloaded data should be erased after completion of the specific
project for which the downloading was done. While this suggestion is not
binding and has no legal force, the unique status of CONTU as technical
advisor to Congress and the outstanding reputations of its members
would almost certainly give its "suggestion" considerable force with
judges.[42]

The second test focuses on the nature of the copyrighted work. Some
works are copied inadvertently and necessarily, and their copying will be
considered fair use. For example, a photograph of Times Square
containing as an incidental feature a copyrighted billboard would
probably be considered to be a fair use because of the public nature of the
billboard in such a well-known place. As applied to downloading of data,
however, the "nature of the work" test would seem to refer more to the
fact that the specific factual elements of the work are by their nature in
the public domain. Facts, particularly well-known facts,[43] cannot be
copyrighted, and so one is permitted a more liberal borrowing of specific

facts contained in a database than one would be permitted to copy, for example, a work of fiction.

On the other hand, courts may be persuaded that a use is not fair where the copyright proprietor is forced to charge a high price because there is only a limited market for copies of that work. In this case, the "nature of the work" test coincides with the "effect on value" test, as the nature of the work is that it appeals to a limited audience, and taking away even a small part of that audience affects the value of the work to the copyright proprietor. This issue is one of particular significance to downloading because many of the more specialized databases have only a limited market, and entry of data into those databases is as costly as entry of the same amount of data in a widely-used database. It suggests that the downloading of a "mass-market" database such as Dow Jones would be treated differently from the downloading of a more limited database such as Surface Coating Abstracts.[44]

The third test is the amount of the work that is copied relative to the size of the work. This rule has two faces. First, a very small work of a few words or figures may be copied in its entirety. Second, in the case of a larger work, the amount that may be copied grows with the size of the work, but in a less than linear way. As applied to databases, the first rule is of little relevance, since databases in order to be useful must be larger than one or two records. The second rule has much more importance. As noted in the passages from the CONTU Final Report quoted above, it is generally the case that copying a few records from a large database would qualify, subject to the other factors governing fair use, simply because of the small number of records copied. There is no specific legislative or judicial limit to the number of records that can be copied, but neither is there a "safe harbor," i.e., a number of copies that can be made without fear of infringement.[45]

The fourth test looks to whether the copying reduces the market for the copyrighted work. This test, it should be noted, looks not only to the copying of the specific defendant, but to whether the activity of the defendant, if carried out by everyone similarly situated, would adversely affect the value of the work.[46]

This test is of particular importance to the question of downloading because one of the principal advantages of downloading data is that it enables the user to avoid having to do the work directly in the online database. In the situations described above in the CONTU Final Report, entry of a copyrighted written work into a computer database was under certain conditions allowed as a fair use, but it must be recognized that those considerations would not be present where the work was already available online.

The fourth factor will, it can be predicted, be the most difficult test for a downloader of data to satisfy. Unless, for example, a downloader can show that his own downloading program has essential features not present on the online database, a court is likely to conclude that every use of his or her copy of the downloaded data would, absent the downloading, have been done on the online database, thereby reducing the demand for the copyrighted work on a use-for-use basis. Pleas of poverty on the part of the downloader, that he or she could not afford the cost of repeated online searching, are likely to fall upon deaf ears unless the court is swayed by the extreme "worthiness" of the defendant under the non-commercial use test described above.[47] The reduction in value test may be very difficult for a downloader to pass except where the copying was *de minimis* enough to satisfy the third test.

DOWNLOADING BY LIBRARIES

Mention must be made about copying by libraries and archives. Librarians and archives are covered by a special section, section 108, that allows libraries, archives or their patrons to make copies of copyrighted works if the copying (a) is small-scale, and (b) is believed to be not for profit.[48] This special provision almost certainly applies to downloading of data from databases, but there are some qualifications to this general rule.

First, the copying must not be "systematic."[49] In this context, "systematic" means repeated so as to form a pattern of behavior. It is an open question whether the use of downloaded information kept on a storage device that is part of a library's microcomputer system becomes "systematic" by virtue of repeated use of the database. It may well be that repeated use of downloaded data would qualify as "systematic."

Second, in order to qualify for the benefits of section 108, "the collections of the library or archives [must be] (i) open to the public, or (ii) available not only to researchers affiliated with the library or archives or with the institution of which it is a part, but also to other persons doing research in a specialized field. . . . "[50] Leaving aside the interesting question of how "open" a proprietary library must be in order to qualify for the benefits of section 108, which is a question common to issues of copyright apart from downloading, the question more pertinent to the downloading issue is whether the library's or archives' computer facilities or downloaded databases must be open to the public. "Collection" could be interpreted to mean that the entire collection must be open to the public or to scholars, or it could be held to include only the hardcopy portion of the library. It is quite likely that however a court were to rule on the question, libraries or archives interested in taking advantage of section 108 for the purpose of downloading data would be able to alter or adjust their activities so as to make their computer facilities nominally or actually open to the public or to scholars. Even if, as is most likely, unaffiliated persons using a private library were required to reimburse the library for actual computer charges including computer time, this might in turn diminish the number of subscribers to private databases, since people would be able to use a library's equipment without having to obtain their own. This problem will be mitigated significantly by the low cost and wide availability of suitable microcomputer equipment and peripherals, as described at the outset of this article, as well as by progressive marketing policies by online database services who charge users no minimum monthly fees for access to the database.

HOW WOULD A COURT LIKELY RESOLVE THE DOWNLOADING QUESTION?

As noted throughout this article, there are no hard and fast rules as to whether downloading is prohibited or permitted in all circumstances. There are only a number of clues as to how courts are likely to behave when confronted with the question of whether downloading data from an online database constitutes copyright infringement.

First, the downloading of a single or very small number of facts is not likely to get a user into trouble. The economics of litigation are such that even if such acts constitute copyright infringement, they constitute only *de minimis* infringement.[51] In all likelihood, a database proprietor suing for copyright infringement based on the downloading of a very small number of instances would find a court ruling that he had no copyright in facts themselves or that his copyright was limited to only the arrangement of facts, not the facts themselves.

The downloading of a large number of records but still less than the entire database is not likely to be found to be copyright infringement, especially where the use is non-commercial or where the data is in the public domain. Where the use is commercial, particularly where the user is believed to be one able to pay the full cost of using the database, or where the data itself is not in the public domain, a user is exposed to copyright infringement liability.

A person planning to download large amounts of data from an online database for distribution to others should immediately retain a good attorney. Such a use is almost certain to be found to be infringing, even where the data is in the public domain or where the user is not intending to make a profit on the copy of the original database.

One bellwether of how courts will resolve close cases involving downloading may be in the analogies courts adopt in order to come to grips with this novel question. Two analogies seem relevant to down-loading data, and—as might be suspected—they lead to opposite conclusions.

First, a court could say that when a user subscribes to the database, he or she is "purchasing" a "copy" of the database. If this premise is followed, a judge would apply a long-standing rule of law that says that restraints on alienation—restrictions on a property owner's ability to sell his or her property—are looked upon with disfavor, particularly where the restraint on alienation involves copies of copyrighted works. One of the clearest rules in American copyright law is that your copy of a copyrighted work is yours to do with as you please. If you wish to cut up your copy of the Encyclopaedia Britannica and rearrange all the words in order of their length, you may do so without fear that you have committed copyright infringement. If you wanted to cut out your favorite articles and hang them on the wall of your office, you would not have committed copyright infringement. The essence of copyright is that you may do what you want with your copy, but you may not make more copies of the work in altered or unaltered form without the consent of the copyright proprietor.[52]

Under this view, the downloading of data is but one aspect in using the database, analogous perhaps to the taking of notes as the data streams across the screen of your terminal.[53] The downloading of data would be simply your means of adapting your copy of the database, roughly analogous to cutting up your copy of the Encyclopaedia Britannica and hanging it on the wall of your office. A database proprietor who attempted to prevent downloading except where the downloader would be going into competition with him would be placing an invalid restriction on the user's right to use his or her "copy" of the database.

On the other hand, a court could say that a user's right to use a database is not the right to the physical possession of a copy of the data, but rather is a license to use the database, analogous to a theater-goer's right to view a performance of a play or a movie. Under this view, a user has no right to physical possession of the data, subject to considerations of fair use and the like, but rather has a license to use the database but not to make any copies of it.

Under this view, the downloading of data from a database would be an infringement because the user is not entitled to make copies of the database. The user would be entitled to use whatever he learned from the database, just as the viewer of a play is entitled to use any lessons he or she can draw from the play. Put another way, application of this analogy to downloading of data from databases would allow the user to make use of non-copyrightable elements of the database, but not to the particular expression of the data, i.e., the fact that it is in machine-readable form.

Which analogy would seem more persuasive to a court? Both analogies can be criticized for failing to capture some of the essence of the downloading issue. The "ownership" view depends on an assumption that the database proprietor must "give" the user a "copy" of the database in order for the database to be useful. Such an assumption creates a legal fiction, since in fact the usual contract for access to a database speaks of access, not ownership of a copy. On the other hand, the "license" view places too great a restriction on the utility of an online database such that few people would have any use for the data if they could not at least copy the results of their research for later use. Once you allow copying of results on, say, a printer located next to the computer terminal, what logical difference is there in storing exactly the same information on disk?

There are, of course, counterarguments to all of these points, and it is beyond the scope of this article to resolve them. These two analogies are intended to show two ways that a court would attempt to grapple with the question of whether downloading data constituted copyright infringement.

RESOLUTION OF THE UNCERTAINTY SURROUNDING DOWNLOADING

One of the principal virtues of any legal system is predictability. Predictability allows people to arrange their affairs without fear that they will unknowingly expose themselves to loss or punishment for their acts. Predictability reduces the risks to investors, thereby giving them more inducements to engage in socially useful activities. Not least of all, a predictable and understandable law reduces the need for society to spend time and money litigating over each other's rights and responsibilities.

The present state of the legality of downloading data is such that—except in certain extreme areas—no certainty exists. Much of the blame for this lack of predictability must be laid at the feet of new technology, which has outdistanced even the most recent steps of Congress to address the effects of science on copyright. What alternatives to the present situation exist?

If no action is taken, the result will be judicial resolution of specific cases only as they arise. Courts, by ruling on specific actions involving specific parties, will lay down guidelines that will, ultimately, allow people to form conclusions as to what behavior is permitted and what is not. As a practical matter, however, it must be recognized that in this struggle the online database operators have the upper hand, as they command not inconsiderable legal resources and usually have the power and the right to control where and against whom litigation is brought. For database users engaged in downloading data, many of which users are likely to be small firms or non-profit organizations on limited budgets, resources necessary to establish the right of users to download certain data in certain circumstances represent a direct drain on other activities that form the principal mission of those users. Only group action through trade associations or other entities may be enough to offset the advantages possessed by database operators.

A second solution, not exclusive with the first, is to regulate the use of downloading by contract.[54] Users may be licensed by database proprietors to download some or all of the data desired, upon payment of a fee or royalty to the database proprietor. A third alternative would be to restructure user fees to minimize the financial incentives that encourage downloading. Rather than charge on the basis of connect time or search unit, a database could charge per record retrieved and listed with only a nominal charge for subsequent retrievals of the same data.

Another marketplace solution would be to re-price online database services high enough to recoup the cost of providing the service plus a profit on the assumption that everyone will be engaging in downloading. This policy must be regarded as socially undesirable because it would encourage users seeking copies of the data to obtain them from other users rather than from the database proprietor. In many ways, this is analogous to the toleration of software piracy, where people who buy computer game programs make copies to exchange with their friends. This clearly unlawful activity may represent one of the most pervasive moral problems of our day, as some say that eight illegal copies of some game programs exist for every one legitimate copy. Most copies are made by children, who may grow up believing that the copyright law is something of no relevance to their own personal or professional lives. Tacitly or explicitly encouraging database piracy does not seem a socially desirable solution.

A fifth solution would be a legislative one. Congress could take one or more of several steps in order to clarify the current legal status of downloading from databases.[55] Congress could adopt clear rules as to what could or could not be downloaded, although virtually any rule that does not cause a great burden on users and database proprietors alike would probably be too difficult to enforce.

A second type of legislative solution would involve forced licensing, where proprietors of online databases must accept a copyright royalty paid by users directly or indirectly to the copyright proprietor. Forced licensing is not new to copyright. The law has long required holders of copyright in music to license performance rights to others under certain conditions.[56] Also, cable television operators have to pay royalties for retransmitting certain programs.[57] Jukebox owners must pay royalties to holders of copyrights in music for each playing of a song by a jukebox user.[58] Several compulsory licensing schemes are being discussed now in Congress in the aftermath of the "Sony Betamax" case.[59] One such proposal would involve a fee added to the price of videocassette recorders along with a separate fee added to the price of the videocassettes themselves. While a precisely analogous scheme would be manifestly unreasonable and unjust in connection with microcomputers and disks, it should be possible by statute to grant specifically to database users the right to download some or all types of data, and to establish a reasonable fixed royalty that the Copyright Royalty Tribunal would distribute to copyright holders. The market would then make whatever other adjustments were necessary in the way of contractual provisions or fee plans in order to assure that the rights of both proprietors and users of databases are protected.

Footnotes

1. Shea, "Hard Disks Will Soon Pack Hundreds of Megabytes," *Infoworld* (December 5, 1983):158.
2. Even today it is possible to use videodisks to play back recorded computer data, although this is not very useful since once the data is recorded on the videodisk, the data cannot be erased and recorded over.
3. O.W. Holmes, Jr., *The Path of the Law*, 10 Harv. L. Rev. 457, 461 (1897).
4. Of course, the weight judges usually attach to precedent and to reason makes it fairly certain that once judges begin to rule consistently on one issue, other judges are more likely to follow those rulings. An additional factor for stability in the law is the fact that lower courts are supposed to follow the law as declared by courts above them in the judicial hierarchy.
5. (a) Copyright protection subsists, in accordance with this title, in original works of authorship fixed in any tangible medium of expression, now known or later developed, from which they can be perceived, reproduced, or otherwise communicated, either directly or with the aid of a machine device. . . .
   (b) In no case does copyright protection for an original work of authorship extend to any idea, procedure, process, system, method of operation, concept, principle, or discovery, regardless of the form in which it is described, explained, illustrated, or embodied in such work. 17 U.S.C. § 102 (1982).
6. 17 U.S.C.§ 401 (1982).
7. *Id*. § 405.
8. *Id*. § 102.
9. *Id*.

10. The Commission is known by the acronym "CONTU." This report, submitted in 1978, will be cited hereafter as "CONTU Final Report."

11. CONTU Final Report 41.

12. H.R. Rep. No. 94-1476, 94th Cong., 2d Sess. 54 (1976).

13. 17 U.S.C. § 102 (a)(1982).

14. H.R. Rep. No. 94-1476, 94th Cong., 2d Sess. 53 (1976). Note however that whether a work in a computer memory is fixed for the purpose of being eligible for copyright protection is separate from the fact that a copy in computer memory of a copyrighted work can be an infringement.

15. See the discussion of compilations and collective works, below.

16. U.S. Const. art I, § 8, cl. 8.

17. 17 U.S.C. § 302 (1982). In the case of copyright by institutions, the term is the lesser of 75 years after publication or 100 years after creation. For works copyrighted before January 1, 1978, the term may be less than for works created on or after January 1, 1978, but in any event not less than 28 years after the copyright of the work. Id. § 304(a).

18. CONTU Final Report 41-42.

19. There are other defenses to infringement besides fair use, but these are beyond the scope of this article.

20. 17 U.S.C. § 101 (1982).

21. *Id.*

22. "Copyright in a derivative or collective work covers only those elements contained therein which are original with the copyright claimant." 1 Nimmer on Copyright § 3.04 (1983 ed.) (footnote omitted).

23. 17 U.S.C. § 101 (Supp. V 1982).

24. Of course, government-established databases with nothing but government-created works are likely to be maintained only by such agencies as the Department of Defense, the Central Intelligence Agency, or the National Security Agency. Penalties for copyright infringement will be only a secondary concern to unauthorized persons who are caught downloading data for their own use from such databases.

25. Grove Press, Inc. v. Collectors Publication, Inc., 264 F. Supp. 603 (C.D. Cal. 1967).

26. Donald v. Uarco Business Forms, 478 F. 2d 764 (8th Cir. 1973).

27. Eggers v. Sun Sales Corp. 263 Fed. 373 (2d Cir. 1920).

28. 400 F. Supp. 228 (S.D.N.Y. 1975).

29. Millworth Converting Corp. v. Slifka, 276 F. 2d 443 (2d Cir. 1960). *See, e.g.*, 1 Nimmer on Copyright, § 3.03 (1983 ed.).

30. Alfred Bell & Co. v. Catalda Fine Arts, 191 F.2d 99 (2d Cir. 1951).

31. The interrelationship arises because it is easier to consider the answer to one of the other questions in order to answer the larger question of infringement where the copyist selected and altered the material from the other party. It is evident that an answer to one of the two secondary questions leads to a complementary answer to the other secondary question. Courts often address one of the secondary questions at length in order to arrive at a conclusion regarding the more general question posed in text of whether selection and alteration of the format is an infringement or not.

32. 91 F.2d 484 (9th Cir. 1937).

33. 415 F. Supp. 682 (E.D. Pa. 1976).
34. *See also* Hoehling v. Universal City Studios, Inc., 618 F.2d 972 (2d Cir. 1980), in which a movie distributed by Universal borrowed from factual research done by Hoehling on possible causes of the destruction of the dirigible *Hindenburg.* The Second Circuit held that while Hoehling's theory was based on historical facts he had discovered only with great effort, he was not entitled to copyright protection for the facts themselves.
35. 1 Nimmer on Copyright § 3.04 (1983 ed.). Cases following this line of reasoning include New York Times Co. v. Roxbury Data Interface, Inc., 434 F. Supp. 217 (D.N.J. 1977) which despite the names of the parties did not involve the copyright in downloaded facts, but rather involved whether the defendant could maintain an index based on names cited in plaintiff's newspaper.
36. CONTU Final Report 41.
37. *Id.* at 40, 42.
38. *Id.* at 42.
39. CONTU's Final Report was, to be sure, a "first cut" at the question of downloading of data from databases, and necessarily lacks the advantage of experience gained in the last few years, as the technology has improved to the point where downloading is feasible and potentially significant.
40. CONTU Final Report 40 n.166.
41. *Id.* at 40.
42. The erasure of data also makes the use more likely to satisfy the fourth test of not reducing the market for the copyrighted work.
43. See above for a discussion of the ability to copyright little-known facts under a "sweat" theory.
44. Surface Coating Abstracts is derived from World Surface Coatings Abstracts, published by the Paint Research Assn., and is available on DIALOG. *See* H.R. Rep. No. 94-1476 at 73-74 (1976).
45. Compare the situation in text with the case of photocopying for classroom use, where guidelines are clear, if somewhat irrational. See Agreement on Guidelines for Classroom Copying in Not-For-Profit Educational Institutions, *quoted* in H.R. Rep. No. 94-1476(1976) at 68-71. The guidelines permit the copying of an entire prose article, story or essay if it is less than 2,500 words long, but if it is 2,500 or more words long only the lesser of 1,000 words or 10% of the work (but not less than 500 words).
46. But in Williams & Wilkins Co. v. United States, 487 F.2d 1345 (Ct. Cl. 1973). *aff'd by an equally divided court*, 420 U.S. 376 (1975), the Court of Claims in deciding whether the copying of medical research articles by the National Library of Medicine looked only to the copying done by the National Library of Medicine, and not to copying that would be—and subsequently was— soundly criticized, and is not likely to be followed in the future. See 3 Nimmer on Copyright § 13.05 [E] (1983 ed.).
47. The tension between the non-commercial use test and the reduction in value test is arising more often now because of the explicit recognition in the new copyright act that educational uses are specifically in the favored category. But where the only market for a copyrighted work is in education, the reduction in value test should be given greater weight. This is a point of

particular tension in the educational software industry, because many schools have begun buying a very small number of expensive educational programs and copying them for use in all of the microcomputers in the school system. It is not entirely certain how the courts will resolve this dilemma when it comes before them, although the egregiousness with which some schools have behaved in this matter should weigh heavily against them.

48. There are a number of qualifications and exceptions to this rule that are beyond the scope of this article. The rules for libraries and archives are perhaps the second most specific in the new copyright act, with only cable television singled out for more careful treatment.

49. 17 U.S.C. § 108 (g) (2) (1982).

50. *Id.* § 108 (a) (2).

51. The copyright law does not provide for statutory damages between zero and $50,000, depending on a number of factors, even where a copyright holder cannot show specific damage. 17 U.S.C. § 504 (c) (1982). A court may also award court costs including attorneys' fees. Id. § 505.

52. But be alert that this principle does not apply to certain types of musical or audiovisual works, where the author is presumed to retain the right to publicly perform the copyrighted work.

53. But even the taking of notes may be a copyright infringement. See 3 Nimmer on Copyright § 13.05 [E] [4] [a] (1983 ed.).

54. But see the discussion of preemption of contract law remedies discussed on page 59.

55. Perhaps more workable, given the rapid change in technology and the slow pace with which Congress deals with copyright issues, would be for Congress to empower the Register of Copyrights to promulgate copyright law by regulation in accordance with certain broadly-drawn purposes. The regulatory process could be subject to the notice and comment provisions of the Administrative Procedure Act, 5 U.S.C. § 551 (1982), to ensure procedural fairness to all parties. While not without its flaws, such a system would be expected to be markedly more flexible than the present system, which relies entirely on legislation only when Congress is made aware of a pressing need to amend the copyright laws.

56. 17 U.S.C. § 115 (1982).

57. Id. § 111.

58. Id. § 116.

59. Sony Corp. of America v. Universal City Studios, Inc., 104 S. Ct. 774 (1984).

Additional Readings—
Microcomputers in Online
Searching

Beaumont, Jane and Krueger, Donald, eds. *Microcomputers for Libraries: How Useful Are They?* Ottawa: Canadian Library Association, 1983.

Casbon, Susan. "Online Searching With a Microcomputer—Getting Started." *Online* 7 (Nov. 1983):42-46.

Chen, Ching-chih, and Bressler, Stacey E., eds. *Microcomputers in Libraries.* New York: Neal-Schuman, 1982.

Ensor, Pat, and Curtis, Richard A. "Search Helper: Low-Cost Online Searching in an Academic Environment." *RQ* 23 (Spring 1984):327-331.

Janke, Richard V. "BRS/After Dark: the Birth of Online Self-Service". *Online* 7 (Sept. 1983):12-29.

Look, Hugh E. "Evaluating Software for Microcomputers." *The Electronic Library* 2 (Jan. 1984):53-60.

Mason, Robert M. "Current and Future Microcomputer Capabilities: Selecting the Hardware." *Microcomputers for Information Management* 1 (March 1984): 1-13.

Mason, Robert M. "The New IBM PC AT, IBM and Apple LANs." *Library Journal* 109 (Oct. 15, 1984):1903-1904.

Ojala, Marydee. "Knowledge Index: a Review." *Online* 7 (Sept. 1983):31-34.

Rorvig, Mark E. *Microcomputers and Libraries: A Guide to Technology, Products and Applications.* White Plains, N.Y.: Knowledge Industry Publications, 1981.

Stout, Catherine, and Marcinko, Thomas. "Sci-Mate: A Menu-Driven Universal Online Searcher and Personal Data Manager." *Online* 7 (Sept. 1983):112-16.

Tenopir, Carol. "Database Access Software." *Library Journal* 109 (Oct. 1, 1984):1828-1829.

Tenopir, Carol. "Full-text, Downloading, and Other Issues." *Library Journal* 108 (June 1, 1983):1111-1113.

Toliver, David E. "OL' SAM: An Intelligent Front-End for Bibliographic Information Retrieval." *Information Technology and Libraries* 1 (Dec. 1982) :317-326.

Woods, Lawrence A., and Pope, Nolan F. *The Librarian's Guide to Microcomputer Technology and Applications.* White Plains, N.Y.: Knowledge Industry Publications, 1983.

There can be little doubt that the widespread adoption of online reference services has wrought dramatic changes in library and information centers. These changes affect virtually every aspect of service management from the type of staff that is hired to the titles of journals ordered, from the scope of services offered users to the design and implementation of pricing policies. Some of these changes were anticipated and their introduction eased by skillful planning. In most instances, however, they just happened as the inevitable result of the adoption of computer technology for the reference function.

One of the first impacts of online bibliographic searching was on the role and self-esteem of the reference librarian. The scheduling of appointments with users for the negotiation interview often in a specially designated office, the mystique associated with computer use, and the fact that users were actually paying for an information product all served to enhance the professional image and self-esteem of the librarian. The role of the librarian was no longer perceived as being restricted to the confines of the library's collection but was that of an intermediary between the inquiring user and the vast information store accessible on huge databases. Whereas initially the fear was that jobs would be lost to automation, in fact the workloads in public services increased necessitating larger staffs, albeit with new skills, attitudes, and behaviors.

As the volume of online searching increased, so did demands for original documents. A surge in photocopying, interlibrary loan, and circulation followed. More subtle changes occurred in acquisitions as titles of journals purchased shifted to reflect the citations retrieved in online bibliographies. Other budgetary reallocations became necessary as accommodations were made to meet the new demands for staff training, equipment, and resources. The institution of user fees meant that many libraries for the first time became involved in business transactions: charging policies had to be clarified, costs accurately determined, and accounting procedures implemented. Statistics gathering gained a new importance as did expertise in market research and promotion strategies. In retrospect, then, all aspects of service provision and management were affected.

While habits, opportunities, and work flows were all subjected to the impact of technology, greater freedom also became possible as what could be done was no longer constrained by physical files. Of equal importance was the flexibility and adaptability displayed by the librarians who experienced these changes in the early days, just over a decade ago. Having witnessed the early disruptions with some skepticism, their attitude to more recent innovations has become pragmatically philosophical.

Though the impact of the first decade of online retrieval has been pervasive, even more impressive changes in the management and delivery of online reference are anticipated in the future. The application of expert systems, artificial intelligence, and built-in help and tutorial facilities to online bibliographic retrieval will facilitate searching not only for the professional but for the burgeoning end-users as well. Also expected to swell the numbers of direct users are improvements in front-ends, automatic sign-on, dialing, and reconnect capabilities. This increased user access will undoubtedly continue to influence the way the role of the information specialist evolves. The role, rather than being reduced or eliminated, will become a highly sophisticated one as systems continue to improve, expand, and multiply.

These enhancements will allow simplified searching of multiple files, searching of larger consolidated databases, electronic delivery of offline prints, and messaging and conferencing capabilities enabling users to communicate with vendors, producers, and each other. Improvements in communications will make possible higher access speeds, faster response times, and greater overall reliability. Increased baud rates, smart terminals, and downloading of searches will lead to new charging schemes. There will be a move away from using connect time as a basis for charging, toward an emphasis on the quantity of output retrieved as the result of a search. As new charging schemes come into effect between vendors and institutional users, new end-user fee structures will be devised. Though costs for communications may be decreasing, it is unlikely that total costs will go down as producers try to recover lost revenue from shrinking subscriptions to hard copy products and as library and information centers seek new sources of revenue, or at least cost recovery, to bolster retrenching budgets.

As user expectations for service alter and expand, managers will be pressured to reconsider and revise their goals, objectives, and policies to more closely match the new demands of their users. If they fail to recognize the continuing impact of the computer on their operations or are too hesitant in their responses, commercial competitors will infiltrate their information domain and perhaps even threaten their very survival.

The authors of the articles that follow have assessed the effects that the expanding use of computers may be expected to have in some detail. Pat Ensor examines the new ways of doing reference work and speculates about possible future developments. She discusses tertiary databases, cooperative reference, knowledge-based systems, full-text storage and searching, data manipulation, the creation of inhouse files, and speculates about the future role of the librarian.

Simone Klugman explores the ways in which the new services generated by online retrieval capabilities interact with more traditional reference work. She describes the problems resulting from the reluctant merger including staff anxieties, overburdened work schedules, user frustrations, and hardware breakdowns. In spite of her candid assessment of the drawbacks, however, Klugman concludes on an optimistic note, convinced that online retrieval holds exciting prospects for the future development of reference services.

The impact of online services, has, of course, reached beyond the individual library or information center. Online services have profoundly changed virtually every component of the information industry. Astute managers must be aware of these changes, their influence, and devise effective strategies to cope with them. In their article, F.W. Lancaster and Herbert Goldhor show the effects that online services have had on subscriptions to printed publications. Finally, Richard P. Kollin and James E. Shea conclude this part and the volume with five major trends in the online industry that in their view will profoundly effect information delivery in the future. For more on the impact of online services, the reader is referred to the Additional Readings.

The Expanding Use of Computers in Reference Service

Pat Ensor

Computers have become an integral part of the functioning of libraries across the country in the last decade. Their effects have been felt strongly in reference departments, primarily through the availability of online database searching. There are currently available at least 55,000,000 references in 400 public databases.[1] In a recent survey of college and university libraries in thirteen states, 48 percent of them did online searches.[2] Online databases are here to stay, and use of them will continue to expand.

TODAY'S ISSUES

Librarians are learning that databases are simply another type of reference tool. This idea must be accepted before it is possible to explore the incredible potential of computers in reference service. The services already available have had many implications for libraries. Increased costs for equipment, personnel, and access to the information systems have, of course, been incurred. Users of the services seem to be expecting more of the library—they expect the library to have the resources identified for them by the computer. Identification of materials not owned leads to more strain on interlibrary loan. In addition, the nature of database-searching services allows for more exact measurement of user satisfaction with the service. Research in this area has implications for improvement in all areas of reference service since much can be learned about the user's view of the library and the librarian.

One of the most controversial problems faced by librarians in the offering of online database searching is: should we charge for searches?

Reprinted by permission of the American Library Association from *RQ* 21 (4):365-72 (Summer 1982); copyright © 1982 by the American Library Association.

Most libraries charge fees covering at least part of their costs, though many librarians will agree it would be nice if they didn't have to. John Linford has stated that charging is justifiable for patron-specific services that cost the library money.[3] Access to databases can be seen, however, as simply a new form of reference aid. Databases are a tool available in general to users rather than a patron-specific tool. Libraries are gaining access to more online indexes than they could get in printed form, and there is, and will be, more and more information that is only available online. This is especially seen in the growth of numeric databases. Charging fees deprives people of access to some materials and to the computer's "expertise" in searching. Studies have shown, reasonably enough, that far more people would use these services if they were free, and we are depriving ourselves of a large group of potentially satisfied customers. Students, particularly undergraduates, are an untapped user group, but fees would have to be low or nonexistent for them to use online searching. Use of this service would also expose them to other reference services.

Practically speaking, it is currently impossible in many places not to charge fees. In accordance with ALA aims for free search service in public institutions, the State University of New York at Albany tried to do free searching, but eventually had to start charging for printouts.[4] There is evidence that searchers are more efficient when the user is paying for the search, but perhaps we should aim for a higher view of service for its own sake in this area, instead of using this as an excuse for fees.[5] As Peter Watson told us in 1978, though, this should be considered a transition phase. Librarians should, of course, seek all possible forms of alternate funding and work on building support for the ideas of the importance and the moral right of access to computer services in reference. He sees fees for online services as "ethically wrong, politically unwise, educationally unsound, and economically inefficient."[6] Free online searches have proven to be feasible at California State College at Stanislaus. The librarians decide when a computer search is more appropriate than a manual search in any particular situation. They have even been able to discontinue some indexes that are infrequently used and are accessible by computer.[7] The possibility exists in some libraries of reallocating acquisition funds on a regular basis. John Brewster Smith and Sara Knapp call for lower charges by owners of broad-appeal databases, hoping that use will increase and make up the difference.[8] This would be of some help to libraries and their patrons. If fees continue to be charged, particularly at present high levels, more and more library users will be denied access to the expanding capabilities of computers in database searching.

Currently there are services offered by database vendors that are not being made available to users, or, if they are available, they are not being publicized. Susan Evans and Maurice Line demonstrated in 1973 the usefulness and desirability to social scientists at Bath University of current-awareness services, yet now when libraries have the capability of offering selective dissemination of information, or SDI, through database vendors, many of them ignore it. In the Evans-Line study, participants were given cards citing relevant new articles, documents, books, and so on. Current awareness services were rated as very useful by thirty-one out of forty-one people. When the project was over, two departments offered to help continue the service with their own funds.[9] More recently, a study showed that 70 percent of the people who had been receiving free computer SDI would want to continue it even if charged for it, while 90 percent would want it if it was free.[10] Another study showed that use of current-awareness services leads to more success and productivity and computer SDI is the best current-awareness method for counteracting the scatter of information found in interdisciplinary fields.[11] Yet a 1978 survey of database searchers showed that 63 percent didn't use SDI, though they knew it was available, and 14 percent didn't even know about it.[12] It would seem wise for libraries to offer and publicize SDI to users even if they do have to charge for it, since it is available to libraries at least through DIALOG and Orbit, and users would probably appreciate it. Using the Orbit SDI service, one can specify up to six databases, set a time period for deletion, limit the number of printed citations, have the results delivered to any address, and change strategies. There is a small charge for each stored statement and for each execution. DIALOG's service is similar, but it is only available on fifteen databases.

Another service currently available is online ordering of documents to be provided by database suppliers and information brokers. This involves more expense that should be incurred by the buyer of the document, but users should at least be made aware of it.

TRENDS FOR TOMORROW

Computers will become an ever more useful tool in reference, both through vendors and locally. They will become increasingly sophisticated in their capabilities in reference service and yet, at the same time, increasingly easy to use. Certain recent trends in the use of computers in reference will become more prevalent, and some new developments will become more widely available.

We can, of course, expect more of what we've already got. We will be doing more searches on more databases with more records and more services. The creation of tertiary databases, which are composed of records from other databases, will give us added ways to access information. This is a very useful approach in making available information in a mission- or problem-oriented field, such as alcohol studies and studies of violence and inflation, since these areas cut across disciplines. The Women's Education Equity Communications Network developed a tertiary database in women's educational equity that draws on thirteen existing databases. They surmounted the technical problems of reformatting and reindexing citations to produce an internally consistent database. They also overcame the administrative problem of developing agreements with database owners for the use of part of their databases.[13] This kind of approach will become more common in the future.

Cooperative reference is increasingly being done with online database searching. Libraries that have online searching agree to provide it for patrons of libraries without this service. Usually it is determined at some point that online searching is the most appropriate method of service. This kind of cooperation can lead to increased communication and shared resources, and give more people access to a useful reference tool. There are problems—the service can be used inappropriately, requests can be misunderstood—but this kind of cooperation is a growing trend. It is possible with two telephone lines and two terminals, one of each in two cooperating libraries, to carry out online reference on the phone. The terminals can communicate with each other during the search, as can the two libraries.[14] However it is actually handled, cooperative online reference will increase.

The online searching services now available will continue to become more sophisticated in their capabilities. Research is being done extensively in the area of fuzzy sets—that is, sets without clear boundaries, where there is no sharp transition from membership to nonmembership. Work is being done to develop the capability to search databases using fuzzy (or imprecise) terms—for example, "recent," "old," and "many."[15] This is one of many moves toward the development of very intelligent database systems. An experimental program has already been developed that allows the computer to recognize citing statements in the stored text of documents. Retrieving citing statements gives more information about the cited document, and, more importantly, gives more terms to be searched. Searching words from citing statements with this program increased recall from 60 percent to 80 percent of the relevant documents.[16] "Knowledge-based systems" are being developed that capture the knowledge and reasoning processes of specialists in various fields to allow the computer to assist in performing difficult tasks.[17] This increase in the computer's "intelligence" has great implications for the future.

Capabilities are being expanded in another area—that of document full-text storage and searching. Decreased costs of storage, decreased costs and improvements of optical character recognition equipment, an increase in the percentage of publications captured in computer-readable form at the point of origin, an increase in the number of publications prepared by electronic data-processing techniques, and an increase in the use of computer-assisted publications will lead to the availability of more full-text material in machine-readable form.[18] After copyright problems are overcome, this material should become available for full-text searching and viewing and then for direct document delivery to the end user. Full-text searching capability has already been developed for several databases. There was a great need for it in the area of law, where the context in which a term is used is particularly important, and several legal databases have full-text searching. The National Library of Medicine is developing an experimental system for the electronic scanning and storage of documents in biomedicine and their subsequent retrieval and transmission.[19] An increase in full-text storage and document delivery may be made possible in the future by using sophisticated systems that perform computerized microform retrieval and transmit document facsimiles.[20] As computer storage costs continue to go down, full-text searching and storage will become increasingly available.

Online manipulation of data in databases is being done more and more on private databases, and this will probably become an option available to librarians. The availability of computerized census data has shown the usefulness of retrieval and manipulation of numbers in a data collection. The University of Florida libraries have administered a Census Access Program since 1971 with good results.[21] Librarians who are not in libraries that have such facilities should know that they are available and be cognizant of the possibilities for census-data manipulation. The most advanced work in the online manipulation of data in databases has been done in private databases. The Clearinghouse of Information on Child Abuse and Neglect puts data gathered in annual surveys on child-abuse programs into their database. Statistical analyses of the data can then be done by database users; tables and graphs can be prepared from the manipulated data.[22] The Bureau of Labor Statistics has a statistics database called Labstat, which provides access to 145,000 economic time series, including statistics on employment, productivity, and prices. The user can do simple and complex operations on data. Data can be retrieved and displayed, simple statistical operations can be done and data can be formatted in, for example, line charts.[23] These capabilities are becoming increasingly available.

Work is being done on personalizing database systems in various ways. This would involve adjusting databases to fit users. Online keyword in context indexes can be formed for the user. Work is being done to make database systems multilingual. A small, special-purpose information retrieval service called ACQUIRE has been developed at Keio University in Japan; it allows the user to store and retrieve personal information. The user can form his own database by inserting his own data, or by selecting records from an existing database.[24] The techniques developed in this kind of research will undoubtedly have implications for library use of computers in reference.

This increased sophistication will also influence the development of local databases in reference departments, an area in which work is already being done. Although centralized, large-scale, shared computer systems have generally been used during the first two decades of computing, this has not always been completely satisfactory. Technological changes since the early seventies allow for the remedying of this situation. Hardware costs have dropped drastically, and modular software structure techniques have been developed. Great computing power is available more cheaply in micro-and minicomputers. Arrangements incorporating dedicated micro-and minicomputers linked to a host or hosts are becoming more common. Such an approach lowers operational costs over the long run. In reference, this would allow local operations to be done on a local computer that is also serving as an "intelligent terminal" for a database system. It is becoming increasingly obvious that having a local computer, probably a microcomputer, can be very valuable to a reference department. Microcomputers can be used for word processing and in preparation of local bibliographies, indexes, etc., and they can be used in increasing effectiveness in online searching—by storing and manipulating searches and search results and by gathering statistics. A local computer would also make possible local networking, electronic messaging, and online bibliographic instruction. Local databases of different libraries can be linked to allow sharing of reference knowledge and to increase communication between libraries.

Probably the most important use of a local computer would be for an in-house database. The Reference Librarian Enhancement System developed at UCLA is such a system. In reporting on it in 1979, Bivins and Palmer pointed out three areas in which reference service could be enhanced in providing immediate data (fact retrieval) and pointers to data: recording and organizing unavailable or inaccessible data (non-current ephemeral data or data available from local resources), finding new reference sources, and recording search strategies for everyone's use. A local database would identify sources of data and would record data not easily available elsewhere. Computerized files, easily maintained and updated, could contain such things as information on the library, a directory of local contracts, information on other collections in the region, and instructions, procedures, and manuals. The Reference Librarian Enhancement System includes an operating-system file, a fact-retrieval file, and a search-strategy file, and is accessed by a general, controlled vocabulary. The search-strategy file, in addition to identifying obvious relevant sources, will identify new sources, esoteric sources, and nonprint sources. The system allows easy storage of new records, easy alteration of existing records, addition of new descriptors, and creation of more pointers to new and existing records. Use of the Reference Librarian Enhancement System has led librarians to review sources more carefully and record transactions involving ephemeral data more systematically. It has led to more structure and coherence in user/librarian interaction due to the precision required by the computer. Users, of course, benefit from the wider range of sources available. Librarians are able to share expertise, identify collection gaps, use systematic techniques, and use an advanced tool. Even student assistants have benefited from the sharing of expertise; the system is also used as a training tool for them.[25,26] Other places have developed local databases. The Pikes Peak Library District has a system that identifies library, community, and state and national resources. The Primate Research Center at the University of Washington uses a local database to keep records on its monkeys.[27] A computerbased medical information system, COSTAR, has been designed to perform data management functions needed by a group practice in the care of ambulatory patients.[28] A Palo Alto hospital has a microcomputer-based data management system. The Health Information Sharing Project of Syracuse, New York, uses a computerized resource directory to make available "fugitive" resources, such as reports, studies, and data files in the community.[29] An automated model file of twenty-five human-service agencies has been developed at the Wake County Department of the Library in North Carolina for use in giving information and referral. Computerization is particularly useful in this application because it allows easy updating and the creation of specialized reference tools.[30] Many in-house specialized bibliographic databases are being produced.

A reference department generally has three choices of method in implementing a local database project: microcomputers, minicomputers, and private database services. All are capable of text editing, indexing, electronic messaging, and computer-assisted instruction with the right software. Entry to the system should be easy, as should addition, modification, and retrieval of records. The system should be as user-friendly as possible to allow patron use when the librarian isn't there. Automatic monitoring of this use will be very helpful. Microcomputers cost less and provide local control, flexibility, and dedication to in-house use. If the department has access to a minicomputer, larger file capacity and more sophisticated programming features will be available. Fairly complex integrated data management systems are available on mini-computers. Access could be a problem, though, if the minicomputer isn't dedicated to reference department use. A private database service can provide for storage of files with large numbers of records requiring sophisticated retrieval techniques and noncontinuous access. This method allows less flexibility and versatility, though. The method chosen will depend on the needs of the reference department.

Online information retrieval systems are being made much easier to use. It is very difficult to deal with the variety of command languages, subject vocabularies, and capabilities of multiple systems and databases, and no user will be able to search well on more than a small group of familiar databases on a familiar system. Attempts are being made to remedy this with the development of user interfaces such as menus, natural language search capabilities, interface translators, help/explain commands, standard message formats, universal data languages, and graphics. Menu-based systems, in which the user chooses from lists of options, are currently being researched, especially in business applications. A menu-based system called BROWSE has been developed to access an online catalog; it is fast, easy, and inexpensive to use.[31] Natural language searching, or speaking English to the computer, greatly simplifies the search process. It promises to have a profound impact on bibliographic retrieval. It will enable large numbers of end users to interact directly with information retrieval systems, using their own particular, unrestricted professional jargons. Queries would also be transportable across multidisciplinary files. Medline is the first large database for which this capability has been developed; other work in this area has been done on an experimental basis on small to medium-size databases, but the research wasn't put to use on large systems. The prototype program CITE, or Current Information Transfer in English, developed by Tamas E. Doszkocs of the National Cancer Institute and Barbara A. Rapp of the National Library of Medicine, is fairly fast, uses only a reasonable amount of the computer, and is transferable to other files. The online searcher can enter a search in natural language, that is, English sentences, paragraphs, phrases, term lists, or a combination of these. There are no special syntactic requirements. In this system, the English query is processed by the same method used to produce the Medline file. Search terms are also identified by checking the query against a list of terms derived mainly from the actual term distribution in Medline. After an initial set of documents has been retrieved, the subject headings assigned to those documents are incorporated into the search strategy for later iterations of the search.[32] The Malaysian Rubber Producers' Research Association's database, MORPHS, also has natural-language searching capabilities. Its vocabulary developed gradually, until it approached that of the natural language, and since indexing and retrieving became easier, the natural language capability was formalized.[33]

Some people have called for standards in interactive languages to make them less variable and confusing. This would involve standard technical terms and symbols in search/query negotiation, instructions, output, and supervisory control. Next would come a code of practice with recommended ways to operate. In the long-term view, an effort would be made in the area of dimensional standards, for interchangeability. Standardized commands were strongly desired by surveyed database searchers and 69 percent said they would probably use other systems if standardization was done, but it seems unlikely at this time that database vendors would agree to standardize their commands.[34] Much more promising work is being done in the area of user-oriented transparent systems, which would contain convertors or translators so that the user would not need to understand all the specific differences of databases, systems, command languages, vocabularies, and access protocols. All systems would look alike to the user, and databases would function as if they had the same vocabulary. Work has been done at the University of Illinois on the design of the Total Transparent Information Retrieval System. This system is put into effect by transparency aids that automate various functions. These include selectors, convertors, evaluators, analyzers, and routers.[35] Some experimental transparency aids have already been developed. CONIT, developed at MIT, is an aid to the user in operating a retrieval system; it also automatically saves all searches and can rerun them easily, it does automatic keyword/stem searching, it can tailor searches for individual databases, and an automatic database selection capability is being developed.[36] The Vocabulary Switching System is also being developed at Batelle's Columbus Laboratories. It translates user requests into useful search queries across databases with little user intervention.[37]

The aim of all these efforts is not just to make searching easier for experienced intermediaries, but also to make searching possible and even easy for the inexperienced end user. End users will almost inevitably begin to do their own searches when the system is easy to use. The ACQUIRE System is intended to be used by people with no prior knowledge of information retrieval or the system. Using the CONIT system, inexperienced searchers were able to retrieve some relevant documents in a reasonable amount of time. It is only a matter of time before the end user will receive some instruction from the librarian, then do his own search, just as he currently searches printed indexes. It has been found in several studies—at the Congressional Research Service,[38] on the Individualized Instruction Data Access project,[39] and by medical librarians[40]—that people will, with training, do their own database searching on terminals in their work area. At the Congressional Research Service, 72 percent of the people trained in the use of the Scorpio database continued to use it, 88 percent of them at least once a month. Training sessions and user assistance were provided in this project, as in the others, but they still took less time than doing the searches. Given access to an easy-to-use system, many users will probably do their own searches.

THE FUTURE

Ideally, in the future, users will do free (to them) online searches with the aid of the librarian, if necessary, on databases that are sophisticated in access techniques, yet very easy to use. Every good-size reference department will have its own microcomputer for ready reference and word processing. Everyone at least will have access to computerized reference through cooperative networks. These projections of current trends won't all necessarily be realized, and situations can always change drastically, but these are some hopes for a stimulating future.

All of the mentioned innovations and improvements in computer capabilities can potentially be used to improve reference service. What actually comes into use depends not only on technological innovations and human creativity, but also on societal constraints. Librarians need to try to play more of a part in determining developments in online services. We also need to pay more attention to research done in the area of user satisfaction with online services and make more contributions of our own in this area. What makes a user satisfied or unsatisfied with a search? Do we know a good search when we see it? The librarian's view is needed more in research in this area. No matter what course the use of computers in reference service takes, though, it is bound to be exciting.

Footnotes

1. Martha Williams, "Online Retrieval-Today and Tomorrow," *Online Review* 2 (December 1978):355.
2. Marcy Murphy, "Organizational Communication: Managing Online Services in Libraries," in *Communicating Information: Proceedings of the 43rd ASIS Annual Meeting, 1980* (White Plains, N.Y.: Knowledge Industry Publications for the American Society for Information Science, 1980), p. 44.
3. John Linford, "To Change or Not to Change: A Rationale," *Library Journal* 102 (October 1, 1977):2010.
4. Sara D. Knapp and C. James Schmidt, "Budgeting to Provide Computer Based Reference Services: A Case Study," *Journal of Academic Librarianship* 5 (March 1979):13.
5. Michael D. Cooper and Nancy A. DeWath, "The Effect of User Fees on the Cost of Online Searching in Libraries," *Journal of Library Automation* 10 (December 1977):317.
6. Peter Watson, "The Dilemma of Fees for Service: Issues and Actions for

Librarians," in *ALA Yearbook 1978* (Chicago: American Library Association, 1978), pp. xxi-xxii.

7. Paula J. Crawford and Judith A. Thompson, "Free Online Searches Are Feasible," *Library Journal* 104 (April 1, 1979):795.

8. John Brewster Smith and Sara D. Knapp, "Data Base Royalty Fees and the Growth of Online Search Services in Academic Libraries," *Journal of Academic Librarianship* 7 (September 1981):207-8.

9. Susan Evans and Maurice Line, "A Personalized Service to Academic Researchers: The Experimental Information Service in the Social Sciences at the University of Bath," *Journal of Librarianship* 5 (July 1973):214-32.

10. Kathryn Chaloner and Ann de Klerk, "A Comparison of Two Current Awareness Methods," in *Communicating Information: Proceedings of the 43rd ASIS Annual Meeting, 1980*, p. 92.

11. Katherine H. Packer and Dagobert Soergel, "The Importance of SDI for Current Awareness in Fields with Severe Scatter of Information," *American Society for Information Science Journal* 30 (May 1979):133.

12. Nolan F. Pope, "Database Users: Their Opinions and Needs," *Special Libraries* 71 (May 1980):267.

13. Matilda Butler and Ted Brandhorst, "Construction of a Tertiary Database: The Case of Women's Equity Communications Network," in *Communicating Information: Proceedings of the 43rd ASIS Annual Meeting, 1980*, p. 174.

14. Hillis L. Griffin, "Dial Your Problems Away: Reference Service by Telephone to Libraries Large or Small," *Illinois Libraries* 60 (April 1978):350.

15. Valiollah Tahani, "A Conceptual Framework for Fuzzy Query Processing-A Step Toward Very Intelligent Database Systems," *Information Processing and Management* no. 5, 13 (1977):289-90.

16. John O'Connor, "Citing Statements: Recognition by Computer and Use to Improve Retrieval," in *Communicating Information: Proceedings of the 43rd ASIS Annual Meeting, 1980*, pp. 177-79.

17. L.C. Smith, "Implications of Artificial Intelligence for End User Use of Online Systems," *Online Review* 4 (December 1980):288-89.

18. Williams, "Online Retrieval-Today and Tommorrow," p. 358.

19. George R. Thoma, "Compression Techniques for Document Storage and Transmission," in *Communicating Information: Proceedings of the 43rd ASIS Annual Meeting, 1980*, p. 97.

20. George McMurdo, "The Interface Between Computerized Retrieval Systems and Micrographic Retrieval Systems," *Journal of Information Science* 1 (March 1980):348.

21. Ray Jones and Barbara Wittkopf, "Computerized Census Data: Meeting Demands in an Academic Library," *RQ* 19 (Spring 1980):251.

22. Ruthann Bates, Karen Kinnear, and Richard Roth, "Analysis of Program Information by Using an Online Search and Retrieval System," in *Communicating Information: Proceedings of the 43rd ASIS Annual Meeting, 1980*, p. 223.

23. Rudolph C. Mendelssohn, Steven R. Roman, and J. Harvey Trimble, Jr., "Labstat: The Bureau of Labor Statistics Data Base and Information

System," in *Information Choices and Policies: Proceedings of the ASIS Annual Meeting, 1979* (White Plains, N.Y.: Knowledge Industry Publications for the American Society for Information Science, 1979), p. 301.

24. Kimio Hosono, "Development of a Personalized Information Retrieval System by Using APL Programming Language," in *Communicating Information: Proceedings of the 43rd ASIS Annual Meeting, 1980*, p. 77.

25. Kathleen T. Bivins and Roger C. Palmer, "REFLES (Reference Librarian Enhancement System)," in *Information Choices and Policies: Proceedings of the ASIS Annual Meeting, 1979*, pp. 58-65.

26. Kathleen T. Bivins and Roger C. Palmer, "REFLES: An Individual Microcomputer System for Fact Retrieval," *Online Review* 4 (December 1980):357-65.

27. Jose-Marie Griffiths, "Applications of Mini and Micro Computers to Information Handling," in *Communicating Information: Proceedings of the 43rd ASIS Annual Meeting, 1980*, p. 308.

28. N. Justice, G.O. Barnett, and P.D. Beaman, "COSTAR—A Medical Information System for Ambulatory Practices," in *Information Choices and Policies: Proceedings of the ASIS Annual Meeting, 1979*, p. 357.

29. Marta L. Dosa and Bissy K. Genova, "Policy Implications of Health Information Sharing," in *Communicating Information: Proceedings of the 43rd ASIS Annual Meeting, 1980*, p. 109.

30. Loretta K. Mershon, "A Model Automated Resource File for an Information and Referral Center," *Special Libraries* 71 (August 1980):336-37.

31. M.S. Fox and A.J. Paley, "The BROWSE System: An Introduction," in *Information Choices and Policies: Proceedings of the ASIS Annual Meeting, 1979*, p. 184.

32. Tamas E. Doszkocs and Barbara A. Rapp, "Searching MEDLINE in English: A Prototype User Interface with Natural Language Query, Ranked Output and Relevance Feedback," in *Information Choices and Policies: Proceedings of the ASIS Annual Meeting, 1979*, pp. 131-36.

33. Colin Bell and Kevin P. Jones, "Towards Everyday Language Retrieval Systems via Minicomputers," *American Society for Information Science Journal* 30 (November 1979):334-35.

34. Pope, "Database Users: Their Opinions and Needs," p. 268.

35. Martha E. Williams and Scott E. Preece, "Elements of a Distributed Transparent Information Retrieval System," in *Communicating Information: Proceedings of the 43rd ASIS Annual Meeting, 1980*, pp. 401-2.

36. Richard S. Marcus, "Search Aids in a Retrieval Network," in *Communicating Information: Proceedings of the 43rd ASIS Annual Meeting, 1980*, pp. 394-96.

37. Robert T. Niehoff, "The Optimization and Use of Automated Subject Switching for Better Retrieval," in *Communicating Information: Proceedings of the 43rd ASIS Annual Meeting, 1980*, p. 397.

38. Jeffrey C. Griffith and Nancy Prothro Norton, "Training Congressional Staff to Search the SCORPIO Online System," in *Communicating Information: Proceedings of the 43rd ASIS Annual Meeting, 1980*, pp. 348-50.

39. M. Karen Landsberg et al., "A Joint Industrial-Academic Experiment: An

Evaluation of the IIDA System," in *Communicating Information: Proceedings of the 43rd ASIS Annual Meeting, 1980*, pp. 406-8.
40. Winifred Sewell and Alice Bevan, "Nonmediated Use of MEDLINE and TOXLINE by Pathologists and Pharmacists," *Bulletin of the Medical Library Association* 64 (October 1976): 382-91.

Online Information Retrieval Interface with Traditional Reference Services

Simone Klugman

1. THE LIBRARY ENVIRONMENT

In this paper I shall be dealing with a large university library setting, one in which the collection is basically in the humanities and social sciences and I shall be focusing on the reference function of that library. I shall define the reference function as broadly as possible, as encompassing all the direct public services activities in which the library engages in facilitating the pursuit of knowledge and in the provision of information. These activities generally consist in instruction in the use of books and libraries, such as explaining the library's catalogs or describing bibliographies. They also include helping with the deciphering of mystifying citations and the decoding of cryptic lists. And finally they entail the supplying of factual information, mostly out of books such as encyclopedias, directories, dictionaries or the like. The reference librarian's role, therefore, is not merely that of providing appropriate answers to specific questions, but is also that of catalyst in the process by which research in progress absorbs research accomplished. That, at least, is the accepted professional credo. Unfortunately, in many university libraries, the sheer number of people seeking guidance or specific solutions to problems, the pressures on librarians of other duties, such as book selection or processing assignments, the restrictions imposed by formal reference desk arrangements with telephone enquiries pouring in, often severely limit the amount of time and energy one person can devote to a question and hence the effectiveness of the solution proferred. In many instances one is only able to offer quick first aid and hope that the problem might cure itself or be solved elsewhere. In this environment of budgetary constraints and limited staffing, circumstances have led many university

Reprinted with permission of Learned Information Ltd. from *Online Review* 4 (1980):263-272.

reference librarians to make a virtue out of necessity and to stress the instuctional or "how-to-do-it" aspect of their mission, thus creating a mystique to the effect that total service is somehow damaging to a patron's moral fiber and that information acquired the hard way is more beneficial. Yet as Samuel Rothstein said "information is of crucial concern to many people. For businessmen, legislators, researchers and scholars it is more important that they have it than that they learn how to acquire it . . . The chemist no longer blows his own glassware and the doctor no longer takes temperatures: why should they not have the librarian conduct literature searches for them."[1]

This then is the environment into which online information services are being introduced.

2. ONLINE INFORMATION RETRIEVAL

Mechanized searching did not originate in libraries. This new capability was the result of a convergence of several distinct developments in which libraries were latecomers. The government as a promoter of research results, the abstracting and indexing services looking for more efficient ways to print their product, and systems developers such as Lockheed Information Services as exploiters of database searching capabilities and sellers of the resulting commodity—all these forces shaped the product long before librarians entered the game. In the beginning much of the searching was of the batch variety and was done by the database producers themselves in response to information profiles and for fees. Examples of such services are University Microfilm's Datrix service which supplies bibliographies of dissertations tailor-made to individual specifications. Another such program is the Philosopher's Index PIRS which also furnishes custom searches on request. Online searching was also accomplished in the academic community through information processing centers such as Computerized Information Services which operated at the University of California. The libraries' role was then strictly that of an intermediary; they transmitted requests and explained and described available services. Such centers still exist, although the one at the University of California has since withered away as most of its functions, excepting the acquiring and programming of databases, were absorbed by the various campus libraries.[2] Still another purveyor of computerized literature searching is the commercial information broker who, for a rather large fee and for profit, performs information gathering tasks which include online searching for individual clients. Given the emergence of these diverse information suppliers, libraries might have decided to continue to be interested onlookers; or they might have gone in the opposite direction and opted for subscribing to tapes, acquiring on-site computers and providing the software for their utilization. Instead, they took advantage of the work already performed by the government and the private sector and hooked themselves into the circuit by remote telecommunications. Just as libraries no longer index their own periodicals, so they can rely on centralized and more efficient ways to participate in the online bibliographic network and become actively involved relay stations.

3. THE MERGER

For many libraries the arrival of online bibliographic services in their midst was like that of an adopted child. Was it really wanted? Would they be able to support it? Would it fit in? Would parents and child be compatible? I shall try to examine how online searching survived in this environment, how it modified it and what it can expect to absorb from it as it continues to grow. As the first step of its integration into a new family, the baby which came into the library labeled 'online searching' was quickly renamed 'computer reference services.' It was soon apparent that, just as typing catalog cards was a more efficient alternative to handwriting them, using terminals to retrieve articles or reports from databases was simply another, often more convenient way of doing something librarians had traditionally engaged in, namely the looking up of information in indexes and bibliographies. The databases themselves were computerized versions on tapes or discs of such old-time library dwellers as *Psychological Abstracts* or *Comprehensive Dissertations Index*. Of course databases are not always exact replicas of printed products. Some, like ABI/Inform or the New York Times Information Bank, have no printed counterpart, others, like Public Affairs Information Service Bulletin of Medline, are combinations of several printed tools. Since manipulating information in this format is much more complex than reading a printed page, "the role of the intermediary in the service transaction was far more complicated and delicate than had been anticipated."[3] Librarians had to undergo rigorous training to enable them to use the new tools effectively. This training also embraced detailed knowledge of the coverage, scope, comprehensiveness and indexing practices of the various databases. And whereas it had been possible for reference libraries to survive without ever having had to master the intricacies of arrangement of the *Philosophers' Index*, for instance, and to simply refer users to it when needed, the advent of computerization forced them to learn in minute detail all the features of the databases and their print products, thereby greatly enhancing their effectiveness as reference consultants. For instance, it was not until the *Social Science Citation Index* became computer searchable, that I finally conquered my aversion for its repellant format and learned to appreciate its many virtues. The printed version thereby became doubly useful to the library.

Much has been written about another aspect of reference, the interviewing process; if we consider what is involved in interviewing for online searching, I think a complete convergence of these two processes will emerge. The interviewer needs to understand the question, break it into logical components, isolate its key elements and eliminate irrelevancies; he or she also must find out how much information is needed, at what level, how soon, where the enquirer has already looked and with what results. All these fact-elucidating techniques are, or should be, the stock-in-trade of every good reference librarian. Here too those skills acquire a new importance with online searching, since overlooking any of those steps might have immediately visible disastrous consequences. Here too the benefits of a more rigorous discipline will carry over and enrich the librarians' ability to deal with information requests of all kinds. Here then is an immediate by-product of absorbing online searching, namely job enrichment for librarians. There are other good reasons for offering online bibliographic services in a library setting and one of them could perhaps be labelled 'user enrichment'. Information is not a commodity which can be sliced into neat little packages, but must often be garnered from many disparate sources. In this respect computer searching and traditional services can complement each other, each offering what it is best suited to accomplish. The information in many databases is relatively recent and when retrospective sources are also needed, both manual and online searching will have to be performed. Some disciplines are not yet completely covered and others not included at all in databases and the researcher in literature, anthropology, film or even history might benefit most from expert guidance in the use of printed bibliographies. Very often a student may have come to the library with some misconceived notion about computers performing push-button magic and producing instant answers to questions. Since most of the databases at present are bibliographic ones and do not provide answers *per se*, but only citations to documents, the librarian, whose role it will be to disillusion such a student, will be very glad to have the back-up reinforcement of a collection of encyclopedias, dictionaries, directories and biographies at his or her disposal. Very often, hearing about this new gadget brings a patron to the library who had never set foot in it before, and who in the course of his visit will stumble upon many marvellous sources of information he had not dreamed existed.

Reference librarians can also suggest literature searches to patrons whose questions seem particularly suitable, but who had not known the service existed. If what is needed is very recent and the printed indexes have not yet come out or have not cumulated, it might be much more practical to sit at a terminal and retrieve the information effortlessly and conveniently than to pore through many weekly or monthly issues of indexes. Very topical subjects sometimes have not yet acquired subject headings and the free text capability of online searching can be a tremendous help in unearthing otherwise elusive information. 'The quality of life,' 'work humanisation,' 'no-growth,' 'reverse discrimination' were once new topics and references to them could only be found through key words in titles or abstracts. How else would one uncover articles on self-insurance, vernacular architecture or self-fulfilling prophecies? Some of the regular users of such printed bibliographies as the *MLA Annual Bibliography* or *Art, Modern,* which use a broad subject categories approach, were delighted to learn that they could now find articles on such specific topics as 'dreams in literature,' 'parody or allusion' or on 'artists who had painted self-portraits.' To take another example: A search for all American dissertations on Jack London can be performed manually or online. If one chooses the manual method, one will need to use many volumes of the *Comprehensive Dissertations Index,* look under several academic departments for the key 'London,' disregarding references to the city of London.

It would take time and patience and the time spent would be the researcher's not the librarian's. On the other hand, a computer search on the same topic can be delegated to a librarian who can run it rapidly, effectively and relatively cheaply. Depending on the requestor's preference either method can be used. So what emerges here is a picture of a continuum of information where no clear demarcation lines can be drawn between computer searching and traditional reference services and where there is a frequent spill-over of one activity into the other. An information or research question often escapes beyond the confines of one medium to encompass other resources available in the library environment. The fact that the large research library can also provide delivery of the full text items uncovered by the search must not be overlooked. J.S. Kidd says "Users can experience profound frustration if they are presented with their heart's desire in the form of an impressive list of patently relevant titles, only to be told that some are unobtainable . . ."[4] There seems therefore to be a clear affinity between online searching and university libraries.

In addition, another issue which confronts large research or university libraries makes it even more imperative for them to be concerned with electronic information transmission, namely the impending demise of the traditional card catalogue. This venerable institution, like the dinosaur, has grown too bulky and unwieldy to continue to be an effective means of displaying bibliographic information. The issuance of the second edition of the *Anglo-American Cataloging Rules* and its implementation by the Library of Congress will undoubtedly administer the *coup de grace* to this elderly organism. A new bibliographical era, with new forms of life, will emerge. Online access will probably be found in some shape or other in most research libraries. Automation will provide both the impetus and the vehicle for standardisation and the sharing of bibliographic information across institutions and even across nations and we will see the flourishing of large-scale regional cooperation, if not the birth of a national bibliographical network. Already many California libraries contribute to RLIN (Research Libraries Information Network) (nee BALLOTS) and OCLC (Ohio College Library Center) cataloging and many reference librarians routinely query those databases for verification of information or subject searching.[5] Through those computer-based bibliographic networks libraries share their resources and quick information on book availability is already at our fingertips. A convergence of the two separately evolved online systems is inevitable, the one providing references to journal articles, reports dissertations or conference papers, the other information and location of books and eventually journals.[6] Book publishers have also been active in building and maintaining databases. "The Association of American Publishers' Book Distribution Task Force recently issued a request for proposals for a study of the need for a comprehensive database of book title information."[7]

If a U.S. National Library Network is ever developed, it will have the capability of interconnecting all major bibliographic databases regardless of origin and ultimately large-scale electronic communication of information will become commonplace.

4. PROBLEMS

(A) Human Problems

Let us now consider some of the problems which reference services and libraries in general are facing as the result of introducing online searching. Not every reference librarian has wholeheartedly embraced the new development, in fact many have done their best to ignore it. Because libraries and books are almost synonymous, the non-book format of the operation has made the hurdle sometimes hard to jump. In our institution, the demand for the service began slowly, therefore only some of the staff was trained. This resulted in a polarization at the reference desk and for a long time non-searching librarians, upon hearing the words 'computer' or 'literature search' would tune out, start panicking and look around for a searcher to relieve them of the questioner. Searchers realized that it was up to them to help their colleagues break out of this negative pattern. They tried to do this by reporting on new developments at staff meetings, giving workshops and demonstrations, and providing staff with as many aids and tools as feasible: Database thesauri, lists of journals indexed, directories of databases and services. They also wrote promotional brochures and provided price lists. Gradually, the knowledge gap diminished. As new staff are recruited into reference service out of library schools, it is hoped that they will have had the necessary courses on online searching and eventually everyone at a reference desk will have the minimal competence needed to access databases. Some librarians are also hesitant to use the new technology because of fear that they do not have the technical background to understand computer operations. It is of course desirable to have some idea of what is happening in the system in response to a set of commands. However, just as one can cook by following a recipe without worrying about the chemical reactions taking place, one can learn to use databases as a quick information-finding device by following a step-by-step routine.

(B) Administrative and Economic Problems

Another problem librarians are facing is that of fitting online searching into an already overburdened schedule. Far from wiping out librarians' jobs, automation has opened up new possibilities and has drawn librarians into an involvement with research projects considerably more time-consuming than a routine explanation of the uses of the *Humanities Index* or of *Historical Abstracts*. Interviewing for online searching often takes longer than a regular reference interview. Search strategies must be constructed and executed, results analysed and discussed with the users, etc. Time must be allocated to continuous training, since systems are complex and continually changing, new databases are being added all the time, indexing practices and retrieval programs constantly being modified. In addition, a whole new administrative superstructure has been generated by the service. Online reference services must be fully documented if they are to gain acceptance from administrators, since they have to compete for funds in a world of shrinking budgets. Statistics must be kept of number of questions, staff time spent, break-down by kind of users, fees charged etc. Accounting procedures have to be set up. The fee structure must be monitored so that it fulfills the institution's aim, whether it be full or partial recovery. Promotion must be planned so as to exert some control over the demand for the service, avoiding overload or underuse. Given this immense investment, it is not surprising that the growth of the service has been uneven and that some branch libraries have not yet been able to stretch their resources to accommodate it.

So far I have deliberately steered away from the question of fees and all the controversy the question has generated. I shall touch upon it very briefly, because it could easily become the subject of another paper if treated in depth. Here again, faced with the dilemma of, on the one hand, continuing in the tradition of free access to information and, on the other, being able to absorb a costly and labor-intensive service, many libraries took the position that charging fees was a lesser evil if the alternative to it was not to provide the service at all. Some funds are usually allocated to this activity, so that some free searching does occur at the librarians' discretion when this is the most efficient solution to a problem.[8] Some institutions have been able to secure government grants for launching this activity. In the Berkeley area a group of public libraries have formed a cooperative network to share resources and services and have obtained a grant for this purpose which includes the provision of online services. Since none of them has either the equipment or the trained personnel to perform the searches, they have contracted with our University to run them. It is an experiment and time will tell whether the demand will justify more direct involvement on the part of public libraries.[9] At the same time it affords university librarians opportunities for practice on a diversity of questions.

(C) Problems for the User

Reference librarians, like Janus, now keep one face turned toward the user to absorb his or her information in all its ramifications and the other toward the system to transform the query into schematic formula and to extract answers to it. This gives them a more participatory role in academic research. But what of the library patron who used to stumble upon his own information in printed sources and who was reared by a succession of librarians into self-reliance and may even have learned to enjoy it? He now finds himself faced with two intermediaries: the vendor who has taken his favorite index and shaped it into a different animal and the librarian who used to be a dim figure in the background, but to whom he now has to confide his research topic and on whose ability to comprehend it he has to rely. Obviously the search results will vary depending upon which system the librarian has access to or has chosen to use. Results will also vary depending on the person who performs the search. Misunderstandings will occur which sometimes will be costly and will create resentment which only goodwill on both parts and the progressive acquisition of skills by the librarian will mitigate. Perhaps at some future time the systems will become simple enough and cheap enough for direct use by researchers. Certainly this will eventually be true of online catalogues. At the moment, however, there are not too many signs pointing in the direction of commercial vendors tailoring their services to the occasional inexperienced researcher. Opinions are divided on the merits of this situation. Some see this new dependence as an obstacle in the researcher's path. So far, researchers have seemed willing enough to discuss their projects with librarians and whereas they would never have admitted to ignorance in the matter of printed indexes, they often seem quite relieved at not having to concern themselves with the mechanics of the search or at not having to keep up with the proliferation of new databases. The service is still too new to assess its real impact on the information-finding opportunities of what librarians call "the end-user" and this aspect of it has not yet been fully documented.

(D) Document Delivery Problems

Online searching has significantly affected libraries in yet another fashion. Since information can now be retrieved at a faster pace, the library is faced with a new burden: an increased demand for the documents uncovered by the search. The impact is felt first at the reference desk where patrons with printouts suddenly appear to have the results interpreted to them and ask for assistance with locating journals, dissertations etc. Large libraries can probably supply most of the documents out of their own collections, provided they are not out to another borrower or mysteriously missing, but in many cases a great deal of interlibrary borrowing is generated, the effect of which is felt far from the epicenter of the search. Sometimes the operation reveals documents which are so recent that the library has not yet ordered or received them or not yet extracted them from the bowels of its various processing units. Therefore new pressures develop which affect acquisition, cataloging, reference, circulation and interlibrary lending staff and put a further strain and demand on collections.

(E) Hardware Problems

Everyone associated with the process of electronic retrieval has a repertoire of anecdotes illustrating examples of acute frustration due to 'down time,' telecommunication problems, terminal misconfiguration, uncooperative printers and a myriad of other tales of woe. A card catalogue or a printed index occupy a solid and comforting physical space and are normally ready to oblige and divulge their contents whereas our electronic appliances seem to fall prey to a multitude of mysterious maladies and bouts of autistic uncommunicativeness for which we have as yet no household remedies. We would do well to acknowledge the vulnerability of these systems and the necessity of back-up methods of retrieval.

5. FUTURE PROSPECTS

In spite of all these difficulties, libraries and online searching seem to have achieved a viable symbiosis, but it is not unreasonable to ask ourselves what improvements and modifications librarians would like to see in the future as their newest adopted child moves toward adulthood. Unfortunately, libraries are not the only customers of online services and they find themselves in a seller's market without too much power to affect prices or quality control. Competition sometimes results in cheaper rates. To some degree this has happened, with BRS entering the field in 1977, concentrating its efforts on group contracts with large academic users and stocking only heavily used databases. Libraries have also joined in consortia for bulk subscriptions at discount prices. Competition has resulted in some modest improvements in features and capabilities as well. Lockheed has modified its 'search' and 'save' modules to bring them in line with those offered by BRS and SDC. It is now working on a free-text truncation capability, again because it was available on BRS first. Conversely BRS is modifying its 'root' structure to make it as effective as the Lockheed "expand" feature. In this context, some vendors are more customer-oriented than others. BRS, through its user groups, has been somewhat more receptive to implementing new features. The Information Bank, on the other hand, whose product is more oriented to the business community than to the academic one, has been rather unyielding and has successfully resisted substantial modi-fication of its rigid and cumbersome Prompt system. As matters stand now, there is a crying need for standardization, both across vendor systems and within each system, in the way the various databases are accessed and programmed. For instance, we librarians have traditionally called our controlled vocabulary "subject headings." If the information industry prefers to use "descriptors" we can accept that, but we see no need to carry diversity so far as to also accomodate "indexed terms." We are not opposed to learning sophisticated retrieval techniques but we do balk at remembering that to end a search on Lockheed you "logoff", but on SDC you must cry "stop" whereas the Information Bank would like you to say "Z" followed by "A" and BRS will not terminate your search until you have told it to be " . . . off." Nor do we see any great virtue in learning three or four different truncation symbols (? $ #). A standard citation format for each type of document would also be of great help and there is no excuse for the poor bibliographic citations some database producers, such as Sociological Abstracts for instance, inflict on us. Since so many indexing services cover the same journals, a method for eliminating duplicate citations needs to be devised; in addition an international standard bibliographic description for articles would be welcome and perhaps even an international standard article number. Vendors and database producers can also lift some of the burden of document delivery from libraries by offering a better and cheaper access to the documents themselves. To some degree, this has happened with such services as ERIC and NTIS where one can go directly from the citation to a microfiche version of the document itself without any intervening steps. There are document delivery services such as ISI's Original Article Tear Sheet, but at $3.50 per article it is not an ideal solution. In the future, documents could perhaps be viewed or selectively printed online using interactive television and push-button video telephones.[10]

Libraries in the social sciences and humanities would like to see more non-bibliographic databases for answering factual questions. Such databases already exist for numerical or statistical data or chemical properties. Some fact-finding databases are also being used in medicine, business or demography. In some systems such as LEXIS, full text of documents is directly searchable. Directory-type information is an obvious candidate for online searching and a step in this direction has been taken with the provision of foundations and grants information and the addition of the Encyclopedia of Associations to the Lockheed list of databases. Remote access to various organisations' files could result in extensive referral services or in a capability to view college catalogs online for instance. A master index of biographical information, containing brief sketches and citations to further information would also be very helpful and quotations and literary concordances, to name but a few more candidates, could be added to our desiderata list.

As more libraries enter the field of online searching and become adept at exploiting the potential of the new services, librarians should continue to press for more user-defined functions and more effort should be directed toward improving the performance of vendors and database producers.

The most exciting implication for the future of library-based online reference services is the possibility of finally breaking out of the rigid 'instruct only' mode of service into a philosophy of total service. A dentist does not show his patient how to fill his own teeth. Samuel Rothstein says . . . "The task of tracing and using scientific literature has become considerably more difficult . . . The effect is to justify a place for an intermediary between the research man and his literature, and to suggest that the location of information almost necessarily becomes a specialized function devolving upon specially assigned personnel."[11] The reference librarian, now ably assisted by his new sorcerer's apprentice, can become that necessary information specialist.

Footnotes

1. Samuel D. Rothstein, "Reference Service: The New Dimension in Librarianship," in *Reference and Information Services—A Reader*, ed. Bill Katz and Andrea Tarr (Metuchen, N.J.: Scarecrow Press, 1978), pp. 12-23.
2. Jeffrey J. Gardner and David M. Wax, "Online Bibliographic Services," *Library Journal* 101 (September 15, 1976):1827-32.
3. Jerry S. Kidd, "Online Bibliographic Services: Selected British Experiences," *College and Research Libraries* 38 (July 1977):285-90.
4. Ibid., p. 290.
5. Richard W. Blood, "Impact of OCLC on Reference Service," *Journal of Academic Librarianship* 3 (May 1977):68-73.
6. Mary P. Ojala, "Using BALLOTS as a Reference Tool," *Online* 2 (October 1978):11-19.
7. Sandra K. Paul, "What is a Database ... And Why Should I Care?" *Publisher's Weekly* 216 (July 1979):38-39.
8. James A. Cogswell, "Online Search Services: Implications for Libraries and Library Users," *College & Research Libraries* 39 (July 1978):275-80.
9. James M. Kusack, "Online Reference Service in Public Libraries," *RQ* 18 (Summer 1978):331-34.
10. Budd L. Gambee and Ruth R. Gambee, "Reference Services and Technology," in *A Century of Service: Librarianship in the United States and Canada*, ed. Sidney Louis Jackson, Elenor B. Herling and E.J. Josey (Chicago: American Library Association, 1976), pp. 169-91.
11. Samuel D. Rothstein, "Reference Service: The New Dimension in Librarianship," p. 19.

The Impact of Online Services on Subscriptions to Printed Publications

F.W. Lancaster and Herbert Goldhor

The impact of online searching on subscriptions to printed publications has recently been given some consideration in the professional literature. Barwise,[1] in the most complete analysis so far conducted on the interaction between printed products and online databases and the effect of this interaction on pricing policies, concludes that online services have so far had a negligible effect on sales of printed products. On the other hand, he points out that there is great uncertainty about the possible impact in the period 1978 to 1985. In a survey of use of five databases peripheral to medicine, Timour[2] discovered little evidence of a decline in use of the printed products since online access had become available to major biomedical libraries. Indeed, for some databases at least, use of the printed product is said to have increased. His own attitude, however, seems to favour cancellation of at least the more expensive printed services:

> But considering subscription prices of $2,565 for *Biological Abstracts* and $3,700 for *Chemical Abstracts*, plus binding costs for each, one can conjecture that a reallocation of these subscription fees would go far in making more online searches available and would save a substantial amount of shelf space in the process.

Pfaffenberger and Echt[3] analyzed the use of the printed *Science Citation Index* and its machine readable equivalent, Scisearch, in one academic library. They concluded that, even with recent royalty increases and the fact that reduced royalty rates apply to subscribers to the printed product, the volume of use favoured cancellation of the subscription and complete reliance on online access for current searches.

Reprinted with permission of Learned Information Ltd. from *Online Review* 5 (1981): 301-311.

Stanley[4] has reported the results of a questionnaire survey completed by directors of information services in 55 chemical, petroleum, pharmaceutical and manufacturing companies. Large, medium and small corporations were all represented. Slightly more than half of these organizations (actually 52%) reported the cancellation of at least one hard copy subscription as a result of the availability of the equivalent[5] database online. It is noteworthy that virtually no information service that has failed to cancel a subscription is at present giving serious consideration to the cancellation possibility. On the other hand, several of those organizations that have discontinued some printed subscriptions are now considering cancellation of further titles. This suggests the existence of two camps within the information services/library field: some directors seem quite happy to substitute electronic access for print on paper while others still look at online services as complementing print on paper rather than substituting for it. There is also evidence in Stanley's study that the availability of a database online has prevented some organizations from entering a new subscription to the printed equivalent. Other evidence of a migration from print to online use has been presented by Trubkin.[6]

Some further evidence has been presented by the database producers. Creps,[7] for example, in discussing the *Engineering Index* situation, has reported that revenue from sale of printed products is still growing, but very slowly, while revenue from sales of magnetic tapes is growing "erratically." Online royalty income, however, is described as "growing rapidly." Use of the online database is now increasing at the rate of 23% per year. A similar situation exists with *Chemical Abstracts*.[8] Here, subscriptions to print on paper still account for 80% of revenue. The number of subscribers to the printed service is declining but revenue from sales is actually increasing, at about 10% per year, due to ever increasing subscription prices, now set at $5,000 a year. Nevertheless, while revenue from print on paper is increasing at 10% a year, that from online use charges is now growing at 25% a year. As of 1979, these online revenues amounted to about $1.8 million a year.

In an effort to cast some further light on the impact of online services on sales of print on paper, a study was performed by the Library Research Center, Graduate School of Library Science, University of Illinois, in the period October 1979 to February 1980. It was decided to poll 200 libraries—50 large university libraries, 50 smaller university libraries, 50 US Government special libraries in science and technology, and 50 private industrial special libraries. The first group was randomly selected from the membership list of the Association of Research Libraries. The second group was chosen from the National Centre for Education Statistics, *Library Statistics of Colleges and Universities: 1976 Institutional Data (1978)*, Table 1, pp. 13-67 (omitting libraries outside the 50 states). Since the minimum requirement for ARL membership is 800,000 volumes, each library in this second group had to have fewer volumes than that and had to be identified as a university library. Within these restrictions, the 50 libraries were selected through use of a random number table.

The third and fourth groups were both chosen at random from Margaret L. Young *et al.*, eds., *Subject Directory of Special Libraries and Information Centres*; Vol. 5, *Science and Technology Libraries* (Gale, 1977), pp. 1-101, but with exclusion of all libraries of academic libraries and state government libraries.

The four samples were drawn in early October, and the questionnaire (with an identifying number), cover letter and stamped self-addressed envelope went out simultaneously to all 200 before the end of October. A second mailing of the same three items (with cover letter marked "Second request, please respond") went out before Christmas 1979 to about 100 libraries that had not responded.

The questionnaire was a simple one, including only four items. It asked each library to indicate which of 36 printed databases are subscribed to and which of 27 machine readable databases, the equivalents of the 36 printed tools, they make some use of. It asked which, if any, of the 36 printed tools had been discontinued within the past five years, and whether or not the decision to discontinue had been influenced by the availability of online access, and which, if any, printed services other than the 36 listed had been discontinued in the past five years as a result of the availability of the equivalent database online. Finally, it asked each library to indicate if it is now considering cancellation of any

TABLE 1 Response Rates

		Returns			
		Total		Usable	
Type of library	Number	No.	%	No.	%
1. Special libraries in science and technology in the Federal Government	50	41	82	33	66
2. Nongovernmental special libraries in science and technology	50	34	68	30	60
3. Research libraries that are members of the Association of Research Libraries (ARL)	50	41	82	39	78
4. University libraries that are not members of ARL	50	48	96	44	88
TOTALS	200	164	82	146	73

subscriptions to indexing/abstracting services where this decision has been influenced by the availability of the database online. Responding libraries were also given the opportunity to comment on the broad question of the probable transition from print on paper tools to online access.

As shown in Table 1, a high rate of return (73%) of fully usable questionnaires was achieved. 'Fully usable' here refers to questionnaires from libraries giving all of the data requested. For some of the analyses, however, the base for the data extracted is 164 (all returns) rather than 146. The returns from academic libraries were greater than those from the non-academic community.

Table 2 shows the percentage of responding libraries in each category claiming to make some use of online search services. These figures should be treated with some caution in terms of further extrapolation. It would be tempting to conclude that about 77% of all special libraries in science and technology in the U.S. are now making some use of online services. This may or may not be true. One suspects that the group of non-respondents may include a higher proportion of libraries that make no use of online services. The figure of 76 to 77% may thus be somewhat inflated.

A comparison of Table 3 with Table 4 shows some similarity between the printed databases most held by the responding libraries and the databases used online by most libraries in this group. It is important to note, however, that the tables do not in any way reflect *volume* of use of the various sources. The ranking merely reflects number of libraries owning each printed source (Table 3) and claiming to make some online use of each database (Table 4). The discrepancy between the 36 items of

TABLE 2 Percentage of Responding Libraries Making Some Use of Online Services

Special libraries in science and technology in the Federal Government	76%
Nongovernmental special libraries in science and technology	77%
ARL member libraries	100%
University libraries not members of ARL	88%
TOTAL	85%

TABLE 3   List of Databases Held in Printed Form by 164 Responding Libraries. Ranked by Number of Libraries Holding

Rank	Database	Libraries
1	Chemical Abstracts	107
2	Dissertation Abstracts International	97
3	Biological Abstracts	96
4	Congressional Record	93
5	Engineering Index	86
6	Pollution Abstracts	83
7	Physics Abstracts	82
8	Psychological Abstracts	82
9	Government Reports Announcements	81
10	PAIS Bulletin	81
11	Resources in Education	77
12	Science Citation Index	76
13	Historical Abstracts	75
14	Electrical and Electronics Abstracts	73
15	Current Index to Journals in Education	71
16	Social Sciences Citation Index	68
17	Weekly Government Abstracts	67
18	Bio Research Index*	67
19	Computer and Control Abstracts	65
20	Library and Information Science Abstracts	65
21	Bibliography and Index of Geology	63
22	American Doctoral Dissertations	60
23	Bibliography of Agriculture	55
24	Environmental Abstracts	53
25	Metals Abstracts	53
26	Foundations Grants Index	51
27	Food Science and Technology Abstracts	45
28	PAIS Foreign Language Index	36
29	Energy Information Abstracts	35
30	World Textile Abstracts	28
31	Federal Register Abstracts	28
32	Petroleum Abstracts	21
33	Alloys Index	21
34	Management Contents	20
35	World Patents Index	4
36	Central Patents Index	3

*Now Biological Abstracts/RRM

Table 3 and the 27 of Table 4 is accounted for by the fact that some of the machine readable databases are equivalent to two or more of the printed sources. It is also important to recognize that this study was restricted to major databases for which the machine readable versions have more or less direct printed equivalents. Databases existing in machine readable

TABLE 4 List of Databases Used Online by 164 Responding Libraries. Ranked by Number of Libraries Using

Rank	Database	Libraries
1	National Technical Information Service	112
2	CA Condensates or CA Condensates/CASIA*	102
3	Scisearch	97
4	Comprehensive Dissertation Index	96
5	COMPENDEX	95
6	BIOSIS Previews	92
7	ERIC	88
8	INSPEC	87
9	Psychological Abstracts	84
10	Management	81
11	AGRICOLA	80
12	Social Scisearch	76
13	Enviroline	71
14	PAIS International	69
15	Pollution	69
16	Energyline	67
17	LISA	67
18	Historical Abstracts	57
19	Foundations Grants Index	56
20	Geo Ref	56
21	METADEX	53
22	FSTA	49
23	FEDREG	40
24	C Record	37
25	World Textiles	34
26	TULSA	25
27	WPI	18

*Now CA Search

form but not in printed form, or vice versa, were excluded from the investigation.

Although the tables show definite similarities, there are also some differences. In particular, it is possible to identify certain databases held by many libraries in printed form but used by few libraries online (the *Congressional Record* is a notable example) as well as some databases used by many libraries online but held in printed form by comparatively few. The Management database, for example, is used by 81 of the libraries while *Management Contents* is held in printed form by only 20. This phenomenon is shown more clearly in Table 5. Here, each database included in the study is listed (A) along with the printed tools considered equivalent (B). The remaining columns list the number of libraries using the tool online only (C), the number subscribing to print only (D), the

TABLE 5 Comparison of Online Use and Subscriptions to Printed Tools

A Database	B Printed equivalent	C Online	D Print	E Both	F Neither
AGRICOLA	Bibliography of Agriculture	28	3	52	81
BIOSIS Previews	Biological Abstracts* Bio Research Index†	10	14	82	58
CA Condensates (CHEMCON) or CA Condensates/CASIA‡	Chemical Abstracts	12	17	90	45
Comprehensive Dissertation Index	Dissertation Abstracts International* American Doctoral Dissertations	12	14	84	54
COMPENDEX	Engineering Index	26	17	69	52
C Record	Congressional Record	5	61	32	66
Energyline	Energy Information Abstracts	39	7	28	90
Enviroline	Environment Abstracts	27	9	44	84
ERIC	Resources in Education* Current Index to Journals in Education	15	5	73	71
FEDREG	Federal Register Abstracts	30	18	10	106
Foundation Grants Index	Foundation Grants Index	17	12	39	96
FSTA	Food Science and Technology Abstracts	19	15	30	100
Geo Ref	Bibliography and Index of Geology	8	15	48	93
Historical Abstracts	Historical Abstracts	5	23	52	84
INSPEC	Physics Abstracts* Electrical and Electronics Abstracts* Computer and Control Abstracts	21	17	66	60
LISA	Library and Information Science Abstracts	24	22	43	75
Management	Management Contents	64	3	17	80
METADEX	Metals Abstracts* Alloys Index	19	19	34	92
NTIS	Weekly Government Abstracts* Government Reports Announcements	18	18	94	34
PAIS International	PAIS Bulletin* PAIS Foreign Language Index	11	23	58	72
Pollution	Pollution Abstracts	9	23	60	72
Psychological Abstracts	Psychological Abstracts	11	9	73	71
Scisearch	Science Citation Index	32	11	65	56
Social Scisearch	Social Science Citation Index	16	8	60	80
TULSA	Petroleum Abstracts	15	11	10	128
WPI	Central Patents Index* World Patent Index	14	1	4	145
World Textiles	World Textile Abstracts	15	9	19	121

*In the case of databases for which there are two or more printed equivalents, columns D and E do not add up to the totals for the printed equivalents given in Table 3. This is because, in the present table, columns D and E add up to the number of libraries subscribing to *at least one* of the printed equivalents. In Table 3, on the other hand, subscribers to each printed tool are separately identified.

†Now Biological Abstracts/RRM.

‡Now CA Search.

number both subscribing and using online form (E) and the number neither using online nor subscribing (F). C plus E equals the number of libraries using the database online, while D plus E equals the number owning in print form. The discrepancy between C and D represents the magnitude of the difference between libraries using a database only in online form and those using it only in print form.

The major purpose of our study was to determine the extent to which the libraries surveyed have cancelled subscriptions to printed tools within the past five years. These data appear in Table 6. The figures are to be viewed with some caution. First, they reflect cancellations of subscriptions but not necessarily cancellations of all subscriptions in a particular library. Thus, a large academic library may have cancelled one

TABLE 6   List of Printed Databases Discontinued Within the Past 5 Years by 164 Responding Libraries. Ranked by Number of Cancellations

Rank	Database	Cancellations
1	Engineering Index†	11
2	Chemical Abstracts‡	9
3	Bio Research Index*	7
4	Physics Abstracts	7
5	Science Citation Index	7
6	Pollution Abstracts	6
7	Bibliography of Agriculture	6
8	Dissertation Abstracts International‡	5
9	Metals Abstracts	5
10	Biological Abstracts	4
11	Weekly Government Abstracts	4
12	World Textile Abstracts	4
13	Environment Abstracts	3
14	Bibliography and Index of Geology	3
15	Electrical and Electronics Abstracts	3
16	Social Science Citation Index§	3
17	PAIS Foreign Language Bulletin	3
18	Computer and Control Abstracts	2
19	Government Reports Announcements	2
20	PAIS Bulletin	2
21	Congressional Record	1
22	Resources in Education	1
23	Current Index to Journals in Education	1
24	Foundations Grants Index	1
25	Library and Information Science Abstracts	1
26	Alloy Index	1
	Total	102

†Monthly issues or complete subscription
‡One or more sections cancelled
§In one case only a cumulation was cancelled
*Now Biological Abstracts/RRM

subscription to *Chemical Abstracts* but may still hold one or more subscriptions to this tool. Secondly, as the footnotes to the table indicate, some cancellations may not be complete cancellations. In some cases, for example, the monthly issues to *Engineering Index* may have been cancelled but the annual volume retained (or vice versa). Likewise, certain libraries reported the cancellation of a particular section of *Chemical Abstracts* and it was not always clear if this was the only section subscribed to. The best that can be said for the data is that, on the surface at least, they indicate loss of income to the publishers from sales of printed tools, a loss that the publishers themselves recognize and report. Unfortunately, we do not know how many of the responding libraries entered new subscriptions to these titles during the same period. We suspect that this factor may be insignificant, but cannot be absolutely sure.

Another defect of our study (to be remedied when repeated some two years from now) is that we did not determine how many subscriptions to each service are held by the responding libraries. Consequently, it is not possible to estimate with certainty the extent to which the cancellations have contributed to loss of income to publishers from this group of libraries. Consider, for example, the *Bio Research Index* (now *Biological Abstracts/RRM*). Table 3 shows that this is now held by 67 libraries and Table 6 shows seven cancellations in the past 5 years. If each of the 67 libraries holds only one subscription to this tool, and if no new subscriptions have been entered by the responding libraries in the past five years, it would be possible to say that, within the group of respondents, subscriptions to *Bio Research Index* have declined almost 10% (7/74) in the past five years. Unfortunately, we cannot make this assumption with certainty. We suspect, however, that a loss of subscriptions in the range of 5 to 10% is probably true for the titles at the top of the list of Table 6. Moreover, this trend is likely to continue as shown by the data in Table 7, which indicate titles 'under consideration' for

TABLE 7   List of Printed Databases Which 164 Responding Libraries Are Now Considering Cancelling and Decision Is Influenced by Availability Online

Rank	Database	Number of libraries
1	Chemical Abstracts	7
2	Government Reports Announcements	4
3	Engineering Index	3
4	Science Citation Index	3
5	Electrical and Electronics Abstracts	2
6	The following titles were each mentioned by a single library: Biological Abstracts, Dissertation Abstracts International, Environmental Abstracts, Index Medicus, Encyclopedia of Associations, Monthly Catalog of US Government Publications, Economics Abstracts International, Commonwealth Agricultural Bureaux Abstracting Services, Excerpta Medica, Food Science and Technology Abstracts, Psychological Abstracts, Physics Abstracts, National Union Catalog, Surface Coatings Abstracts, US Patent Gazette, Pharmaceutical News Index, PAIS Bulletin, Social Science Citation Index, Pollution Abstracts	

cancellation among the responding libraries, where this consideration is influenced by the availability of equivalent databases online.

Another restriction on the data of Table 6 must also be recognized. The cancellations reported are cancellations for all types of reasons, not just because of the availability of equivalent databases online. As Table 8 illustrates, less than 10% of the 102 cancellations are due solely to availability of online access, although about 40% of the cancellations (9 + 33) have at least been influenced by the availability of equivalent databases online.

Of the 102 cancellations reported, approximately 60% were cancelled by the academic libraries. The cancellations, by groups of libraries, are as follows: 23 in special libraries within the Federal Government, 18 within private special libraries, 31 in ARL member libraries, and 30 in other university libraries.

Another question in our survey asked the libraries to identify printed databases, other than those listed, that have been discontinued in the past 5 years where the decision to discontinue was at least influenced by accessibility online. Twelve further titles were mentioned. Of these, however, only one, *Excerpta Medica*, was mentioned by more than a single library. *Excerpta Medica* subscriptions have been cancelled by three of the responding libraries in the past 5 years.

What do these data mean? Clearly, subscriptions to many secondary services in printed form are declining. However, the reason for this phenomenon is only partly attributable to the availability of these tools online. Much more important is the fact that subscription costs are increasing while the relative purchasing power of many library budgets is declining. The data do, in fact, suggest that online services have so far had rather little direct effect on subscriptions to printed services. Whether or not this effect can be termed 'negligible' is a matter of personal interpretation.

TABLE 8   Reasons for Cancellation of 102 Subscriptions

	Number	%
Solely influenced by availability online	9	8.8
Partially influenced by availability online	33	32.4
Not influenced by availability online	60	58.8

The comments of the respondents, however, suggest that there is a 'hidden' effect of online services on sales of printed products, an effect that is not clearly demonstrated in our data. It is clear that, while some libraries at least are reluctant to discontinue a printed tool that may have been subscribed to for many years, online services are having some effect in preventing certain institutions from entering new subscriptions to services in print on paper form. This is particularly true of new libraries, those that have emerged in the 'online age.' As one government respondent points out:

> Because our library is relatively new and specialized, it is not a matter of discontinuing subscriptions, but rather of not subscribing initially.

Another respondent, the librarian of a small special library in an academic environment, was even stronger on this point:

> We simply never ordered them in the first place. Our library is only 4 years old and the availability of online services has made us want *all* of them! For us, print subscriptions are obsolete.

This library holds only one of the 36 print services listed on our questionnaire and is considering discontinuing this one. An almost identical situation was reported by another library subscribing to only one of the printed tools:

> Our library is three years old. Online indexes have been utilized from the very beginning.

Another pertinent comment from an industrial library suggests that some libraries are just now beginning to question their policies *vis-a-vis* the printed tools:

> We went online in 1974. It took us until 1979 to begin to question our rationale for continuing the published editions. This may be the last year we buy them (1980).

Within the academic environment it seems that there are two major barriers to the substitution of online access for paper access. The first is the fact that libraries are unable or unwilling to absorb the full cost of online searching. The second is that present online services seem generally to be regarded as unsuitable for unmediated use. The following quotations echo the views of several of the academic respondents:

> We expect to continue our subscriptions to the printed versions until online access is possible without a librarian as intermediary.

We would cancel printed versions of some files only if the library could absorb the cost of all needed computer searches, which we cannot afford at this time.

I don't think that's likely to happen in a university environment until online access is demonstrably cost effective compared to subscription in 'real dollar' terms and online searching systems become simple enough for end users to conduct their own searches.

Since we currently must charge for computerized searches, the cancellation of a printed index in favour of an online database would work a hardship for those unwilling or unable to pay. We would take this step only if the library found it economically feasible to absorb all costs.

Should our users ever become proficient at searching online bases themselves—perhaps it will happen more quickly than we imagine after experience with an online catalog—we would cease subscribing to a variety of A/I services.

From all of this, it seems reasonable to conclude that the availability of online access has so far had a rather minor effect in causing libraries to cancel subscriptions to print on paper. Nevertheless, there is evidence to suggest that increasing numbers of libraries are now beginning to question their policies concerning subscriptions to print versus online access, and that cancellations may occur at an accelerated pace in the future. Moreover, loss of subscription income to publishers as a direct result of online access exceeds that due to cancellations alone since the availability of a database online may prevent the initiation of new subscriptions by certain information services.

It is clear that the future attitude of librarians on this important matter is also going to be affected by the rising costs of printed subscriptions relative to rising costs of online services:

If the publishers of the paper indexes keep raising prices 20-25% per year, it's a cinch we will start dropping the lesser used paper subscriptions and absorb the costs of connect and staff time to search online free for users on demand.

It may be that the transition from print on paper to electronic access in information services may actually proceed through three recognizable though overlapping phases:

(1) Existing libraries adopting online use of databases
    (a) not held in printed form, or
    (b) not available in printed form.

(2) New libraries/information centers adopting online access in lieu of subscribing to print versions of well established publications. Some existing libraries preferring online access to *new publications* where such publications are also issued as print on paper.
(3) Existing libraries discontinuing printed subscriptions in favor of online access.

The first two phases have already been reached. The third phase is just beginning. It still seems entirely possible that a rather substantial move into the final phase of this evolution will occur within the next ten years. The process of conversion from print to electronics will be accelerated by (a) simplification of search procedures to reduce the need for intermediaries, (b) increasing availability of terminals to provide ready access to online services, and (c) changing attitudes among librarians regarding the proportion of the budget to be allocated to subsidizing print on paper access versus the proportion to be allocated to subsidizing online access.

Footnotes

1. T. Patrick Barwise, *Online Searching: The Impact on User Charges of the Extended Use of Online Information Services* (Paris: International Council of Scientific Unions Abstracting Board, 1979).
2. John A. Timour, "Use of Selected Abstracting and Indexing Journals in Biomedical Resource Libraries," *Bulletin of the Medical Library Association* 67 (July 1979):330-35.
3. Ann Pfaffenberger and Sandy Echt, "Substitution of SciSearch and Social SciSearch for Their Print Versions in an Academic Library," *Database* 3 (March 1980):63-71.
4. W. G. Stanley, "Changing Revenue Patterns from Online Use," paper presented at the national Information Conference and Exposition, NICE III, Washington, D.C., April 1979.
5. We have used the term "equivalent" although we recognize that "most equivalent" or "comparable" may be preferred terms. Sometimes the machine readable database is not exactly equivalent to its printed counterpart (e.g. it may exclude abstracts or have a slightly different scope).
6. Loene Trubkin, "Migration from Print to Online Use," *Online Review* 4 (March 1980):5-12.
7. John E. Creps, Jr., remarks made at the National Information Conference and Exposition, NICE III, Washington, D.C., April 1979.
8. Informal discussions with Ralph E. O'Dette and J. C. Dean, Chemical Abstracts Service, October 1979.

New Trends in Information Delivery*

Richard P. Kollin and James E. Shea

In the way of a preface to our comments and predictions regarding new trends in information delivery, we would like to mention first our reasons for choosing these particular trends. There is a common element in each of the following examples that imparts to them an important and pivotal characteristic for the information industry. It is vital that we as systems designers and producers recognize this vital characteristic before we proceed with large commitments of capital and personnel. The element common to each of the following trends is that to a great degree the direction finally taken will not be 'technology controlled' but 'market controlled.' It is a common and maybe universal mistake made by developing industries when they let what it is they *can* do and *can* deliver dictate to them the features of their product. With their technological skills and managerial zeal they forget that it is not what they can produce that is important but what the marketplace is inclined to buy. In the information industry the question should not be simply what or how much more data we can deliver, but how do we make it accessible and convenient to use in addition. At this juncture 'convenience' is probably the key word. Does anyone still recall the great promise that was being held out for the micrographic library? The technology represented by the idea was wonderful, but the concept ignored the fact that the micrographic library was inherently inconvenient to use. With that as an introduction, we will attempt to identify and describe very briefly some of the areas to watch for in information delivery.

There are five major trends or areas of controversy in the online industry as it exists today. The first involves the evolution of system convenience. The earlier 'unforgiving' systems, which didn't allow the user to make errors in spacing, grammar, and choice of synonyms and abbreviations, are now capable of translating certain errors into the

---

*Based on a presentation delivered at the Fall Meeting of the Association of Information and Dissemination Centers (ASIDIC) in Philadelphia, 19 September 1983.
Reprinted with permission of Elsevier Science Publishers B.V. (North-Holland) from *Information Services and Use* 4 (1984):225-227.

requirements of the system. The newer 'friendly' systems issue prompts to the user and provide help screens or menus. Examples of such systems include Knowledge Index, BRS/After Dark, and the Dow Jones network. Be assured that others will follow, and when they do, they might be called 'reactive systems.' Reactive systems will learn from the user, and store the user's interactions for later sessions. User idiosyncrasies will become important search refinements rather than barriers to retrieval effectiveness. The controversy inherent in this trend toward system friendliness lies in the implied challenge to the role of the search intermediary. No longer will the intermediary be the sole interpreter between the user and computer. This is not to say that the intermediary will become a dinosaur. Intermediaries will evolve into a new role and possibly function as online managers.

The second major trend involves the development of procedures to handle information overflow. As we have all discovered, the most highly 'relevant' paper is not always the best paper for one's needs. Nevertheless, some rough measure of usefulness must be applied to the results of a typical search. Ranking algorithms are being developed that impose an order on search output according to potential *user* relevance. One such method was developed by the European Space Agency on their ESA-IRS System. The technique, called "zoom," represents a new dimension in information retrieval. It analyzes an initial list of retrieved items for elements, such as vocabulary terms, adjacent terms, author names, etc., and determines which elements are most characteristic of the list. The zoom procedure can then be used either to search a database for additional items containing the key elements or to rank the items on the initial list according to the number of key elements each contains.

The third major trend concerns the relative development of the passive versus the active system. Active systems involve a direct, intentional, interaction between a user, whether it be the ultimate consumer of the information or an intermediary, and the online system. Passive systems involve fixed, but updatable profiles, against which incoming information is compared, selected, and automatically forwarded to the user. While active systems appear to be more attractive at first glance there is one key factor that might slow their universal adoption which is often overlooked. This factor can be termed 'keyboard aversion.' A large New York magazine publisher, interested in getting into the information business, commissioned a survey of corporate officers and managers, people who were potential end-users of business systems. The results indicated that although 89 percent of the sample considered themselves to be either good or fair typists, only 13 percent would use a terminal keyboard to search privately, and only 6 percent would permit colleagues to observe them searching. The results might be considered predictable. Members of generations represented by the sample probably consider the use of a keyboard demeaning and essentially clerical in character. Peer pressure can be a strong impediment to change even though change would improve information delivery. One might argue that the new generation, because of their familiarity with micro-computers, will be less inclined to experience keyboard aversion. This might well be true. It might also be true that once introduced to user-friendly and menu-driven systems scientists and laboratory personnel will show little of the bias exhibited by business people. To the scientist, published information is at the heart of his or her work; to the business person it is more tangential. Whatever the case, the point is that designers of information delivery systems should consider seriously the market they have in mind. An active system might be more appropriate for one market and a passive system more appropriate for another.

The fourth trend to be mentioned is the development of 'gatewaying.' A gateway is a link from one vendor to another vendor or data-base publisher that is transparent to the end-user. Perhaps as significant as the sophisticated technology involved is the spirit of cooperation being displayed by the various publishers and vendors. Publishers will be able to lock arms and unite complementary data bases to the benefit of both themselves and the user. The mounting of a data base at a single location and permitting multiple gateway access to it has two colossal impli-cations for the end-user. The elimination of duplicative data bases will ultimately lower the cost of online information, and the amount of information accessible to the end-user will increase dramatically.

Trend five involves the emerging technology of videotex. The chief question is whether the consumer will ultimately select for home use the relatively expensive, multi-purpose personal computer with its memory and software on-site or the less expensive, single-purpose videotex terminal that permits interactive use with intelligence resident in a mainframe through a television set. As of today no definable trend has emerged. The edge seems to go to videotex in Europe and Canada; in the US and Japan, it is to the microcomputer. I predict that eventually the videotex system with its superior graphics capability and lesser expense will predominate. It is being demonstrated now in the Miami area, through the Viewtron experiment, that nearly all of that which home users want, e.g. electronic catalogs, computer games, home banking, etc., can be supplied by videotex. Also demonstrated is a decided disenchant-ment with the personal computer, with its high start-up costs, relative complexity, rapid obsolescence, and rather illusive home applications. Undoubtedly there will be many professional applications for the microcomputer, but it seems to have a definite disadvantage when compared to videotex for the average consumer. The trend should be watched carefully, for it has serious implications for those involved in information systems design.

All of these observations should be taken for what they are—guesses (albeit based on some experience) as to what the future will hold for us in information delivery. Perhaps we should be satisfied with knowing why we went wrong in the past. This itself is no easy undertaking. As a commemorative to past folly and for the study by future generations, we propose the establishment of the Edsel Museum of not-so-state-of-the-art innovation. Into it will go optical coincidence cards, McBee card sorting needles, and micrographic libraries. I wonder if there is any similarity between the McBee sorting needle and videodisc storage technology.

Additional Readings—Impact of Online Services

Clayton, Audrey. "Factors Affecting Future Online Services." *Online Review* 5 (August 1981):287-300.

Cogswell, James A. "Online Search Services: Implications for Libraries and Library Users." *College & Research Libraries* 39 (July 1978):275-80.

Duchesne, R. M.; Guenter, D. A., and Tsai, S. *Ownership of Machine-Readable Bibliographic Data*. Ottawa: National Library of Canada, March 1983.

Gardner, Trudy A. "Effects of Online Databases on Reference Policy." *RQ* 19 (Fall 1979):70-74.

Guskin, Alan E., Stoffle, Carla J., and Baruth, Barbara E. "Library Future Shock: The Microcomputer Revolution and the New Role of the Library." *College and Research Libraries* 45 (May 1984):177-183.

Line, Maurice B. "The Future of Libraries in the Information Transfer Chain" *Information Services and Use* 3 (Summer 1983):11-22.

Nesly, Glend S. "Online Databases: Effects on Reference Acquisitions." *Library Acquisitions: Practice and Theory* 5 (1981):45-49.

Neufeld, M. Lynne. "Future of Secondary Services." *Online Review* 7 (Oct. 1983):421-426.

Sperr, Inez L. "Online Searching and the Print Product: Impact or Interaction?" *Online Review* 7 (5), 1983:413-420.

Trubkin, Leone. "Migration from Print to Online Use." *Online Review* 4 (March 1980):5-12.

Contributors

Alice H. Bahr is Project Librarian, Government Publications, Muhlenberg College, Allentown, Pennsylvania.

Marcia J. Bates is associate professor in the Graduate School of Library and Information Science of the University of California at Los Angeles.

Richard W. Blood is Assistant Library Director for Technical and Circulation Services, San Francisco State University.

Roger W. Christian is coauthor with Pauline Atherton of *Librarians and Online Services*.

Pauline Atherton Cochrane is Professor, School of Information Studies, Syracuse University.

Walt Crawford is manager, Product Batch, at the Research Libraries Group, Inc.

Pat Ensor is Coordinator of Database Searching, Indiana State University, Terre Haute.

Carol J. Fenichel is Director of Library Services, Philadelphia College of Pharmacy and Science.

Herbert Goldhor is Director of the Library Research Centre, Graduate School of Library and Information Science, University of Illinois.

Mary M. Hammer is Librarian, Holland Library, Washington State University.

Stephen P. Harter is Associate Professor, School of Library and Information Science, Indiana University.

Eileen E. Hitchingham is Coordinator of Evaluation Resources, Oakland University Library.

William Joseph Jackson is a Reference Librarian, University of Houston Library.

Simone Klugman is Reference and Collection Development Librarian, University of California, Berkeley.

Jean E. Koch is Director of the Urbana Muncipal Documents Project, Urbana Free Library, Urbana, Illinois.

Richard P. Kollin is with the Institute of Scientific Information, 3501 Market St., Philadelphia, PA 19104

Frederick W. Lancaster is Professor, Graduate School of Library and Information Science, University of Illinois.

Louise R. Levy is a Marketing Information Specialist, Market Information Research Service (MIRS), AT & T Bell Laboratories.

Mary Jo Lynch is Director, Office for Research, American Library Association.

Doris B. Marshall is an information consultant since retiring from her position as Information Scientist, Ralston Purina Co.

Jean K. Martin is Library Manager, Molycorp Inc., Los Angeles.

Magdeleine Moureau is Head of Documentation Centre, Institut Francais du Petrole, Cedex, France.

James Rice, Jr. is Associate Professor, School of Library and Information Science, The University of Iowa, Iowa City.

Stanley J. Shapiro is Professor of Marketing, Faculty of Business Administration, Simon Fraser University, Vancouver, British Columbia.

James E. Shea is with the Institute for Scientific Information, 3501 Market St., Philadelphia, PA 19104.

Renata Tagliacozzo has retired from the position of Associate Research Scientist, Mental Health Research Institute, The University of Michigan.

Carol Tenopir is Assistant Professor, Graduate School of Library and Information Science, University of Hawaii.

Martha E. Williams is Professor, Coordinated Science Laboratory, University of Illinois, Urbana-Champaign.

Thomas S. Warrick is an attorney with the firm of Pierson Semmes Crolius and Finley. Address: 1054 Thirty-first St., NW, Washington, DC 20007.

Name Index

Personal names conform to the following code:
  a = author of article included in this volume
  b = name cited in bibliography of article
  f = name cited in footnote or reference of article
  r = name cited in additional reading
  t = name mentioned in text of article

Adams, A.L., 247t, 248t, 250f
Ashbury, H.O., 173f
Atherton, P., 5t, 7t, 9t, 11f, 12f,
  13f, 23r, 89t, 92f, 93f, 126-136a,
  137t, 139t, 141t, 151t, 156f, 157f,
  251r
Atkinson, H.C., 114r
Atwood, R., 219t, 226f
Auster, E., 251r

Back, H.B., 44t, 48f
Bahr, A.H., 137-157a
Barker, F.H., 49f, 191r
Barlow, D.H., 172t, 174f
Barnett, G.O., 358f
Baruth, B.E., 389r
Barwise, T.P., 372t, 384f
Bates, M.J., 238-250a, 239t, 249f
Bates, R., 357f
Bauer, C.K., 158r
Beaman, P.D., 358f
Beaumont, J., 341r
Beeler, R.J., 191r
Beisner, K., 288t, 293f
Bell, C., 358f
Bellardo, T., 87t, 92f, 112f
Bement, J., 166t, 173f
Benefeld, A.R., 137t, 157f, 219t, 226f
Bennett, J.L., 45t, 49f
Berger, M.C., 251r
Berk, R.A., 94t, 95t, 112f
Berry, J., 183f, 184f

Bevan, A., 359f
Bivans, M.M., 4t, 11f
Bivins, K.T., 352t, 358f
Blair, D.C., 240t, 249f
Blair, Jr., J.C., 283t, 286t, 289t, 291f,
  292f
Blood, R.W., 197-214a, 212t, 371f
Blue, R.I., 70r
Bonn, J.H., 5t, 12f
Borgman, C.L., 23r
Borko, H., 77t, 85f, 112f
Boss, R.W., 287t, 293f
Bourne, C.P., 104t, 108t, 112f, 113f,
  114r, 227f, 245t
Boyce, B.R., 112f, 191r
Boyle, H.F., 191r
Brandhorst, T., 39b, 43t, 48f, 357f
Bressler, S.E., 341r
Brooks, H., 279t, 292f
Brown, C.P., 212f
Bryant, E.C., 217t, 225f, 226f
Buckel, W.L., 70r
Budd, J., 191r
Bunge, C.A., 78t, 85f
Burgess, J.G., 6t, 12f, 70r
Burton, H.D., 42t, 48f
Butler, M., 357f

Caldwell, J., 88t, 93f
Calkins, M.L., 4t, 5t, 11f, 12f
Callahan, D., 251r
Capodagli, J., 176t, 183f

Subject Index